Peacock Richard Atkinson

# Physical and historical evidences of vast sinkings of land on the north and west coasts of France

Peacock Richard Atkinson

**Physical and historical evidences of vast sinkings of land on the north and west coasts of France**

ISBN/EAN: 9783337202484

Printed in Europe, USA, Canada, Australia, Japan

Cover: Foto ©Andreas Hilbeck / pixelio.de

More available books at **www.hansebooks.com**

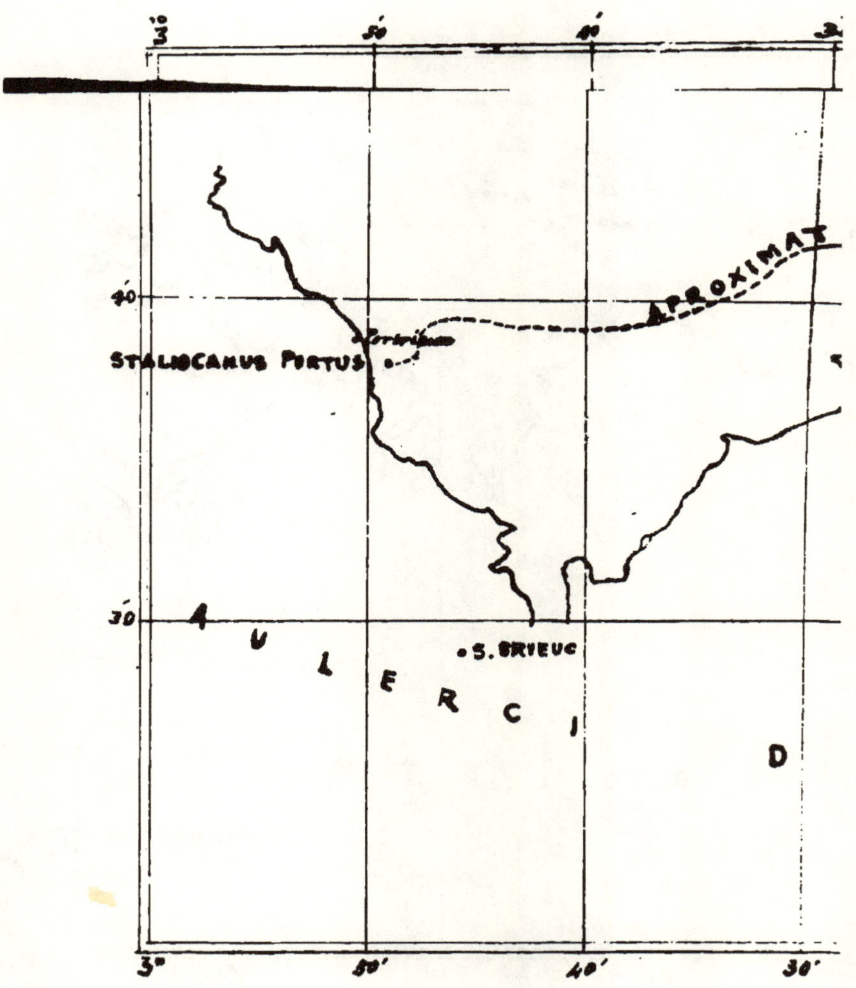
3°
50'
40'
40'
STALIOCANUS PORTUS
APROXIMAT
30'
AULERCI
S. BRIEUC
D
3°
50'
40'
30'

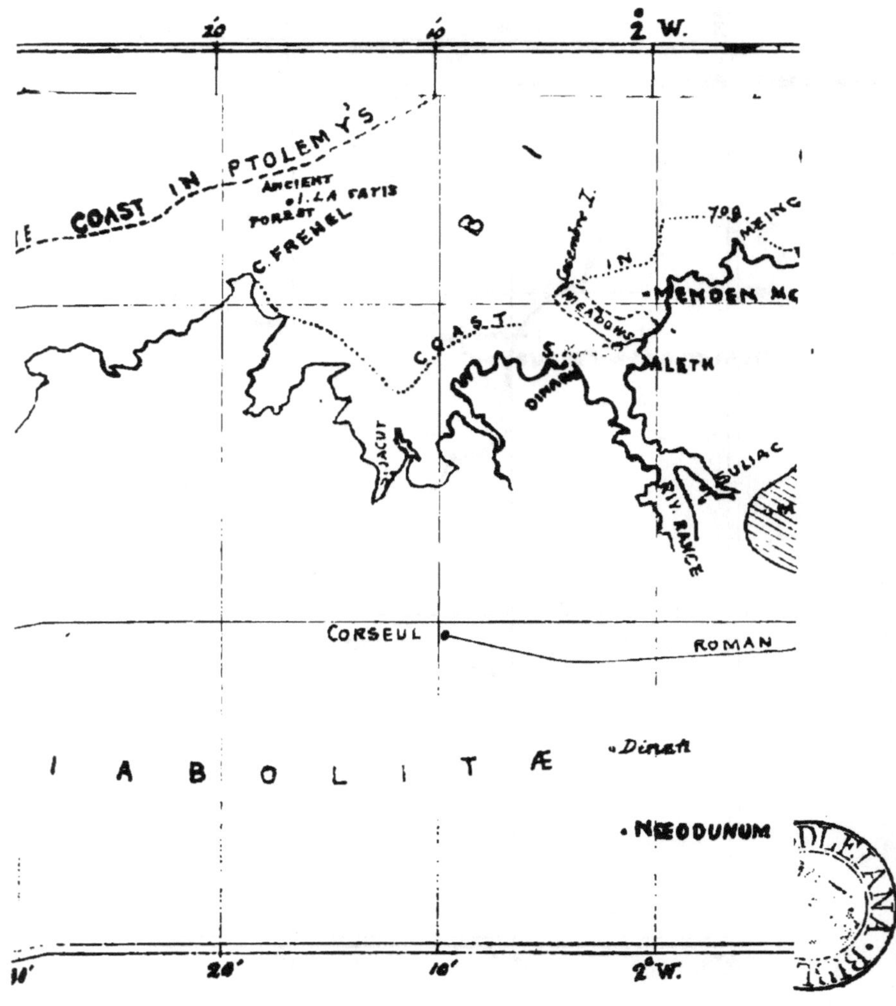

20
10
2 W.
COAST IN PTOLEMY'S
ANCIENT
I. LA FATIS
FOREST
C. FRENEL
B
Cezembre I.
IN
MEADOWS
MENDEN
COAST
S.
ALETH
DINARD
JACUT
RIV. RANCE
CORSEUL
ROMAN
Dinan
I A B O L I T Æ
NEODUNUM
20'
10'
2° W.

No 1.
S. MOACKS MONASTERY
CANCALLE PT
LHAN-KAFRUTH
TAURAC OR CAURAC MONT
DRAGEY
AVRANCHES
GENEST
TOMBELENE
S. MICHEL
BEAUVOIR
PONTORSON
CARFANTIN
DOL
L'ILE MER
ROAD
50'
40'
30'
25'

# PHYSICAL AND HISTORICAL EVIDENCES

OF VAST

# SINKINGS OF LAND

ON THE

## NORTH AND WEST COASTS OF FRANCE,

AND

## SOUTH WESTERN COASTS OF ENGLAND;

WITHIN THE HISTORICAL PERIOD.

COLLECTED AND COMMENTED ON BY

R. A. PEACOCK, Esq., Civil Engineer.

*Republished from the Artisan, Engineering Journal,* 1866, 1867; *with corrections and additions made since.*

"All these were joined together in the vale of Siddim, which is the salt sea."—Genesis xiv, 3.

"Therefore will we not fear, though the earth be removed, and though the mountains be carried into the midst of the sea; though the waters thereof roar and be troubled, though the mountains shake with the swelling thereof."—Psal xlvi, 2, 3.

LONDON;

E. & F. N. SPON, 48, CHARING CROSS.

1868.

J. COUTANCHE, PRINTER, HILL-STREET, JERSEY.

# PREFACE.

WHEN the present writer undertook the task of which the present volume contains the results, he contemplated nothing more than the publication of a colored Map exhibiting the Geology proper, of Jersey. It soon became evident however, that Geological events of peculiar character, and extending over a large space; must have occurred within the Historical period. And these being intensely interesting, and involving no small amount of labour and research; it was found to be the best course to limit the present volume to, at least, *a partial* development of those events.

It would be impossible for any one however great his abilities and acquired knowledge, to form a sound judgment on the facts and inferences contained in this volume, without first reading it through in order from beginning to end, and then carefully considering it as a whole. The author has endeavoured by Evidences and by arguments, to prove every opinion which he advances. In fact the work is of a structural character. Proceeding cautiously and carefully he tried to establish each step, before going on to the next. A recent publication of his, on Steam, has received sanction from some highly distinguished men of Science, and it would at all events be *fair*, to read what is about to be stated first, and then condemn or approve as the case may require.

In attempting to elicit Truth from the many interesting facts collected, the author has been obliged to pursue it to within the limits of each of the nine following sciences :—Antiquarian, Astronomical, Civil-engineering, Conchological, Geographical, Geological, Greek and Latin, Historical, Philological. And where his own knowledge did not reach the small degree necessary for the purpose, as in Conchology and Philology, he thankfully acknowledges willing help received from J. Gwyn Jeffreys, Esq., F.R.S., F.G.S., in the former science; and in Philology from M. Edouard le Héricher, Régent de Rhétorique, Avranches—George Métivier, Esq., Guernsey—and Professor Williams of Lampeter College.

The author has often been met with the remark, —" It must have taken you a deal of time." It would be well if the gentlemen who have made this remark, would employ at least some of their leisure in attempting to add however little, to the sum of scientific knowledge; rather than waste the whole of that leisure in amusements.—It has also been said repeatedly, "It is all copied from books." Not quite so. It has been gleaned wherever it could be found: from books, MSS., and maps, from the local knowledge of others kindly communicated and duly acknowledged, and from the author's own studies and observations, made for the purposes of generalizing and drawing conclusions, and giving correct explanations, for the Advancement of Science. Even if it had been possible for one man to have personally discovered all the facts quoted, such personal discoveries would only have added to his difficulties in obtaining credence. As it is, he has the guarantee of many authorities—some of them of great eminence—for the facts stated. And their good faith has this farther guarantee, that for the most part, they had no idea of the purposes to which their statements would be applied.—Again, it has been said, "If there ever had been such catastrophes, History would have said so." History *does* say so, scores of times. It is only because History has been written and read without having been fully understood; because those who wrote and those who read have *seen* or related without *perceiving;* that the curious and important facts which it is the business of this volume to explain, have not been perceived and explained before. It is surprising to find that (though only in rare instances) men of Science have refused to believe in ancient Histories, Chronicles and Records, which often mutually corroborate each other and which plainly indicate Sinkings of land, though the writers make no attempts to explain the phenomena they narrate. The gentlemen referred to have with misplaced ingenuity, sought to explain away such phenomena, with the object of getting rid of them in reality; though there can be no doubt that their objections were made in perfect good faith. Their disbelief, does not signify that it is not true that the Sinkings took place at the times stated in this volume; but that the gentlemen themselves have incautiously, while knowing almost nothing of what History unfolds and disbelieving what they did know—committed themselves to a contrary opinion. It has been the custom of some of them to allege, not from any authority, but of their own mere motion, that "The Sinkings have not taken place within the Historical period." Let us take a few very modern examples of Sinkings:—In 1692 the town of Port Royal in Jamaica, and a thousand acres of land in its vicinity, were submerged to a depth of fifty feet. Great changes of level were caused by the Lisbon earthquake of 1755, in particular the site of the then new quay became water 600 feet deep. In 1783 the town of Guatemala in Mexico, was swallowed up with 8000 families. From 1783 to the end of 1786 fissures, ravines, landslips, falls of the sea-cliff, new lakes, and other changes were caused by the earthquakes of Calabria. In 1811 the valley of the Mississippi from New Madrid to the mouths of the Ohio (fifty miles) was convulsed so as to create lakes, islands, and new water channels.* Mrs. Somerville, relates (*Physical Geography*, 1858, p. 156) that in 1772 the greater part of one of the largest volcanic mountains of Java, was swallowed up after a short but severe combustion; a luminous cloud enveloped the mountain on the 11th of August, and soon after the huge mass actually disappeared under the earth with tremendous noise, carrying with it about ninety square miles of the surrounding country, forty villages, and 2957 of their inhabitants. In 1815 the town of Tombora in Sumbawa, was submerged by heavy rollers from the ocean. She says (p. 166) "In the present day elevation is going on in many places, especially on the Moray Firth and the Channel Islands." She

* Quoted chiefly from Page's *Advanced Text book of Geology*, p. 349.

gives a general reference to Sir C. Lyell's works on Geology—(in which plenty of other instances of modern Sinkings may be found) but the Channel Islands does not occur in the Indexes. The writer has lived a dozen years in Jersey, but has never seen or heard of any recent elevations. It is of no avail to say "The Sinkings you specify all took place in Volcanic countries." Because the Channel Islands and Cornwall are also Volcanic countries, that is to say—they all consist of Igneous rocks. And if the Volcanoes are not *active* in the present day, they were so formerly, as is proved by the upheavals of granite, syenite, and porphyries (and by the abundance of felspathic ash) *which doubtless left cavities below them.** Besides, the well known Sinkings (and risings) in northern Europe, are not in Volcanic countries. Why then may not Sinkings have occurred on the coasts of the English Channel and Bay of Biscay—and in the Channel and Bay themselves—again and again in the Historical period? How can any one refuse to believe the scores of mutually corroborative testimonies to that effect which will now be produced? "Whenever a new and startling fact is brought to light in science, people first say, it is not true." The author has experienced the

* See "*Eleven reasons* (old, or new, or newly put) *why there must be cavities in the crust of the Earth*," in the Steam Tract, published by the author in 1866, p. 46, &c., with Preface published in 1867.

truth of this dictum of Agassiz. With respect to that distinguished man's other dicta, that people next say "It is contrary to religion," and lastly that "everybody knew it before"—such allegations have not been made in the present case, because it is obviously impossible they can apply. It is nothing new, to meet with those who will believe nothing which disagrees with their own ideas; but that is not philosophy. No doubt a few will continue in the predicament specified in the old rhyme:

> "A man convinced against his will,
> Is of the same opinion still."

The writer states his authorities and gives reasons for his inferences therefrom: and washes his hands of responsibility. Nevertheless he proposes to support anything which may seem to him to be misapprehended. Instead of being reluctant to believe that the Sinkings about to be described, can really have occurred within the last nineteen centuries, We ought rather, while remembering the many Elevations and Depressions of land which have occurred at all periods, and all over the Earth, and remembering the well known axiom that, "all geological changes are due to causes still in operation"—willingly to believe in the Sinkings, if substantiated, as in the present case, by a reasonable amount of proof.

The reader cannot fail to observe, that whatever the nature of each piece of evidence, or its date, or whosoever its author; the whole body of evidences tends to prove one and the same thing. Such universal concurrence can never happen unless the thing concurred in is the truth. Evidences must prove, some one thing and some another, in order to afford sound reason for doubt. The whole matter is therefore explainable only on the supposition, *that the ground has Sunk as stated.*

No catastrophes appear to have taken place among the Channel Islands for more than five centuries, nor about S. Malo for more than four centuries. The localities are as safe as the average of places in temperate climates, and much more safe than many densely inhabited places in volcanic countries.

The mode of proceeding in this investigation is, to interpret fairly certain facts stated in Julius Cæsar's Commentaries on the Gallic war, and in other authors of the Roman period. In connexion with many other Histories and Records of Middle Age and Modern dates; including observations and statements by the author's contemporaries and facts observed by the author himself. Being an attempt to ascertain, so far as may be practicable in a case abounding with difficulties, the extent of the vast changes of land into sea which have certainly taken place among the Channel Islands and at various places on the coasts of France and England—since Cæsar's time. The surprising circumstance is, that the Sinkings are so extensive, so recent, and previously so very little (if at all) suspected. As a matter of convenience, the testimonies have been taken in inverse order of time, commencing with the Modern, and progressing backward through the Middle Age and Roman authorities. Partial investigation led only to unbelief and controversy, and consequently a sifting as complete as circumstances permitted became a necessity. This sifting has disclosed many proofs all pointing in one and the same direction; namely to establish Sinkings more extensive and deeper, than were at first stated. As questions arise more than once on Engineering points, the author mentions that, professionally, in early life he paid a fee to a firm of land-surveyors (one of whom, Mr. William Johnson, now resides in Jersey) to learn the art of measuring and mapping land. He afterwards was connected in professional business as a Civil-engineer, with the late celebrated Engineer Robert Stephenson, M.P., F.R.S., and his partners, under whom as Engineers-in-chief, he executed a large amount of constructive engineering work.

It is evident that the only satisfactory course is, to consider this volume as a whole. To controvert individual statements of fact, even if that could be done successfully, would have no more effect than to kill individual soldiers, for it would leave the army still unconquered. A (necessarily) very brief statement of the Evidences in their then imperfect state, was read to the Geological Section of the British Association at Birmingham on Sept. 9, 1865; * which elicited from the distinguished President Sir Roderick Murchison, the remark that the author "had gone far to prove his case," an opinion which no one present seemed to doubt. Certain objectors have stated their views with all kindly feeling in the interest of scientific truth; and the author has endeavoured to answer them in the same spirit and with the same object. On those principles when pointing out what he conceives to be errors, he does so without mentioning names, except in one unavoidable case † which is however of the most friendly character. This little Volume would never have existed, if it had not been for the advantages afforded by the British Association for the Advancement of Science.

* See *Transactions of Sections*, Brit. Assn. Report, 1865, p. 70.

† The circumlocution of avoiding the mention of the gentleman's name, was found to be quite unmanageable.

The Scripture Quotations on the title page seem to refer to Sinkings of land.

The author has the greatest pleasure in acknowledging the invariable kindness and communicativeness, which he has experienced on all hands. His warmest thanks are due and are now offered, to the gentlemen whose names follow alphabetically (or to their relatives if deceased) who have lent him books, manuscripts or maps, or have given him local information, or have in other ways contributed to the stock of materials contained in the work. But no one of these gentlemen is responsible (except in the very slight degree stated from time to time in the body of the book under each of their respective names) for the inferences drawn, or for the conclusions arrived at; which are solely attributable to the author. The following is an

*Alphabetical list of names of gentlemen who have supplied the author with local information, &c.*

The late J. P. Ahier, Esq.—The late Col. Aubin. —Mr. John Aubin, St. Clement's.—Capt. Babot. —Rev. Henry Bell, Nottingham.—Rev. Richard Bellis.—Mr. John Briard, St. Ouen's.—T. W. Clarke, Esq., of Her Majesty's Customs.—The late F. G. Collas, Esq., St. Martin's.—Capt. de Caen. —The late Charles de Ste. Croix, Esq.—M. Delalonde.—Frederick Etheridge, Esq., F.G.S., Government School of Mines, Jermyn Street.—The late Messrs. Falle, Royal Square.—Phillip Le Feuvre, Esq., La Hougue.—M. Hacquoil, Postmaster, St. Ouen's.—M. Edouard le Héricher, Régent de Rhétorique au Collège d'Avranches.—J. Gwyn Jeffreys, Esq., F.R.S., F.G.S.—Rev. G. J. le Maistre, Grammar School, St. Aubin's, Medallist, T.C.D.—F. C. Lukis, Esq., Guernsey. —The late F. C. Lukis, Esq., M.D., F.R.S., Guernsey.—Thomas Mansell, Esq., M.D., Guernsey.—Mr. G. H. Mauger, St. Lawrence.—George Métivier, Esq., Guernsey. — Edward Mourant, Esq., Samarès Manor.—P. W. Nicolle, Esq.—H. C. Ogle, Esq., Ireland Scholar, Magdalene College, Oxford.—Capt. George Orange.—William Pengelly, Esq., F.R.S., F.G.S. — Mr. Piquet, Chemist. — Capt. Ranwell, R.N. — Capt. John Richards, R.N., Chief of the Admiralty Survey of the Channel Islands.—T. W. Rose, Esq.—P. J. Simon, Esq., Receiver of her Majesty's Rents.—Edward Simpson, Esq., Bristol.—William Smith, Esq., C.E., F.G.S., F.C.S., proprietor of the Artizan, a valuable Engineering Journal, in which the first ten chapters of these papers first appeared.—Edward de la Taste, Esq., —F. B. Tupper, Esq., Guernsey.—The late Vice-Admiral White, R.N.—H. C. White, Esq., F.G.S. —Professor Williams, Lampeter College.—If any names have been omitted it is through inadvertency.

The following is the list of Subscribers, omitting only two who desired to withdraw their names. Those marked * are deceased, or have left Jersey, or are unconnected with the Channel Islands.

R. P. Marett, Esq., Attorney-General of Jersey. —*H. E. Jerome, Esq., Major, 27th regiment.— *Rev. John Simpson, D.D., Derbyshire.—*Miss Dewe, ditto.—*Miss Simpson, Clifton.—*Rev. Henry Bell, Nottingham, two copies.—Rev. F. Godfray, D.C.L.—H. C. White, Esq., F.G.S.— Col. Turner, Gorey.—Mr. Piquet, Chemist.—Mr. Bryant, Coal Merchant.—Rev. J. J. Balleine, two copies.—M. Blood, Esq., M.D.—Rev. G. J. Le Maistre, St. Aubin.—P. Marett, Esq., Avranches, Jersey.—*Thomas Marsh, Esq.—Henry Redstone, Esq., Emerald Villa.—Phillip Le Feuvre, Esq., La Hougue.—Rev. Philip Guille, St. Martin's.— Rev. Edward Guille, St. Luke's.—Rev. A. J. Murray.—*Capt. Woolhouse.—W. H. Gardner, Esq., 8, Elizabeth Terrace.—Mr. Trebeck, Elm Bank, St. Saviour's.—*Col. Hyslop.—Capt. De Caen.—H. L. Manuel, Esq.—Mrs. John Barbenson.—Rev. C. H. Bateman.—*Col. Aubin.— Thomas Rose, Esq.—*Rev. J. W. Braikenridge, Clevedon, two copies.—Elias Neel, Esq., Jurat.— *Mr. Philip Falle, three copies.—Capt. George Orange.—Charles Philip Le Cornu, Beaumont.—

*Mrs. General Huthwaite.—*Rev. Dr. Henderson. —*J. Gwyn Jeffreys, Esq., F.R.S., F.G.S.

The author has no means of judging at present, whether such parts of the Channel Islands as are now above water—have sunk at all since Cæsar's time, or not.—Any communications bearing on the subject of the volume, will be thankfully received.

The Steam Tract referred to and this volume on Sinkings, are sometimes bound up together, because they are naturally connected. The former proves at p. 46, &c., that the crust of the Earth abounds with cavities, the latter proves that Sinkings have taken place which could not have happened unless the cavities had afforded a *locus in quo.*

*R. A. P.*

*Jersey, October,* 1867.

# CONTENTS.

NOTE.—*The numbers following refer to the numbers of the Articles, except where they obviously refer to Chapters, Dates or Pages.*

## Chapter V.—Pages 37 to 60.

### Geographical changes in the bay of Mont S. Michel and near St. Malo, much within the Historical period.

60. Abbé Desroches in his *Hist. du Mont S. Michel*, 1838, states that scientific men believe that Jersey, Guernsey and Alderney belonged to the continent. He attempts to prove that in the Celtic language, Neustrie (Normandy), and Vestrie (Britanny) signify that the two Provinces had been separated from each other by some convulsion of nature. The like is stated in the anonymous *Essai sur l'Hist. de Neustrie*. 61. The Abbé states that Genets 5 miles west of Avranches, near the sea, formerly possessed many churches; those of St. Sebastien and St. Catherine were submerged, the ruins of St. Anne and St. Lawrence still exist. I do not agree with his opinion that Cæsar's sea-fight with the Veneti took place in the Bay of Mont S. Michel.

62. Abbé Manet's work, *de l'état ancien............ et de la Baie du Mont S. Michel et de Cancale*, 1829. His well deserved honours. He records that the Forest of Sciscy was overwhelmed by the sea in the year 709 without accounting for its having remained much under water, ever since. I worked hard for a month in the British Museum to collect evidence. Abbé Manet quotes sixteen authorities to prove the former existence of the Forest of Sciscy; of which I verify one half, and have laid them before the reader.—63. He says, History does not permit us to entertain the least doubt of the former existence of the Forest of Sciscy. Bay of Mont S. Michel, was not a Bay until the year 709. Other submergences since the year 709, occurred in the years 811, 842, 891, 1163, 1244, 1247, 1356, 1437, 1827.—64. He attributes the effects in 709 to a "terrible *north* wind," another writer states that the direction of the wind was *different:* environs of Chausey first yielded: *all disappeared under the waters, except the mountains* WHICH NOW FORM ISLANDS; and a portion of forest and meadows spared for a time on the coast near Avranches. The course of the river Couësnon altered, (evidently by sinking) and gave to the Ocean nearly all the part of the Bay which belongs to Normandy. *See description in Art.* 64, *and Map No.* 1.—65. The island la Catis, spacious ancient forest, now lost.—66. Details of the catastrophe of 709.—67. This catastrophe evidently a sinking of the land.—68. Names of parishes sunk.—69. Nearly forty square miles of sunken land in Britanny recovered by embanking.—70. Mr. Trollope names five cities, now

Brest, but with a former mouth of the Loire now submerged and lost, &c., &c., &c.

CHAPTER VII.—Pages 72 to 80.

115. Ptolemy gives no positions at or near the Northern Channel Islands.—Sunken land goes out of sight and is therefore difficult to identify.—Percée rock (covered at high water) near the south end of Herm. Facts stated and reasonings thereon.—118. Mr. F. C. Lukis disbelieves that the rock has ever been a gate-post. M. de Gerville gives a copy of a charter proving that in 1440 there was a body of Friars Minors settled in Herm. My remarks.—119. My argument that the pierced stone would have been an odd and awkward apparatus to fasten a boat to, as suggested; and also that *that theory* does nothing to account for the apparent road now existing. —120. If the pierced rock was formerly above high water, then a gate *may* have hung there.—121. Mr. Lukis's statements as to peat and trunks of trees found on the N.W. of Guernsey as far as low water; and on the S.E. of Vale Castle. His belief that these submerged Forests may date with the same catastrophes which have created the peat beds on the north and west of the approximate shore of Britanny and Normandy. My arguments on the significant names "Roque *au Bois*" and "Grunes *du Bois*." Mr. Lukis's testimony that when the cromlech at L'Ancresse Bay was constructed, the sea was at a greater distance from the site of the hill than at present. He says the whole neighbourhood bears marks of the inroads of the sea. Great importance of these arguments of his, which are corroborative of Sinking. The argument of Mr. W. B. Herapath, F.R S., is also corroborative of Sinking. Dr. Mansell and Mr. Lukis refute the statements that there are remains of walls in the sea bottom near the isle of Lihou, or a submarine tower near Herm.—122. Is there any originality in my investigations? The Royal Geographical Society did not publish an abstract of these papers as was expected.—123. The late Mr. J. P. Ahier's statements and theories.

CHAPTER VII, continued.—Pages 80 to 82.

124 to 126. Dr. Fleming's theory inapplicable to the present case.

CONTENTS.

CONTENTS.

### CHAPTER XIV.—Pages 143 to 156.

# ERRATA, ADDENDA, AND CORRIGENDA.

Title page for "Psal" read "Psalm" in 7th line from bottom.

Page 10. For period of Roman occupation of Britain, see *post* p. 31.

Page 6 line 1 for "admissible," read "inadmissible,"

Same page, line 16, after "respects" introduce a semicolon.

Same page, line 17, for "flowed" read "flowed"

Same page, 7th line from bottom, for "hydraulic" read "hydraulio."

Page 7, end of 9th line from bottom for "clay," read "clay-."

Same page, line 22 from top, and 8th line from bottom, and *elsewhere*, for "Viellett" read "Vieillet."

Same page, line 28, and *elsewhere*, for "Quarternary" read "Quaternary."

Page 10, line 10, for "*απιςία*" read "*απιςιας*."

Same page, last line but 3, instead of distinguishing the articles in the Appendix by letters of the alphabet, they are distinguished by the numbers of the pages referred to.

Page 13, line 15 for "wate" read "water."

Page 16, line 28, the word *Percer* refers to "piercing" a road from St. Ouen's Church to the shore.

Page 17, fourth line from bottom, it is common to refer losses of land to Hurricanes and High Tides, the writers forgetting that both these combined entirely fail to account for *permanent* submersions.

Page 18, line 15, for "des" read "de."

Page 20, line 27, for "Sandworms" read "The Teredo."

Page 21, Article 32, the italics are mine.

Page 26, line 10, for "Quelkou," read "Quettehou"

Same page, line 11 for "Titahou" read "Tatihou"

Ditto, line 26 for "miason" read "maison"

Page 28, line 27 for "*Historie*" read "*Histoire*"

Page 30, line 12 for "north-eastern" read "north-western"

Ditto, line 24 for "lienes" read "lieues"

Page 32, line 30, for "Constantiui" read "Constantini"

Ditto, line 8 from bottom for "eratiene" read "erateine"

Page 33, end of last line but 4, insert a period after "*nameless*"

Page 34, end of 5th line from bottom for "general's" read "general"'

Page 35, line 29, for "interpretatton" read "interpretation"

Ditto, end of 3rd line from bottom read "*Neustria Pia*, p. 712"

## ERRATA, ADDENDA, AND CORRIGENDA.

Page 37, insert "37" at top of page
Ditto, line 13, for "respective" read "respectively"
Page 38, last line but 6, for "Scisey" read "Sciscy"
Page 39, line 11 include the word "ninth" in a parenthesis thus (ninth)
Page 40, line 5 for "attention" read "intention"
Ditto, line 33 for "600" read "300"
Ditto, line 7 from bottom for "Duraud" read "Durand"
Ditto, line 5 and 6 from bottom, *dele* the words "In my MS." to "coasts" inclusive.
Page 41, last line for "Mauet" read "Manet"
Page 42, line 6 for "Laumeur" read "Lanmeur"
Page 43, last line, but one of text *dele* the words "the words New Channel are a little out of place"
Page 44, last line but 7, for "Briandi" read "Briand"
Page 55, last line of text, it appears from *Principles of Geology*, 1868; that St. Pol-de-Leon was only overwhelmed with drifted sand.
Page 57, last line for "100..2" read "104..3"
Page 64, line 31 and 32 for "by him in the centre column" read "immediately before"
Ditto line 4 from bottom for "Plate 307" read "Maps 1 and 2"
Ditto, line 3 from bottom *dele* the words "of the table"
Page 67, line 36 for "48°" read "49°"
Page 68, line 1, for "17" read "25"
Ditto, line 9, for "north east" read "N.N.W."
Page 70, line 8 from bottom, for "Dinau" read "Dinan"
Ditto, line 5 from bottom, for "Aulircii" read "Aulerci"
Page 75, line 10, between the words "many places" insert "other"
Ditto, line 21, for "1869" read "1859"
Ditto, line 7 from bottom, for "certain of" read "certain degree of"
Page 76, line 28, for "Genas" read "Genus"
Page 78, last line but 3, I was an invalid at the time and unequal to the fatigue of preparing suitable Maps.
Page 79, line 5, for "south-each" read "south-east"
Ditto, after making other obvious printer's corrections, place "(?)" after "Calais" and again after "la Hague"
Page 82, line 14, for "shnnned" read "shunned" and for "Igenuity" read "ingenuity"
Page 86, lines 10, 11, *dele* the words "The original Greek is quoted in the MS. Appendix, pure and simple."
Page 87, line 4, *dele* "*"
Page 88, line 11 from bottom insert " after forests

## ERRATA, ADDENDA, AND CORRIGENDA.

Page 89, line 3 from bottom, for "in chapter XVI" read "hereinafter"

Page 105, line 18 the obscure words mean "Channel Islands"

Ditto, line 19 ditto ditto "stated in these papers"

Ditto, line 20 ditto ditto "not less than £200"

Ditto, line 27 ditto ditto "best way we can"

Ditto, line 28 ditto ditto "very significant"

Ditto, line 30 ditto ditto "it would."

Page 109, last line but 3, for "Antonimus" read "Antoninus"

Page 110, line 6 from bottom, for "Art. 205" read "p. 107"

Page 112, last line but 4 for "Britannica" read "Britannia"

Page 120, line 11 for "(Art. 133)" read "page 89"

Ditto, second paragraph "Art. 209" is in one of the Chapters not yet printed.

Page 121, line 14 for "Henry" read "Charles"

Ditto, last line but one, for "rean" read "read"

Pages 123—124, from "Volume II" to "after their time," all this, amounting to nearly a page, may be omitted; being chiefly superseded by the sequel.

Page 127, line 4 for "xlviii" read "xliii"

Page 132, line 12 for "lines" read "worms"

Page 133, *dele* * and foot-note

Page 142, line 5 for "Eviodia" read "Evodia"

Page 147, line 8, for "than" read "then"

Page 158, line 2, for "ascendancy" read "ascendency"

Page 165, line 13 from bottom for "Vol. V, p. 346" read "Vol V p. 346."

Page 173, line 17 for "*Massoniuss's*" read "*Massonius's*"

Ditto, line 30 for "antiquititibus" read "antiquitatibus"

Page 175, line 4 for "putuaverint" read "putaverint"

Ditto, line 13 for "Archery" read "Achery"

Ditto, line 30 for "oœlesti" read "cœlesti"

Page 180, line 8 for "linconuenient" read "l'inconuenient"

Page 183, line 32 for "Aqutanico" read "Aquitanico"

Page 185, line 7 fot "137" read "127"

Ditto, lines 10, 11 *dele* "down to the words voisinage de Granville inclusive, are" and insert instead "is"

Page 187, line 13 for "geolagical" read "geological"

Page 190, line 22 for "still—We" read "still,—we"

Ditto, same line *dele* "then"

# ON VAST SINKINGS OF LAND.

---

## INTRODUCTION.

The sinkings about to be considered had not taken place as early as Ptolemy's time (the first half of the second century), but some of them had occurred before 550, for Jersey is known to have then been an island. It is mentioned also, and for the first time in history, as an island under the name of Cæsarea in the Roman Itinerary (so called of Antoninus), as Thomas Gale, D.D., F.R.S., well observes in commenting on his Itinerary of Britain. The Itinerary must have been added to from time to time, just as new railways are from time to time inserted in Bradshaw's Railway Guide as soon as they are opened for traffic. For it is obvious that no British Roman Roads could have appeared in the Itinerary before Cæsar's first invasion of Britain B C. 55, and it is equally obvious that the British Roman roads must have been inserted from time to time as they were made, during the 500 years of the Roman occupation of Britain. The Itinerary contains the name of Constantinople four times, though the inauguration of that city did not take place until A.D. 330, six years after its commencement. But Antoninus Pius died A.D. 161. The separation of Jersey from the continent probably took place between 15[illegible] and 350 A.D.

By the time the reader has finished the perusal of these papers, he will have noticed how unanimously all things point to one and the same conclusion—a sure test of truth.

## CHAPTER I.

1. *Average level of the sea is stationary, it is the land which rises or sinks.* There are many instances of trunks of trees with roots attached, and of other purely terrestrial products, having been found at considerable depths below high water amongst the Channel Islands. They are generally when *in situ*, covered with sand and consequently not often visible. The wood looks fresh and not much discoloured in St. Ouen's Bay, as if it had not been immersed more than five or six centuries, which is the fact. Near St. Helier's the submarine relics of an ancient forest are mostly decayed in consequence of exposure to the weather. There is a good deal of historical evidence, which will be laid before the reader, that considerable tracts of land formerly existed where there is now only water, or bare rocks. It is equally true that there are no banks of shinglo, that is of rounded pebbles, at all approaching in numbers or magnitude to the relicts of large districts which had been simply washed away; and if they had been washed away the trees must necessarily have gone also. But the trees have not gone, on the contrary, very many have remained *in situ*, consisting of greater or less portions of the trunks with roots attached, and inserted in the sea bottom where they grew, and consequently the ground has *not* been washed away. Some of these roots and stumps of trees, as well as remains of buildings, have been found evidently *in situ*, in the bed of the sea below low water, where the rise of an equinoctial spring tide is 42ft. It is out of the question to suppose that these trees could ever have grown where they were covered with salt water to that depth or nearly so, twice in every twenty-four hours. And it is also an axiom in geological science, though some geologists have forgotten it, that wherever there is any alteration in the relative levels of land and sea, the average level of the sea is always stationary, and it is necessarily the land which has risen or sunk, as the case may be. This axiom will be proved both by direct appeals to the reader's understanding, and by the deliberate opinions of distinguished geologists. For which opinions the reader is referred to Sir C. Lyell's *Manual of Geology*, 1855, p. 44, 45; and to Mr. A. B. Jukes's *Manual of Geology*, 1857, p. 203, 204. Also in the "Scheme for establishing the Royal Society," by Sir Isaac Newton; (see his life by Sir D. Brewster, vol. I, p. 91). Sir Isaac speaks of "the rising or falling of mountains and islands." Thus we see that the greatest philosopher who ever lived well knew that land rises and sinks. Influenced by these considerations, the present writer publicly announced in Jersey, that extensive sinkings of land had taken place since Julius Cæsar's time, and gave two public lectures to that effect in March, 1862.

2. In the deep rock cutting, or in military phrase, the "covered way," south of Fort Regent, near the town of St. Helier; are some remains of a raised beach at the top of the cliff on the west side; about 30ft. long and 8ft. thick; consisting of well rounded, water-worn pebbles. The place is

well known to the inhabitants of the town as the scene of a sad accident. A few years ago a soldier and his sweetheart fell from the cliff, and were both killed. The highest part of this beach has been found by the spirit level, to be 101ft. above the highest part of the neighbouring present beach. But of course we must not suppose that the sea has ever attained 100ft. above present high water since Noah's flood. A "raised beach," means that the beach has been raised, not that the sea level has altered.

3. But there is another reason why it is quite impossible to believe that the sea has ever been 100ft. above its present level since Noah's flood. The surface of the oceans and seas comprises an area of 110,849,000 square miles.* To raise the sea level over all that surface would require about 2,100,000 cubic miles of water, for it is certain that it would be impossible to raise it in one part without raising it all over. Where could all this water have come from, or where did it go to?

4. Again, in St. Ouen's Bay, on the west of Jersey, trees have been seen *in situ*, as will presently be proved, below extreme low water where the greatest rise of tide is 42ft. And supposing them to have originally grown a little above extreme high water, we shall have a difference of about 50ft. to account for. Now, as before, we must not conclude that the sea level has ever been 50ft. lower than at present; we have no right whatever to suppose so from any records. And, physically speaking, to have brought it up to its present level would have required an accession of 1,050,000 cubic miles additional water. Where could all that water have come from?

5. Any theory of the sea level having risen 50ft. since the year 1356, which will be proved to have been the date of the submersion of St. Ouen's forest, is quite inadmissible and impossible.

6. Again, if the sea level ever was raised 100ft. (since Noah's flood), every part of every continent and island in the world which was less than 100ft. above the present sea level must have been simultaneously covered with water. But it is certain no such simultaneous catastrophe ever took place since Noah's flood. The question can be still more decisively refuted with regard to any supposed rise or fall of sea level. Thus—

7. Can the sea level rise 50ft. above its usual height at the Channel Islands without also rising about as much along the south coast of England? No.

Can the sea level rise 50ft. above its usual height along the south coast of England without also rising about as much at London Bridge? No.

If the tide rose 50ft. above its usual height at London Bridge, it would of necessity drown half London. Has such a catastrophe ever happened since Cæsar's time? No.

If the like queries are put with respect to the tide *falling short* of its usual level by 50ft. at the Channel Islands and south coast of England, the answers must still be—No.

---

* Lyell's *Principles of Geology*, 1853, p. 125.

For if the sea level was to have been 50ft. below its usual level at the mouth of the Thames, then the tide could never have entered the Thames at all. Is it true that the tide has ever failed to enter the Thames since Cæsar's time? No.

Then, if the present writer proves that the relative levels of land and sea have altered (suppose 100ft. or more) since Cæsar's time amongst the Channel Islands and on the neighbouring French coast, it will necessarily follow that the land must have risen or sunk, as the case may be? Yes.

The errors here combated have been advanced by *geologists* (amongst others) which ought never to have been the case.

8. The following is another of these wild impossible suppositions. The greatest rise of tide in St. Ouen's Bay is about 42ft. But a gentleman gravely suggested in reference to the fact of the late Admiral White having seen two or three stumps of trees a little below extreme low water, that though the roots were below low water, the trunks may have been above *high* water! That is to say, allowing for the roots having extended a few feet into the bottom to support the trunks and keep them above high water, the roots must have extended about 50ft. vertically downwards from the trunks. For all the world like the peasants of the Landes stalking about on their long stilts! Besides, this wild conjecture violates the facts of the case, for the remains of the trunks, as well as the roots, were below extreme low water.

9. There seems to be a great reluctance in more quarters than one to admit that any stupendous events have taken place during the historical period among the Channel Islands; and a disposition to attempt to account for the interesting phenomena about to be stated by very simple, but either totally inadequate, or totally impossible causes. These attempts have already in part, and will be from time to time set forth, to give the reader an opportunity of forming his own judgment.

10. Why should any geologists object to risings and sinkings when they well know that nothing has been, and is, more common in all ages and in every part of the world? Why should they object to a sinking of twenty, or even more, fathoms when they know that marine fossils have been found at an elevation of more than 8,000ft. in the Pyrenees, 10,000ft. in the Alps, 13,000ft. in the Andes, and above 18,000ft. in the Himalaya; Captain R. J. Strackey found oolitic fossils 18,400ft. high in the Himalaya.* And the late Professor Forbes says Illampu or Sorata (Andes) 24,812ft. high is fossiliferous to the summit.† Granted that subterranean action was, generally speaking, on a grander scale of intensity in former geological periods than it is at present: and so the immense heights named are on a grander scale than the hundred and odd feet now contended for: ought geologists who know that coal, a vegetable substance once growing on the surface of the earth, is now found at 2,000ft. and more below that surface, to object to these alleged sinkings on account of

* Lyell's *Manual of Geology*, 1855, p. 4.
† *Quarterly Review*, January, 1863.

their magnitude? They know that the grander effects in ancient epochs were caused by the very same motive powers still in action at the present day. They know also that this sinking of twenty odd fathoms is not otherwise a grand event, than because it is perhaps the greatest, both in extent and depth, of any which has hitherto been known to have occurred in the historical period.

11. *The Low District Theory.*—But other views have been held than alterations of the level of the sea, and equally untenable. On the north-west of Guernsey, as we learn in a very valuable work, from the observations of a gentleman very likely to have made himself well acquainted with the facts.* Duncan's history states, and the present writer has personally assured himself of the accuracy of the statement, that peat is dug at very low tides.† This peat is justly supposed to have been derived from some catastrophe affecting the coast of the island, as well as the other islands, and the neighbouring coast of France where similar events have occurred, at some unknown date or dates. Whole trunks of trees have been found imbedded in this peat, and there is no doubt this timber grew where it was found. "This district was probably extensive, and enclosed a large portion of Rocquaine Bay, the Hanways or Hanois rocks (a dangerous reef which extends about two miles from Pleinmont Point) and the extremity of the island of Lihou. It may have passed beyond the Bays of la Perelle, Vazon, Cobo, the north-western limit of the Clos du Valle, including the whole extent of the Braye." The writer quoted is an accomplished geologist, naturalist, and antiquary; and he says in the "Archæological Journal" (what makes him one of my best witnesses) when speaking of a Cromlech at L'Ancresse Bay, on the north of Guernsey, as follows:—"At the period it was constructed the sea was at a greater distance from the site of the hill than at present, for *the whole neighbourhood bears marks of the inroads of that element:* the near approach of the sandy hills around it was caused by *those events which have so materially changed the coast of these islands, as well as that of the opposite continent.*‡ This district may, for the purpose of a calculation, be roughly stated (taking only that part of it which is contained within the watershed line on the chart, and its continuation by a dotted line) to have comprised a space of sea of various breadth, from a few hundred yards to a mile and a quarter wide, from the Hanois rocks (which are 1¼ miles west of the most western point of Guernsey)—along the north-western coast as far as the dotted boundary extends. We shall in due time have reasons for believing that the land extended still farther into the present sea in both directions. So far the author quoted and the present writer are agreed, but not so in respect to the sentence quoted in the following paragraph.

It is submitted to the reader that the proposition contained in the

---

* Duncan's *History of Guernsey*, p. 516-17.

† Tupper's valuable *History of Guernsey*, p. 37, gives 1750 as about the date when the peat and trees were first discovered.

‡ The *italics* are the present writer's. The eminent author in question thus clearly establishes the fact that great changes have taken place and diminished the extent of land.

following quotation, is admissible, because it is impossible. He says, "that the whole [of the peat and trunks of trees] was the produce of a low district which was protected from the power of the Atlantic wave by rocks and silted materials at a certain distance from the present coast line."

Now that supposed mass of rocks and silted materials must have been watertight, else the sea water would have percolated through it, and have made the supposed low district a lake, and if so the trees could not have grown there. On the other hand, if the supposed natural embankment was watertight, we are met by another insuperable difficulty derived from the following considerations: Guernsey consists of igneous rocks like the Isle of Bute, where rain guagings have been taken, and the produce of the streams has been measured all the year round.* The result was found to be that *a little more than half the annual rain flowed off by the brooks and streams.* That is to say, in Bute, an island very similar to Guernsey, in all respects in 1826, 23·9in. out of the whole quantity of 54·4in. rain, flowed off. And applying this fact to Guernsey, where the annual rain-fall averages 35in.† we shall have an annual "flow" of about half a yard in depth. And assuming by way of illustration the most probable situation for part of the supposed low district and natural embankment, the latter would have extended as shown on the map, in an irregular line say five miles long from Port Pezerie, by Rocquaine, Lihou Isle, la Conchée, Modiere, to Grand Roque. And would have had an average breadth of about half a mile clear of rocks. It would follow then that the total "gathering ground" comprised between the "watershed," or summit ridge of the hills of Guernsey; and the supposed line of natural embankment (marked on the map by a broken line) would comprise 9,934 acres. This multiplied by half a yard deep would give an annual discharge of about 24 millions of cubic *yards* of water, into the supposed low district. This large quantity would have filled the supposed lake of 5 miles long and half a mile wide, to the average depth of 9ft. 3in. This is only the produce of one year. At the end of next year the depth would have been twice as great, namely, 18ft. 6in. This must necessarily have been fatal to the trees, and the low district theory ought to be abandoned.

In early life the present writer paid a fee to a firm of land-surveyors, to learn the art of measuring and mapping land. He afterwards was connected in professional business as a civil engineer, with the late highly distinguished engineer, Robert Stephenson, F.R.S., and his scarcely less distinguished partners, Messrs. Bidder and Gooch, under whom, as engineers-in-chief, he executed many important engineering works, and is not without experience in hydraulic engineering. Those who are not familiar with the method stated, of viewing the question, are informed that calculations are made in this way by hydraulic engineers, when planning reservoirs to supply towns. A more familiar method of arriving at a con-

---

* See Beardmore's *Hydraulic Tables*, 1852, p. 30.

† The late F. C. Lukis, Esq., M.D., F.R.S., of Guernsey, kindly volunteered to send the present writer this result of about fifteen years' rain gaugings.

clusion, is to remember that the whole of the brooks and streams of the district, whatever their number, would have been perpetually running day and night, from year end to year end, into the supposed low district. And it is obvious that if you wish to fill a reservoir, you have only to allow a few brooks to run into it perpetually day and night.

11A. The diagram shows the nature of the change which has taken place, the tides are shown as they are at Jersey; but no particular place is intended to be represented; and the diagram is not drawn to any scale horizontally. Some thirty years ago a line of levels was very carefully carried across the peninsula, from near Lyme Regis on the English Channel, to East Quantockshead on the Bristol Channel, under the auspices of the late Professor Whewell, to ascertain if there was any, and if so, what difference in level between the half tides of the two channels. And the difference of level was found to be practically nothing. A detailed account is contained in one of the volumes of Philosophical Transactions of the Royal Society.

REFERENCE.—*a* High water; *b* low water of a Spring tide. The rise represented is 39ft., but the greatest Springs rise 42ft. at Jersey. *c* high water; *d* low water of a neap tide. Rise 14ft. *E* half tide level, *invariable.*

12. *Remarkable angularity of the marine rocks on the west and south of Jersey.*—It is observable that in the Banc du Viellet, on the south of Jersey, comprising the large extent of about ten square miles, as well as in the Bay of St. Ouen's, both which tracts of rocks, except the tops of a very few of the loftiest of them, are covered and uncovered at every tide: the rocks so covered and uncovered are more angular than rocks which are high above the sea, and have been exposed to the weather during the whole Quarternary period perhaps; though every one knows that the action of the tides, particularly in storms, is much more effective in rounding off the angles of rocks than mere weather. A gentleman suggests that pieces of stone are continually broken off the marine rocks by the violence of the sea, and that in consequence sharp angles are continually left to the rocks. To this it may be answered that it is true there has been a considerable amount of breaking off of pieces of rock, but, if that were all, those pieces ought to have become rounded by the action of the sea, and there ought to have been considerable banks of *rounded* gravel; but there is nothing of the kind worth mentioning in either locality. The rocks of the Banc du Viellet consist of hornblende, granite, sienite, and porphyry, and, in St. Ouen's Bay, of crystalline clay, slate. They may be observed in the case of the Banc de Viellett, which Poingdestre's statement (to be presently mentioned) naturally leads one to expect, namely, that though there are abundance of fragments chipped off, neither they nor the fixed rocks have *had time* to become rounded. You may find one in a hundred subangular, and one in five hundred rounded, or, still more rarely, an oval or elliptical pebble well rounded; but having been only exposed to the action of the sea probably since the year 1356, they are of course much less rounded than if they had been so

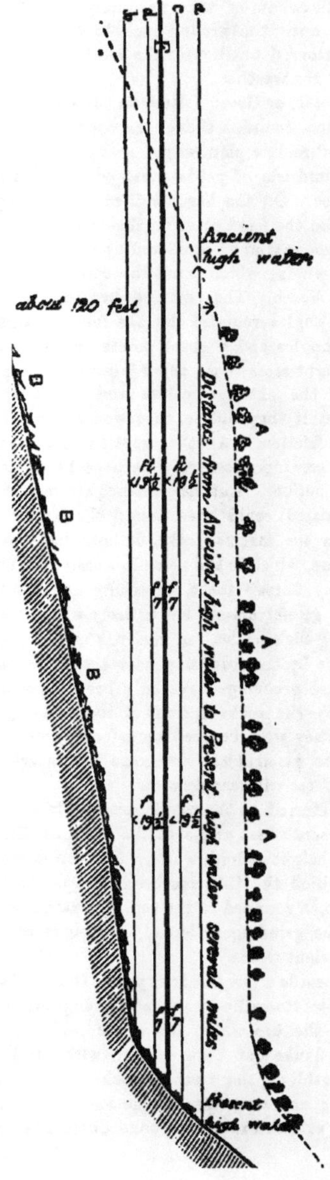
Ancient high water
about 120 feet
Distance from Ancient high water to Present high water several miles.
Present high water
A
B

exposed during the whole of the quartenary period. I say they were covered with soil until the ground sunk in that year, and the angles of the rocks were preserved until after the soil had been washed away, even from the action of the weather.

About Isle la Motte, or Green Island, on the south of Jersey, the angles of the rocks are less rounded though exposed to the action of the sea, than at the Fairies' rock, a picturesque group of porphyry rocks on the mainland, some hundreds of yards north of Green Island, and quite out of reach of the sea. On the beaches themselves, the pebbles are a good deal rounded, as also the fixed rocks on their west and south, by reason of the action of the coarse sand when stirred by the waves under the influence of the prevalent winds; which is not the case (except on rare occasions) to seaward of the beach. The chimæra has been started, that Fairies' Rock has had its angles rounded by the feet of sight-seers. But on the contrary, the angles and highest points are rounded where it would be dangerous for sight-seers to go, and it is certain that people will seldom, if ever, stand on the extreme points and edges, which are the parts rounded; and even if they did so, they would be cautious and still, and exercise very little friction. Another gentleman has suggested that the phenomena under consideration, may perhaps be explained by the supposition of glacial action. But he does not attempt to show how glacial action (if it had existed) could have caused the land rocks to have been more rounded than the marine rocks, if both had been exposed for an equal length of time, which is the point in question. The present writer has examined many Jersey rocks, especially on the north side of the island, for signs of glacial action, but entirely without success. There is a good example of "slickensides," or one rock grooving another by sliding down it,—to be seen by the road side near the entrance of the village of L'Etacq. But these groovings have only been exposed to view for some half dozen years, by the rocks in front of them having been removed to widen the road. They were covered up before by other rock, and it was quite impossible for glaciers to have come in contact with them. But there is no end to these wild conjectures.

The reader is referred to the bathing rock, a large mass of granite on the beach at the south-east angle of the town of St. Helier, which is covered to half its height at high water. The top is more rounded than the eastern flank which the tide reaches. The flanks on the south and west sides are as much rounded as the top, in consequence of their having been exposed to the grinding action of the sands of the beach, when stirred by the prevalent winds.

Proceeding westwards a few hundred yards, the reddish-topped tract of sienite rock opposite Roseville-street, is very angular everywhere; but it is less angular on the top which the waves seldom reach than on the flanks. As if the flanks had been covered with earth and so protected. The like may be said of the tract of rocks to the west, and also of a tract further south; and very few of the small loose pieces lying about can be said to have attained so much roundedness as even to entitle them to be called sub-angular. The like is true as to marine rocks of St. Ouen's Bay.

The Royal Geographical Society are about to publish a somewhat full abstract in their journal, of that which is about to be given in detail in these papers. The writer sent them a stereoscopic view of some beach rocks at Pontac on the south coast of Jersey (the only copy he had), which shows the angularity in question. And a local firm of photographers have promised to take more views to illustrate this very interesting fact.

13. It would be well on the present occasion to remember the words of Hesiod, "Πιστις δᾶρἅ δμῶς καl απιστla ωλεσαν ἄνδρας."—"Faith and no faith have equally ruined men." And while we try to hit the proper medium between believing too much and believing nothing, we ought to be cautious *not* to explain away in the sense of getting rid of, and not to refuse to believe things which are quite possible and sanctioned by abundant evidence; although they may perhaps not accord with our preconceived ideas. Milton's rule which he gives in the preface to his "History of England" appears to be sound, and it will be followed in this series of papers. He says: "That which hath received approbation from so many I have chosen not to omit. Certain or uncertain, be that upon the credit of those whom I must follow. So far as keeps aloof from impossible and absurd, attested by ancient writers from books more ancient, I refuse not, as the due and proper subject of story."

Everything appears to have been honestly related in the present case, and one circumstance often corroborates another preceding. And there certainly has not been a grand conspiracy amongst chroniclers and historians, continued through nineteen centuries, to forge records for the purpose of deceiving posterity.

At the same time we ought to remember with the illustrious Polybius,* that it is in vain to attempt to gather history from individual circumstances. He says, "Particular relations are by no means capable of yielding any clear or extensive view into general history; the only method which can render this kind of study both entertaining and instructive, is that which draws together all the several events, and ranges them in their due place and order, distinguishing also their connection and their difference." He very justly compares the study of a particular history, to the study of a particular member of the human body. In either case, we should certainly fail to obtain a complete knowledge of the whole.

NOTE.—Notwithstanding the answers to objections and the general clearing of the ground in this paper; the facts to be stated are so extraordinary that the writer has felt it desirable that as little as possible should depend only on his own *ipse dixit*. He has, therefore, copied out many important passages from classical, middle age, and modern authors, as guarantees of his good faith in correctly quoting and faithfully translating; which passages he therefore calls voucher A, B, &c. But it would not be fitting to load the columns of *The Artizan* with Greek, Latin,

* Polybius, a Greek historian, died about 124 B.C. Many statues were erected to him.

and old French. Translations of the whole, or great part of them, will be given. And the vouchers themselves can be printed as an appendix, if ever the demand should arise for the republication of the Memoir in a volume.

---

## CHAPTER II.

### *The Sinkings have been sudden, not continuous.*

18*a*. The catastrophes about to come under consideration, have not been gradual and continuous, consisting of so many feet and inches per century; as is the case on the south of Sweden. The country to the north of S. Malo is described by the historian as having been "swallowed up in an instant;" whilst the vast tract of Britanny inundated, but afterwards recovered by embanking, appears to have gradually sunk from day to day for several days, without any sudden shock of the nature of an earthquake. The sinkings about Jersey in 1356, so far as can be gathered, appear also to have been sudden; of the nature of the more ancient sinking about Elizabeth Castle, there is no record. With regard to those about Guernsey, there does not appear to be any record either of the time or the manner of their occurrence.

I have before me "A Survey of the Islands of Guernsey, Sercq, and Herm, with the surrounding dangers," by Capt. Martin White, R.N. (Published by the Admiralty, August 30th, 1822, and corrected by Capt. White to 1840. Scale about 2in. to a geographical mile.) Also a "Chart of the English Channel Islands, Guernsey, Herm, and Serk, surveyed by Commander Sidney and J. Richards, Master R.N., 1859-62," with corrections to March, 1864, on a scale of about 4in. to one geographical, or sea mile. And by drawing corresponding lines on each chart across the Great Russel Channel, from Sercq, &c., on one side of the Channel to Herm, &c., on the other side of it, the following table of greatest soundings has been obtained, Capt. White's soundings, which he gives in fathoms, having been first reduced to English feet.

| Capt. White.* | Messrs. Sidney and Richards.† | Differences. |
|---|---|---|
| ft. | ft. | ft. |
| 168 | 127 | 41 |
| 180 | 141 | 39 |
| 168 | 124 | 44 |

From which it appears that, although Captain White's datum is three feet lower than that of Messrs. Sidney and Richards, he makes the soundings about 40ft. in addition, greater than they do. How this difference has arisen I do not know, but am certainly not at all disposed to attribute it to

* Capt. White's "soundings denote the depth in fathoms at low water equinoctial tides."
† "Soundings in feet at low water, mean springs, equinoctial springs fall 3ft. lower."

so great a shallowing of the water as 43ft. in the short space of twenty-four years. In Little Russel Channel, between Guernsey and Herm, I find no material difference between the two series of soundings.

I shall, doubtless, be expected to express an opinion what probability there appears to be of farther sinkings. And my view is this. Since there is no proof that any sinkings have taken place for 510 years about Jersey, and probably as long at the Northern islands, and for at least four centuries near St. Malo, I am under no apprehensions. I reside with my family literally within a stone's-throw of the sea on the south of Jersey, the house floor not exceeding 10ft. above the highest tides, and think myself as safe as in the average of localities of the *temperate* regions of the earth; and of course safer than in the *torrid* regions, where volcanoes and earthquakes are so much more common. I am disposed to compare these localities to a discharged gun. It has been discharged, and is consequently as harmless as any other combination of wood and iron.

14. *Sinkings in St. Ouen's, St. Brelade's, and St. Aubin's Bays, on the west and south of Jersey.*—The weight of what is said, depends a good deal on the ability and probable extent of knowledge of him who says it. Looking at Mr. Poingdestre's testimony from this point of view, it may safely be affirmed that he was a learned and pains-taking antiquary, and a gentleman of great abilities and acquirements. He makes no claim to be a geologist; in fact, in his time, geology was only struggling by the efforts of Steno, Scilla, Plot, Lister, Leibnitz, and Hook,* through clouds of error and conjecture into the dignity of a science.

*Biographical.*—John Poingdestre was born in Jersey in 1609. He became a Fellow of Exeter College, Oxford, and was one of the best Greek scholars in the University. He was ejected from his fellowship for his loyalty by the Parliamentary visitors. His skill in languages, his acquaintance with the civil and Roman laws, and his other acquirements, introduced him into the Secretary of State's office under Lord Digby, where he continued until the affairs of Charles I. had grown desperate. He afterwards assisted in the defence of Jersey and Elizabeth Castle against the "rebels," as Falle calls the Parliamentary forces. After the Restoration he was made Lieutenant-Bailly of Jersey, and died in that island, in his eighty-third year, in 1691. He had from his earliest days been collecting all the historical antiquities he could find in print or upon records.†

He is the author of No. 5,417 of the Harleian MSS. of the British Museum, which is a historical sketch of Jersey, consisting of 44 folios or leaves, quarto size, bound in Russia leather, and profusely gilt over the backs. There is no date. It is written neatly and clearly since Camden's time, for the first chapter commences with the words:—"The isle of Jersey in Mr. Cambden's accompt," &c. On the first fly leaf occur the following words, in a different handwriting, and evidently ancient:—"This did belong to King James I had it from Coll. Grahme." The title of the book is "Cæsarea, or a Discourse of the Island of Jersey in two parts. The first an accompt

* Lyell's *Principles of Geology*.
† See Falle's *History of Jersey* and its preface by the Rev. Edward Durell; Tupper's *History of Guernsey*, &c.

of it as it is at present. The second Some Historicall observations relating to antiquity." He presented this MS. to King James II. on his accession to the throne, which event occurred February 6th, 1685. The date of the book is important, because, as we shall presently see, Poingdestre mentions that "the sea hath overwhelmed within these 350 years the richest soile" of the parish of St. Ouen's. Deducting 350 from 1,685 gives 1,335, which is an answer to those who allege that there have been no sinkings in this locality within the historical period. We must necessarily adopt the date 1356 for the submersion of St. Ouen's forest, as there is direct testimony to that effect. Of course Poingdestre's period of 350 years from 1685 embraces 1356. He says in the same sentence that the land extended "very farre into the sea," which, in connection with other testimonies to be hereinafter given, is an answer to those who contend that the lost land was a mere narrow belt along the present coast. Though the present writer neither affirms nor denies the well-known tradition that the only wate between Jersey and France was once capable of being crossed by a plank, ·et neither does Poingdestre disprove that tradition by showing that Jersey as been an island ever since Antoninus' Itinerary, (so-called) was written. ·rst, because if an island at *high* water, the space between it and France ny have been dry or nearly so at *low* water; it being possible to cross even y'at extreme low water, without going into water more than about four fathoms deep. And second, because as will be seen presently, Jersey was pro·bly part of the Continent in Cæsar's time, and still later.

1 The following is an important extract from Poingdestre's MS.

"Of things detrimentall."

"CHAPTER XV.

"Iave been ouer prolixe in discoursing of those things which may be of some auty or advantage to the Isle of Jersey. Bona fides requires that I shouldot conceale the other things, which may seem to be of the some deform or disadvantage to it. It cannot be denied but that the said Isle of Jers is much beholding to the sea, yt supplies it so abundantly with bread a firing, that is with Vraic an excellent fewell and manure for ye grour both burn't and unburn't, besides fish, navigation, and other conveniency which ye sea affoards. But if one consider the great diminucions which ye ·d Island hath suffered both of old time and lately by inundations and ·ls, it will be hard to say whither those advantages or those losses be y ·eater, for first it appears by history that ye Islet nowe about a mile dista rom the land was about eleven hundred years ago ioyned to it:* for St. aglorius settled himselfe there or erected a Schoole of Christianity, ·ch was continued until at last it was converted into an Abby, of whic he shallowness of the sea between that small Island and ye Towne, and along ye coast towards St. Albin, and between ye fort there and ye n part of y land, is noe contemptible testimony: [?] If soe, it is not h to guesse what a tract of good land hath been lost by that incroachmen the wator. Next it is acknowledged, and ye records

* This gives the dat the separation in 485. We shall find further on the year 687 given. And the Edito the MS. *Chroniques de Jersey*, writing in 1832 (p. 242), says it happened 1175 years a hich gives the date 657.

of those times testifye it, that in ye parish of St. Ouen, the sea hath overwhelmed within these 350 years the richest soile of that parish, that is a vale from beyond the Poole towards Lestac in lenght, and in breadth from the hills very farre into the sea, and that to this day stumpes of oakes are found in ye sand during the Ebbe, and some ruins of buildings among the rocks: the like whereof is also seen in the Bay of St. Brelade." It will now be convenient to interrupt the quotation from Poingdestre, in order to corroborate him; and, in passing, to mention the following interesting fact, for which I am indebted to my friend, T. W. Clarke, Esq., of her Majesty's Customs. He says four trees, one of large size, were seen in the Bay of St. Brelade's, in April, 1866, lying in the sand, near the centre of this bay and at about half tide mark.

16. A paper, of which the following is a copy, was given to the present writer in February, 1860, by Mr. George Mauger, of St. Lawrence Parish, Jersey, who said he had copied it from the "*Gazette de l'Isle de Jersey*, du 28 Avril, 1787, imprimée par Math. Alexandre":—

"*Troncs d'Arbres* decouverts à St. Ouen, Jersey, pendant l'Hiver, 1786.

"Il faudrait posséder une philosophie plus qu'humaine pour concevoir les révolutions étonnantes qu'a subies la face du globe, depuis le commencement des temps jusqu'à present: je n'entends pas des revolutions politiques; c'est du naturel que je veux parler.

"Ce petit pays que nous habitons nous en fournit des preuves assez curieuses. Les troncs et les racines d'arbres qui se sont decouverts l'hiver dernier, par l'agitation de la mer, dans la Baye de S. Ouen, et qui sont encore visibles, nous fournissent un sujet de contemplation dans des tems fort reculés. On voit des milliers d'arbres couchés les uns près des autres dans cette baye, depuis la Corbière * jusqu'aux deux bancs de sable à quelques milles du plein de la mer.† Par ces débris antiques on ne peut douter que tout ce terrein, aussi bien que celui au-dessus, appelé les mielles, n'ait été autrefois de riches prairies et des forêts épaisses, qui ont été submergées par quelque événement extraordinaire. Parmi ces arbres on en voit de forts gros, et on assure qu'après une tempête de certains vents, ils viennent si au-dessus du sable qu' il est fort difficile pour des chariots de passer.‡ Peut-être les Bayes de S. Helier, de S. Clement et de Grouville qui sont étendues, ont-elles subi le même sort, et que la mer qui n'est aisée dans ces endroits là ne nous découvre rien de semblable; car il est à remarquer que ce n'est que rarement et après de gros vent que ceux dans la Baye de St. Ouen sont rendus visibles."

The "mielles" is now called "les Quenvais." This is still high above the sea, having only been submerged by sand drifted from the shore.

On Great Bank the soundings are from 7 to 9 fathoms at low water and the greatest rise of tide is 42ft. And if we suppose the original forest to have been 10ft. above high water (it can hardly have been less), we shall

* The S.W. angle of Jersey.

† Rigdon Shoal and Great Bank are respectively about two and three miles from high water.

‡ The beach was then a public road.

have a sinking of at least 100ft. It will presently be seen that the three bays he names "were subjected to the same fate" of having sunk.

17. *St. Ouen's Bay.*—On the 26th April, 1861, at St. Aubin's, Jersey; the Rev. G. J. le Maistre, head master of the grammar school there, and medallist, T.C.D., made the following statement, which the present writer took down in writing. He said that, "fifty or sixty years ago his father, who is now dead, saw a good many stumps and roots of trees, standing apparently *in situ* where they had grown, below low water. They were near L'Etacq village at the north end of St. Ouen's Bay. When his grandfather, now also dead, took his father there, he looked out for the remains of a brick house which he had formerly seen, and more particularly for a stone trough for watering cattle. From which he (the Rev. G. J. le Maistre) infers that his grandfather must have previously seen these things in the same part of the bay as aforesaid. His grandfather was born in 1754."

18. Vice-Admiral White, a resident of Jersey, and who has since died there on July 2nd, 1865,* was formerly Capt. Martin White, R.N., and by direction of the Lords Commissioners of the Admiralty he made a survey about 1822, which he corrected up to 1840, with very numerous soundings of the Channel Islands seas; from which, with the assistance of some soundings from the beautiful large scale charts of the French Government, the map annexed has been prepared, and the statements contained in these papers have been obtained. On May 22nd, 1860, he personally stated to the present writer that "in taking soundings he saw two or three stumps of trees in St. Ouen's Bay, a little outside of low water. They were fixed in the soil, or sea bottom, near la Pule or Pinnacle."

18*a*. After several personal attempts to find in St. Ouen's Bay at extreme low tides stumps or roots of trees, the writer has not succeeded in finding any except at and on the beach, at a maximum depth of about 8ft. below high water. On May 18th, 1859, on the beach a few hundred yards south of L'Etacq village, there was an old oak lying prostrate with its root south and top north, a little below high water. On July 4th, 1859, the writer measured along the beach of St. Ouen's Bay, from the westerly angle of the British Star Hotel, 1,250 yards southward, and at that place there commenced a space of beach extending 115 yards southward by 20 yards wide, on which trees had formerly grown, for there were both stumps and roots. One tree must have been a very large one. Generally the stumps were gone, but there were abundance of roots radiating from the places where each tree had stood; and at about a quarter of a mile further along the beach were other stumps of trees. The whole are often covered up and hidden by the shingle, being covered and uncovered by the tides. The present writer's not having seen any terrestrial remains far out in St. Ouen's Bay is of no importance, because, as has been stated, there is plenty of good and reliable testimony of gentlemen who have seen them.

19. On April 27th, 1861, Mr. Le Feuvre, of Le Hogue, St. Peter's parish, Jersey, personally informed the writer that there are quantities

---

* This amiable gentleman and accomplished scientific officer attained the ripe old age of eighty-four years.

of submerged trees in St. Ouen's Bay, due west of the pond. He has seen two *in situ*, with upright trunks broken off at two or three feet high. He and the writer went to look for them at low water of an equinoctial spring tide, but they were covered up, as they often are, by the wind and waves having drifted sand over them.

St. Ouen's pond is about opposite the *middle* of the bay, the village of l'Etacq and the tower-like rock called the Pinnacle being at the *north end* of the bay. Thus a second submerged locality is identified.

20. The late Mr. Daniel Janvrin, a banker of St. Helier, then at an advanced period in life, who with his forefathers were natives and inhabitants of Jersey, on May 14th, 1860, personally informed the writer that his great-grandfather remembered there being a forest at La Pulente, at the *south end* of St. Ouen's Bay; and that his said great-grandfather either paid or received, he does not remember which, a corn rent on account of it. This must have been a payment, not a receiving, because the forest belonged to the Crown. It is known that John Wallis (Seigneur), proprietor of the sunken forest of St. Ouen's, forfeited his estates to the Crown for joining in the Earl of Warwick's rebellion. The Earl and he were both killed at the battle of Barnet, which is known as a matter of history to have occurred in 1471.

21. February 21st, 1865, Mr. P. J. Simon, receiver of the Queen's rents in Jersey, informed the writer as follows, by reference to his books of account:—"There were rents payable for allowing pigs to go into the former forest of St. Ouen's Bay, but those rents are not now collected. The small rent of three sous payable three times a year for a right of road from St. Ouen's church to the shore, called *Percage*, has been erroneously supposed to have been paid for the pigs, under the supposition that it meant *Pourcage*. But *Percage* is probably derived from *Percer*, to pierce, or break through. He does not know any manor called La Braquette, but there may be a house of that name in St. Ouen's parish. The fiefs Handoys, in the parish of St. Lawrence, Grainville, and Pesnel (which last is very small), in St. John's parish at Mont Mado, and Morville and Robilliard, in St. Ouen's parish, along with the former forest in St. Ouen's Bay, were formerly all comprised in the Seigniory of St. Germains, of which more presently. The payments made for the pigs come under the head of "Herbage," but the books contain no details of any animals in especial. Mr. Simon has no doubt that there was once a forest in St. Ouen's Bay."

22. Mr. Simon's statement will have prepared the reader to believe that such statements as the following, may be heard now and then in the parish of St. Ouen's, as is really the case. On the 7th July, 1859, the writer accidentally met at the village of St. Ouen's, Mr. John Breard, of St. Ouen's parish, aged 83; who stated that his brother, who had died a few months before, used to pay a rent for the privilege of putting his pigs into the forest of St. Ouen's, though it had long since been destroyed by the sea. It is well known that royal rights are never lost, so long as it is thought proper to enforce them.

23. In 1826, "A brief description of the Island of Jersey," was published by Messrs. Le Lievre, publishers and booksellers, St. Helier. The author's

name is not given, but it is known.* And it is known also that he was a gentleman of ability, and that he had intimates in official positions, who were well qualified to give him authentic information. He says, page 13, speaking of the Bay of St. Ouen's: "At a period not more remote than the end of the fourteenth century, or beginning of the fifteenth century, groves of oaks and fertile meadows occupied a portion of the bay, now proudly triumphed over by the usurping billows. At some particular seasons of the year, when the tide recedes to a greater distance than usual, the stems of trees are still observable, and what will cause us still further to lament the inundation, what once were the habitations of men. As the irruption from its force must necessarily have been sudden, and its progress rapid, we scarcely need speculate on the fate of its inhabitants. That the calamity was very extensive, and the loss of property great, is known with a certainty which it would be vain to doubt. A record is still in existence granting to an inhabitant of the parish, the privilege of feeding his herds of swine in the forest of St. Ouen's, and the following extract from a patent issued in the reign of Charles II.,† gives many particulars of the district now lost, and affords us some information respecting the proprietor of the greatest part of the territory thus calamitously inundated. The fief Morville and Robilliard, being a part and parcel of the fief of St. Germain, in the island of Jersey, appertained anciently to a gentleman of the name of John Wallis; his manor was situated on the same fief in the valley and country of a village called l'Etacq, on the borders of the sea, and was called the manor of la Braquette, near which there was a forest of oak and other large trees, on the east and north of the said manor, which is now below high-water mark. The said valley and manor have for many years been covered by the sea; nevertheless, when the sea goes down, there are still seen remains of the said manor; and after a tempest and damage caused by the sea, is found a quantity of large oak trees, where formerly was the said valley of l'Etacq. After the sea had so over-run its bounds, the said Wallis retired to the parish of St. Laurence, in the said island, where he built a chateau, now in ruins, which is called the chateau of St. Germain." St. Lawrence is the central parish of Jersey.

24. The following most interesting and important statement was given me by Mr. George Mauger of St. Lawrence. Quoted from the *Almanach de Jersey* for 1849, of which I have not been fortunate enough to obtain a copy.

(Extrait d'un Ancien Manuscrit.)

*Ravages causés par la Mer à Jersey.*

"En l'année 1356, dans la paroisse de St. Ouen, la mer engloutit un assez riche canton de terrain. Les Registres de l'Echiquier font mention d'un peuple qui habitait cette portion de terre.

"La Forêt de la Brequette fut renversée et engloutie par l'affreux ouragan d'alors.

"En ladite année 1356, John Maturins était Gardien de Jersey (aujourdhui Governeur), et Guillaume Hostein était Bailli de cette dite Isle.

"En l'an 1495, un grand banc de sable fut jeté par une tempête au plein de la mer qui monta et couvrit et ensevelit cette longue étendue de terre à l'ouest de la dite Isle, laquelle ressemble à un désert; et suivant toutes les apparences, que le grands vents de l'Ouest qui soufflent ici dans toutes les saisons et une partie de l'année, ont élevé le sable qui a causé ce désastre.*

"Il y a environ 1134 ans que la petite Ile où est bâti le Chateau Elizabeth fut détachée de la terre ferme, vers l'an 687." This gives date 1821; *i.e.*, 1134 + 673 = 1821.

"N.B. Par une ancienne tradition, il est pretendu que la maison de M. de St. Germains fut ensevelie sous les sables de l'Ouest de ladite Ile, et qu'ensuite ayant fait mesurer l'île en longueur et largeur, il fit bâtir une maison au milieu, située on la Paroisse de St. Laurens, laquelle porte encore aujourdhui le nom des St. Germains; mais je n'ai jamais rien vu qui autorise cette tradition."—From the Jersey Almanack, 1849, p. 99, publié par Perrot et Huelin, au le Bureau de la Chronique.

25. There are extant eight or ten copies in MS. of a M.S. of the date of 1585, entitled *Chroniques de Jersey*, by an anonymous writer, who was probably one of the de Carterets of St. Ouen's Manor, one of the most distinguished families of the island. A copy of one of these was published in Guernsey, in 1832, by Mr. George Syvret, and republished in Jersey by Abraham Mourant, Ecrivain, in 1858, who gives ten pages of errata, addenda, and corrigenda to the 1832 edition. The Rev. Edward Durell, then rector of St. Saviour's, in Jersey, republished, in 1837, Falle's *History of Jersey*, and he says the Chroniques "is a valuable performance, the publication of which is an important acquisition. As to their veracity, it is confirmed by the Records (of Jersey) in many particulars.† and there is little doubt that most, if not all, of their chivalrous embellishments are true." Mr. Durell reminds us that in virtue of his right as one of the twelve rectors of *The States*, he had access to the Records. It appears from Chapter III. of the printed edition of the Chroniques of 1858, that Robert de Norton and William de la Rue, Commissioners appointed by King Edward III. in 1331, ascertained that at that date, amongst the possessions of the Seigneurs named, the then Seigneur of St. Germain's (p. 12), possessed the fiefs "Granville, Morville, Handois et Pesnel." By the politeness of Mr. T. W. Rose, the writer has been enabled to peruse one of the MS. copies which belongs to him, and which has every appearance of being as old as 1585, and which contains the statements above given, and enumerates the seigniory and fiefs as follows:—"Le Seigneur de St. Germain, Grainville, Morville, Handoyo, etc., and Fieu Pesnel." And afterwards, "St. Germain, Handoye, Grainville, le fieu Penel, le fieu Cheney, et le fieu de Morville."

It is stated in *Chroniques de Jersey*, p. 236, not as part of the ancient

* This sentence has nothing to do with the sinking, it refers only to the drifting of sand from the shore over the Quenvals, with which the latter is still covered about three yards thick.

† A great quantity of the Jersey Records was unfortunately burnt many years ago.

MS., but as part of "a Historical abridgement concerning the isles of Jersey Guernsey, Auregney, and Serk," by George S. Syvret, that, "In the parish of S. Ouen, the sea has swallowed up a very rich district within about 400 years," [this would give the date 1432, as he writes in 1832, but 1356 was probably the correct date] "which one may compare to the parishes du Valle and St. Sampson, in the Isle of Guernsey, and this country is now called the Bay of St. Ouen," &c.

The forest of St. Ouen's no doubt belonged to a Wallis, Seigneur of St. Germains, at the time of the submersion.

It has been suggested that the rocks about Elizabeth Castle have probably experienced no change *since* the building of St. Helier's Hermitage, which still exists with its arched stone roof in very fair repair, because, it is said, such a change would probably have fractured the building, if not brought it down entirely. From Lecanu's *Hist. des évêques de Coutances*, p. 48, we learn that St. Helier was martyred in Jersey about A.D. 578. This argument, however, is by no means conclusive, because the hermitage is very small, and the rocks may have quietly and slowly settled down without any shock, as we shall see in due time that leagues of land settled down in Britanny, day by day, and *so quietly* that nobody suspected the ground was sinking.

26. The word "Grune" and its plural "Grunes" will be observed to occur a good many times on the annexed chart. It is an obsolete French word signifying *low marshy ground*, and is perhaps the equivalent, or it may be the origin of our English word "Ground," which is still pronounced *Grund* by the country people in the north of England. And Grün is *the green* in German. Metivier of Guernsey says, "The root Grune is Cymric, Gröyn, pebbles, ridge of pebbles formed by the sea; bas-breton, green gravel. And though it is not contended that the fact of many marine rocks being now called "Grunes" is of itself conclusive evidence that those rocks have been dry land within the last nineteen centuries, yet neither, on the other hand, would it have been right to omit all mention of the circumstances just stated. The following is a descriptive account of the positions of some grunes in St. Aubin's Bay, which could not be conveniently marked on the chart for fear of over-crowding. Petite Grune is 9-10ths of a mile W. by S. of Noirmont Tower. Grand Grune, 1 mile S.W. by W. Grunes Vaudin S.W. rocks, 1½ mile S. by W. Grunes aux Dards, 9-10ths of a mile S.S.E. Grunes St. Michel, 1½ mile S.E. by E. Grunes de Port, ½ mile E. These are bearings (true, not magnetic), from Noirmont Tower, which is at the western extremity of St. Aubin's Bay. Trois Grunes are 1½ mile S.E. by S. from Elizabeth Castle. The word Grune has been inadvertently applied on some of the charts to high marine rocks; which is no more true than it would be to call the top of a mountain, a valley. Further remarks on "Grune" appear in Art. 145.

*Note.*—Mr. George Metivier of Guernsey, an eminent etymologist and philologist, objects to this interpretation of *Grûne*; for reasons given by him which will be quoted hereafter, as well as the answers to them. Several other etymologies will also be considered, hereafter.

27. Capt. Ranwell, R.N., informs the writer that he was at Jersey with

his ship in 1812, and there were then to be seen stumps of trees near low water mark, in the north-west part of St. Aubin's Bay near St. Aubin's Tower. He did not see them, but several of his ship's company saw them. The highest tides rise in St. Aubin's Bay 42ft.

28. The writer has been credibly informed that two or three years ago, stumps of trees were found in the bottom, which the tide never leaves, outside of St. Helier's harbour, near Crapaud rock.

29. The following has been communicated by Mr. Manger, of St. Lawrence:—

" *Chronique de Jersey*, du Mercredi, 7 Avril, 1847

"Les excavations que l'on fait en ce moment pour asseoir les fondations de la Nouvelle Chaussée du Nord viennent ajouter des preuves incontestables à l'appui de l'assertion de plusieurs historiens, que les rochers sur lesquels sont construits le Château Elizabeth et l'Ermitage formaient jadis partie du littoral, c'est-a-dire que le grand espace connu sous le nom de Baie de S. Aubin était recouvert de terre et élevé au-dessus du niveau de la mer haute. A cinq ou six pieds de profondeur, les ouvriers trouvent une riche terre végétable et une profusion de racines d'arbres en parfait état de conservation. Nous devons ajouter, dans l'interêt de nos agriculteurs, que cette terre, qui doit être un excellent engrais, est à la disposition de ceux qui voudront en prendre pour leur usage."

Mr. Jurat Nicolle says that nuts, as well as stumps and roots of trees, were found in sinking the foundations of the new pier.

30. May 7th, 1865.—The present writer examined the sandy surface where the brook runs down on the north-west of the long pier of the new harbour of St. Helier, and found numerous remains of trees. They were mostly decayed, and contained numbers of sandworms, which were devouring them. There were several parts of trunks of trees of from one to five yards long, lying prostrate on the sand in a direction about north-west and south-east. Some of these trees when entire had been as thick as a man's body. Had one stump with parts of the roots dug up, and brought it away, and afterwards exhibited it before the Geological Section at Birmingham. Am not certain of the species, but think it is birch. Another larger stump was attempted to be got up; the interior from its great resistance must have been sound; it was probably an oak. The spade broke, and the writer was not sorry to leave this stump *in situ*, where it is to be hoped it will long remain as an interesting record of the remarkable position of an ancient forest. Many of the remains of the trees are quite rotten, and must soon be carried off by the action of the sea. The trees extend from about where the brook issues from the pier wall, south-westwardly and parallel to the wall, to a place about 180 yards short of the principal angle of the wall near the wooden shed. One large trunk of a tree, about three yards long, the upper half of which is gone, lies transversely across the brook opposite the highest part of a low expanse of rock, where the greatest rise of tide must be about 18ft. or 20ft. Some of the stumps of trees are in an upright position with roots inserted in the sandy loam; such was the one brought away. The trees can be seen from the parapet of the pier

without going down upon the sand, and it is to be hoped that gentlemen will be very moderate in taking away specimens, otherwise these curious and important relics must soon become extinct.

Saturday, Sept. 2nd, 1865.—Re-examined those stumps, and took one of them (oak), and exhibited it, as well as the former one, to the Geological Section at Birmingham, when reading a paper on the subject on Sept. 9th. It was decayed, except the heart, which was light brown, nearly the natural colour, and was generally thought not to have been long submerged.

31. To the south-westward of the Engineers' Barracks, which are at the south end of the Fort Regent, is a rock called *Les Quesnais*, *Quesne* signifying in the ancient language the modern *Chêne*, an oak, and *Quesnais* means a wood of oaks, *i.e.*, plural number, as if formerly there had been a forest of oaks there. The Quesnais is a full mile seawards, from present high water. It is covered at high water. At all events, it is right to have stated these circumstances, whether it be true that Les Quesnais once formed part of the Isle of Jersey, or not.

In the "reference" to the Diagram last month the following explanations were omitted:—A A A, position of the forest *before* the ground sunk; B B B, position of forest *after* the ground sunk.

More than twenty years ago the writer had tide staffs erected in Morecambe Bay, and, except when the water was disturbed by strong winds, he found half-tide level was at a uniform height, both in spring, neap, and medium tides.

32. It will now be convenient to continue the quotation from Mr. Poingdestre's M.S., commencing at the point where it was interrupted in Article 15:—"But of late years, within the memory of most men, two great rocks lying one behind the other in the sea at a place called Le Hoc, in St. Clement's parish, the nearest of which is severed from the land a bowshot at full sea, were *ioyned to it*,* and served many men yet alive to drye vraic upon; *which in former times was the fate of a great tract of land neere Mont Orgueil Castle, called le Banc du Viellet, which appeareth above water at halfe ebbe, like an island, at some distance from the maine land.* As for the sands, because the hurt from them is caused by westerly winds (which blowe the greatest part of the year in these islands), and drive them from the seawards upon the land, theire disaster is not seen but in the westerne parts, and espĕlly in the parishes of St. Ouen and St. Brelade; but greater in the last, even at the very top of it, which of a long time is utterly covered therewith a great depth, that it is hideous to behold, and of no use or profit at all, being above the third part of that parish. Not to speake of the harme don by those sands in y^e parish of St. Helery from y^e very town to y^e bulwark of St. Lawrence, which is not a little; all y^e bay of St. Ouen, *formerly full of meadows and good arable ground*, is within these fewe years quite spoiled by y^e sands, from the sea to the very hills, and become of noe value. The fabulous reports which

* The Italics are by the present writer. These rocks still exist, the tops covered with grass.

have ben concerning the cause of those sandy banks are not worth being any more published." * It will now be necessary to interrupt the quotation again to produce farther evidences.

33. A few hundred yards east of the Hot Sea Baths, on the south coast of Jersey, is "the new slip," or inclined paved slope across the beach, for the convenience of carts passing to and fro between land and low water. Measuring along a line parallel to the outside edge of the top of the coping on the western side of this slip, and 17ft. distant westwardly from the said outside top edge, for a distance of 922ft. from the wall which forms the north boundary of the beach southwards, you arrive at the roots of a large tree, probably an oak, lying prostrate and imbedded in the sand. The roots are on the south, and the top towards the north, the length of the remains of the tree is 19ft., the diameter above the roots 2ft. 4ins. A thick fragment of root projects on each side at the extremity. The trunk of the tree is by spirit level 22ft. below greatest high water. It is probable this tree grew where it lies.—July 17th, 1865.

34. A few hundred yards farther east than this tree, about two or three years ago, Mr. Rose, the proprietor of the Baths, states that he saw four small trunks of trees in an upright position, at about the same distance from the north side of the beach, and that he has a portion of one of them in his museum.

35. In March, 1864, Mr. John Aubin, of St. Clement's, had his boat-load of vraic unloaded into a cart near the two great rocks at Le Hoc, mentioned by Mr. Poingdestre, and the cart had nearly been upset in consequence of the wheel running against the stump of a tree, of which there were two or three about 12ft. below high water, and 50 yards north-east of the nearest of the said rocks. These stumps of trees were afterwards removed by order of Mr. Le Mare, the Constable. The locality is immediately south of the New Pontac Hotel.

36. At or near Grand Roque, which is on the south coast, near the south-eastern extremity of Jersey, there are said to be other stumps of trees, but the writer has not seen them. All these four places are parts of the Banc du Viellet. At Grand Roque, or La Roche, as we shall see in the next article, there were once a church and village called Luneville, which have now totally disappeared, and which must have stood upon the Banc du Viellet. The Banc extends two miles south and two miles east into the present sea, from the south-east angle of Jersey, therefore "that great tract of land," when it *was* land, gave a coast line considerably nearer France than at present. We shall also find the French coast extending farther *west*, and other far more striking circumstances. I cannot depend on the hydrographical accuracy of any of the ancient maps, and, therefore, do not refer to them as authorities; they will, however, be referred to more particularly, that the reader may know what maps are meant and their dates.

* This, and the whole of the two sentences preceding, refer not to any sinking of land, but to its becoming covered with drifted sand. But the latter is the direct consequence of the former events. For when the vegetation had decayed on the sunken tracts, after they had been for some time daily covered by the tide, there was nothing to prevent the sand from drifting.

## CHAPTER III.

### The Ecrehous and Dirouilles.

37. The Ecrehous islets are six English miles north-east from the north-east angle of Jersey. Maitre Isle, the principal islet, is now very small; by measurement on May 20th, 1864, it was found to contain only 2a. 2r. 15p. within high-water mark, of which part is entirely destitute of soil, and there are only 2a. 0r. 34p. productive. Its highest point is stated in the late Admiral White's "Sailing Directions," 1846, p. 223, to be 36ft. above high water, though it did not appear to the writer to be so much. The island produces only grass and a quantity of luxuriant plants of the *Lavatera arborea*, or sea tree mallow. There is neither shrub, nor bush, nor any fresh water. Its extreme length and breadth are 188 yards by 100 yards. It contains a few huts for the temporary occupation of those who go to gather seaweed and to catch lobsters during a few weeks of summer, also parts of two walls which once formed an angle of the ancient chapel. The whole group of the Ecrehou rocks (for the rest are mere rocks without soil) is about 3 miles long from east to west, and nearly 1½ mile from north to south; and at a little distance to the westward commences another group of naked rocks called the Dirouilles, occuping a nearly circular space of about 2 miles in diameter. Maitre Isle must necessarily have formed part of a much larger island within the last six centuries, for various reasons. For though it is now not fit for being permanently inhabited, for want of wood and fresh water, which are not to be had at a less distance than six miles, and on account of its smallness, it had once a sufficient number of inhabitants to induce the diocesan to send two monks to celebrate mass daily in the chapel; because, as the Rev. G. J. Le Maitre well observes, at S. Lo, in the Archives is a parchment referring to the tithes to be received from the curè of the "parish" of the Ecrehous in Jersey, from which he justly infers that, as it was a *parish*, there must necessarily have been *cure of souls*, and consequently *inhabitants*. And there is also, he says, another parchment referring to a village and church of Luneville, in the parish of Grouville at la Roche (ad rupem). These have been referred to in the previous article.

38. Only one angle of the chapel of Maitre Isle now remains; the site of the rest of the building has been destroyed by the tides, which prevents any judgment being formed of its original extent. The late M. de Gerville, of Valognes, a learned antiquary who studied western Normandy for forty years, and copied five or six thousand pages of records of cathedrals, monasteries, chateaus, and hospitals, published a pamphlet entitled "Recherches sur les Iles Normandes du Cotentin en général et sur la mission de St. Marcouf en particulier." In this pamphlet he says that one of the Ecrehou isles "was in 1203 sufficiently considerable to contain a church in which mass was to be said every day; which in 1327 had still a chapel of our Lady of enough importance to cause the

abbot of Val Richer to have it served by two monks; which in 1687 * presents still the ruins of this chapel, and which in this day has ony its ancient name given to uncultivated and uninhabited rocks. The rest has been swallowed up by the sea." And giving the following reference, "Ex Gall. Christ., t. xi., Inter Instrum. Ecc. Bajoc., col. 94," he quotes in the pamphlet (which is without name or date, but which was printed by the late Messrs. Falle, of Royal Square, Jersey, within the last twenty years), a copy in Latin of a charter dated 1203, by which Peter de Pratel gives to God and to the monks of the Church of Holy Mary of Val Richer, for the salvation of the soul of John, the illustrious king of England, who gave him the islands, and for the salvation of his own soul and those of his father and mother and all his ancestors, the isle of Escrehou in its entirety to build there a church (basilicam) in honour of God and blessed Mary, so that divine mysteries may be celebrated there daily, and the abbot and monks are also to possess whatever they shall be able to build up and erect in the said island. And he also grants to them whatever may be given to them in charity by his men of Jersey, Gernesey, and Aureney, and confirms his grant in the presence of eight witnesses named and many others.. In the same volume of Gallia Christiana, M. de Gerville says it is recorded in col. 447 that Gabriel . . . . , abbot of Val Richer, sent two monks in 1337, on Thursday before Palm Sunday, to keep and preside over the chapel of Blessed Mary of Escrehou. This is the last we hear of the practical use of this church or chapel. The original Latin is quoted in my M.S. appendix, but it would not be fitting to load the columns of THE ARTIZAN with it.

39. In a book of the King's rents in Jersey, made in August and September, 1607, by Sir Robert Gardner, knight, and James Hussey, —now in possession of F. G. Collas, Esq., of St. Martin's—folio 5, is an account of wheat rents due for Ecreho from the heirs of Jean le Hardy, gent., and others, which corroborates the fact of there having been a priory or chapel in Ecrehou, for he gives a list of wheat rents "due for the Prio-y of Ecreho payable yearly in manner and forme as the aforesaid wheats of the Daughter of Carteret," &c., namely, from John Grey, John Hubert, and Edward la Cloche—in the whole V cabots.

40. One of the boatmen who rowed the writer to Ecrehou on May 20, 1864, namely, Thomas Biampied of Rozel, stated that he had seen, in 1861, a stump of a tree which he thought stood where it grew, about 300 yards east of the rock called Gros Tète, where the tides are about 41 feet. Gros Tète is about half-a-mile north-west of Maitre Isle. Joseph Blampied of the Glory Inn, Rozel, also a boatman, has seen stumps of trees fixed in the gravel about at extreme low water between le Viél rock and le Bègue; these rocks are somewhat farther to the north-west than Gros Fète. In sailing amongst the rocky islets of the Ecrehous, it was observable that there was not a sufficient amount of gravel banks to account for the land

* I saw at the British Museum Marriotte's Map of this date, which shows the chapel about the centre of the Isle. The Map is on a very small scale.

having been washed away. The only gravel bank lies about half a mile north of Maitre Isle, in the island Marmotiére which consists of two barren rocks (the southerly rock is granite containing minute specks of silver, and has several huts upon it). A ridge of gravel extended from one of these two rocks to the other at the date named, and was triangular in cross section, and was estimated to contain about 12,000 cubic yards of gravel. Every storm alters the form and position of this bank, which appears to be entirely inadequate in bulk, to justify the belief that the island has been washed away; and if it had been washed away, it is quite impossible that the stumps of trees could have remained sticking in the bottom. If we suppose it to have sunk upwards of 41ft., the stumps of trees would previously have been above high water, where they doubtless grew, and the island would have been large enough to have produced both wood and water, and it would have been habitable and worth inhabiting. It is certain that without a much larger and loftier "gathering ground" than there is at present; there never could have been a sufficient supply of fresh water. It will be seen that these reasonings, which naturally arise from the premises, are confirmed by the actual facts narrated in Article 41, where it is stated as a matter of history, that in consequence of a certain catastrophe in 709. Chausy became an island, *so did the Ecrehous, but of a very great extent which it has not maintained.** From about the year 860, as we also gather from Article 41, to about the year (suppose) 1356, there can be little doubt that the Ecrehous and Dironilles formed one considerable island. The present sea being very shallow amongst the islets, the island, or islands, would necessarily before sinking, have contained some hundreds of acres at least. The last date of sending monks to the chapels, namely, 1337, admits the belief that it was submerged about, and perhaps exactly, at the same time as the forest of St. Ouen's. In fact Poingdestre's expression is "within these 350 years," meaning that it was less than 350, which is quite consistent with the belief that the sinkings at the Ecrehous and Dironilles, as well as those on the south and west of Jersey, may all have occurred in 1356.

41. In the vast researches which Lecanu, in his preface, describes himself to have made (and which are detailed at length in my MS. Appendix), for the purpose of his *Hist. des Evêques de Constances*, whilst he places in 709 the principal submersion of the Forest of Sciscy, he says:—"Yet it was not till the year 860 that the forest was totally submerged; then the isles of Jersey, Guernsey, and Alderney found themselves very much farther separated from the continent than before; Chausey became an island, *so did the Ecrehous*, but of a very much greater extent which they have not maintained." Lecanu is, at any rate, an unprejudiced witness as respects the sinking, for he had no notion of anything of the sort. For he attributes the submersions only to a "south-west wind which blew constantly for many months with great violence, and accumulated the waters of the ocean in such quantity "on our shores, that the [equinoctial] tide of March,

* Lecanu's Evêques de Coutances, p. 448.

assisted by all its impetuosity, overpassed the ordinary limits and over-ran a vast extent of country."! Causes, it need scarcely be said, totally inadequate to the effect.

THE WORD "HOU" AND ITS SIGNIFICATION.

42. Amongst the Channel Islands, some of the islets, now too small and rocky to be inhabitable, have as part of their names, *hou* or *ou*, which according to M. de Gerville, in the Teuton or Danish language means "house." M. Edouard le Héricher too in his Glossary on Germanic Origins, says that *hou* is a common affix to topographical names in the sense of habitation, the "house" and he gives examples Néhou, Quelkhou, Pirou, Bléhou, Lihou (rock of Granville), Titahou (isle of).

If these things be so, the fact is very significant. For then we have Ecre*hou*, or the Ecre-"houses." Dir-*ou*-illes, or "the house-isles. Also Brecq-*hou* near Sercq, Bur*hou*, near Alderney, Jet*hou*, near Herm, and Li*hou*, west of Guernsey. Plainly meaning that there were once plenty of *houses*, and, consequently, of *inhabitants*, in the places named, where there is now *scarcely either house or inhabitant.** M. de Gerville (in effect) concurs, and he further says as follows:—

"Mais pourquoi, dira-t-on, ces terminaisons sont-elles affectées aux plus petites îles, tandis que les plus grandes, comme Guernesey ou Jersey, conservaient le leur? C'est suivant moi, justement parce que les grandes îles avaient conservé une population plus étendue, et que les pirates se trouvaient plus a l'aise dans les lieux inhabités. A l'embouchure de la Seine, et particuliérement dans l'île ou presq'île de Jumièges, on trouverait d'autres exemples de ces terminaisons en *hou*. Je me rappelle entr'autres celle de Koni-hou, qui, dans la langue du Nord, signifie miason du roi. Ce roi pouvait bien être un roi de mer, ou un capitaine de vaisseau, ou tout simplement le nomme d'un homme qui s'appelait Le Roy."—*Pamphlet*, p. 14 and 15.

Mr. Metivier informs me that "As early as the reigns of Robert and Wilhelm (William) Guettehou, or Jethou (the Chetel-hou in the cartulary of *Cerisium, Cerisy*) had an '*hospes*,' '*hospitem suum*,' of course, a 'hou' or house."

43. The following passage, which is quoted from p. 525 of *Duncan's History of Guernsey*, and written by F. C. Lukis, Esq., of Guernsey, an accomplished geologist, naturalist, and antiquary, tends to prove (especially by the parts which I have caused to be printed in Italics) that the islet

---

* A statement of the population at various periods is now given.

Statement of the numbers of inhabitants in Herm and Jethou; obtained from the census of 1851.

| Years. | HERM. No. of persons. | JETHOU. No. of persons. |
|---|---|---|
| 1821 | 28 | 9 |
| 1831 | 177 | 14 |
| 1841 | 38 | 6 |
| 1851 | 46 | 3 |
| 1861 | | |

The "adjacent islands" mentioned besides, as containing inhabitants, are "Le Marchant" and Serk (Great and Little)." Ecrehou Dir-ou-illes, Brecqhou, Lihou, Burhou, are not named, evidently because they contain no inhabitants in modern times.

of Herm was once densely populated, though its whole population in 1851 was only 46 souls. He says:—"The common limpet (patella vulgata) is very abundant on the rocks, and appears to have been used as an article of food to a greater extent than at present. The quantity of shells exposed over the surface, or occasionally dug up, *shows the vast use of these by the early inhabitants*, and in some places they are found *at a distance from the cottages* and at a depth of many feet below the soil. Beds of limpet shells are not unfrequently cut through in the island of Herm, where it is difficult to account for their accumulation."

M. de Gerville (pamphlet p. 36) gives a copy of a charter "extracted from the Cartulary of Cherbourg, and the archivist has since communicated to me the original." (A copy appears in the MS. Appendix). There was, in short, in 1440, a convent of cordeliers established (or then existing) in the isle of Herm. But the cordeliers probably did not use much of so poor a food as limpets. It will be shown afterwards by reference to *Cæsar's Commentaries on the Gallic War*, that there is reason to believe all these islets may have been numerously inhabited, and by persons who would eat limpets, as others did at and before Cæsar's time. If so, the beds of limpet shells are not surprising—they are probably *shell middings*.

In Cæsar's Book 3, Sec. 12 (quoted heareafter) we find that when the works of the Romans overawed *one town*, the inhabitants carried away all their effects in their numerous ships and betook themselves into *other nearest towns*, and so baffled him during great part of summer. It will be shown that these transactions took place at the Northern Channel Islands, *not* near Vannes.

Everything can be accounted for, if there has been, as I say there must have been—a general sinking. The losses of land on the west and south of Jersey, and at the Ecrehous and Dirouilles; the former existence of groups of houses, *i.e.* towns, and the existence of shell middings—where there are now scarcely either houses or inhabitants—can all be perfectly well understood, if we admit that there has been a *general sinking*. Other things, about to be stated, can also be well understood on the same principle.

---

## CHAPTER IV.

*Losses of land on the Norman coast, on the west and north-west of Coutances.*

44. From *Tableau Historique de la Civilisation à Jersey*, par John Patriarche Ahier (now deceased), 1852, p. 97, we learn as follows:—

"The Seigneurs of Mont Chaton near Regneville, possessed at the end of the river which passes by Coutances, for all time the fishery of this little river as far as Roqui, a rock well known which is now two leagues in the sea.* Conformably to their title they had fished for all time also in the sea, as far as that limit; but their administration commenced an action in 1789 founded on this, that their right of fishing could not extend beyond the river; and two months before the Revolution, they established before the Parliament of Rouen; first, that their title gave them the right of fishing as far as Roqui, the place where the river of Coutances discharged itself into the sea. Second, that since a long time, it is true *the sea had invaded the land bordering on this river*,† but that that had not destroyed their right of fishing the ancient bed of the river. Third, that otherwise there existed still all along the ancient shores *the trunks of willows visible in the water*, which thus settled the limit where the right of fishing could be exercised. By these reasons the Seigneur of Chaton won his action, and the Parliament confirmed to him his right of fishing. This decree may be found in the Archives of France, the last volume of decrees of the Parliament of Rouen. Plees has so stated p. 10 of his "History of Jersey."

It is quite true that Plees gives a summary of the facts now stated about the fishery, at p. 11, in his *Account of the island of Jersey*, published in 1817.

45. Mr. Ahier informed the writer that only a few years ago a fisherman dredging for oysters near the international oyster boundary (a part of which is marked on the Chart), brought up the stump of tree with portions of the roots attached, which was identified as a plane tree. It was obtained about opposite the centre of Jersey, and therefore about four miles from the present French shore.

46. M. Lecanu who published his *Historie des Evêques de Coutances* at Coutances, in 1839; gives a preliminary chapter on the means, end, and method of his work, and mentions by their names his very many authorities.‡ Saying at p. 6 :—" Such is the immense quantity of materials among which we have chosen, piece by piece, the elements of this history." And at p. 10, he says, " We have pruned off all which appeared to us disputable, all that which we have thought uncertain; and if now and then we have inserted doubtful statements, we have cautioned the reader. We have laid aside all that which appeared to us to have little interest; and as such all the writings and private charters, which have no value for antiquaries; a great number of very small facts, of guarantees about particular acts and dates. In fact of guarantees we have preserved only those which were useful to fix the chronology." After all this judicious sifting and selection, he informs us at p. 14, *without any caution*, as follows :— " A vast marsh called Chesey (Scissiacum), covered with forests, filled up all the space now occupied by the Ocean from the coast of Britanny as far as Cherbourg, or the Val de Saire, widening itselt at the side of Chausey

* It is 2¼ English miles by the sailing charts, and is called *Ronqué* on the English chart and *Ronquet* on the French chart.
† The italics are the present writer's
‡ The names are recited in the MS. Appendix.

and Jersey over a depth now unknown." And at p. 21, speaking of the forest of Sciscy, he says:—"The dimensions of this marshy ground cannot now be defined; but this is what we know: in the first place we have assured ourselves that from S. Pair* to Cape la Hague there exist very numerous stumps of trees rooted in the clay of the shore."

47. It will now be convenient to continue the quotation from Mr. Poingdestre's MS., commencing at the point where we left off in Art. 32. He says: "Neither will I here mention another yet more fabulous tale of the coniunction of Jersey to Normandy by a bridge or without a bridge, which never was unlesse it were before the flood. It is very certain that above eleven hundred years agoe it was bestowed upon St. Sampson, Bishop of Dol, under the appellation of Island, and that it was in Antoninus his Itinerary called an Island, above two hundred yeares before that. But yet for all that, I dare say that whoever shall look with due reflexion upon y[e] most craggy Coast of St. Clement, at a low Ebbe, and then behold an infinite number of different rocks close one by another, will not be much out, for beleeving that soe many bones of mother Earth were not at first created naked; and consequently that the sea hath by degrees as long running worne and diluted that earth w[ch] was about them; leaving onely that part behind which it could not dissolve."

I agree with Mr. Poingdestre that the Banc du Viellet was "not at first created naked." And I agree also "that the sea hath by degrees as long running worne and diluted that w[ch] was about" the rocks. I say that the soil has been washed away since the ground sunk and brought it within reach of the tides. To the rest of his statement I partly object, and say that it requires farther explanation; and will now attempt to bring the matter correctly under the reader's consideration.

### PTOLEMY, THE GEOGRAPHER, GIVES REASONS FOR BELIEVING THAT JERSEY WAS PART OF THE CONTINENT IN HIS TIME.

48. In pursuing this interesting investigation, it was obviously of great importance to ascertain whether the promontories, harbours, mouths of rivers, &c., of which Ptolemy gives (in his own way) the latitudes and longitudes; were or were not correctly laid down by him. Because those positions were clearly points in the ancient coast lines, and if he had laid them down correctly, we should at once have a vast amount of information bearing directly upon the present question. And, supposing him to be correct, we should know the situation of the coast as it existed in the first half of the second century, which was the time when he flourished. After considerable further research beyond what has hitherto been narrated; it became clear that such vast losses of land had occurred since his time on the northerly and westerly coasts of France, that it was doubtful whether any positions on the present coast of France could be identified as the places indicated by him. And ultimately the centre of the Isle of Wight (which he and other ancient writers call Vectis), and the Lizard Point

* About two miles south of Granville.

(which he calls the Damnonian and Ocrinum promontory) were fixed upon as bases, or points of departure, in which there had probably been little or no alteration in longitude since his time, but there must have been alterations in latitude which have been allowed for, and are explained hereafter. He gives, in his own way, the latitudes and longitudes of these two points, and their modern latitudes and longitudes having been obtained from the British Ordnance survey, it was clear that his latitudes and longitudes could now all be reduced to modern, which was accordingly done, and the results will be given in a future chapter. Two important positions of his, on the north coast of Britanny, successfully stood this rigid test, namely, the Gobæum promontory of the Osismii; which is well known to be the north-eastern angle of Britanny, and Staliocanus Portus, which fell all but exactly where is now the small harbour of Portrieux. At the Gobæum promontory, the existence of stumps of trees and remains of buildings, bear witness to the fact of the land having extended somewhat farther north than it does at present. Allowing for which, Ptolemy's and the modern positions are very nearly identical. This ought to give us confidence in his approximate correctness on the north of Britanny. And accordingly his "Mouth of the river Argenis" and his "Mouth of the river Tetus" have been laid down upon the chart (as the reader will find), which of course was done by means of his latitudes and longitudes being reduced to modern. But there are farther corroborations of the correctness of his position of the mouth of the Argenis. Mr. Abier affirms, at p. 98, that Mont S. Michel was once "dix lienes de l'Océan," which is nearly the distance from the Mont to the mouth of the Argenis. When asked for his authority for the statement, he could not remember. M. Bonissent, also, Membre de la Société Géologique de France, &c., in a pamphlet called "Essai Géologique sur le Departement de la Manche," published in 1860, speaks of Mount S. Michel being "en pleine forêt, à dix lieues de la mer." I have not been in communication with this gentleman, and consequently cannot give his authority for the statement. If the position of the mouth of the Argenis is right, the position of the mouth of the Tetus is not likely to be far wrong. By the former it will appear that France once extended farther west than it does at present by seventeen miles, and by the position of the latter that the land extended more than thirty miles farther west than it does now. There are other corroborative circumstances, presently to be detailed, tending to prove that Jersey was connected by dry land with the Continent since Ptolemy's time. Such being the case, there is no necessity to debate about the existence, or not, of the bridge mentioned by Mr. Poingdestre.

### The Roman Itinerary, so called of Antoninus.

49. In the Itinerary; *Cæsarea* is Jersey, *Sarmia* Guernsey, and *Arica* Alderney; by common consent of commentators. This is the first mention of Jersey in History, and Mr. Poingdestre seeks to fix a date by means of the Itinerary, but that is plainly impossible—it was added to from time to time like Bradshaw's Railway Guide of the present day. The

paragraph following contains a few facts gathered chiefly from Wesseling's Preface to the Itinerary, which contains a large mass of very valuable comments, on the authorship of the Itinerary, by about seventy learned men. The several dates I have added.

Alexander the Great, born 355 B.C. had his βηματισαι or measurers of his journeys. Some other materials for an Itinerary existed as early as Polybius's time, 124 B.C. Strabo, who died A.D. 25, Pomponius Mela who flourished about A.D. 45, and Pliny, the elder, who lived from A.D. 23 to 79 laboured very diligently in this business. Metius Pomposianus who lived A.D. 81-96, represented the whole world on parchment. Maginus, the Tyrian, and Ptolemy, the geographer, laboured hard in preparing materials that were suitable for an Itinerary. The Romans penetrated the whole of Britain in the first century after Christ and vacated it and Armorica (Britanny) A.D. 409.*

Now, it is certain that there could be no Roman roads in Britain before Cæsar's first invasion, B.C. 55, and that new Roman roads would be made in Britain from time to time and added to the Itinerary, until about Gibbon's date, namely, the beginning of the fifth century. The name of Constantinople occurs four times in the Itinerary, although that city was not inaugurated until A.D. 331, after having been six years in building.

Cæsarea, or Jersey, was therefore not necessarily inserted in the Itinerary until the fourth, or even the beginning of the fifth century; and there was consequently plenty of space of time for Jersey to have become an island between that date and Cæsar's invasion of Gaul, which happened more than half a century before the commencement of the Christian era. Indeed, in the two and a half centuries accruing between Ptolemy's time and the evacuation of Britain and Britanny by the Romans, the sinkings now under consideration may have occurred, and probably did occur. His positions of the mouths of the Argenis and Tetus would appear to justify us in believing so. Next month further reasons will be given for believing that Jersey was since Ptolemy's time an integral part of the Continent.

## Farther reasons for believing that Jersey was, since Ptolemy's time, an integral part of the Continent.

50. The following is an extract from Mr. Poingdestre's MS., commencing at folio 36. He says, speaking of the Channel Islands:—

"Not much knowledge of them can be expected before the conquest, seeing there is so little preserved since. Except the Records in the Tower and at Westminster, there is hardly anything reliable. This darkness has deterred others but it has instigated me to farther research especially in MSS. of the lives of the Saints, which amongst many fabulous things, contaeine many truths."

I hope in due time to convince the reader that a good deal about the Channel Islands (though they are not referred to by their names) may be

* See Gibbon. Vol. 5, p. 346, who quotes Zosimus.

gleaned from ancient Classical authors. The following is not a copy, but an abstract with quotations, in continuation of the second part of Mr. Poingdestre's MS.

51. He has first tried to ascertain the old names of the islands. For "of what use," says he, "would it be to know the feates of Cæsar in Gallia, if I did not know that Gallia means France?" He supposes "Cambden is the first who wrote that Jersey is an island in ye. British Ocean, which in Antoninus' Itinerary is called Cæsarea and that Jersey or Gersey is but a contraction of that name as Cherbourg or Gerbourg is of Cæsaris Burgum; a very good example, if Burgum or Burgus were a Latin word near Cæsar's time. His [Camden's] conjecture has been followed by all others, and I do not intend to oppose it. I wonder, however, that not long after Antonimus it should be called by the name of Augia which can in no way have been derived from Cæsarea." We learn the former name from a donation of four of these islands to Sampson, Bishop of Dol, in which this pretended Cæsarea is called Augia and in French Angic. "This donation is found in the life of that Bishop which I have seen in written hand very ancient, and in Latin and is attested by Bertrand D'Argentre in his History." If it be doubted that this Augia is Jersey, Mr. Poingdestre says he will remove that doubt by a fragment taken out of the Abbey of Fontenelles by Du Chesne in his third volume of *Scriptores Coætanei Hist. Franc.* "neere as ancient as Charlemagne* concerning Geroaldus one of the abbots there. Is enim (sayth he) quadam legatione fungebatur iussu Caroli Augusti, in Insulam cui nomen est Augia, & est adjacens pago Constantino. If he had pointed at Jersey with the finger he could not have shewed it more plainly: for Gregorius Turon: Aimoinus and Papirius Masson, speaking of Jersey without naming it, call it, the first Insulam maris quod adjacet Civitati Constantinæ, the second Insulam maris quæ adjacet Constantiæ, and the third Insulam Constantini littoris. No other island than Jersey can be meant. Guernezey "is out of the way: Chausey† (which is the likelyest next to Jersey) is an inconsiderable plot of earth or rocks rather, unsuitable to such an employment as is spoken of in that Fragment, and not so much adjacent to Coutance as to Aurenches on the coast Britany:"‡ and Alderney is farther off: much less he thinks can Serc be meant, for Jersey lies between it and Coutances. Paulus Æmylius, he says, is mistaken in calling it Insulam Constantiensis Diœcesis: for at the time of which he speaks it was not part of the Diocese of Coutances, but of that of Dol. "This name hath had many synonyms in ye. world, from Homer's time (in whose workes we find Augeia eratiene) downewards, and in our time both upon the lake

* Crowned A.D. 800, died 814.

† A very large proportion of each of the three extensive groups of rocks called respectively Chausey, Minquiers, and Grelets; is within reach of high tides and is consequently entirely destitute of earth.

‡ I am under the necessity of differing from Mr. Poingdestre here. The centre of Chausey rocks is five miles nearer to Coutances than to Avranches, and both Coutances and Avranches are in *Normandy*.

of Constance, where are two small islands of that name, and in Normandy itself Le pays d'Auge, called by Cenalis, Normannia Augiaca, that is (sayth he elsewhere) Coele † Normannia, Normandy the hollowe, for Auge in old French signifieth a Trough or other such hollow thing, and for that reason this name may possibly have been anciently given to this Island, because of the many great Valleyes which are to be seene there from one end to the other."

52. I interrupt the abstract and quotations from Mr. Poingdestre to remark that the trough, or hollow, may, and probably did, signify the depression now occupied by the sea between Jersey and Normandy. Cenalis is speaking of *Normandy*, not Jersey; and the only *considerable* hollow anywhere near Jersey in that province is the one in question between Jersey and Normandy. Cenalis clearly could not have meant the *very small* (not "great") valleys through which the Jersey brooks run, when he spoke of "Normandy" the hollow. I cannot agree with Mr. Poingdestre either in the following passage, where he thinks that Jersey was called Augia *before* and *during the time of the Romans having to do in these parts*, for reasons which will be stated after concluding the abstract and quotations from his MS. He says:—"I am apt to beleeve that Augia was the true genuine name of this island, and that long before y[e] Romans had anything to doe in those parts, and that it was continued among y[e] natives all along the Romans' time; and after theire departure untill the Norman Dukes that the Roman name was received, but with a corrupt way of pronouncing it" as Gersui, Gersoi, and by Vaicce in his verses written in the time of Henry II. "Gersui," also Gressui, Gresoi. Matthew Paris calls it Gersea, and a MS. chron. in the library at Oxon, Gerzy. In the Tower and Westminster records it is "Jereseye," which he thinks is in imitation of the Saxons, and gives several illustrations.

53. Wace the poet was born in Jersey at the commencement of the twelfth century, and died in England about 1180. He says that the celebrated Danish chief, Hasting, landed

"En Auremen, en Guernesi.
En Saire, en Erin, en Gersi."

Hasting's landing was in 838 according to one authority, and in 856 according to another. But Wace calls the islands by the names of his own period, which might, or might not, be the names current in Hasting's time.

54. It is not a little significant that during a certain period which terminated legally but not popularly, at the middle of the sixth century, Jersey is described as "an island of the shore of Coutances" as if it had *no name*. It cannot but be regarded as surprising, and as a fact which requires to be accounted for, that an island which even yet contains about 47 square miles after heavy losses of territory, should have been *nameless*

---

† This is evidently meant for the Greek word Koile (feminine of Koilos) *hollow*. Exactly for the same reason a part of Syria is called *Cœle Syria*, namely because of the immense "hollow" of the Dead Sea, which is more than 1,200 feet below the Mediterranean.

Childebert, King of France, about the year 550, gave to Sampson, Archbishop of Dol "certain islands and lands in Normandy, de Rimoul, Augic, Sargic, and Vesargic, which are islands on the coast, for I have seen it" D'Argentre says "in ancient letters."* These islands no doubt were *Rimoul* Alderney, *Augic*, Jersey, *Sargic* Sercq, and *Vesargic* Guernsey. Alderney is still called "remui" in Andrea Biancos' Chart, found by Mr. Rawdon Brown among the Venetian State papers, date 1436, but supposed to be still older. Bianco gives "rocha toba" for Jersey, "quasquit" for the Caskets, and "cabo de g" (the g having an abbreviation over it) which doubtless means "the cape of Guernsey," as it is written against the S.W. angle of that island. The map comprises all the north of Europe, and is of the scale of 100 miles to an inch. Neither this Chart, nor Blaews' "Sea-Mirrour" date 1625, nor Dumaresq's map of Jersey 1694; can be relied on as hydrographically correct. The latter exhibits a remarkable promontory at the S.E. angle of Jersey, three miles long, by a quarter of a mile wide, unlike anything now existing. The map of Jersey in Camden's Britannia, exhibits the same promontory, but only a mile and a half long, which however the text does not explain. I think the promontory only means part of the Banc du Vieillet.

M. de Gerville supposes that the names Augia, Angia, Agna, Angey, Aucey, and Agen, signify along with Gersey, or Gery, a habitation by the water. And that Cæsarea is an origin derived from flattery.

It is well known that in Celtic, *Ey* signifies an island, and *As* signifies water. May we not conclude that the Romans were obliged to give the island a name, that it might be inserted in their Itinerary, and that they appropriately called it after their great general and first emperor, who had to much distinguished himself in the neighbourhood? And that this must have happened at some period between the middle of the second century (Ptolemy's time), and the abandoning of Armorica or Britanny by the Romans in 409;† they would have no occasion to trouble themselves to name the island *after* they had abandoned the neighbourhood? The Gauls would have no occasion to name the island until King Childebert gave it to Sampson, when doubtless the necessity was felt of giving it a name.

55. *Neustria Pia*, or Pious Normandy, by the Abbé du Monstier, 1663, is called in Watts's *Bibliographical Dictionary* "an important and valuable work, similar in its plan to Dugdale's Monasticon." At p. 155 I find the passage quoted by Poingdestre (Art 51) "For the abbot [St. Gernoldus] by command of Charles Agustus [father of Charlemagne] discharged a certain embassy in an island of which the name is Augia, which a race of Britons (Brittonum) inhabits, and is near the town of Coutances, over which at that time a certain person of the name of Amvvarith was general's (Dux), &c. It is stated also in Neustria Pia, p. 154 that Gernoldus died on the Kalends of July in the year of Christ 806. And that his embassy to

---

* *Hist. Bret*, folio 114 B

† Gibbon, Vol. 5, p. 346.—Nennius gives a different date as will be seen hereafter.

Augia was in 787. And Falle the historian of Jersey, is also of the opinion that Jersey is meant by the passage, which he quotes from *Hist. Franc.*, Lib. 3, cap. 26, (the date must have been about 574) "a certain island of the sea which is adjacent to the city of Coutances." If Augia did not mean Jersey, that considerable island would still have been without a name, which is incredible. Yet we shall find some confusion in the passage next following (which is translated from Neustria Pia), between Sciscy or Chausey, and Jersey. For he speaks of "Sisciacum" and "Gerzay," as if they were the same island, which is of course a mistake.

56. *Confusion between Sciscy or Chausey, and Jersey*, ("*Scisciacum.*") "Thither afterwards S. Pretextatus 17th Archbishop of Rouen was banished by command of King Chilperic, at the instance of Queen Fredegunda: he is driven out into exile* into an island of the sea (writes Gregory of Tours) which is adjacent to the city [civitati] of Coutances. But that island was called Brenciana, commonly Brency;† situated in the Ocean sea near the shore of the city [civitatis] of Coutances, in Lower Normandy, if we believe Tillius.‡ But in the antiquities of the MSS. of Normandy, it is named Gergia, or Gersayum, and *Sisciacum*, in French *Geray* and Chezay; according to Cænalis, in [reference] to the same Prætextatus.§ It was afterwards inhabited by Franciscan brothers, but thence by heretics, being profligates they were compelled to settle themselves out of sight near Macropolis; the aforesaid bishop Cænalis thought, and more rightly, that it was some island, [and] was that, where in those ancient times the noble monastery, Sciscy, of S. Paterne stood, now altogether overthrown and levelled." *Neustria Pia*, p. 67.

57. In the life of S. Sampson, ‖ we read the following curious passage. The Chronicler says, "a certain island *lately* established" (insula quædam super fundata), as if he meant that it had lately become an island. The context, however, is unfavourable to this interpretatton, how could Pyrus, or any other man, establish or make an island so large? May not the sentence rather mean, that Pyrus established in, or endowed the island with, some religious house? "But there was not far from this monastery a certain island lately established by a certain excellent man and holy

---

* "Lib. 1, Histor. Franc. cap. 18."

† The origin of this word signifies an *excretion* or *remnant*; a very approprpriate name, which ever of the two islands it is applied to. By the kindness of Frederick Crank, Esq., I am enabled to quote a case in Persia, observed in 1836, between Shiraz and Ispahan; where part of the plain Yezd-de-Kost, three to four hundred yards in breadth and many miles in length, has sunk to the depth of from sixteen to twenty yards—and where large masses of rock still rest on each other in the most fantastic and apparently precarious positions. Close adjoining is a fort bearing a similar curious name, *i.e.*, Pok-yu-Kollah, or "excrement fort;" the inhabitants of Teheran informed him, that discharges of gas or steam took place from the cavities under the fort, whilst the earthquake was in operation. The banks of the Roymungal, one of the largest rivers of the Soonderbuns in the south of Bengal, within his own observation, "have risen considerably." And "in many parts of these rivers at low water, the traces of the brick foundations of buildings are plainly discernible; and in the Chattiya river which branches out of the Thakoorannee, a very old brick tower of 90 or 100ft. in height, still stands." It is to be hoped that Mr. Crank will very soon carry into execution his plan of writing out a full account of these interesting places, illustrated by plenty of his beautiful pen and ink sketches.

‡ "Tillius in Chronico de Regib. Franc. ad ann. 582." See also Neustria Pia, p. 712.

§ "Tom. 3. Hierachiæ Eccles. Neustriæ MS."

‖ *Vita S. Samsonis act. SS. Bened.* Sæc. 1, p. 171.

Presbyter Pyrus by name, in which island also I have been, with whom, I say, Sampson wished to live."

58. Aimoin, the monk of S. Germain,* also says (p. 183) "Prætextatus, Bishop of Rouen, is accused" (and at p. 190) . . . "he is banished into exile in a certain island of the sea which is near the city (civitati) of Coutances." In the annals of Massonius, p. 55, "He is banished into an island of the shore of Coutances." In Robert Gaguin's *Hist. Franc.*, fol. xxii B, "and thus Prætextatus is banished by design. Whom when seized the king commands to be kept in prison. From whence when freed he almost escaped by night; troubled by abuse and wounds they at length banish him in an island of the diocese of Coutances."

In all this there is nothing in favour of Chausey being the island meant, except that it is about, only half as far from Coutances, as Jersey is. Jersey may, without doing any violence to language, be termed "an island of the shore of Coutances." We find as follows in Steeven's supplement to Dugdale's Monasticon:—"Bernard d'Abbeville, to avoid being chosen Prior of St. Cyprian's, proceeded to the borders of Britanny, into the *peninsula* of Chaussey, on the north side of that province."

I think Jersey must have been meant, both because Chausey was a peninsula (not an island), and for several other reasons. Those reasons are as follows:—*First*, in Art. 54 Augia *must* mean Jersey, in the enumeration of the islands given to Sampson. And Augia is identified (Art. 55) as the island "near the town of Coutances," to which Charlemagne's father sent an ambassador. *Second*, as Poingdestre well observes (Art. 51) "Chausey, which is the likeliest next to Jersey, is an inconsiderable plot of earth," for a great prince to have sent an ambassador to; it is much more probable that the embassy was to Jersey. *Third*, if Augia does not mean Jersey, Jersey was *ignored* as well as nameless, which is incredible.

59. The important point to be gathered from all this discussion is that Jersey must have been the island meant by the description that it was near the city (or shore) of Coutances, *as if it had no name*, which is a very improbable circumstance, *if* it had been an island from time immemorial. To recapitulate. The Romans were obliged to give it a name to insert in their Itinerary, and they very appropriately called it Cæsarea. King Childebert was also obliged to name it when he gave it to Sampson in 550, and he called it Augia. A certain amount of sinking must therefore have occurred at the east of present Jersey, in order to have entitled it to a name *Augia* derived from *Auge*, "a trough, or hollow." About the same date, namely, in 582, Jersey was called Brenciana, or Brency, which signify "a remnant." But Gregory of Tours who was then living (for he was born about 544, and died in 595) *did not know it by any name*, for he of course was not consulted about a gift of certain distant islands to a neighbouring archbishop. The transaction no way concerned him, and he had evidently never heard by what name Childebert conveyed Augia to

* Aimoini Monachi, *Hist. Franc.*, Paris, 1567. Morery's Dictionary says that this History was written by another Aimoin, a monk, of Fleuri, in the 10th century.

Sampson. All which tends to prove, and Ptolemy's positions of the mouths of the rivers Argenis and Tetus completely prove, I submit, that *Jersey had only lately become an Island.* The "line of shallowest soundings" on the map, must therefore have been a *watershed* previous to the separation of Jersey from the Continent. And it may be quite true (though I accept no responsibility in the way of guaranteeing it) that the diocesan in his journeys to and fro between Coutances and Jersey—could cross by a plank, the small brook which may have been the only intervening water between Jersey and Coutances. If that was so the *final* sinking must have taken place since the year 1000; for we find that the Channel Islands were transferred from the diocese of Dol to that of Coutances "by one of Rollo's immediate successors, apparently Duke Richard II. or III.," who ascended the throne respective in the years 996 and 1026.*

---

## CHAPTER V.

### Changes in the Bay of Mont S. Michel, and near S. Malo.

60. Abbé Desroches published his *Hist. Du Mont S. Michel* "aprés les chartes, cartulaires, et manuscrits, trouvés au du Mont S. Michel, à la Tour de Londres, et dans les Bibliothéques de la France et de l'Etranger," in 2 vols. 8vo. Caen, 1838.† In Vol. 1 p. 4, he says:—

"Anciennement les iles de Jersey, de Guernsey et d'Aurigny tenaient à la terre ferme: c'est sentiment des savans." In a future chapter when Cæsar and Diodorus are treated of, reasons will be submitted for believing that all was *dry at low water in their time*, from Guernsey and Alderney to the continent. Passing over two unimportant sentences we come to the following paragraph, in which he attempts to prove that in the Celtic language both the words Neustrie (Normandy) and Vestrie (Brittanny) signify that the two provinces had been separated from each other by some convulsion of nature. As the present writer is not skilled in Celtic, the passage is simply quoted for the reader's own judgment. Abbé Desroches says:—"Une preuve que la Neustrie fut separée de la Bretagne, dans les temps les plus reculés, ou du moins qu'on l'a cru, c'est que ce changement a ete désigné en langue Celtique. Le nom de Neustrie est formé du Celtique *an ev ze tre* ou *ter.* le gué ou la rupture faite par les eaux, causée par l'extension de l'Ocean Brittannique, sur les terres de la baie où sont d'un côté le Mont St. Michel, et à l'opposite les côtés du Cotentin et de l'Avranchin.‡ Le mot Vestrie est le même que *ev ze ter*, rupture faite par les eaux."

---

* See Tupper's *History of Guernsey*, p. 31, 34.
† 575g 23, *Brit. Mus.*
‡ The Cotentin extends from Cape la Hague to some point between Coutances and Avranches, and the Avranchin extends from that point to Pontorson.

*Note.* I find these last two sentences, nearly word for word the same, in *Essai sur l'Hist. de Neustrie.* Anonymous, Paris 1789, 12 mo. 1st Vol. p. 3.

The Abbé refers his readers to "M. le Brigant de Quimper."

61. He says, speaking of Genets, now an inconsiderable village near the sea, five miles west of Avranches:—"Cette ville posseda plusieurs églises. Celles de St. Sebastien et de Ste. Catherine *ont été submergées*; il subsiste encore des ruines de celles de Ste Anne et de Brion sous l'invocation de Ste. Laurent." And he thinks that the ancient city Dariorigum was not Vannes on the west of Britanny (nor anywhere near it), but was Vains two miles west of Avranches, and that Cæsar's sea-fight with the Veneti took place in the Bay of Mont S. Michel. For many reasons, as will hereafter appear, I am of a different opinion.

62. The late Abbé Manet published at S. Malo in 1829 a small 8vo. volume of 183 pages, entitled *De l'etat ancien et de l'etat actuel de la Baie du Mont S. Michel et de Cancale, &c.* This work he informs us "was crowned and honoured by a gold medal worth 400 francs by the Royal and Geographical Society of France, at its solemn assembly of the 28th of March, 1828." Abbé Manet certainly rendered great service to science, by collecting and narrating as a Historian, many important physical facts. He appears to have had no thought what was really the cause of the sea's overwhelming the forest of Sciscy, on the occasion of an equinoctial spring tide propelled by a strong north wind. And especially he assigns no reason why the water did not ebb off again. Nor why that which was the Forest of Sciscy until the year 709, has been navigable sea ever since. It may be that the weight of the vast mass of water brought upon the country (now submerged) on that memorable occasion, was the proverbial last feather's weight which broke the camel's back, and caused the land to settle down into some cavity beneath: especially as a diligent search in the works of chroniclers and historians has entirely failed to discover any reason for believing that there was an earthquake shock. Some think Manet has been too credulous. Partly to satisfy himself on that point, but chiefly to obtain what other evidence he could, the present writer devoted a month's hard work at the British Museum reading room, in July and August 1861, in searching and making extracts, and had a fair measure of success. Of sixteen authorities quoted by the Abbé in his Note 26, to prove the former existence of a Forest called Sciscy in the Bay of Mont S. Michel; about one half of those references have been examined and verified by the present writer. The particulars gathered are about to be laid before the reader, from time to time.

63. Abbé Manet says that the former existence of the Forest of Scisey, or Chausey, is a fact of which history does not permit us to entertain the least doubt. And indeed if history is worth anything, there can be no doubt whatever that this forest once existed, and that an immense tract of it has been for about eleven centuries and a half under water, at every high water. He says (and he is justified by several chroniclers who wrote previous to the tenth century, in saying so), that the Bay of Mont S. Michel

did not exist as a bay until A.D. 709. He says also that there have been [at least] five distinct catastrophes of permanent submersions of land. Namely, in the sixth century, the seventh century, 709, 811, 842,* and 891; and a seventh appears to have occurred in 1163. According to a pamphlet published in 1860, entitled "Essai Géologique sur le Département de la Manche," par M. Bonissent, member of the Societé Géologique de France, a reference is given to the twenty-first volume of Dom Bouquets' "Historians of France," that about the year 1244, a formidable tide inundated our shore anew, and extended as much 24 kilometres, or about 15 English miles over the land, and so completed the destruction which began in 709, being an eighth sinking. Mr. Metivier says a ninth submersion "is mentioned by our countryman Dumaresq, in 1247, there was likewise an earthquake.† A tenth, as we have seen, occurred around Jersey in 1356. Of the date of the submersion west of Guernsey there appears to be no record. And an eleventh submersion took place on the north of S. Malo about 1437; since which date apparently all has been stationary, except on the west of Britanny, where a twelfth sinking took place so lately as 1827.—*See Manet, p. 76, foot note.*

64. Of all these, that of 709 appears to have been by far the most completely recorded; of the effects of previous "inundations" there appears to be no record. Abbé Manet describes the inundation of 709 as having been unhappily sustained by a terrible north wind: another writer says the direction of the wind was different. The invasions commenced at S. Pair, the Abbé says, which is a small village about two English miles south of Granville. "The environs of Chausey first yielded to its attack, and the tempests continuing to unite their fury to the efforts of the subsequent tides, produced at last the most frightful changes. *All disappeared under the waters, with the exception of the mountains which form the islands.*‡ and a portion of the forest intermingled with meadows, which was spared for a time on the coast of Avranchin." * * * "The storm changed the course of the Couësnon and gave to the ocean nearly all the portion of the bay which belongs to Normandy."—*Manet, p.* 11.

It destroyed all the land to a point distant three English miles westward of Cape Lihou, near Granville; as well as the land enclosed by an imaginary, nearly straight line, drawn from the said point to the promontory of Cancalle. This boundary line on the map is copied from one of Manet's maps. But the ravages of the sea in 709, were not confined to this. It began again, he says, in "le Verger" in the Commune of Cancalle and destroyed all the land between the present coast and the line on the map marked, *Coast line in A.D.* 709, extending from le Verger to

---

* The chronicler of Fontenelle was a witness that from the 22nd to 29th Oct., 842, the islands were visited by a violent earthquake and rumblings, which engulphed the sea-shore of the Cotentin, or that part of Normandy which is in the diocese of Coutances.—Tupper's *Hist. Guernsey*, p. 28.

† There was an earthquake Feb. 13th, 1247, in London, in diocese of Bath and Wells, also felt in Piedmont, Savoy, and Syria.—See Dr. Mallet's "Earthquake Report," vol. xxii., Brit. Ass.

‡ The italics are the present writer's. the passage gives direct, though unconscious, testimony that the ground had sunk.

Cape Frebel, being 21 miles in length and often as much as 2 miles wide. The submerged part first mentioned averages about 18 miles long by 9 miles wide, so that in the whole there was a loss of about 200 square miles, in the districts named. Beyond Cape Frebel, Manet says, he has no attention to follow it. Not quite the whole of the land in question was destroyed in 709, the isle of Cesembre was still joined to the continent in 1108, and a tract of meadows extending from S. Malo to Cesembre, 2½ miles in length and called the meadows of Cesembre, was part of it covered by the sea in a moment in 1163,* but the whole was not finally lost until about 1437, which is the date of the last account we have of it. Abbé Manet's description has enabled the writer to describe these meadows on the chart.

65. The island la Catis, 10 nautical miles north-west of S. Malo, was formerly surrounded by a forest which the River Rance passed through. And there was formerly in the sea to the westward of Lannion (which town is 67 miles westward of S. Malo) "an ancient spacious forest." And as we shall find presently, a vast quantity of trees was washed up on the coast of Morlaix in 1812. These were probably some of the last named forest.

66. Abbé Manet says, p. 12, the sea in 709 swallowed up "all the flat country which was in view of the town of Aleth.† We are certain the disaster there was considerably greater, since this territory was much more populous than the other. Its devastations commenced at Cape Frebel, which disappeared in a moment. The assault of the waves carried away also at the same instant all the space occupied by the shores of S. Jacut. It made breaches in five or six places in the long chain of rocks, which exist from the east of Cesembre to the point of Mingar in S. Coulomb,‡ and gave passage to the torrent. At last the lands which joined the two arms of the River Rance were overwhelmed in their turn, and the new deluge rapidly gained an entrance to what is now the harbour of S. Malo, and of which this town, as well as that of St. Servan, form the two sides, one on the north and the other on the south. It formed there a separation of about 600 toises § in its least extent—that is to say from the south part of the rock of Aaron ‖ to the opposite point which we now call Nais, or Naye. It spread itself afterward on one side into the meadows called la Hoguette and des Joncs which border the high road leading from la Hoguette to Paramé, and on the other side into all that extent which we now call Marais Rabot, Little and Great Marshes, &c. It extended even to the heights of Paramé, Tertre au Merle or mountain of St. Joseph, la Grand Rivière, and even Frotu and du Vallion,

* August 2, 1163, an earthquake is recorded, but it was in Anjou. See *Chroniques de Saumur et d'Augers*; *Dom Bouquet*, t. 12, p. 482; *Martène et Duraud*, t. 5, p. 1145; *Labbe*, t. 1, p. 279. In my MS. Appendix is an account of all earthquakes at all likely to have operated on the French coasts.

† The cite part of S. Servan.

‡ Four miles west of the Point of Cancalla.

§ 640 yards.

‖ On which S. Malo stands.

as you go to Château-Malo, and Saint-Meloir. The Rance which was only a large stream from Aleth to Dinan, acquired by the same event, a considerable breadth and depth to above S. Suliac, a town about mid-distance between those two places.* The district he describes (exclusive of the part between Aleth and S. Suliac) extends to about 5 miles east of S. Malo by perhaps half as much in breadth.

67. Is not this remarkable swallowing up, devastating, disappearing in a moment, carrying away at the same instant, making five or six breaches in a chain of rocks, and so giving passage to the torrent: just such a description as a faithful chronicler might be expected to give, if the ground was sinking and he did not know it?

68. At p. 11, 12, the Abbé says:—"The storm changed the course of the Couësnon, and gave to the ocean nearly all the portion of the bay which belongs to Normandy.† It gained the whole of the parishes of St. Benoit-des-Ondes and la Fresnaye, even to the marshes of Dol, which it succeeded in completely destroying in 811 at the approach of autumn; it desolated and destroyed the parishes of Cherueix, S. Broladre, S. Marcan, Ros-sur-Couësnon, and S. Georges-de-Grehaigne. In the meantime it respected still at these two epochs (709 and 811) different portions of territory which it has swallowed up since, and which we shall recite in note 51." In note 51 he states as follows:—" Beyond, the environs of the Herpins and the Fillettes have ceased to exist, having been undermined in their turn; the sea spared then as we have already said, the little village of Porz-Pican, and a certain extent of neighbouring territory, which are no more to be found. The principal parishes which from this time have successively paid tribute to its rage are those of S. Louis, Mauny, and la Feillette, which still existed at the commencement of the 13th century, as is attested by different donations of land situated on their borders, to the Abbey of Vieux-Ville in Epiniac, and by the Synodical books of the Bishopric of Dol, which have continued to mention the names until 1664."

69. Thus the sea overwhelmed about ten parishes (some of which have been recovered by embanking) and we shall have accounts of the loss of several more presently. It inundated all the tract of land from the Bay of Mont S. Michel nearly to Dol, comprising 26,000 acres,‡ or nearly forty square miles in extent. Sir John Herschel ("Outlines of Astronomy," 1864, p. 816), gives the toise as 6·394593 British feet, which would give only 24,751 acres, which are equal to about 38⅔ square miles. Manet says in his note, that the embankment by which this vast tract has been recovered was first commenced in 1024. The tract can be seen on the map. It is mentioned in Trollope's "Summer in Britanny, p. 187, that the embankment is sixteen miles in length. Abbé Manet says six leagues, and that it was not all constructed at once.

* These places are all between the River Rance and the Bay of Mont S. Michel, but the scale of the map is too small to admit of their respective situations being exhibited.

† The places about to be named by him are all comprised in the Bay of Mont S. Michel and in the tract inundated.

‡ "20,599 journaux et 13 cordes submersibles (le journal de 1280 toises carées)."—See "Manet, p. 99.

70. In his vol. ii., p. 103, &c., Mr. Trollope, who was a diligent collector of old Breton legends, mentions the ancient cities of Lexobis, Ys, Tolente, and Occismor "of which the mere names survive." Their sites are doubtful, and a fruitful subject of dispute to the Breton antiquaries. He mentions also, p. 113, that in the extensive sands of S. Michel—not Mont S. Michel—but near Laumeur on the north of the department Finisterre, "once existed, according to the local traditions, a flourishing town called Kerfeunteun, or the town of the fountain." He says, p. 358, that constant and immemorial tradition has fixed the site of the city of Is, or Ys, "in the immediate neighbourhood of the Pointe du Raz." More as to this alleged city in a future chapter.

71. The lost territory described in Art. 64 previous, as well as the 40 square miles mentioned in Art. 69, were covered, Manet says, with a thick and sombre forest, namely, *the forest of Sciscy*. It has been mentioned, he proceeds, by Latin authors as *Sciciacum nemus*, in French, Sciscy, now changed into Chausey.

71*a*. I have had doubts about re-publishing the following legend which occurs at p. 159 of Dr. Hairby's Book, and it has in fact been added to an otherwise completed section of the MS. The principle of altering nothing, and suppressing nothing, settled the question in the affirmative. Passing over all about S. Michael, Satan, and the angels, the rest is very like a graphic description of what the action of the sea must necessarily have been when the ground was sinking.

*Legend of Mont S. Michel, A.D.* 709. "St. Michael unable to banish Satan from the world, wished to place the sea between him and the two rocks,* and for this purpose he ordered it to approach and surround them with its waters. The mandate was not immediately obeyed, but from that moment fearful signs appeared in the air; globes of fire rushed through the dark shades of night; groanings and lamentations which seemed to come from the bowels of the earth, were heard; the wind howled through the forest trees: the rains fell and all nature seemed to wait some great crisis. These alarming prognostications continued till the month of March; when the rivers Selune, Sée and Couësnon simultaneously overflowed their willow-bordered banks, carrying shepherds, herds, and people with them into the sea. The ocean sympathised, driven by a boisterous north-east wind, it burst through its banks and forced a way into the hollows, uprooted the forest, levelled the surface, filled the vallies, created new land, defaced the old, rose like a water spout in one place, and glided along the earth like a serpent in another, *the angels pushing it forward with their hands* [!]. It mounted, it reared like a horse under the lash of the whip, its white main floated in the air as high as the clouds. Thr two Mounts were not protected from its wrath. The waves clung to their sides as the wasp does to the flowering almond: the waters stripped them of their verdure, of their fresh covering of broom, mingled with white roses, tore from their heads their plumes of vervain, they ate the flesh to the

* Namely Mont S. Michel and Mont Tombelene.

bone. And when peace was again restored to the country, when the calm—the first fruit of the tempest—shone forth in a brilliant day, nothing was to be seen but a vast sea, in the midst of which were two black and naked rocks, such as one of them now is, and the other would be if without its mural dress."

SINKINGS IN THE BAY OF MONT S. MICHEL, AND ON THE NORTH COAST OF BRITANNY.

72. *Ancient roads in the Forest of Sciscy.*—"Two great military roads or routes, of which one started from Condate, now called Rennes, and the other from Corseul, were re-united at Hayes de Dol, between S. Leonard and Carfantin. There they formed a single road which proceeded by La Mancelière in Baguer Pican, traversed the forest in all its length, and joined Crociatonum, the capital of the Unelli, situated apparently in the parish of Aleaume, one-quarter league from Valognes, in the Cotentin. For the rest, this desert filled with wild beasts, as history explains (prœbens altissima latibula ferarum)* "was originally scantily peopled by other creatures scarcely human, namely, by certain half savage pagans, to whom in Christian ages succeeded a crowd of anchorites, who retired to the forest to serve God more freely far from the tumult of the world. Adjoining this profound forest, was another, which was in fact only a prolongation and continuation of the former. Its proper name, if it ever had one, is unknown to us; but it is certain, by history and from the remains which are found in it still in our time, that it extended with some slight interruptions almost from the Bay of Verger, mentioned above, to Cape Frehel." So far Manet. On the authority of Dr. Hairby, in his History of Mont S. Michel, 1841, we know that the learned antiquary, M. de Gerville, says that this destroyed country was crossed by a Roman road, which led from S. Pair to Rennes. In the Bayeux tapestry (temp. William the Conqueror), there is a view of eight warriors on horseback, preceded by three men on foot, who are crossing the River Couësnon, near Mont S. Michel. This was simply a crossing on the sand, there is no reason to believe there was any such elaborately formed road as the Romans were accustomed to make, and the circumstance has nothing to do with the sinkings. The Couësnon, which is the boundary between Normandy and Britanny, used sometimes to pass on the Breton side, and sometimes on the Norman side of the Mont as the action of storms determined. A few years ago a new channel was formed for the river, faced with stone at the sides, which leaves the Mont on the Norman side of the Couësnon. The making of this channel gave rise to a circumstance which is illustrative of our subject. A French countess, one of the ancient nobility, claimed compensation for the portion of sands taken for the channel, as having been part of a former estate belonging to her family. Her claim was admitted and compromised. This channel is shown on the map by a black line; the words New Channel are a little out of place.

* Abbé Manet mentions in his note 30, the horn of a stag, with many antlers, and 19 French inches long, which was found in the recovered territory in 1814, buried 3 or 4 French feet deep. An entire head of the Urus (mentioned by Cæsar), is also said to have been found.

73. *Vast quantities of trees from the sands of Mont St. Michel, &c.*—Abbé Manet gives personal testimony in his note 26, as to "the immense quantity of trees of all species, which have been disinterred for ages from the sands of Mont S. Michel, on the coasts of Granville, and especially in the marshes of Dol, &c., where the sea does not impede the workmen. Those trees, which are commonly oaks, have preserved their form, their bark, and some of them even their leaves. Their long sojourn in the mud has, in the meantime, altered their substance a little; and given them when they are burnt, a sour odour which causes hoarseness, but when the water which has penetrated them is evaporated, their wood which was soft, becomes compact, and acquires great hardness. It takes almost the polish of ebony, which it resembles in colour; and makes very pretty furniture." It is used for espaliers and in the construction of houses, which are especially to be seen in the Isle *de Mer*, which place is in 1° 51′ W. long., and 48° 33½′ lat., 3½ *miles inland.* The name, of course, signifies that the place was once surrounded by the sea. The inhabitants of the marine islands near S. Malo call these trees "canaillons," the workmen call them "coërons." "During the famous hurricane of 9th January, 1735, the agitation of the sea was so great on the sandy shore of Mont S. Michel that it ejected from the sand a prodigious quantity of these logs (billes), which were always found lying from north to south, which proves, independently of history, that these trees were not thrown confusedly here and there, but that the tempest to which they owed their ruin, blew from the north."* This alleged direction of the prostrate trees is not concurred in by other authorities. Manet states, p. 36, that the shifting sands of Mont S. Michel have been penetrated in different places more than 50ft. without finding their bottom. And he says also, in a footnote on the same page, that "In 1780, according to M. Blondel, a ship was stranded near Mont S. Michel. It sunk in such a manner that it was swallowed up entire; and it all, even to the masts, disappeared in the space of a few days."

"The places named the Grand Bruyère and the Cardequint, between Mont-Dol and the Isle Mer, are especially remarkable for the acorns, beechmast, hazel nuts; &c., well preserved; which one encounters at 6, 8, and 10 [French] feet deep; from which [the abbé thinks] it is natural to conclude that the entire overthrow of the forest of Scisсy in this part, was not effected until the approach of autumn. The custom of the borderers, in order to discover the stumps, is to sound the earth with long spits of iron, and to dig in the places where the spits prove a resistance."—Manet p. 53.

74. *Farther proofs of the inundations in Britanny.*—Abbé Manet, informs us in his note 50:—"It is common and notorious," says M. Briandi Bertrand, rector of S. Guinou, in the procès-verbal of the commissaries sent on the 23rd August, 1606, by the parliament of Bretagne to prove the state of the country, "that anciently the sea covered all the marshes of Dol at every high water; it reached as far as the town of Carfantin, against the cemetery, and for this reason it was called the Port of Carfantin. * *

* See Abbé Manet's Book, p. 53. This storm, he says (p. 100), caused the sea to surmount the top of the embankment, and flooded a vast extent of Britanny.

We can say also this much of this village, also called the Port, that it is at 5 or 600 toises to the south of Cendres, near Pont-Orson; and where, as a proof which dispenses with all others, one does not encounter still very near, the black earth, but that white mud, which proves the long sojourn of the ocean on all the places of which we have spoken. And what is more, is, the marshes of Boucé, Aucé, and others going towards Antrain, bear themselves the symptoms of the terrible invasions of 709 and 811; and it is a fact as curious as authentic, that in 1789, at the time of the enclosure of these marshes, there were found buried in the Tangue, the remains of a barque, with a quantity of shells of the same species as those with which the sands of Mont S. Michel are filled."

75. The following extract from *The Acts of the Saints of the order of St. Benedict* confirms the fact of the former existence of the forest of Sciscy (and the same statement appears in Neustria Pia, but under dates 548 and 550). It says,* "Year of Christ 565, April 16, Seculum I., p. 152, 153. From the M.S. volumes. 1. The most reverend Bishop Paterne of Poitiers. . . . 4. When this man of God had passed the 13th year of his pontificate, one day of Easter when he wished to visit his brethren in the forest of Sescy, he fell sick. But in like manner S. Scubilio fell sick in the monastery of Mandan. Then the messengers meeting him advise the blessed Scubilio to undertake the journey, that he might meet his brother. But an arm of the sea † being interposed, he was not able to ford it at night. But when there was about three miles of space between the two saints, they both died in the same night." And Laut (or Lauto, who was Bishop of Coutances from 525 to 566) ‡ "when he came to visit the place before eight days, brought to the cathedral the blessed Paterne from Sescy, and performed the funeral ceremonies." According to *Neustria Pia*, p. 57, Paterne died April 15, 562, aged 83. And according to Manet, he died in 570. Plees gives at his p. 322 the following, which he extracts from the Roman Catholic breviary, and which corroborates the fact of the former existence of the Forest of Sciscy:—"In the 6th century St. Père, or Paterne, and St. Scubilion came from Poitiers into Neustria (Normandy), and established themselves in the diocese of Coutances; but having desired to pass into a neighbouring island, to live in very great solitude, they were detained by the Christians of Sisci, who besought them to remain amongst them to uproot idolatry. They consented, and founded the monastery of Sisci. Afterwards St. Père having been elected Bishop of Avranches, came at the age of 82 years to visit the said monastery. He died the day before the fête of Easter." §

M. Boudent-Godelinière, Secretary to the Archæological Society of Avranches, in his *Mont S. Michel* p. 19 informs us that "M. Rouault, curé de S. Pair, says in his *Hist. des évêques d'Avranches*, that Saint Leoncien third bishop of this city (elected in 500), often travelled all over the frightful and vast solitude of Scycy, to preach the gospel; and that Saint Gaud died at

---

* See voucher H. in M.S. appendix for the original Latin.
† Possibly one of Cæsar's estuaries, to be mentioned hereafter.
‡ Lecanu, *Hist. des Evêques de Coutances*, 1839, pp. 31 and 37.
§ See MS. appendix, p. 609, for the original Latin.

Scycy in 525, where is now the commune of S. Pair. He had quitted the bishopric of Evreux to live in this retreat, and S. Pair worn out by old age and labours, returned to Avranches from Scycy to die with his brethren about 540; and that under S. Romphaire sixth bishop of Coutances (in 566) S. Sénier, anchorite in the desert of Scycy, afterwards bishop of Avranches, having come to this ancient solitude to visit his brethren, fell sick and died. One could add to this list the name of many other historians." And his own conclusion is, that it is evident that formerly the Bay of Mont S. Michel as covered with forest which extended to a greater or less distance.

76. M. Ogée, geographical engineer of Bretagne, says in his *Dictionnaire Historique et Geographique de la Province de Brétagne*, 1778; that the best known cenobites who have inhabited the Forest of Sciscy are Saints Brieuc, Sampson, Sulia, Magloire, Budock, Broladre, Hildent, Colomban, Meloir, Pol-de-Leon, Tugdwal, Corentin, Malo, Aaron, Goad, Aroaste; and it is from the residence of these anchorites that many parishes of these districts have taken their names. Manet repeats some of these names, and gives a few others in addition at p. 56 with some particulars, viz., "M. Rouault, in his *Abrégé de la vie des Evêques de Coutances*, p. 51, says 'that the deserts of Sciscy and Nanteuil,* situated at the two extremities of the Cotentin, have produced so great a number of anchorite saints that one might make an entire legend of their lives.' But the most celebrated of which the *Hist. ecclesiastique de Normandie* (Trigan, t. 1, p. 78, 128, 131, &c.) makes mention are (omitting Paterne already named), Saint Gaud bishop of Evreux, and S. Aroaste priest, who both died in Sciscy forest about the year 491; Saint Senier or Senateur, also bishop of Avranches, who died on the 6th or, according to others, on the 18th or 26th Sept. 570; finally St. Pair or Paterne the younger, native of the Cotentin, who was brought up in his infancy in the monastery of S. Pair the elder, from whence he passed to that of Saint-Pierre-le-Vif near Sens, and was assassinated in the forest of Sergines 12 November, 726 by some robbers whom he wished to convert, '*he lived long enough to be witness of the great catastrophe effected in 709 by the sea in the environs of Chausey*.'"

At vol. ii., p. 40, Ogée says:—"The territory of Dol presents irregularities on which we ought to remark. It proves the great physical revolutions of another district of Britanny. Mont St. Michel, Tombelaine, the Isles of Jersey, Guernsey, Chosey, Alderney,† and all the little isles which are on the borders of this coast, formed in times very distant part of the continent. We know that in times less remote from us, *a vast forest extended from the environs of Coutances to the rocks of Cesembre above St. Malo* (a direct distance of 38 English miles). The first epoch at which the sea took possession of this immense extent of coast is unknown to us; but we know that the destruction of the Forest of Sciscy ascends no higher than the year 709. This inundation is the origin of the marshes of Dol, of which the length is eight leagues (about 23 English miles), from E. to W., and the breadth, one or two leagues from N. to S. The industry of men has tried

* Near the sea on the coast of Bessin.

† It will be shown hereafter that the northern Channel Islands were islands at the time of Cæsar and Diodorus.

to rescue this plain from the sea, which would invade it again in the absence of the embankments which have been opposed to it. A thousand proofs attest this ancient usurpation of the sea. The marshes of Dol are filled with overturned trees, often hidden by a very small quantity of earth. The trees which are the most common are oaks, which have preserved their form, their bark, and sometimes even their leaves. The long sojourn which they have made in the marsh has very much changed their substance; when they are taken out their wood is black and soft; but when they are exposed to the air they become compact, acquire a great specific gravity and an extreme hardness. The mere motion of flow and ebb often uncover these trees in the sandy shore." A prodigious quantity of insects and plants of all species, he says, died and rotted in the marshes.

"Another plain, named La Bruyère, situated between Dol and Chateauneuf,* which the sea has covered and which it has abandoned, made equally part of the Forest of Sciscy. The inhabitants of the neighbourhood have dug up for almost eight hundred years, and have not yet ceased to draw out trees well preserved. The excavations made present constantly leaves and fruits of trees of a forest,—acorns, beech-mast, hazel-nuts, stones of cherries. The barks of trees are so well preserved that one recognises, without difficulty, their species. The shells of the land and sea are almost everywhere mingled with the earth. In the middle of this plain there is an extensive pool, called the pool of St. Coulman, or Colomban.

77. Manet says, p. 9, that there is a rock called l'Evêque, in' the middle of the Bay of Guesclin [west of Cancalle Point] which can only be walked on at low water of spring tides, but which was formerly a strong place. Possibly the little port of Winiau was situated there, or near the ancient canal of Guyoul. It is certain that all the old writings up to 1032, when it ceases to be mentioned, agree in saying that this port was not far from Cancavan, which is our modern Cancalle. The shoals of Petit Pointu and the environs of the Isle Chevret, and the Isles Conchées, Cesembre, Harbour, and Laubras, were well peopled. They are now mere islets, great parts of them having sunk, and are, perhaps, with the single exception of Cesembre, which contains very few inhabitants, entirely unpeopled.

These small islands are north and north-east of S. Malo, between the present coast and the coast line of 709. Other small, and now uninhabited islands, are in the coast line of 709, between Cesembre and Cape Frehel.

78. In *Neustria Pia*, p. 371, is given a most remarkable account of Mont S. Michel, date 709. It says, "This *rock* anciently was a *mountain*," (Hæc rupes antiquitus Mons erat, are the words) "surrounded with woods and forests, extended to six miles in length by four in breadth, on one side contiguous to the main land, on the other to the ocean sea, distant from the city of Arboretana four leagues, on the confines of Normandy and Armorican Britanny. It was called the Mountain in the Storm of the Sea, or the Mountain in the Tomb, at whose foot some hermits had fixed their habitations." On this mountain, he says, S. Ausbert, bishop of Avranches, built a church dedicated to the Archangel Michael, in 709. This bishop at the

*On the N.W. of Dol.

same time, sent three messengers to Naples to obtain certain relics. Neustria Pia then says, p. 372:—"Whilst, therefore, the said messengers in performing their journey spent a year, God permitting, the sea surmounted and prostrated the wood, though very large; and filled up with sand the places adjacent to Mont Tombelène. But the messengers having returned on the 16th October, they wondered so much to see the woods replaced by sand, that they thought they had entered into a new world." *

Du Moustier gives the following references in his margin:—"Glaber, lib. 3, Histor. cap. 3.—Sigibertus in Chronic Ann. 709.—Petrus de Natalib. lib. 9. Catalog. Sanctor. cap. 71.—S. Antonius 3 part. Histor. Titul. 13 cap. 6. § 30.—Constantiense Breviarium MS. Bajocense Vvernerus in Fasciculo temporum ad ann, 704.—Nicolaus Aegidius, in Annal. Franc. sub Childeberto I. ann. 544.

The ancient author Nennius also mentions the top of Mont St. Michel under the name "verticem Montis Jovis" in capital letters, as if it was a mountain of importance.

We see, then, that in 709, the Mont † was six miles long, by four broad. It is now, according to Dr. Hairby's plan, which has every appearance of being correct (scale, five chains to an inch), nearly a circle, averaging no more than 354yds. diameter (equal to 1,112yds in circumference, and 20½ acres horizontal area). What has become of the rest?

79. In the *Acts of the Saints*, which Watts in his *Bibliographical Dictionary*, says "is a valuable compilation of ancient monuments, which throws much light upon the most obscure part of Ecclesiastical History"; we read as follows, in the M.S.S. of an anonymous writer before the 10th century:—"Year of Christ 708, Oct. 16, Seculum III, part 1, p. 86. Concerning the situation of the place; at first, as we can know from truthful writers, it was enclosed by a very thick wood, far from the ocean (the Chesnian codex has it 'distant as it is estimated eight miles from the Ocean') and distant six miles from the tide, affording profound hiding places for wild beasts. * * The sea which was a long way off, rising little by little, prostrated all the magnitude of the wood by its force, and heaped together all things into the resemblance of its sand, affording a means to the people of the earth, that they might relate the wonderful things of God." In the same work it is said, under the same date:—"Concerning the arrival of the reliques. In the meantime the chief messengers returning after a long journey, to the place from which they had set out, on the very day on which the building was completed, in the western parts of the Mont now mentioned; as if they had entered into a new world, which they had left at first *filled with a thicket of briars*."‡

80. The forest of Sessy is often mentioned in the *Acts of the Saints* and in *Neustria Pia*.

81. In Abbé Desroches' *Hist. du Mont S, Michel*, p. 72, he quotes three several M.S.S. of the Mont, all of an earlier date than the 10th century; namely, Nos. 24, 34, and 80, each stating that the sea was six miles distant

* The original Latin is quoted in the M.S. Appendix.
† Mont S. Michel.
‡ The original Latin is in the M.S. Appendix.

from the Mont: "Milibus distans sex." The Mont is now about 4½ miles from extreme low water; eastward, it is now 3 miles from the Mont to the general line of coast.

The *Chronicle of Sigibert* the monk of Gemblours which embraces the period from A.D. 318 to 1113, gives an account of the building of the church of Mont S. Michel in 709, by Aubert, bishop of Avranches, in honour of Saint Michael.

82. In fact, say the *Memoirs of the Celtic Academy*,* "the actual sands of Mont S. Michel were a portion of the continent covered with wood. The river Couësnon traversed this great forest, which was equally watered by the Ardée and the Sée, which overflowed into the marsh."

83. Manet says (p. 96) that a constitution of Louis le Débonnaire, date 817, in which that king, speaking of the convents of his kingdom, which owed to his army gifts of money without men, puts at the head of the list:—"Monasterium sancti Michaelis marisci primi," that is, "the monastery of S. Michael of the first marsh." As if there was then some of the marsh remaining, or otherwise, as if there were more marshes than one. And Lecanu, in his Histoire aforesaid (p. 22), speaking of "Monasterium marisii primi," says in a foot note:—"This Charter is the gift of the Abbey of Mont S. Michel, of a monastery situated very near the Mont, and called the 'monastery-of-the-first-Marsh' (in latere montis) on the side of the mountain." And on p. 21 he says, "in the environs of Granville, the sand on the shore of the ocean bears still the name of the marsh."

Thus we have had abundance of proof that there was an extensive forest surrounding Mont S. Michel, and called the forest of Sciscy, which is now sea.

84. The late Admiral White personally informed the present writer, that in the performance of his duty of taking soundings, on a rock called Le Banc Parisien (at six miles west-south-west of Cape Lihou or Granville Point), the highest part of which is only eight feet below low water; he brought up with the sounding lead, pieces of the thin lead used for glazing windows, with fragments of glass in it. And he saw stones which he thought might have formed a part of a building.—Now the testimonies quoted heretofore, and to be quoted hereafter, and the reasonings thereon, have not had, and will not have, as any part of their object, to bolster up either this, that, or the other theory. The writer cares for nothing but the truth, and that he will diligently seek for, totally regardless where that search may land him. He has suppressed nothing, and will suppress nothing, which appears relevant and worth recording. And, accordingly, he very willingly lays before the reader, the following objections to Admiral White's statement. One of the writer's friends says, "to be candid, I still give very little credence to the glass and thin lead having belonged to a submerged *abbey* or *church*.† If really drawn up with the lead, they more probably were aboard a vessel which was wrecked or foundered in the neighbourhood. But the story is possible." Now on the other hand, glazed

* Tom. iv., p. 384, 8vo. Paris, 1809.
† Neither the Admiral nor the writer said anything about the *nature of the building* the former mentioned church windows, only to show that the lead was glazing lead.

leaden widows are very unlikely things to be aboard of any ship, either as cargo or for use. Such windows are usually, perhaps always have been, prepared on the spot or in the neighbourhood, and consequently would not be likely to have been carried by sea. Another friend says, "the lead may have been drifted to the top of the rock by the action of the sea in storms." This is impossible, lead being eleven times, and glass three times, as heavy as sea water. On one side of the rock the minimum depth of water is 36ft., on the other 60ft. Even if storms could affect the sea bottom in those places at those depths, which is very improbable; their effect would rather be to bury the glass and lead amongst the sand and brown shells which form the bottom. The following objection has been suggested by a third friend, who is a naval officer. He knew a case where a piece of sheet lead was affixed to the bottom of a ship below the water line, and after the ship had sailed for some time, it was found that the lead had entirely disappeared, having been corroded away by the action of the constituents of salt water, as he thinks. May not the friction of the water against the lead, whilst the ship was sailing, have worn away the lead? If so, Admiral White's lead *being stationary*, might possibly have existed under water since 709. The question is submitted to chemists and other experts, whether or not the lead would have existed as described for 11½ centuries? At the same time it ought to be borne in mind, that even if it should be a general opinion that the lead could not have existed so long, that circumstance would only invalidate one, out of scores of testimonies.

85. Admiral White also stated, that on one occasion when he was afloat, near Fort Rimains (south of Cancalle Point), the weather being calm and the water very clear, he saw at the bottom "divisions," which he took to have once been garden fences. To this the friend first named in the preceding article, objects as follows:—"I hold that the garden fences or trenches *must* have disappeared with the action of the sea, in the course of a thousand years, even although sheltered by the promontory of Cancalle. If a trench were dug in St. Aubin's Bay, I am sure it would fill up in the course of a winter." To this the present writer answered, under date June 30th, 1860. "I entirely agree with you that if a trench were dug on St. Aubin's sands it would very soon fill up, because those sands are laid bare at low water, and exposed to very violent action of the waves in storms. But at 15ft. or more below extreme low water, where the "divisions" not "trenches" were seen, and where they are so well protected by Cancalle Point, is the very perfection of tranquility, because at equal depths the pressure of water is exactly equal in all directions." A cubic foot of sea water weighs 64¼lbs., which gives a pressure of 964lbs. per square foot, at 15ft. average depth; which being applied to the divisions *equally in all directions*, is a pretty good guarantee for their stability. The gentleman then quoted the low district theory, disposed of in Art. 11. And when the objections referred to in opposition to that theory, were stated to him, his reply was, that he was not a scientific man. Not long after, a paper to the like effect, showing that the low district theory is an impossibility, was sent by post by the present writer to the author of that theory, And an offer was made at the same time, either to consider his answer confidential, or

to print it side by side with the reasoning against it. But up to the present moment, Sep. 15th, 1866, no answer has been received from the author of the theory.

### D'ARGENTRE, THE HISTORIAN OF BRITANNY.

86. We learn as follows from *Morery's Historical Dictionary*, Amsterdam, 1702:—"Messire Bertrand D'Argentre, lieutenant-general or grand seneschal of Rennes, was one of the most illustrious ornaments of his family, which was one of the most noble and considerable of this province. He was learned, magnificent, honourable, liberal, and the most generous friend in the world. He composed learned Commentaries on the Customs of Britanny, which the most skilful, and amongst others the famous Charles du Moulin have given their great praise. We have also of his a History of Britanny, which he undertook at the instance of the states of the province. He died 13 February, 1590, aged 71." This eminent man, in describing the course of the river Couësnon as the boundary between Normandy and Britanny, uses the following remarkable expressions, namely, that at the time he refers to, the river meeting the reflux of the sea, "is constrained to yield to the strongest, and flowing over the land which it finds *below* it, is so spread out that it has submerged one or two leagues of the best country of Britanny." And he says, farther, that the sea "every morning increases," so much so that on one particular morning "it ruined more than four leagues of very good land, and more than 100,000 livres of proprietors' revenue,"* namely, of the annual value of £7,500 sterling. The writer's belief is, that the ground was *quietly* settling down day by day, and nobody suspected it. How could the sea have overwhelmed it then, and never before on any other hypothesis?

87. A large collection of accounts of earthquakes has been made for the purposes of this work, embracing all that could be found, for the period between the third and seventeenth centuries. All that are at all connected with the northerly and westerly coasts of France are stated in the MS. Appendix. It does not appear that any of the sinkings can be identified as the effects of earthquakes. We ought not to be surprised at these occurrences passing almost, and sometimes altogether, unnoticed, because they happened mostly before geology had become a science, and consequently before such events were understood. The inhabitants could only observe that, whereas yesterday the given tract was land, to-day it was sea. Sir Charles Lyell † describes the sinking of a tract of land, called the Runn of Cutch, at the mouth of the Indus, 2,000 square miles in area; it sunk in a few hours. And he quotes Sir A. Burnes as stating that "these wonderful events passed unheeded by the inhabitants of Cutch;" for the region convulsed though once fertile, had for a long period been reduced by want of irrigation, so that the natives were indifferent as to its fate. A similar indifference appears to have occurred on the coasts of France, almost with the single exception of records kept in monasteries—all honour to the monks for their care and thoughtfulness,—there appears to be no record at all of

* D'Argentre, *Hist. Bret.*, 1611, folio 41 F, &c., quoted in MS. appendix.
† *Principles of Geology*, 1853, p. 461.

the sinkings about Guernsey farther than that the submarine gorban or peat was first discovered about 1750, being the first record of the event.* Is it not probable that other catastrophes of the same nature may have taken place in the localities in question, without having been noticed, at least without being recorded at the time they occurred?

88. Manet relates (p. 102, 103) an entertaining anecdote quoted from the author of the *Observations on the desert of Scisey*, who gives the date 1685. A priest of the diocese of Dol being aware of the tradition that in a place now occupied by the sea there was formerly a parish called St. Louis, mischievously sent word to Rome, that the cure was vacant by death and was in the gift of the Pope. On receipt of this news, the registers were consulted, and it was found to be perfectly clear that this parish had been presented to by previous Popes. It was put to competition and fell to a priest of Lower Britanny, who went immediately to take possession. But what was his surprise when he arrived in front of Mont S. Michel, and the place was shown him *amongst the sands*, where the pretended parish was formerly situate. His only course was to make attestation of the state of the case and return it to Rome, and then seek another benefice."

89. *Testimony of S. Pair, the poet.* The following is from Dr. Hairby's *History of Mont S. Michel.* Guillaume de S. Pair, a monk of Mont S. Michel, wrote in verse in the 12th century a history of the Abbey, &c., from which it appears that the Mont had once been surrounded by a celebrated forest which he calls "Quokelunde," [perhaps *Coquillunde*, land of shells, according to Abbé Desroches] where there was once abundance of venison. but where there is now nothing but fish. And that it was an easy walk from Avranches to Poelet and to the city of Ridolet, which last according to M. Edouard le Héricher is probably the very ancient city of Aleth, bordering the river Rance, on the west of S. Servan. Camden and D'Argentre call it "Quidalet."† Manet says it has also been called "Wic-Aleth," and that it was surrounded by walls as early as 250 B.C. It has also been called "Guich-Alet." M. de la Rue says he believes the historical details of the poet, for he wrote under the eye of his abbot Robert de Thorigney, a learned annalist who could not easily be deceived; and that the MS. was taken to England during the French revolution. Robert de Thorigney, otherwise called Robert du Mont, was the 15th Abbot of Mont S. Michel, from 1154 to 1186.‡ Here is an extract from the poem:—

"Desous Avranches vers Bretaine
Qui tous tems fut terre grifaine,
Est la forêt de Quokelunde
Dunt grant parole est par la munde;
"Ceu qui or est mer et areine,
En icels tems est forest pleine
De mainte riche venaison
Mes ores il noet, li poisson

---

* *Annals of the British Norman Isles*, by John Jacobs, Esq. 1830.
† Camden's *Britannia* p. 1512, edition 1722.—D'Argentre's *Hist. Bret.*, 1611, folio 113
‡ *Hist. de l'Avranchin*, par M. Edouard le Héricher, Vol. 2 p. 230.

Dune peast l'en très bien aler
Ni estu est ja crendre la mer
D'Avranches dreit à Poelet
A la cité de Ridolet.
En la forest avait un Mont, &c.
* * * *
Uns jouvencels, moine est del Mont
Deus en son règne part li dunt,
Guillelme a nom de St. Paier
Escrit en cest quaier,
El tems Robeirt de Thorignié
Fut c'est romans fait et trové," &c.

90. From *Mont S. Michel*, par M. Boudent-Godolinière, 1845, p. 14, we learn as follows:—"The poet, M. Chateaubriand adds, fixed the irruption of the sea in the reign of Childebert," which was from 511 to 558, according to Morery's Dictionary. M. Boudent-Godelinière who was secretary to the Archæological Society of Avranches, also says, after quoting S. Pair's verses aforesaid, at p. 16:—"To these probabilities, in favour of the existence of a forest in the Bay of Mont S. Michel, one may add all the great number of trees which it is certain have been found, all blackened, buried nearly everywhere, not only on our sandy shores, but *also under the waters in the part of la Manche, situated between Agon and Jersey.*

NOTE.—Agon is a village near the coast of Normandy, west of Coutances, Manet's coast line (shown on the map), at the beginning of the year 709, is not a little surprising by the great extent of sinkings which it indicates. But Ptolemy will soon convince us that those are but a small fraction of the sinkings which have really taken place during the last seventeen centuries.

### SAINT MALO AND NEIGHBOURHOOD.

91. D'Argentre says*: "One finds that in times past the town of S. Malo was not all sides surrounded by the sea, which always since then has gained upon it very far at this side, so that the marshes which were between the town and Sesember (which is an island about two leagues distant,† in which there is a convent of Cordeliers) was terra firma, and it appears by the accounts of the revenues of the bishopric of the chapter of this church, that the receivers had made a charge and discharge of the revenue of the marshes between the town and the convent of Sesembre, and even now the receivers have had a chapter of accounts of monies due and not received. And there is found in the registers of the "Senechaussée" of Rennes,‡ that formerly there was a trial between the Duke and the bishops, for the pasturage of the above-mentioned marshes; where the Duke pretended that his people had the right of leading their cattle in common."

---

* Hist. Bret., Folio 72A, 1611. (And M.S. Appendix, p. 635.)
† It measures 2¼ English miles on the French Chart.
‡ D'Argentre himself was Seneschal.

92. On this Manet remarks at p. 105:—"What the Historian of Britanny says here, was practised for a long time to maintain possession of the land *in case the sea had retired from it*,* is very certain, and perfectly agrees with the original pieces from which we are about to recite some extracts. A register of the chapter, in fact, commencing in 1415, reports formally that a certain person was condemned for having let his cattle escape inte the meadows of Césembre. Under the date of 1425, the same register contains an account rendered the preceding year, by the Jean Billart named, receiver of the Chapter-house, which charges him with having received 21 livres 8 sols of Colas Gochard, farmer of the meadows of Césembre. It contains another account signed, by Dom Pierre Billart, in 1437, who at this period (the last, probably, of these meadows) had again farmed them at 30 sols to one called Charles Cauchart. Finally, in 1486, the same Pierre Billart, or another of the same name, 'does not account, and does not charge himself with the farm of Césembre, because the said receiver has not enjoyed it.'" Between 1437 and 1486, probably about the former date, the meadows appear to have sunk.

93. Manet proceeds (p. 106):—"One could, if there was need, add to all these historical and physical demonstrations, that in the different statements rendered to the dukes and kings by our bishops, until the 29th December, 1689, all the range of rocks named les Portes, the isles of Césembre, Harbour, Great and Little Bés, les Marais, Talards, &c., are designated as if they were dependencies of the ecclesiastic Lordship of S. Malo, and not as appurtenances of the ducal or royal domain, like other isles situated in the sea and the rivers; and that these statements were always received by the chamber of accounts without blame or dispute, which would certainly not have taken place if the pretensions of our prelates had not rested on a notorious fact, namely, that this skeleton of a continent which had been devoured; from all antiquity made part of the territory of the churches of Aleth and S. Malo."

He says at p. 5 that S. Malo was originally situated in the middle of a marsh.

94. Manet also gives (p. 13) the boundaries of the meadows of Césembre, long known by the name "Prairies de Césembre," namely, "les Herbières, les Rats, la Pierre-aux-Anglais, Dodehal, les Coquières, les Hongréaux and la Roche-aux-Dogues." And he says the meadows have for their base the actual rocks called the "Bons-Hommes," to which, of course, must be added Césembre itself. The meadows are defined on the map, and doubtless would have appeared in Bianco's chart, referred to in Art. 54, if its hydrography had been correct, which it is not; and if its scale had been large enough. But the scale is only an inch to 100 English miles.

95. "Submarine trees on our shores are covered with about two feet of mud at extreme low water, at S. Suliac and the Bay of Dinard drawing near the Little Port—if we may believe M. Brisart who says he has seen them more than once. In nearly all the other slopes which border the

* This apparently affords a clue to the origin of the famous neutrality, of which more presently.

coast on the west, these stumps are scarcely deeper buried; especially in the sands of Port-Blanc, of la Garde-Guérin, of la Fosse-au-Veau in Saint Lunaire, and of Port-Hue in Saint-Briac.*

96. M. Ogée, Geographic engineer of Bretagne, says:—† "The sea has insensibly gained in this part a very vast territory, and whilst it has retired from the coast, to the south-west of Bretagne,‡ it has invaded the lands situated at the north of the province. A famous trial between the Dukes on one part, and the Bishop and Chapter of S. Malo on the other, informs us that the land situated between the city and the Isle of Césembre, which is distant about a league, and that which is situated between the city of Aleth and Dinard, [which latter is opposite to Aleth on the other side of the Rance] offered to view Meadows and Marshes which belonged to the Chapter. The Duke of Bretagne claimed these domains; but the decision of Judges of the Sénéchaussée of Rennes was not favourable to him, and the receivers of the Bishop and Chapter have made mention [of the meadows and marshes] again and again, although they have obtained no revenues. *This is a very wise precaution for the maintenance of their rights, in case they might some day become of value.*"

This last sentence which we have italicized intimates a belief in the possibility of the land rising again, and shows that the former owners still lay claim to the lost lands. And the sea which covers them is in consequence, not a part of the high sea, but is private property and consequently neutral; which will be treated of in the chapter on neutrality.

97. *Parishes and other places now missing.*—In Articles 68 and 69 preceding, we have specified ten parishes destroyed (though some of them were afterwards recovered by embanking); Ogée in Vol. 2 of his *Dictionary* says that Tommen or Thomen (which is some three miles south of Cancalle Point) now only a rock, was until the 14th century a parish of the same name of great extent. The parish of Bourgneuf was not submerged until about the 15th century. The sea uncovers sometimes under the sandy shore, portions of walls which formed the houses of villages which it has destroyed. The inundation of 709 was not the only fatality in this country; we know that the parishes of S. Louis, Mauny la Feillette, and Paluel existed until the 12th century. Gifts of property situated in those parishes, made to the Abbey of Vieuxville, attest their existence. The synodal books of the bishopric of Dol, bear their names up to 1664. A violent hurricane uncovered in 1735§ some ruins of Paluel submerged in 1630; a vessel for holding holy water of the ancient church, was found; and the wells in which were preserved some vessels of tin. One distinguishes still the streets and foundations of the houses of this town. He also mentions|| that at S. Pol-de-Leon (much to the west of

* Manet p. 90.
† See his Dictionary, Vol. 4, p. 266.
‡ He doubtless refers to the Aunis, to be hereinafter described.
§ See Art. 73 ante.
|| Vol. 4, p. 362. And Manet p. 103.

S. Malo, but on the north coast of Britanny), "one only parish named the Minihi, formed out of seven which existed formerly." There was also the parish of Ecrehou "in Jersey," see Archives of S. Lo quoted already; and the parish of Vivier, all situated on the north of Britanny except Ecrehou. In all no less than twenty parishes appear to be missing, without including any of those which must have been lost on the west coast of Normandy.

98. There are missing the great village of St. Anne, a town called Moulin du Buot, St. Etienne du Paluel, of which the streets and ruts of carriages could be distinguished so lately as 1735. The isle of Herpin and Port of Winiau are also missing. In 1427 an earthquake is said to have overturned part of Nantes, and swallowed up thirteen villages near Dol. The cities of Tolente and Occismor and Ptolemy's Habour of Staliocanus are now gone. Under the heading "Ptolemy," we shall see that the Harbour Staliocanus was probably identical with the present Harbour of Portrieux.

### As to the Depth of the Sinkings.

99. *Lost Monasteries and Town, and Comments.*—Manet and others give the names and positions of several monasteries, and the former gives (p. 59) also the name of a "Bourg" or town, which were once standing in that part of the forest of Sciscy now overwhelmed by the sea. The monastery of St. Moack's, he says, is five leagues from Dol going towards Chausey and one league north-north-west of the *Bourg de Lhankafruth.* The writer has therefore placed the Bourg on the great military road, at a place which agrees very nearly with Manet's description of its situation; the line of the road itself is copied from one of his maps. The monastery is of course placed a league north-north-west of the Bourg. At the Bourg there is now about six fathoms of water at low water, and at the monastery (which falls close to Manet's coast line previous to 709) there are between seven and eight fathoms at low water. Manet says that Rivallon brother to Judicaël* king of Bretagne, had in the Bourg one of his hunting boxes. Violent as he was, in a fit of passion, he caused the monastery of S. Moack to be burnt; but afterwards being penitent he re-established it in a better state, at the suggestion of S. Thurien or Thuriave, bishop of Dol.†

100. St. Scubilien founded the monastery of Menden 1,600 toises (3,410 yards, nearly two English miles), north-north-east of the isle of Aaron, on which S. Malo stands, which Manet says must be carefully distinguished from Mandan, which is near Chausey. The sounding at *Menden* at low water is by M. Beautemps-Beaupre's chart, 24 French feet, eqval to 25½ English feet.

*Note.* Manet gives in one of his maps a league as 2,400 toises. And in Sir John Herschel's *Outlines of Astronomy,* 1864, p. 716, the toise is stated at 6·394593 British feet. Hence a French league is equal to 5,115⅜ yards. These measures we have adopted.

* Judicael succeeded Alain le Long, who died A.D. 690, *Morery's Dictionary.*

† Manet gives a reference, Gallet, *Mem sur l'orig des Bret. Armor,* ch. 6, n. 18.

101. The monastery of Taurac or Caurac was 1700 toises to the east of Cancalle Point, or 2 English miles and 203 yards. At this place there are about 9 fathoms at low water.

102. M. Edouard le Héricher, who has extensive philological and local antiquarian knowledge, says the monastery of Mandan was six miles [west] from S. Pair (a village on the coast two miles south of Granville); at that place there are 5½ fathoms at low water.

103. Now supposing the positions of these monasteries and Bourg to have been correctly given, they evidently help to an approximation to the amount of sinking; because if we assume the Bourg and each monastery to have originally stood, say ten feet above the highest tides (they can scarcely have been less), and add to that the rise of tide and the sounding for each place, the sums will approximate to the total sinkings. And first, it will be convenient to give a table of the greatest rises of tide, which is very different at different places, for the very same mechanical reason which makes the tides of the Bay of Fundy and Chepstow, the highest tides in the world, namely, because the great impetus with which the water flows during the rise of an equinoctial spring tide into a channel which rapidly narrows, causes the water to take in *height* what it cannot take in *breadth*. And thus, while the space between Cape la Hague and the north-western angle of Britanny is 150 miles, the tide is driven into a corner near Mont S. Michel, and so its rise becomes 54ft., whilst at Cape la Hague it only rises 20ft.

Rises of the Highest Tides in the triangle formed by Cape la Hague, Ushant, and Mont S. Michel.

| | English ft. | in. |
|---|---|---|
| Ushant... | 10 | 0 |
| Near Roscoff, in longitude 4° W. of Greenwich | 13 | 10 |
| At 3° west longitude, on N. coast of Britanny | 15 | 4 |
| S. Malo | 46 | 0 |
| Near Mont S. Michel | 54 | 0 |
| At the Minquiers | 47 | 0 |
| At Granville | 49 | 7 |
| Jersey | 42 | 0 |
| North of the Dirouilles... | 41 | 0 |
| Guernsey | 30 | 0 |
| Cape la Hague and the Caskets, each | 20 | 0 |

Approximate Amounts of Sinkings.

| | Soundings at low water. | | Above high water. | | Rise of tide. | | Total Sinking. | |
|---|---|---|---|---|---|---|---|---|
| | ft. | in. | ft. | in. | ft. | in. | ft. | in. |
| Bourg of Lhan Kafruth | 36 | 0 | 10 | 0 | 54 | 0 | 100 | 0 |
| S. Moack's Monastery | 45 | 0 | 10 | 0 | 54 | 0 | 109 | 0 |
| Menden Monastery | 25 | 6 | 10 | 0 | 46 | 0 | 81 | 6 |
| Taurac or Caurac Monastery | 54 | 0 | 10 | 0 | 54 | 0 | 118 | 0 |
| Mandan Monastery | 33 | 0 | 10 | 0 | 50 | 0 | 93 | 0 |
| | | | | | Average | | 100 | 2 |

But "Bourg" indicates a village or town *on a hill*, or in an *elevated situation:* and there may be seen on the sailing chart (from which our map is copied) within the space which appears to have sunk, occasional soundings of 11 fathoms or 66ft., which reckoning, as before, would give a sinking of 130ft. So that the actual sinking may have been greater than any of those given in the table. And, at any rate, it would not be correct to take the average, because that would bring the original positions of S. Moack's and Taurac *below* the level of high water, which cannot have been the case. Ought we not rather to take the maximum, and say the sinking in the Bay of Mont S. Michel has not been less than 118ft.? And, in fact, it may have been considerably more, if Abbé Manet's statement, given in the following article, can be depended on.

104. *Ancient and modern heights of Mont S. Michel.*—Abbé Manet (p. 60) correctly describes Mont S. Michel as an enormous block of granite (the present writer observed that the rock contains shining scales of mica) he says it is singular in all respects. "N'a pas moins de 200 pieds de hauteur, sans compter ce qu'y ont ajouté les ouvrages de l'art. Les géometres qui, en 1775, dressèrent le plan de ce mont, lui donnèrent 450 toises de tour sur le grévage, 180 pieds seulement d'élévation jusqu' au sommet du roc, et *en totalité* 400 *pieds depuis le niveau de la grève jusqu' à la lanterne du clocher;* mais nous avons d'autres bonnes autorités pour les mesures que nous avons determinées. Du haut de ce panorama, dont tout l'ensemble, *dans son état primitif, avait* 565 *pieds d'élévation*, les personnes qui sont en bas ne peuvent être reconnues, et semblent autant de pygmées qui rampent à l'entour." That is to say, if Manet is correct, there is a difference between the height in 1775 and the height in its primitive state of 165 French feet, which are equal to 175ft. 10in. English. Dr. Hairby (p. 128) says that the whole height to the top of the towers is 378ft. And that a large dyke before the entrance gate [to the island] traced by the sea in 1822, exposed the end of a causeway paved with large stones, ten feet below the surface of the sand. This causeway led to the entrance gate.

If we add this 10ft. to Dr. Hairby's 378ft. we shall still have a less height than that of 1775. In Art. 71 we have the chronicler in Neustria Pia, thinking that the Mont formerly deserved the title of a *Mountain*, whereas when he wrote he conceived that it was sufficient to call it only *a rock*, as if its height as well as its length and breadth had been considerably reduced. In the margin of the text of Neustria Pia are given references to Glaber, Sigebert, Peter de Natalibus, Catalogue of Saints, S. Antonius, Breviary of Coutances, &c., which have already been quoted in Art. 78. The Sinkings have been deeper, doubtless, and have extended to unknown distances seaward and thinned, perhaps to nothing, on land.

The present writer is well aware that some of his friends will say:—"We do not believe Abbé Manet's statement of its primitive height." Abbé Manet having departed this life, cannot now be asked for his authority for the ancient measure which he gives. Will the impartial reader believe that he *forged it?* Probably not. If not, there are 175ft. 10in. difference between the ancient and modern heights to be accounted for, which may perhaps be due in small part to difference in heights of buildings. For the writer observed on August 27, 1862, that the top of a small spire had been taken off. He has laid before the reader, as to the former height of Mont S. Michel, all the information he possesses, and there he must leave the matter.

Observe, if nothing had happened except an inundation caused by an equinoctical tide impelled by a strong north wind, why did not the water ebb off again, and leave the ground dry though covered with prostrate trees? Why has the Forest of Sciscy remained 11½ centuries under water, unless because the ground has sunk? Again. From the creation to A.D. 709 is about 4,700 years; consequently there had been about 9,400 equinoctial spring tides during that period. But there are only thirty-two points of the compass, consequently during equinoctial tides, the wind must have blown from each point of the compass on an average 293 times. Therefore, there must have been a north wind of more or less force 292 times before the catastrophe happened. Why did it never happen before? Is it not the only way to explain these things—"*The ground has sunk?*"

## Losses of Land on the North Coast of Britanny, farther West.

105. At two leagues west from Lannion (which is in 48° 45′ N. lat. and 3° 30′ W. long.) in the middle of a great bank of sand, called now, Grève de S. Michel, at the entrance of the village of S. Michel a stone cross was fixed on a rock, and the site of this bank of sand was once occupied by a very spacious forest. M. Ogée describes the same forest in other words as follows:*—"*Plestin;* about 6 leagues to west-south-west of Treguier its bishopric. In the year 480, Saint Efflam arriving from Ireland his country, in Britanny; built for the first time the chapel of his name,† which we see at this day on the border of the Grève. We are assured that the Saint descended from his boat precisely in the place where the stone cross stands, which the sea covers at every tide. The country then was nothing but a vast forest, in which this saint built a hermitage, which they say was in the place where the chapel now is. He died 6 November, 512." I think there can be no doubt that the trees, &c. which are mentioned in the following article, as having been cast up near Morlaix (which is in the neighbourhood), must have been parts of this forest.

106. *Trees cast up near Morlaix.*—In the *Gazette* of France, February 22, 1812, is given an extract of the 179th volume of the "Journal of Mines," as follows:—"M. de Fruglaye, who was walking near Morlaix on a sandbank after a strong tempest, perceived the appearance of the sandbank changed. The fine sand which covered it had disappeared, and a black earth was seen in its place, marked by long furrows. It was a

* Vol. 3, p. 369.
† The French Chart shows this chapel at the S. W. angle of Grève de St. Michel.

mass of vegetable remains, among which several aquatic plants were distinguished, and leaves of forest trees. Beneath this bed were rose trees, rushes, asparagus, ferns, and other meadow plants, of which many were very well preserved. Over all this earth were seen trunks of trees in every direction; the greater part were reduced to a kind of earth, and others were in a state of freshness. The yews and oaks were of their natural colour, and numerous birch trees had preserved their silvery bark. All these ruins of an ancient vegetation, buried by a sudden revolution, were placed upon a bed of clay, like that which ordinarily forms the basis of our meadows. M. de Fruglaye, this *Gazette* adds, has pursued his researches over a space of *seven leagues*, and always along the sandy shore he found everywhere the remains of this ancient forest buried.—*Manet*, p. 30, 31.

107. *Unfounded objections.*—A gentleman objects that the submarine trees in St. Ouen's Bay "may have drifted thither, and then sunk." This is impossible. It could not have been the case near Mont. S. Michel and Granville; nor could it have been the case in S. Ouen's Bay, because the roots were inserted in the sea bottom. M. de Fruglaye's trees were avowedly ultimately drifted upon the shore near Morlaix, but where did they come from, and how did they get to the place from which the storm removed them? Now, granted there were plenty of forests in ancient times close to the sea. But *firstly*, how does my friend get all the trees and plants rooted up and fairly afloat on the sea? *Secondly*, if he can get them fairly afloat, how does he *keep in a body seven leagues long* these thousands of yews, oaks, birches, rose trees, rushes, asparagus, ferns, and other meadow plants? *Thirdly*, supposing him to have got over these two difficulties, how does he get everything after having "drifted"—that is *floated*, for an unknown distance, *to sink and remain at the bottom for an unknown time*, until 1812? It is fair to state that the gentleman's suggestion of "drifting" was made off-hand, in the course of conversation. But though he by no means intended anything of the sort, it was in truth an attempt to explain away, in the sense of getting rid of, a piece of evidence which was unfavourable to his own preconceived views.

### Trunks of Trees and Remains of Buildings found on the Shore at the North-Western Angle of Britanny.

108. In the *Histoire de Petit Bretagne ou Bretagne Armorique*, by Abbé Manet, 1834: speaking of the north-western angle of Britanny he says (Note 15 p. 19), "the ebb uncovers still at this day on the shore, trunks of trees and remains of houses." This is a point of importance and will be referred to again under the heading "Ptolemy." Because it proves that the very rigid test to which his latitudes and longitudes have been put, by reducing them to modern and laying them down on modern charts, would in the present instance if no land had been lost, have coincided exactly, perhaps, with the ancient Gobæum promontory.

## CHAPTER VI.

### PTOLEMY, THE GEOGRAPHER.

109. *Biographical.* "Claudius Ptolemy, a celebrated geographer and astrologer in the reigns of Adrian and Antoninus [who reigned from A.D. 117 to A.D. 161], was a native of Alexandria, or according to others, of Pelusium, and on account of his great learning, he received the name of most wise and most divine, amongst the Greeks. In his system of the world he places the earth in the centre of the universe, a doctrine universally believed and adopted till the 16th century, when it was confuted and rejected by Copernicus. His geography is valued for its learning and the very useful information which it gives. The best edition of Ptolemy's Geography is that of Bertius, folio, Amsterdam, 1618."—See Lempriere's *Classical Dictionary.*

110. In Ptolemy's Geography, longitude is reckoned from the west side of the Canary "Isle," which he calls zero or 0°, to the east side of the island Taprobane, or Ceylon; or according to others Sumatra,* which he calls 130°. The modern longitudes in the following table have been obtained from the English Ordnance maps. Admiral White gives (in *Sailing Directions*) the longitude of the lighthouse which is on the *east* side of Lizard Point, by chronometer, 5° 10′ 39″ and its latitude 49° 57′ 18″.

*Note.* There appeared to be so much doubt whether any, or if so which, points on the northerly or westerly coasts of France are unaltered at the present day; that it was thought better to take the Lizard and the centre of the Isle of Wight, of which Ptolemy gives the latitudes and longitudes under other names—as bases or points of departure. And by that means to reduce his points on the French coast to modern latitudes and longitudes, for the purpose of laying them down on a chart. The first part of the following series of Ptolemy's longitudes and latitudes is from Bertius's edition of Ptolemy's Geography, 1618; and the last part from the Lyons edition, 1535.

| — | Centre of Lizard Point. | Centre of Isle of Wight. | Differences. |
|---|---|---|---|
| | ° ′ | ° ′ | ° ′ |
| Ptolemy's Longitudes ... | 12 0 | 19 20 | 7 20 |
| The Modern Longitudes are | 5 12½ W. | 1 18⅓ W. | 3 54⅙ |

Thus, according to the Ordnance Maps, 7° 20′ of Ptolemy's longitude corresponds with 3° 54⅙′ of modern longitude, and is reckoned in a contrary direction. Hence it follows that:—

1° of Ptolemy's longitude is equal to 0° 31·9316 Modern.

1° of Modern longitude is equal to 1° 52·7402 Ptolemy.

His meridian of Greenwich becomes 21° 47·18.

* See Sir E. Tennant's *Nat. Hist. of Ceylon*, p. 67.

### Latitude.

110. Ptolemy reckons latitude as is done at the present day, namely, from the equator as Zero, northwards. He makes the south coast of England *farther north than its true position*, and consequently the latitudes of his various positions on the French coast have been made *farther north in the same proportion.*

The Lizard has perhaps not altered much, *in longitude* since Ptolemy's time (but it may have altered, *in latitude*, as we shall see), being of the rock called Serpentine, a very hard material. But there may have been a wasting away of the Isle of Wight, which if it has been equal on the east and west, would leave the longitude of the centre of the Island exactly in the same spot where it was in Ptolemy's time. And since the eastern and western extremities of the island are of the same geological material, it has not been thought necessary to make any allowance in longitude for irregular waste. But a different course has been pursued with regard to the *south* coast of the island as regards latitude, because being much more exposed than the *north* coast, it has probably wasted considerably more. And the 40″ of the modern latitude of the centre of the island given in the following table has therefore been cancelled. That is to say, a waste of a fraction of a yard annually on the south coast more than on the north, is assumed by the present writer, to have taken place on the average, ever since Ptolemy's time. And for that reason, the Modern latitude of the centre of the Isle of Wight is taken as 50° 39′ instead of the 50° 39′ 40″ given in the following table as obtained from the Ordnance Map :—

| — | Lizard Point. | Centre of Isle of Wight. | Differences. |
|---|---|---|---|
| | ° ′ | ° ′ ″ | ° ′ ″ |
| Ptolemy's latitudes North of Equator ... ... | 51 30 0 | 52 20 0 | 0 50 0 |
| Modern latitudes (Ordnance) | 49 57 28 | 50 39 40 | 0 42 12 |
| | | | 0 7 38 |

From several authorities quoted in the next paragraph and subsequently it is probable that there has been a good deal more wasting and *sinking* on the south coast of Cornwall than at the Isle of Wight, and therefore the 50° 39′ has in the following Table always been used as equivalent to Ptolemy's latitude of the centre of the Isle of Wight in his time, and the *latitude* of the Lizard has not been used at all for the purposes of calculation.

Sir Henry de la Beche in Chapter XIII. of his *Geological Report of Cornwall, Devon, and W. Somerset,* gives about twenty-five pages of very interesting details as to changes of level, &c., and quotes his authorities, for which the reader is referred to the work itself. It is sufficient to prove the allegation just made as to the wasting and sinking, to quote his summary from p. 420 of his valuable book. He says :—" Taking the general evidence afforded by the so-called submarine fossils round the shores of Devon, Cornwall, and Western Somerset, we find that a vegetable accumulation, consisting of plants of the same species as those which now grow freely in the adjoining land, is frequently discovered occurring as a bed at the mouths of valleys, at the bottom of sheltered bays, and in front and under low tracts of land, the seaward side of which dips beneath the present level of the sea, so that the terrestrial vegetation forming those parts of the bed could not have grown at their present levels. Now, as there appears to be the very best evidence that numbers of the roots of trees occupy the situations where they grew relatively to the subjacent ground, and *as these roots are to be often traced as far as the tides recede even at the equinoxes*, we seem compelled to admit that a change in the relative level of the sea and land has taken place since these trees lived on the situations where we now find them." Mr. Pengelly, F.R.S., too, in the report of his paper read at the Bath meeting of the British Association, "On changes of relative level of land and sea in south-eastern Devonshire, in connection with the antiquity of mankind." After having briefly noticed the characteristics of the existing general coast-line, he described a series of phenomena which indicate that "within what is known as the Quaternary Period, the whole of south-eastern Devonshire was at least 280ft. lower than at present; that by a series of slow and gradual upheavals, separated by protracted periods of intermittence, it was raised at least 40ft. above its present level; that these elevatory movements *were followed by one of subsidence*."* Now it has been supposed by some, that the pre-historic human remains, or pre-historic remains of human art, which have been detected upon or among strata so raised or depressed—give some indication of the *period* of such elevation or depression. And the idea has even been entertained, that the presence of pre-historic remains indicates pre-historic risings (or sinkings). It would be a curious coincidence, and one which we have no right whatever to assume; if the remains in question had been deposited by chance or intention, *immediately before the time* of a rising or sinking. It is infinitely more likely that pre-historic remains have been deposited in pre-historic times, and that they have risen and sunk again and again with the land since. And we shall see in Art. 133, that changes of level took place on the south coast of Cornwall, as lately as the beginning of the 9th and end of the 11th centuries; which *render it probable* that the position of the Lizard is farther north now than it was in Ptolemy's time. Which was obliged to be assumed if Ptolemy's positions were to be used at all—and which has accordingly been assumed, to make his latitude of the Lizard consistent with his latitude of the centre of the Isle of Wight.

111. Ptolemy thus treated (consider Art. 112 in connection with this) puts the coping-stone on what has been been stated in Chapter V. His mouth of the river Argenis, which was, of course, a point in the ancient

* "British Association Report," 1864, Transactions of the Sections, p. 63.

coast-line, falls *seventeen miles west* of the present coast of Normandy. And the mouth of his river Tetus (another point in the ancient coast-line). falls *more than* 30 *miles west* of the present west coast of Normandy, And I think leaves no doubt that Jersey was an integral part of the continent in his time. The writer has wished to be moderate in exhibiting restorations of the supposed ancient coast-line in the map, and he has therefore treated the mouth of the river Tetus as a broad estuary, rather than exhibit. the river of narrower dimensions, and (by consequence) the loss of land as having been greater. He believes the Tetus may have been one of the estuaries referred to by Cæsar in the third book of his Gallic War, as will be explained hereafter.

112. Ptolemy's Gobæum Promontory of the Osismii falls very near the north-western angle of Britanny, especially if we allow for the loss of land stated by Abbé Mauet (Art. 108) to have taken place there. His Harbour of Stallocanus is almost identically in the same position as the present Harbour of Portrieux. There are other statements which tend, so far as they can be depended on, to confirm Ptolemy's position of the mouth of the river Argenis. Namely:—*First*, Mr. Ahier (now deceased) states at p. 98 in the volume quoted before, that Mont S. Michel was "at ten leagues from the sea." But when asked personally he did not remember what was his authority. *Second*, M. Bonnissent (quoted before) states in his pamphlet, that Mont S. Michel was left "en pleine forêt, à dix lieues de la mer." I have not been in communication with him and could not ask his authority. *Third*, Lecanu p. 21, says "c'est une autre tradition que le Mont-Saint-Michel était éloigné de plusieurs lieues de la mer, Thomas Leroi l'a inscrite dans ses *Curieuses Recherches*." It may be that the reader has now before him at one and the same time, both the tradition and its *origin*, namely the position of the mouth of the River Argenis; which is nearly "ten leagues" (French) from Mont S. Michel.

113. The left hand column of the table (to be given presently) gives Ptolemy's latitudes and longitudes of the various places named by him in the centre column; and the right hand column gives the corresponding modern latitudes and longitudes (always west of Greenwich) calculated on the principles aforesaid. The present writer's statements and remarks are placed between brackets thus [ ]. It is remarkable that some of Ptolemy's positions are very difficult to understand and that he takes no notice of any island near the French coast; though Pliny the elder (died A.D. 79) who lived near a century earlier, mentions that there were in his time "nearly two hundred islands of the Veneti" between the Seine and the Pyrenees. There are other ancient references to some of these islands as will be seen in due time.

*Note.*—2° 20′ 22″ added to longitudes west of Greenwich give longitudes west of Paris. See Herschel's *Outlines of Astronomy*, 1864, p. 60.

Plate 307 shows, amongst other things, Ptolemy's positions given in the following table, approximately. The text of the table gives the description and distances from well known points and places correctly, as taken from the large scale charts of the French Government. The conclusion I arrive at is, that Ptolemy's figures are sometimes corrupt, and not as he wrote them. For he is clearly correct in some cases as for instance, where he fixes Gobæum promontory and Staliocanus Harbour correctly, relatively to the Isle of Wight (Vectis) and the Lizard (Ocrinum) though there are a hundred English miles of sea between. Though he had neither a quadrant nor a chronometer, it is clear he had some means of fixing latitudes and longitudes with appropximate correctness, independently of actual measurements which, of course, he could not make all the way across the English Channel. It is incredible that he who could fix the places mentioned, so well, should have made such gross blunders as to place the Harbour Vindana and the mouth of the Seine, each many miles in the interior of Gaul. To suppose that some of his figures have been corrupted, would account for the false positions of the two last-named places. Whether he is right with respect to his former coast line on the eastern side of the Bay of Biscay, which he places a whole degree west of the present coast; I must leave to each reader's own judgment. Remarking only two things. First, if his coast line is right, some of the "almost two hundred islands" of the Veneti must have been farther out into the bay than his coast line. And second, it is very remarkable that all his positions between the Isle d'Yeu and the Pyrenees are *uniformly far west* of the present French coast. With respect also to his British promontory Antœuestæum or Belerium, which he places far out in the Bristol Channel, we shall have farther lights on the subject by-and-by.

*Note.*—In the following statement Ptolemy's longitudes and latitudes, in degrees and minutes, are given on the left hand, and their respective equivalents in degrees, minutes, and decimals of a minute, are given opposite on the right hand.

114. (From Bertius's Ptolemy, 1618).

"Antœuestœum promontory, which is also called Bolerium.

Long. 11° 30′ ........................ 5° 28·46′
Lat. 52° 30″ ........................ 50° 48·68′

[In Mr. Keith Jonhson's atlas the Land's End is given as 5° 47′ W., and 50° 4′ N. Ptolemy's position falls far out in the Bristol Channel, and about 51 miles a little to the east of north of the present Land's End. If the Lionesse country really existed in Ptolemy's time, it cannot have extended as far westward, as is shown in the map in the "Churchman's Magazine,* from Land's End and Lizard Point, *to and comprising the Scilly Isles.* Because Strabo who flourished at least a century before Ptolemy, quoting Posidonius, who was still older, mentions those islands as then existing under the name of Cassiterides,† and that they were ten in number.‡ But it is *possible* that the Lionesse may have extended westwards as far as Seven Stones and northwards as far as Ptolemy's Belerium Nor will I shrink from expressing an opinion on the following statements gathered from Camden's "Britannia," &c. It is said that in Camden's

* July, 1863, p. 39. † Book 3, cap. 2, s. 9. ‡ Book 3, cap. 5, s. 11.

time the inhabitants of Cornwall were of opinion that the Land's End did once extend further to the west, which the seamen positively conclude from the rubbish they draw up, and that the land there drowned by the incursions of the sea, was called *Lionesse*. That a place within the Seven Stones is called by Cornish people, *Tregva, i.e.* a dwelling, and that windows and other such stuff have been brought up from the bottom there with fish-hooks, for it is the best place for fishing. That at the time of the inundation supposed, Trevelyan swam from thence (which was certainly a very long swim, being at least fifteen nautical miles, if he swam to the nearest part of the main land), and in memory thereof bears Gules, an horse argent issuing out of the sea proper. Dr. Paris in his "Guide to Mount's Bay and the Land's End," p. 91, mentions Camden's tradition of the Lyonesse (the Silurian Lyonois) "said to have contained 140 parish churches, all of which were swept away by the ocean." He says also that the Scilly Isles are now 140 in number, though only six are inhabited. Before the reader and I part company, I expect to have convinced him of *about a score of sinkings of land* having taken place in the localities referred to in these papers, within the historial period. And that consequently, sinking being the rule and not the exception, there is no reason why there may not have been a country called Lionesse, which sank also. It is also possible that there may once have been a dwelling at Seven Stones, and that in the frequent fishings there with the strong hooks and lines used at sea, some relics of such a dwelling may have been brought up. If the Lyonnesse existed it would contain parish churches. That Trevelyan swam fifteen miles on horseback, is of course incredible. Can this be a mistake of Ptolemy or of some of his copyists? Or can there be any truth in Camden's traditionary Lyonesse country? And if so was it on the north of Cornwall, instead of on the west, as generally supposed?

The Damnonium and Ocrinum Promontory.]

Long. 12° 0′............................ 49° 57·28′
Lat. 51° 30′

[The Lizard Point. *Note.*—The modern latitude and longitude were obtained from the Ordnance map. But the latitude has not been used for calculation for reasons previously and hereafter stated. Ptolemy's latitude reduced to modern is given on the right hand. Art. 109, 110.]

But below a large harbour is the island Vectis (Οὐηκτὶς). of which the middle has degrees.

Long. 19° 20′
Lat. 52° 20′

[This occurs at p. 38 of Bertius's "Ptolemy," and no doubt means the Isle of Wight. Art. 109, 110.

In Lib. II., cap. VIII., p. 50, of Bertius's "Ptolemy," we have as follows]:—"The sides of Lyons Gaul, which are near Aquitania are [thus] called. Amongst the rest that which faces the west and is washed by the ocean, is thus described."

The Harbour Brivates.

| | | |
|---|---|---|
| Long. 17° 40′ | ........................ | 2° 11·55′ |
| Lat. 48° 45′ | ........................ | 47° 10·91′ |

[Falls a little south of the present mouth of the Loire, namely, 5½ nautical miles south of St. Nazaire.* It was, doubtless, in this harbour that Cæsar built the fleet with which he afterwards conquered the fleet of the Veneti.]

The mouth of the river Herius.

| | | |
|---|---|---|
| Long. 17° 0′ | ........................ | 2° 32·84′ |
| Lat. 49° 15′ | ........................ | 47° 39·95′ |

[falls 8½ nautical miles *east* of Vannes,* a position which is far inland. Ptolemy's position can hardly be correct, unless the Herius was a tributary of some larger river.]

The harbour Vindana.

| | | |
|---|---|---|
| Long. 16° 30′ | ........................ | 2° 48·81′ |
| Lat. 49° 40′ | ........................ | 48° 4·15′ |

[falls above 30 nautical miles south of the north coast of Britanny, which can hardly be correct.]

The Gobæum promontory.

| | | |
|---|---|---|
| Long 15° 15′ | ........................ | 3° 28·72′ |
| Lat. 49° 49′ | ........................ | 47° 39·95′ |

[as the name of this promontory occurs again (with a different latitude and longitude which nearly coincide with the present position of the north-western angle of Britanny) with the name of the city Vorganium attached; probably the present latitude and longitude which fall about midway between the Ile de Croix and the continent, mean the city, not the promontory.]

But the side which faces the north near the British Ocean, thus has itself,

After the Gobæum promontory.

The harbour Staliocanus. [Falls very near Portrieux.)

| | | |
|---|---|---|
| Long. 16° 30 | ........................ | 2° 48·81′ |
| Lat. 50° 15′ | ........................ | 48° 39·02 |

The mouths of the river Tetus.

| | | |
|---|---|---|
| Long. 17° 20′ | ........................ | 2° 22·2′ |
| Lat. 50° 40′ | ........................ | 48° 2·21′ |

[the Lyons edition gives the same figures, falls 5 nautical miles north-west of the nearest Minquiers rocks, and more than 30 nautical miles due west of the present west of Normandy. The position ranges well with Great Bank and Rigdou Shoal, formerly forests, a fact very significant. The lower part of the Tetus may have been one of Cæsar's estuaries, to be mentioned hereafter.]

## "BIDUCESIUM" [? BIDUCENSES.]

The mouths of the river Argenis.

| | | |
|---|---|---|
| Long. 18° 0′ | ........................ | 2° 0·91′ |
| Lat. 50° 30′ | ........................ | 48° 52·54′ |

* From Robiquet's Chart " dressée after the Government work, 1858.

falls 17 nautical miles due west of the present coast of Normandy. It was probably the mouth of the river Coüesnon into which the Sée, the Ardée, &c., had previously discharged themselves, as shown on the map. It may also have been one of Cæsar's estuaries.

"VENELORUM." [No doubt the Unelli of Cæsar.]

The harbour of the Crotiatoni.

Long. 18° 50′ ........................ 1° 34·4′
Lat. 50° 50′ ........................ 49° 11·89′

[falls 9½ miles north-east of Coutances, and 1½ miles east of the nearest part of the western coast of Normandy. It may have meant the present Havre de Piron, or the Havre de St. Germain, led up to by one of Cæsar's estuaries.]

The mouths of the river Olina.

Long. 18° 45′ ........................ 1° 37′
Lat. 51° 0′ ........................ 49° 21·57′

[falls 6 nautical miles south-east of Barneville, and 3½ miles east of Port bail. But it may have been at Portbail, which is an ancient place, where the river may have fallen into one of Cæsar's estuaries.]

"LEXOBII."

Næomagus (P. adds, harbour).

Long. 19° 30′ ........................ 1° 13′
Lat. 51° 10′ ........................ 49° 31·25

[Falls 2¾ miles north-west of the Iles-Saint Marcou or Marcouf. There is nothing impossible in this. Manet says, foot note, p. 56:—"One may see, at a little distance from this coast, the two isles to which St. Marcou has bequeathed his name, and *which were themselves then part of the continent*, as M. de la Martinière has well written." These islands are now about 4 nautical miles distant from the nearest part of the coast.]

"CALETI."

[The Greek MSS. do not contain this word.]

The mouth of the river Sequana.

Long. 21° 0′ ........................ 0° 25·11′
Lat. 50° 30′ ........................ 48° 52·54′

[The Seine doubtless. I think the latitude ought to have been farther north. Ptolemy next gives positions of places further east which do not concern us, and he then returns westward over the old ground.]

But the northern littoral side from the river Sequana the CALETÆ possess, whose city is Juliobona.

Long. 20° 15′ ........................ 0° 49·06′
Lat. 51° 20′ ........................ 49° 40·93′

[Falls 27½ nautical miles east of Pointe de Barfleur, and 30 nautical miles north of the present north coast of France. This position is not necessarily incorrect merely because it implies that a vast tract of land may have been lost. The aggregate *sinkings* of the surface of the earth must have been at least as great in aggregate bulk as the *risings*; but present geological knowledge is very far indeed from having shown in detail that the former approach anything near in magnitude to the latter.]

After whom the LIXUBII.

Afterwards the VENELI. (The Unelli, no doubt.)

After these the BIDUCESII (formerly VADUCÆSII).

And the last up to the Gobæum promontory OSISMII, whose city is Vorganium.

Long. 12° 40′* ........................ 4° 51·21′
Lat. 50° 10′ ........................ 48° 33·18′

[There cannot be a doubt that the territory of the Osismii and Gobæum promontory were identical with the north-western angle of Britanny Pliny the elder, in the 4th book of his *Natural History*, section xxxii. says:—"Lyons Gaul has the Lexovii, Vellocasses, Galleti, Veneti, Abrincatui, Osismii—the clear river Loire. But a very beautiful peninsula running out into the ocean from the end of the Osismii, 625 miles in circumference, in the neck 125 miles in breadth. Beyond the Nanneti" —viz., the inhabitants of Nantes. And Strabo says, book iv., chap. 4, sec. 1:—"The Osismii are the people whom Pytheas calls Ostimii; they dwell on a promontory which projects considerably into the ocean, but not so far as Pytheas and those who follow him assert." And Camden, *Britannia*, p. 1523–4, says:—"Over against these (the Scilly islands), on the coast of France just before the Osismii, or Britannia Armorica, lies the Island which Pliny calls Axantos, and which retains the same name, being now called Ushant." The north-western angle of Britanny is, therefore, abundantly identified as the Gobæum promontory of the Osismii. This position falls 3¾ nautical miles west-north-west of the nearest point of France,† which is a near agreement between Ptolemy and the present position of the cape. In fact the two *may* have been identical before the land mentioned by Manet (Art. 108) as having been lost, had disappeared.]

But the western littoral side below the Osismii . . . whose city is Dariorigum.

Long. 17° 20′ ........................ 2° 22·2′
Lat. 49° 15′ ........................ 47° 39·95′

[It is very remarkable that *the name of the people to whom Dariorigum belonged is not given, either by Bertius or in the Lyons edition.* The position falls about 14 nautical miles east of Vannes, and it is known not to have been really in the same position as Vannes.]

Below whom the SAMNITÆ bordering on the river Loire. Ingena.

Long. 21° 45′ ........................ 0° 1·16
Lat. 50° 30′ ........................ 48° 52·54

[Above 30 miles south of the present coast of Calvados, and near Falaise, therefore irrelevant.

* The Lyons edition gives the same longitude and latitude. The promontory is named Cabæum of the Ostimii, by Strabo, book I., chap. iv., s. 6.

† French Government charts, 1841 and 1843.

In the Lyons edition of Ptolemy, 1535, we have as follows:—The position of Juliobona is given with the same longitudes and latitudes, as aforesaid. After whom the Lexobii. After the Veneli. After these the Biducenses. And last, up to the Gobæum promontory, the Osismii. And then *a blank as in Bertius for the name of the people to whom Dariorigum belonged.* The latitude and longitude of Dariorigum are the same as those already given. The Lyons edition also has "Below whom are the Samnitæ, bordering on the river Loire," as in Bertius.]

*The following are from the Lyons edition.*

The mouth of the river Loire.

Long. 17° 40′ ........................ 2° 11·55′
Lat. 48° 30′ ........................ 46° 56·4′

[This gives a position 6 miles west of the Isle of Noirmontier, on the French chart (which does not quite agree with Map No. 2). This former position of the river's mouth would seem to signify that a large tract of land has been lost. We are told by Strabo,* "they say that in the ocean, not far from the coast, there is a small island lying opposite to the outlet of the river Loire, inhabited by Samnite women who are Bacchantes, and who conciliate and appease that God by mysteries and sacrifices." And Dionysius Periegetes Alexandrinus, who wrote a very valuable geographical treatise in the time of Augustus, still extant, corroborates Strabo, by saying: "another tract of small islands, where the wives of men from the farther coast of the famous Amnites having gone, perform the rite sacred to Bacchus." *There is now no island opposite the present mouth of the Loire.*

In Bertius's "Ptolemy" we read as follows]:—" In the middle territory, but more to the west (formerly east) than the Veneti, are the Aulerci Diabolitæ, whose city is Nœodunum,

Long. 18° 0′ ........................ 2° 0·91′
Lat. 50° 0″ ........................ 48° 23·5′

[falls near Dinan, which is given in the index of latitudes and longitudes in Mr. Keith Johnston's Atlas, 48° 26′ N., and 2° 2′ W. And we are told by Cæsar,† that the Aulerci (meaning probably Aulerci Diabolitæ) were one of the *maritime* states touching the ocean; they may, therefore, have extended from the Biducenses to Staliocanus harbour (Portrieux), or still further west, which is quite consistent with Ptolemy's description, since port Staliocanus, with perhaps a small district round it, *belonged to the Veneti*, as Cæsar tells us all the other harbours did.‡ Nœodunum or Dinan is east of Staliocenus. It is of special importance for the present purpose to show, as has now been done, that Ptolemy is probably correct in this part of his record.]

After whom (namely after the Andicavi and Aulircii Cenomani) the Namnetæ, whose city is Condivincum.

---

* Book IV., chap. iv., sec. 6. He died A.D. 25. He lived in the reign of Augustus.
† "De Bello Gallico," Book II., Sec. 34.
‡ "De Bello Gallico, Book III., sec. 8.

Long. 21° 15′ ........................ 1° 0·46′
Lat. 50° 0′ ........................ 48° 23.53′

falls far away to the N.E. of Nantes.

IN THE BAY OF BISCAY.*

The harbour of Sicor.

Long. 17° 30° ........................ 2° 16·87′
Lat. 48° 15′ ........................ 46° 41·8′

[falls in the Ile d'Yeu.]

Promontory of the Pictonii

Long. 17° 0′ ........................ 2° 32·84′
Lat. 48° 0′ ........................ 46° 27·3′

[from Robiquet's large scale chart, 1858. Falls 30 nautical miles nearly due west from the town of Sables d'Olonne, in 75 métres sounding.]

Mouths of the river Canentellus.

Long. 17° 15′ ........................ 2° 24·85′
Lat. 47° 30′ or ........................ 45° 58·3′
47° 15′ ........................ 45° 43·8′

[falls more than one degree due west of the west side of the Ile d'Oleron for the *first* named latitude, and 13 nautical miles due south of, and in the same longitude as the "Plateau de Roche-Bonne." The *second* latitude is 15 nautical miles south of the *first* latitude, and more than 1° due west of the nearest part of the continent. I have considered it to mean the river Charente. The Roche-due-Sud-Est (part of the Plateau de Roche-Bonne) has only a sounding of 18 French feet; so that at all events there is nothing improbable in supposing that it may have been land. The *first* and *second* latitudes are, perhaps, in about 258 French feet soundings. From M. Beaupré's Chart, 1832.]

The harbour of the Santones.

Long. 16° 30′ ........................ 2° 48·81′
Lat. 46° 30′ or ........................ 45° 0·25′
46° 15′ ........................ 44° 45·74′

[falls 1° 10′ due west of the west coast of the department Gironde. Out of soundings. Measured from Mr. Keith Johnston's School Atlas, 1857.]

The Promontory of the Santones.

Long. 16° 30′ ........................ 2° 48·81′
Lat. 47° 15′ ........................ 45° 43·8′

[falls about 1° 14′ west of the "Tour de Cordouan," which is at the present mouth of the river Gironde. From K. Johnston's Atlas.

The following are from fol. 34*b* of the Lyons edition.]

The promontory beyond the west of the Pyrenees which contains degrees

Long. 45° 30′ or 20′ ........................ 44° 2·18′ or
........................ 43° 52½′
Lat. 15° 0′ ........................ 3° 36·7′

---

* From the Lyon's edition, folio 34*b*.

Mouths of the river Aturius.

| | | |
|---|---|---|
| Long. 16° 30′ or | ........................ | 2° 48·81′ or |
| 16° 15′ | ........................ | 2° 56·78′ |
| Lat. 44° 30′ or | ........................ | 43° 4·11′ or |
| 44° 15′ | ........................ | 42° 49·6′ |

Promontory Curianum.

| | | |
|---|---|---|
| Long. 16° 30′ | ........................ | 2° 48·81′ |
| Lat. 46° 0′ | ........................ | 44° 31·22′ |

Mouth of the river Igmanus.

| | | |
|---|---|---|
| Long. 17° 0′ | ........................ | 2° 32·84′ |
| Lat. 45° 20′ | ........................ | 43° 52·5′ |

Mouth of the river Garumna [Gironde.]

| | | |
|---|---|---|
| Long. 17° 30′ | ........................ | 2° 16·87′ |
| Lat. 46° 30′ | ........................ | 45° 0·2′ |

The middle of its length.

| | | |
|---|---|---|
| Long. 18° 0′ | ........................ | 2° 0·91′ |
| Lat. 45° 20′ | ........................ | 43° 52·5′ |

The fountains of the river.

| | | |
|---|---|---|
| Long. 19° 30′ | ........................ | 1° 13′ |
| Lat. 44° 15′ | ........................ | 42° 49·6′ |

[This position is near one of the fountains of the Adour, not near any fountains of the Gironde.]

These are all of Ptolemy's positions, which it appears necessary to mention on the present occasion. The present writer accepts no responsibility in the way either of asserting or denying the truthfulness of these positions in the Bay of Biscay. When we remember that *littoral* shells (four species in one day) were dredged up by Mr. Robert Dawson, at 40 miles west of the coast of Aberdeen, and the vast losses of land heretofore exhibited on the west coast of Normandy, we ought, at all events, to be cautious how we condemn Ptolemy's positions, *merely* on the ground of their great distances from the present coast.

---

## CHAPTER VII.

### The Northern Channel Islands—M. Ahier.

115. Ptolemy, whatever might be the reason, gives no latitudes or longitudes of any places near the northern Channel Islands.

116. *Sinkings difficult to identify.*—It cannot but be remembered that risings of land are very numerous all over the world, and are easily identified by the marine fossils contained. In this way it is known that the whole of North Wales has been sea bottom. But sinkings go out of sight and are often impossible to get at. It is only about 115 years since

the Gorban or peat with its trunks of trees, was first discovered on the west of Guernsey. Though free from water at low water, the trees are generally covered with sand as they are at Jersey, and on the French coasts. And it is quite possible and probable, considering how many terrestrial remains have been found in, or washed up from, the sea bottom — that there may still be many terrestrial remains at the bottom of the Channel Islands' seas, constantly below low water and covered with sand, too. It is, therefore, peculiarly difficult to follow out sinkings, and we must be content with such evidence as can be obtained. Dredging promises to be a prolific source of evidence of sinkings. When we remember the results of Mr. Robert Dawson's dredging just mentioned and that Mr. Gwyn-Jeffreys and his colleagues have had similar successes, we may look hopefully forward to this resource. Before the present writing is in print, Mr. Rose, of Jersey, will doubtless be plying his dredge on the south of that island, in what (as we have seen) there are reasons for believing is the estuary of the ancient river Tetus. Mr. Gwyn Jeffreys dredged up fossil shells in 1865, near the south-east angle of Guernsey.

PERCEE ROCK.

117. Near the south end of the isle of Herm (about one-quarter mile distant) on its west side, is a rock called as above, because it is pierced (*i.e.* percée). In the sketch the spectator is supposed to be looking westward towards Guernsey, which appears in the distance. The boatmen say a gate once hung there, which is a well known tradition. High water of an ordinary tide is about 12ft. above the hole through the upright stone or post, the view being taken near low water. There are certainly many gate posts, similar in form, now in use both in Guernsey and Jersey. There is something like a road in front of the pierced stone or post, of 7ft. wide, and level transversely for a length of 20ft., so that a horse and cart could travel along it with great ease now, for that distance but no farther. The sides of this (so called) road, one side being hidden in the sketch by the large rock on the left, are at right angles with the road itself; that is to say in cross section, the road is horizontal and the sides are vertical, and the depression must, I think, be artificial. The pierced stone does not

appear to have been cut out of the solid, but to have been inserted in the the rock.

118. The writer was favoured in May, 1860, by the receipt of a letter from F. C. Lukis, Esq., of Guernsey, from which the following is an extract:—"The report of a gate hinge being fixed to a rock at the northern extremity of Guernsey has no foundation, beyond the same vulgar notion which is found in other places, both here and in Britanny. There is a similar statement often made of a gate being once placed among the rocks at the south end of the Herm. This is derived probably from an artificial perforation on the prominent rock called La Percée, which most likely had a buoy or float in ancient times attached to it, in order to guide the boatmen into the harbour of la Rosiére." M. de Gerville gives at p. 36 of his pamphlet aforesaid, a copy of a charter extracted from the chartulary of Cherbourg. He says also, "et l'archiviste m'en a depuis communique l'original." The charter being very short, a translation of it is now given:—

"Know all men, that we, brothers of the order of Minors of the Isle of Herm, near Guernsey, of the diocese of Coutances, while living, have renounced and do renounce all right of possession, property, or perpetuity of the said island, nor do we intend to remain to the prejudice or loss of the venerable lords, abbots, and convent of Cherbourg, of the order of S. Augustin there, but the buildings there being made safe by us or our* brothers, if they should happen to expel or remove us from the island in any manner. Given under the seal which we use, and under the hand of the president of the same place, by the advice equally and consent of all the brothers now dwelling in the said island, on Friday, the day after the feast of B. Mary, to wit, of the Assumption, in the year of our Lord, 1440. It is evident as to the interlineation of *nostros*. Given as above. [Signed] F. J. Doube. Verum est."

This convent, therefore, was inhabited in 1440, which would necessarily lead to frequent communications with the neighbouring large island of Guernsey, for provisions, &c., and would cause a necessity for one or more buoys or mooring posts. But 1440 is several centuries later than the date or dates at which, as I believe, the sinking or sinkings about the Northern Channel Islands occurred. Consequently, even if the post was used, as Mr. Lukis supposes, in 1440, it may have been erected as a gate post long before, when the rocks were above high water.

119. Besides, it is submitted, especially to naval men, that the pierced stone would have been an odd and awkward and unprecedented apparatus to have erected for the purpose of fastening a boat or buoy to. Would not a more obvious and natural course have been, to let in and fix with melted lead, a stout iron bolt with a ring attached, into the centre of the large flattish rock to the left? Two men could easily have done this in one tide; but, providing and conveying the stone, cutting the cavity, and fixing the stone in position, would have been attended with a good deal more trouble and

* The word "nostros," *our*, appears to have been interlined in the original.

expense. And, at any rate, the theory of the post having been erected to fasten a buoy to, does nothing toward accounting for the cutting away the rock to a level and rectangular form as before described. The writer has no wish to insist too much on this latter point; such (apparent) excavations have been known to occur naturally, and the present instance is possibly natural. He visited the rock September 6th, 1861.

120. The reader will observe that if the post, &c., were formerly above high water, a gate *may* have hung there. And this theory only requires that the same sort of sinking should have taken place at Percée, which has occurred at so many places. Of course the reader will judge for himself whether the stone has, or has not, been a gate-post. The hole, which is similar in size and situation to those in very many gate-posts, is in the oldest of them filled with a wooden plug tightly driven in, through which the pointed end of the piece of iron, forming the upper hinge of the gate, is driven, and generally clenched on the other side. In modern times the iron hinge is *leaded* into the hole in the gate-post. The gate, if ever there was one, must (according to precedent) have shut, not across the (so called) road; but across the level space which runs from the nearest side of the post to the right. It is said that the hinges of a gate could be seen not many year since on the Hanois rocks, on the S.W. of Guernsey.*

121. Mr. Lukis states, as follows, date May 25th, 1869:—"The littoral deposit of peat [on the N.W. of Guernsey] called Gorban by the natives, is frequently exposed by the tides, and as, in the case of the largest extent of that substance in Vazon Bay, consists almost entirely of low meadow trees, and paludinous vegetation (the hazel nut has been found therein, and I have a seed vessel of a wild damson, probably the *Prunus Insititia*) from that place. The deposit is, however, at present confined within a narrow belt off the shore and usually in the flat portion of the bays of the islands. I have not obtained any peat from soundings in the deep parts of the Russels, or any from the Casket rocks. These submerged forests may date with the same catastrophes which have created the peat beds on the north and west of the approximate shore of Britanny and Normandy. Lately, on the south-east of Vale Castle,† a portion of a peat bed was uncovered by the contractors of the new breakwater, and a quantity of Roman coins (large brass) were picked up by the men."

On this it may be remarked as follows:—How does Mr. Lukis know that the deposit of peat and trees is confined within a narrow belt off the shore? Nothing short of an elaborate series of borings in deep water could have justified his making such a statement; and there is no reason to believe that any such series of borings was ever made: While on the other hand, there is a certain of probability that there *may* have been a wood at as much as 3½ nautical miles west of Guernsey, from the circumstance of a rock there being called "Roque *au Bois*," on the charts; and from the farther circumstance of another group of rocks, half way between it and the shore being called "Grunes *du Bois*." Further parti-

* Tupper's History, p. 28.
† Between Guernsey and Herm.

culars are given in Art. 145, in the latter part of which article reasons are stated showing how very improbable it is that those names can (as has been suggested) have been given in a capricious and unauthorised manner by pilots, fishermen, or vraic-gatherers. Secondly, neither the hazel nut nor the wild damson are necessarily "low meadow trees." Thirdly, the plum tree is one of the family *Rosaceæ*, no fossil plants of which have, according to Agassiz, ever yet been discovered; so that the submersion of the forest must have taken place later than the formation of the most recent fossils. And, fourthly, we shall see at the end of Art. 146, that Roque *au Bois*, and Grûne *du Bois*, cannot have been derived from the deposit at either of them of drift, or wreck wood. Because the two groups of rocks are only dry for an hour or two at low water of spring tides, and consequently, such moveable wood cannot have remained there long enough to give names to the groups of rocks.. It is worth while to requote Mr. Lukis's important testimony from the "Archælogical Journal." He is unintentionally one of my best witnesses in favour of the sinkings. Speaking of a cromlech at L'Ancresse Bay, on the north side of Guernsey, he says:—"At the period it was constructed *the sea was at a greater distance from the site of the hill than at present*, for the *whole neighbourhood bears marks of the inroads of that element:* the near approach of the sandy hills around it was caused by *those events which have so materially changed the coast of these islands, as well as that of the opposite continent.*" The italics are mine. Mr. Lukis and I are agreed as to the facts, and I am trying to account for them, and will presently produce important corroborative testimony, as to these localities, from Julius Cæsar and Diodorus Siculus, who were cotemporaries of each other, and lived some half a century before Christ.

Mr. W. B. Herapath, F.R.S., *On the Genus Synapta,** says that several were found in Bellegrave Bay, on the coast of Guernsey, a little below low water level at spring tides, in a bed of sand about 10in. or 12in. deep. "The sand-bank was dark in colour, and fœtid from the large quantity of decaying animal matter therein. The Synapta doubtless fed upon that refuse material by gorging itself with sand from time to time." Were these fœtid matters the produce of a similar decay of a prodigious quantity of insects and plants, to that which occurred in the submerged marshes of Dol; mentioned in the latter part of Article 72?

On the 13th August, 1866, the writer was sailing from Jersey to England, and a gentleman aboard informed him that there are remains of walls in the sea bottom below low water to the north of the Isle of Lihou, and that Dr. Mansell has seen them. Dr. Mansell, however, in a letter dated Sept. 18th, 1866, states that he has not seen them, and being well acquainted with the locality, he is "quite satisfied that none exist." Another gentleman also spoke to the writer in the Geological Section of the British Association, at Nottingham, and stated that there is a sunken tower off Herm. Dr. Mansell states in the same letter

* Brit. Assoc. Report, 1864. Trans. of Sections, p. 97, 98.

that he has heard a tradition to that effect, "but there is nothing of the kind to be seen now." Mr. Lukis, of Guernsey, has also kindly sent me a long letter on the same subjects, from which I quote, the date is Sept. 22nd, 1866.—"The causeway from the mainland across the low bay of Lihou, exhibits the work of man, and within my memory several fresh *paved paths* have been constructed by the States of this island, for the convenience of carts and horses, during the wracking seasons. These of course may be observed by travellers, or boats as they pass over at full tides, but I have never heard of the facts related in your letter, and I may safely contradict the statement of your travelling acquaintance. My frequent visits to the little Island of Lihou, where I have resided for near two months at one time, whilst prosecuting the examination of the church and priory in 1838, allow me the opportunity of speaking with confidence upon this rumour. In tracing and examining their *egout* upon the coast limit of the island, I am sure that no further, or lower buildings, or walls ever existed.

"As to the peat marsh lands where the 'Gorban' is dug out, no doubt these were once once somewhat below the present meadows, at the foot of the range of hills, and they would, consequently, be more exposed to submergence, whilst the upper level would rather increase from accumulation, or disintegration of the rocks forming the land above.

"The quality of the timber likewise, which is found in our submarine peat, would rather denote a late origin, for we find the birch, the oak, hazel, and prunus; trees subsequent to the *older* periods of the British Channel. Again, the animal bones and stone instruments, which accompany our gorban or peat, bring us into connection with the early history of our race. In the Gorban we find grass, reeds, and paludinous vegetation, which agree with our *recent* period." Of course, the animal bones and stone instruments worked by man in older periods, may have been deposited centuries before the ground sunk, and have sunk with it, in comparatively recent times.

Mr. Lukis proceeds:—"La Rocque Percée is, from its position at the end of a ridge of sunken rocks, round which it is necessary to [sail to] reach the anchorage of la Rosaire, and no doubt it was pierced for the purpose of having a buoy or ballaie float attached to it, to guide the mariner on entering the little bay near it,—a similar rock is said to be seen near the little harbour of la Pezerie, near Rocquaine Bay, which has, from its perforation, been called a gate-post." The concluding sentence of Mr. Lukis's letter, referring to a specimen of an oak tree 20ft. long, which he kindly sends me, is given as the last paragraph of Article 151.

He and Dr. Mansell have effectually demolished the alleged walls north of Lihou, as well as the alleged submarine tower near Herm. I leave it to the reader to form his own judgment as to the signification of Percée rock, from a consideration of Articles 117 to 121, both inclusive.

122. *Is there any originality in this investigation?* The reader will have observed that evidences have been diligently collected, here a limb and there a feature, and that an attempt is being made to build up a truth-

ful record of the former conditions of the localities previous to the vast changes which have certainly taken place. We say the evidences have been "diligently" collected; for if it was worth while to take any trouble at all, it was worth doing as well as the writer could do it. And indeed it was absolutely necessary so far to sift the matter, that no future revelations could affect the doctrines and principles set forth. Farther researches are more likely to bring to light fresh sinkings, than to afford reasons for doubting either the extent or degree of those revealed in these papers. But it has been said, "there is no originality in these enquiries," and that "all is collected from books." This saying is nothing new, a similar delusion occurred long, long ago, which was as follows:—I remember to have read that a portion, at least, of the ancient Greek populace, said there was no originality about the illustrious sculptors, Polycletus, Phidias, and Praxiteles. And that they were only men who knew which block of marble contained a statue, and when they had got the right block all they had to do was to cut away the superfluous marble. That was all, and very comical it was! In the present case an attempt is being made to cut away superfluous ignorance. If any one still thinks it an easy matter to trace vast physical changes like these, through seven hundred miles of space; and nineteen centuries of time; or whether he thinks it easy or not—it is to be hoped in the interest of science, that he will sit down and try in some other case. The sinkings, of the actuality of which I am trying to convince the reader,—when considered with reference to their grandeur and recency combined,—are so extraordinary, that nothing short of thorough investigation can be satisfactory, which has accordingly been aimed at by carefully working out the details. And knowing that the interpretation put upon the events narrated is the true one, I think it my duty in the interest of science, to add to that interpretation whatever force can be derived from the following letter. By previous arrangement with Sir Roderick Murchison, I sent to Mr. Bates, the assistant secretary, an abstract of these papers and a chart, which in due time produced the following letter:—"Royal Geographical Society, 15, Whitehall-place, S.W., March 21st, 1866. Dear Sir,—As it is probable the Council of our Society will order your most interesting paper to be published in their journal, illustrated by a map of the N. coast of France, may I ask you whether you could send us a sketch-map of the coasts, to include all that you think necessary for the elucidation of your paper. The map need only be a rough one, and should specify these soundings, rock-patches, names of places, &c., which are mentioned in your paper, to the exclusion of the vast mass of unnecessary detail existing on the chart you have so kindly sent to the society. Our engravers would produce a map suitable for our journal, founded on your sketch. Yours sincerely [signed] H. W. Bates. R. A. Peacock, Esq." Three suitable maps were duly sent to Mr. Bates.

### M. Ahier's Statements and Theories.

123. In *Tableaux Historiques de la Civilisation à Jersey*, par John

Patriarche Ahier, 1852. The author gives a map exhibiting a much greater tract of dry land in the Channel Islands' seas than now exists. All along the west of Normandy additional land is shown, extending to, and including the Ecrehous and Dirouilles. More land is shown on the west, south, and especially on the south-each of Jersey. And, thirdly, he shows the Minquiers rocks, and all the present sea on the south, south-east, and east of them as land. This (supposed) land is represented as having been crossed in four various directions by Roman roads. And he states, at p. 93, that:—"The line of the continent commenceming at the isle of Ushant, came by a curve to bear upon (s'appuyer) Guernsey and Alderney, which were only promontories of the continent, and thence to Cape la Hague. All the isles and rocks which now occupy the sea in the triangle formed by Ushant, la Hague, and Mont S. Michel, were nothing, then, but elevated points of a considerable portion of the continent which has disappeared since." And he quotes the very few evidences already copied from him, into these papers. His ideas of the supposed method, or methods, of this sudmersion will be best explained in his own words, with which I only agree so far as to affirm with him, that the sinking may have averaged nearly 150ft. in the Channel Islands' seas. The gulfs he mentions are beyond our limits. Ahier says as follows, immediately after the translated passage just given:—

"L'explanation que donnent les savans de la manière dont les eaux ont pu envahir ainsi tant de terres, et surtout couper la crête de Douvres à Calais, est assez simple. Les deux grands fleuves, qui se jetaient dans les deux golfes dont j'ai parlé, serpentaient au milieu de plaines basses et marécageu ses, et sur lesquelles la mer venait sans doute se repandre dans les grandes marées. Les terres étaient détrempées sur les rives du fleuve dans lequel la mer remontait avec impétuosité, entraînant dans son reflux tout le terrain éboulé des bords; ce même travaile se faisait aussi par le Nord dans le grand fleuve qui recevait la Tamise, le Rhin et les mille rivières de la Belgique et de la Hollande, de sorte que dans un temps donné, la mer démolissant tous les jours quelques parties de ses digues naturelles, a fini par s'ouvrir un passage pour se rencontrer entre Douvres et Calais.

"Quant aux terres basses des nos contrées elles avaient aussi subi un amolissement considérable, mais il fallait une révolution soudaine pour que la mer puisse nous submerger. Cette révolution eut lieu, selon les uns, par une commotion volcanique qui affaisa subitement tous nos contrées d'environ 150 pieds; selon d'autres, cela provint d'une crue énorme des eaux du globe survenue par la fonte des glaces polaires. Que ce soit la mer qui ait haussé ou la terre qui se soit affaissée. peu importe; le fait certain c'est qu'n immense territoire fut envahi, et que les Scilly, l'ile de Wight, Guernsey, Auregny, et ce dernier lieu Ouessant, et Jersey, se treuvèrent des îles. Du reste si aujourd, hui la mer boissait de 19 brasses seulement on irait encore à pied de France en Angleterre, d'Angleterre à la plus éloignëe des Scilly, comme aussi d'Ouëssant, à peu près en ligne droite, à Guernsey, Auregney, et la Hague."

Thus, M. Ahier and the present writer agree that an immense tract of land has been lost, but they differ entirely in opinion as to the manner of that loss, except so far as this, namely, that according to one of M. Ahiers' conjectures, the ground has sunk suddenly (affaissa subitement) 150 French feet, which are equal to 164 English feet. That is to say, it *must* have sunk not less than 120 English feet, and port of it *may* have sunk as much as 176 English feet, or thereabouts.

---

## CHAPTER VII.

### Dr. Fleming's Theory not applicable to the Changes on the French Coasts.

124. In the Edinburgh "Philosophical Transactions" * is a very interesting paper entitled "On a submarine forest in the Frith of Tay, with observations on the formation of submarine forests in general." A bed of peat, he says, occurs on the south side of the Frith of Tay, ten miles in length. It is in detached portions to the extent of nearly three miles on the west side of Flisk beach, and upwards of seven miles on the east side. Upon its surface may be perceived the stumps of trees, with roots attached, and evidently occupying the positions in which they formerly grew; many of the trunks and roots occur from 8ft. to 10ft. below high water mark. He says Mr. Watt, of Skail, thinks it may have come to its present position by the removal of a bank of earth 18ft. deep, washed gradually away. To this theory Dr. Fleming well objects that it is not likely that "a continuous bed of peat of nearly an acre in extent would be spared from destruction and suffered to settle peacefully in the Bay of Skail, so as to be covered at flood tide with 15ft. of water."

He quotes the Rev. Mr. Borlase, F.R.S., on a submarine forest observed in 1757 at Mount's Bay, Cornwall, of which more in Article 133. And he says that Dr. Correa de Silva ascribes the depressed position of the submarine forest of Lincolnshire to the force of subsidence, aided by the sudden action of earthquakes.—"Phil. Trans.", R.S., 1799. He says Professor Playfair conceives it to be a part of that geological system o alternate depression and elevation of the surface, which probably extends t the whole mineral kingdom. He is tempted to think that the forest whic once covered Lincolnshire was immersed under the sea by the subsidence of the land to a great depth at a period considerably remote. That it has emerged from this great depth till a part of it has become dry land, but that it is now sinking again, if the tradition of the country deserves any

---

* Vol. ix., p. 419, &c., for 1823, by John Fleming, D.D., F.R.S.E.

credit; and that the part of it in the sea is deeper under water than it was a few years ago.

Dr. Fleming's paper was read June 17, 1822, and at that time he thought the subject was imperfectly understood, and offered the following solution:—

He supposes a lake near the sea shore, with its outlet a few feet above the rise of tide, and that by mud being carried into it by rivulets, and by the growth of aquatic plants, the lake becomes a marsh of sufficient density to support trees. The force of ordinary subsidence, aided by occasional earthquakes, may render the whole tolerably compact, yet the quantity of water present will prevent anything like the ordinary condensation of ordinary alluvial land or soil. Suppose such a marsh to have its outlet lowered, or rather its seaward barrier removed, the extremities of the strata would then be exposed to the sea to a depth equal to the fall of tide, and the water would then ooze out. All above low water mark would collapse, and the marsh would sink below the level of the sea. But the drainage, he thinks, would not be confined to beds above the low water line; those occupying a considerably lower position would be influenced. He says, "for the water in such would be squeezed out, in consequence of the pressure of all the matter above low water exerted during every ebb, in the expulsion of the water at the lowest level, thus permitting the subsidence of the strata to take place to the lowest beds of the morass." He thinks this would account for the depression of the marsh many feet below its original level. And the same explanation "seems equally applicable to the forests of Mount's Bay, Lincolnshire, and Orkney."

125. Now, *first*, Dr. Fleming's objection to Mr. Watts' theory applies still more forcibly to his own theory. How could storms and Atlantic waves spare from destruction, and suffer to settle peacefully, the extensive peat beds containing whole forests of trees, on the west of Guernsey and Jersey, to say nothing of the Bay of S. Michel? The south-westerly waves and storms of the Atlantic are more forcible than those of the Frith of Tay, and the tides are respectively 32ft., 42ft., and 54ft. as compared with 15ft.

*Second*, can the cautious reader really believe that the very extensive submarine forests about the Channel Islands and neighbouring coasts of France, have once been living forests *afloat on lakes?* Is not this far more improbable than to suppose that the land has quietly sunk down, there being so many well ascertained instances of land both rising and sinking?

*Third*, why will he not be content with the "ordinary subsidence," which he admits and which is sufficient to account for everything; for as he has admitted it, he cannot arbitrarily limit its amount?

But, *fourth*, even if we lay aside these three objections which would be difficult to answer,—we should have, even if we made him a present of all he contends for,—the extraordinary spectacle of a forest rising and sinking alternately (to the amount of 54ft. in the Bay of Mont S. Michel) every time the tide flowed and ebbed! And the more so, because if sea water was substituted for fresh water, the buoyant power would be increased, as is well known; by 2lbs. per cubic foot. But the alternate risings and sinkings with the tides, of submarine forests on the coast of France, do not now and never did take place; and they are not true, with respect to the French coasts now under consideration.

126. Elevations and depressions of strata are the *rule* and *not the exception*, and have been so in all ages all over the world. And it is surprising that any theory whatever, provided it be other than rising or sinking of land is suggested; and more than that, suggested eagerly and adopted readily; often in the face of possibility. Any and every wild and improbable supposition has at one time or another been resorted to, but a great fact in nature; namely the very frequent depressions of strata has equally often been shunned. How much ingenuity and thought has been brought to bear (must we not say wasted?) rather than accept the well proved theory of sinking!

---

## CHAPTER VIII.

### Diodorus Siculus.

127. There is passage in the work of the historian Diodorus, which appears to have an important bearing on the question now under consideration. But it has been denied by some that the passage in question refers to the Channel Islands at all. It is now proposed to lay down as fairly as may be, both the reasons for believing that the passage really does refer to the northern Channel Islands, and the reasons which have been alleged against that belief. And, first, it is important to consider who Diodorus was, what degree of knowledge he probably had on the subject; and, thirdly, the probable amount of fidelity in recording that knowledge. His credulity as to the heathen gods and goddesses is only what might have been expected from a heathen, and does not affect the question, of his general trustworthiness. He gives some notices of Gaul and Britain most elaborate and detailed with respect to the former. Which circumstance makes his statements especially interesting and important on the present occasion. For there can be no reasonable doubt that he was in Gaul for a considerable time, carefully observing and recording his observations of men and things: and he doubtless saw the Channel Islands.

128. It is said of him in Dr. Lempriere's "*Classical Dictionary*,"* that he was "an historian, surnamed *Siculus*, because he was born at Argyra, in Sicily. He wrote an history of Egypt, Persia, Syria, Media, Greece,

---

* 12th edition 1822.

Rome, and Carthage, which was divided into forty books, of which only fifteen are extant, with some fragments. This valuable composition was the work of an accurate enquirer, that and it is said he visited all the places of which he has made mention in his history. It was the labour of thirty years, though the greater part may be considered as nothing more than a judicious compilation from Berosus, Timæus, Theopompus, Callisthenes, and others. The author, however, is too credulous in some of his narrations, and often wanders far from the truth. His style is neither elegant nor too laboured; but it contains great simplicity and unaffected correctness. He often dwells too long upon fabulous reports and trifling incidents, while events of the greatest importance to history are treated with brevity, and sometimes passed over in silence. His manner of reckoning by the Olympiads, and the Roman consuls, will be found very erroneous. The historian flourished about 44 years B.C. He spent much time at Rome to procure information, and authenticate his historical narrations. The best edition of his works is that of Wesseling, 2 vols. fol., Amst. 1746."

In 1823, perhaps, Wesseling's was the best edition.

129. Degory Wheare, the earliest reader of history on the Camden foundation, at the University of Oxford, gives a careful statement as to Diodorus, which will be quoted from.* Wheare says, p. 66:—"Diodorus was a celebrated writer and so expert in antiquities, that Greece can scarcely show another that is his equal; which judgment may be confirmed by the elogie [eulogy ?] which a learned divine of our country, a bishop, and well versed in this [history] and all other sorts of learning, is pleased to bestow upon this author. Diodorus Siculus (saith he) is an excellent author, who with great fidelity, immense labour, and a rare both diligence and ingenuity, has collected an historical library (as Justin Martyr calls it) in which he has represented his own and the studies of other men, being the great reporter of human actions; but as Diodorus himself styles it a *common treasury* of things, and a harmless or safe mistress or teacher of what is useful and good. Our reverend bishop might well call it an *immense labour*, for he spent thirty years (as he himself confesseth) in writing this history, travelling in the meantime over several countries to inform himself, running through many dangers as usually happens." Wheare also says, at p 48, that "Lodovicus Vivis, who admires how Pliny could say that Diodorus was the first of the Grecians who left off trifling, when, saith he, there is nothing more idle [than Diodorus's first five books.] But we [Wheare] reply, that learned censor did not well consider that Diodorus himself owns that the history of those times was mixed with many fables, and delivered very variously by the ancients, but he was content to relate what seemed most agreeable to the truth, and yet at last he did not desire that they should be taken for solid truths, but that he

* On the "Method of Reading Histories," by Degory Wheare, translated into English by Edmund Bohun, Esq., and published, London, 1694.

thought it was better to have the best knowledge we could of those ancient times, than to be altogether ignorant of them."

130. Diodorus himself mentions that he was a cotemporary of Cæsar, for in Book VI., chap. ix., he says, speaking of the Rhine, "which in our days C. Cæsar joined (the two banks) with bridges in a wonderful manner, and conveyed across his infantry," as Cæsar himself also relates that he did.* He survived Cæsar and lived in the reign of Augustus.

130. *The subject-matter of Diodorus's History.*—In his first four and part of his fifth book he relates many "traditions" and "fables," as well as many interesting particulars of various personages, peoples, and places which do not concern the present subject. He then gives a highly condensed description of Gaul and the Gauls,† of which the following account and summary will probably satisfy the reader that Diodorus was present amongst the Gauls, observed them closely, and, doubtless, saw the Channel Islands, and the "peculiar" circumstance which he relates afterwards. The translation of his narrative, even when somewhat condensed, occupies five and a half closely written quarto pages, and is too long to be reprinted entire. The recital of a few prominent facts appears to carry with it internal evidencee both of his truthfulness, and of his having been for a considerable time present among the Gauls. One trifling inaccuracy, not at all affecting the present question, is the more remarkable from standing alone, namely, when he says the Danube flows into the ocean. His statement, which has caused so much disbelief, namely, that the winds blow so strong that they propel stones with sufficient force to knock armed men off their horses,—has lately received a remarkable corroboration, the scene of which was the mountain Matterhorn, also among the Alps.‡ Edward Whymper, Esq., in describing his ascent of the Aiguille Vert, says:—"The Matterhorn rains down showers, nay torrents and avalanches, of stones both day and night."

### Abstract of Diodorus's Description of the Gauls.

He describes Gaul, the people, and their number; the many rivers, and whence and whither they flow. Cæsar passed the Rhine "in our days" in a wonderful manner and conquered the Gauls beyond it. He omits for brevity, the names of many navigable rivers. In summer the winds blow from the north and west with such force that they form considerable heaps of stones, as large as the hand can hold, and they knock armed men off their horses. Neither wine nor oil is produced; beer, and honey and water are drank. They get drunk with wine, fall asleep, or go frantic. It is served out from ships or carriages. Coin is scarce. He describes, in detail, how and where they get gold, melt it, and both sexes use it for ornament, namely, as bracelets on their wrists and arms, "torques" of solid gold on their necks, on their fingers as rings, and as gold on their breasts. They all offer much gold to the gods, neither dare any one steal it from the

* "Cæsar de Bello Gallico," Book IV., s. 17, 18; or in some editions, s. 15, 16.
† Book VI (V. in some editions) chapter 9.
‡ See Brit. Ass. report of the Birmingham meeting, 1865. Trans. of Sections, p. 77.

temples, though all are greedy. He describes their persons, their stature, the colour of their hair, and how they dye and wear it, and increase its apparent abundance. Some shave the beard, some grow it sparingly; the nobles shave their cheeks, but let their beards grow. Food lodges in their beards, and drink descends through them as through a canal. They sup sitting on skins of wolves and dogs on the ground, served by boys, and make fires on which there are pots and spits of flesh. They honour brave men with better meat, as the poet says, was given to Ajax when he conquered Hector. They invite guests, asking them after supper who they are and whence they came.* After supper the war of words ends with a fight; they are regardless of life. They believe in transmigration of souls, and throw writings on the funeral pile, as if the dead could read. He then enters into minute details as to their manners and customs in battle, the names and forms of their weapons, and their manner of using them. Some are so regardless of death that they fight naked. They praise their own brave and depreciate their enemies. He relates how they deal with and preserve their dead enemies and booty; their songs and hymns; and unwillingness to part with their dead foes, an action which they ridicule and consider savage and unmannerly. To strike terror they wear various coloured garments, unshorn, called "Braccæ." Their little cloaks of strips are thicker in winter, finer in summer. Earthen vessels are ornamented with flowers. Their shields are as a long as a man, and adorned to suit the taste; some having brazen figures of animals in relief for ornament and safety. Lofty brazen helmets on which horns are printed, or the images of animals engraved, protect the head. They have barbarous sounding horns.† Some use iron breast-plates, some fight naked with the natural weapons. Some have long two-handed swords hanging on the right by a brass chain. The iron of their lances is a cubit or more long, and two hands broad. Their hunting poles have sharper points than swords. They have straight and curved swords, to stab or cut. Their aspects are terrible, their voices grave and stern. Their words are few, obscure, and doubtful; they boast of themselves and despise others.‡ They swagger and detract, inflated in their own opinion; they have good ability, but little of other men's learning. Their bards are musical poets who sing with lyre-like instruments, in praise or dispraise. Philosophers and theologians, called Saronidæ, are much reverenced. Divines foretell by auguries and sacrifices, many think all obey them. While consulting on important events they keep a wonderful chatter. By the fall of a stabbed man, the tearing of his limbs and flow of blood, by ancient observations, they know future events. No sacrifice without a philosopher, sacred rites should be by those of divine nature as nearer the Gods, from whom benefits may be obtained by such intercession. By their advice, peace and

---

* No doubt Diodorus himself was thus questioned.

† There is still a custom of blowing horns made of shells or cows' horns, on St. John's eve and on other occasions. They are also used to give warning before blasting rocks.

‡ See "Cæs. Com.," Book III., s. xviii.

war are made. Poets have so much influence, that even when the army have thrown their darts and drawn swords, not only friends but enemies cease fighting at their intervention; so that though unmannerly and barbarous, anger yields to wisdom, and Mars respects the Muses.

Can there be any doubt that Diodorus was for some time amongst them, that he was a careful observer, or that he saw the Channel Islands?

131. Having now given the reader the best means in my power of judging of the paragraph in the next artic'e, I proceed to lay a faithful translation before him. The original Greek is quoted in the M.S. Appendix, pure and simple. It is copied from Lib. V., par. xxii., p. 267, Carolus Muller's edition, 1842. The passage is exactly the same, word for word in Stephens's edition, who first published the original Greek of Diodorus. The "various readings" are of no importance to the present purpose. The following particular description, of which the first half is somewhat abbreviated, proves that Diodorus either was in Britain personally, or at all events that he had access to *good* information, perhaps from the tin merchants; else whence so much detail? He says: neither Bacchus nor Hercules contended with the Britons in battle, Cæsar first conquered them and made them pay tribute. There is a promontory called Carion,* where it approaches nearest the continent, and another promontory called Belerium, four days sail from the continent. He then describes the form of the island and the length of its sides, and says the Britons use chariots in battle, like the ancient Greek heroes. They have very compact dwellings built of reeds or wood. They lay up corn in the ear, daily grinding enough for use. Their manners are simple, they are honest, and far behind our people in cunning and quick-wittedness. With food simple and of little value, they pass a life estranged from the pleasures of wealth. The north air is cold; they have many kings and princes keeping the peace by turns. But we will speak more particularly concerning these things when we come to the acts of Cæsar by which he subdued the Britons. Unfortunately Diodorus's account of these things is in one of the lost books. The following paragraph (Article 132) immediately follows that of which an abstract has just been given. The reader's attention is specially invited to the passage which I have marked in italics, and which being evidently parenthetical, has been enclosed in parentheses, and a few remarks will be made afterwards. Immediately after the words "acts of Cæsar by which he subdued the Britons," we have as follows:—

132. "But now we will relate concerning the tin produced there. They who inhabit the promontory of Britain called Belerium, are exceedingly hospitable, and on account of the merchants being their guests, are civilised by custom in their mode of life. They procure the tin by ingeniously working the earth producing it, which being rocky has earthy veins in which working a passage and melting [the ore] they extract [the tin]. Forging it into masses like astragals, they carry it into an island

* Kent.

situate before Britain, called Ictis. For the middle space being dried by the ebb, they carry the tin into this (island) in abundance, in carts. (*But a certain peculiar thing happens concerning the neighbouring islands lying in the middle* (μεταξυ*) *between Europe and Britain, for at full sea they appear to be islands, but by the reciprocation of the ebb of the sea and a large space being dried they appear peninsulas.*) Hence the merchants buy (the tin) from the inhabitants, and export it into Gaul. Finally, proceeding on foot through France in thirty days, they carry it in sacks on horses to the mouth of the river Rhone. We shall be satisfied with these statements concerning tin."

Cæsar mentions that he sent Sergius Galba with the twelfth legion, "because he willed that a passage should be laid open through the Alps, by which passage merchants had been accustomed to go with great danger and great tolls."*

133. *Which was the Isle of Ictis?*—Certain eminent authorities are of opinion that the geographical change which has occurred since St. Michael's Mount was "the hoar rock in the wood," cannot have taken place within the last 2,000 years, because, as it has been alleged, this was the island referred to by Diodorus, who wrote before Christ, when he spoke of the Britains carrying the tin into an island situate before Britain, called Ictis.† If St. Michael's Mount was not Ictis, I know of no other competitor, unless it be Wolf Rock. The Rev. W. Borlase, F.R.S., and Sir Henry de la Beche (Report on Cornwall, &c., p. 418), both give us reason to believe that there have been great losses of land within historical times, and the latter adds—"Of the great loss of this land within modern times Dr. Bosse adduces ample proof," to say nothing of Camden, and his tradition of the lost country of the Lionesse. One part of the question is, do not the submarine trees of the Rev. Mr. Borlase (and of others to be specified hereafter), by their comparative freshness, indicate a comparatively modern submersion, like the submarine trees of the Channel Islands, or in the Bay of Mont S. Michel?

Let us hear the Rev. Mr. Borlase. The Rev. William Borlase, F.R.S., read a paper which is published in the "Transactions of the Royal Society," for 1757, p. 80:—"*Of some trees discovered underground on the shore at Mount's Bay, in Cornwall.*" In the said place one day, Mr. B. found the roots of a tree branching off from the trunk in all directions, and on further search, about 30ft. to the west, he found the roots of another tree, but without any trunk, "though displayed in the same horizontal manner as the first. 50ft. further to the north, was the body of an oak, 3ft. in diameter, reclining to the east. On digging about it, it was traced 6ft deep under the surface; but its roots were still deeper than they could pursue them. Within a few feet distance was the body of a willow, 1½ft. diameter, with the bark on; and one piece of a large hazel branch, with its bark on. What the first two trees were it was not easy to distinguish,

* *De bello Gallico.* Lib. III., c. 1.
† "Hardwicke's Report of the Birmingham Meeting," p. 126; and Brit. Ass. Report 1866, p. 71; Trans. of Sections.

there not being a sufficiency remaining of the first, and nothing but roots of the second, both pierced with the teredo, or augur worm. Round these trees was sand about 10in. deep, and then the natural earth in which these trees had formerly flourished. It was a black marsh earth, in which the leaves of the juncus were entirely preserved from putrefaction. These trees were 300yds. within full sea mark; and when the tide is in, have at least 12ft. of water above them. But these are sufficient to confirm the ancient tradition of these parts, that St. Michael's Mount, now enclosed half a mile with the sea when the tide is in, stood formerly in a wood.* That the wood consisted of oak, very large, hazel and willow trees is beyond dispute. That there has been a subsidence of the sea shores thereabouts, is hinted in a former letter;† and the different levels and tendencies observed in the positions of the trees found, afford some material inferences as to the degree and inequalities of such subsidencies in general (?); as to the age in which this subsidence happened (it is) near 1,000 years since at least." In Milner's "Gallery of Nature," p. 387, it is stated that in the time of Edward the Confessor, the rock of St. Michael's Mount was the site of a monastery described as being *near* the sea; and as the storm of 1099, mentioned in the Saxon Chronicles, occurred in the autumn,‡ the submersion of the district has been referred to in that inundation, he says: Vice-Admiral Thevenard in "Mem. relatifs à la Marine," 4 vols., 8vo., An. 8, (A.D. 1800), Vol. II., p. 13, mentions, "la submersion du terrain * * et de la pointe ouest de l'Angleterre * * *au commencement du IX siècle.*" The italics are mine.

I have read, with great interest, the large mass of important and well-condensed facts, by Mr. Pengelly, F.G.S., F.R.S., entitled "Changes of level of Devonshire." It was read at the Bath meeting of the British Association, and is in the *Reader*, of Nov. 19th, 1864, which (thanks to Mr. Pengelly) is now before me, in extenso, corrected by the author. The conclusions he arrives at are (amongst many other interesting things which do not concern the present purpose) that after many subsidences and elevations, "since the last adjustment, the coast line of south-eastern Devonshire has everywhere retreated." And "even in some of the limestone districts, every ebb tide exposes a broad platform of denudation; and in the new red sandstone localities the waves, which at spring tide high water assail the cliffs, break at low water nearly half a mile from them, and thus furnish a rude measure of the minimum of time which has elapsed since the completion of that downward movement which submerged the forests.§ I have no personal knowledge of the locality, and very willingly accept this statement, which plainly proves that the

* See Camden's "Britannia."

† This refers to another paper of Mr. Borlase's, for 1753, p. 324, vol. X., "Phil. Trans. R.S.," in which he says the Scilly Isles *were* ten in number (as Strabo states, Book III., chap. v., sec. 11), but *are now* 140; and where he thinks that for various reasons stated there must also have been a subsidence.

‡ We are not bound to suppose that the sinkings took place in *autumn*, merely because nuts are found; nut shells will take years to decay, especially if slightly covered with leaves, &c.

§ Page 645.

latest sinking there, of which we have certain knowledge, was *long before the historical period* (and, therefore, is beyond the limits, which are dealt with in these papers), because the broad platform of limestone denudation must have taken many ages to produce, as also must the cutting back for half a mile in the new red sandstone districts. I make this general reservation, however, which cannot be too much insisted on, that bones or horns of extinct animals and every other species of pre-historic relic, though it may have been deposited either at the sea bottom or on dry land in pre-historic times, and may have been elevated or depressed with the land again and again also in pre-historic times, yet for all that, while it still lay in situ and not yet discovered by the geologist, there *may have been*, also, one or more risings or sinkings completely within the historical period, in which it partook.

Referring to Mr. Borlase's date of "near 1,000 years since at least," that number deducted from 1757 (the date of his paper) gives A.D. 757; which, observe, is less than half a century later than the great subsidence of 709 on the other side of the English Channel, which we have been considering. And at any rate it is clear that Mr. Borlase's opinion was, that the subsidence had taken place within the Christian period. If, instead of using the *round number* 1,000, he had happened to say 1,048, we should then have had the exact date 709,—the year of the great catastrophe about Mont S. Michel. The trees in Mount's Bay were *so fresh* that the species of several were clearly identified, as we have seen; which circumstance is, of itself, a strong argument in proof of their recent submersion.

Dr. Gibson, the editor of Camden's "Britannia," says that St. Michaels' Mount is called *Careg cowse in clowse*, in Cornish, which means, he says, "the hoary rock in the wood." *Careg* is doubtless the origin of the English word *crag;* and *cowse* is said to mean *cana*, white; and *clowse* obviously means a *close* or enclosure. Mr. Metivier says that St. Michael's Mount was *Carreg Coedh yn clôs*, rock of the wood in the enclosure.

134. *Which islands did Diodorus refer to?* If "the storm" of 1099, that at the commencement of the ninth century (both accompanied by submersions of land), or Mr. Borlase's submersion in the eighth century, are any of them true,—and there does not appear to be reason to doubt the truth of any of them,—then it would follow, that Saint Michael's Mount cannot have been the ancient Isle of Ictis, because, must we not suppose that the mount only became an island at one of those submersions? In that case we must look to Wolf Rock, Seven Stones, or to some island now totally lost, for that ancient island, Wolf Rock, may have been the ancient Ictis, if there be any foundation for Camden's well-known tradition of the Lyonesse country. Cornwall, it is very likely, once extended farther west and north-west; and if that was so, Wolf Rock would have been "opposite Britain," as Diodorus says the Isle of Ictis was. The question of the identity of Ictis will be further considered in chapter xvi.

Diodorus calls his islands "neighbouring" islands (πλησίον νήσους) as if they were islands lying neighbouring to Cornwall, of which he is speaking.

But, on the other hand, he says they were islands "in the middle between," (τὰς μεταξὺ κειμένας) Europe and Britain.

Does he mean first, to limit his meaning to the coast of Cornwall? Or second, does he include all the islands lying neighbouring to the south coast of Britain? Or, thirdly, does he mean the Channel Islands, Guernsey, Sercq, Herm, and Alderney, which are geographically, "the islands lying between Europe and Britain?" We will consider each of these three questions in order.

Ictis was no doubt near the then coast; if it had been so distant that the distance was worth remarking upon for its magnitude, the miners would not have been likely to have carted the tin into the island in such abundance, because the distance would have been too great; and we have no historical authority for believing that there was any other isle than Ictis off the coast of Cornwall, and in that case he would not have used the plural number, and said islands. But more than all, it would have been particularly absurd to describe an island lying near the coast of Cornwall, as "between Europe and Britain," when the whole distance across from Europe (Britanny) to Britain is a hundred miles. We may not impute such an instance of clumsy description to such a man as Diodorus. If he had meant an island or islands near the south coast of Britain, he would doubtless have said so, and never have mentioned Europe at all. If he had meant to include the so-called Isle of Portland and the Isle of Wight, along with Ictis, he would also (if we are to give him credit for common sense) have said "islands near the south coast of Britain," without mentioning Europe at all. He would no more have named Europe than we should say, in describing the position of Ireland, that "it lies between America and Britain," or in geographically describing Waterloo Bridge, that "it lies between the English Channel and the Strand." The reader would not commit either of these two absurdities, and can have no right to impute anything of the sort to such a man as Diodorus. And, secondly, we have no authority for supposing that Portland was other than it is now, namely a peninsula connected to the mainland by Chesil Bank; or that Wight was other than it is now, namely, an island at all times of tide.* And even if we beg the question that the two spaces were then alternally wet and dry (which they certainly are not now) we should still be in the dilemma that the distances (two or three miles each) are too small to have been worth special remark as anything "peculiar." For there must have been hundreds of well-known cases where spaces, as great as those, were alternately wet and dry.

I believe the following is the true interpretation of Diodorus's remarkable passage, and it makes everything perfectly clear and reasonable. If we suppose, as some contend, that μεταξὺ only means "between;" still when we say that anything lies between two other things, we usually mean that it is at or near the *middle*; and thus Guernsey, Sercq, and Alderney, are about half way from Britain to Britanny,

* Suetonius and others will be quoted hereafter to prove that Vectis (Wight) was an island at various early periods in the Christian era.

and must be the islands meant. Much more certainly must Diodorus have meant those islands, if we say with Liddle and Scott that *μεταξὺ* means *in the middle.* For in that case most certainly the northern Channel Islands were meant. The present space between Guernsey and the Continent is twenty-seven miles; and if anything like that extent had been dried at low water, it would have been very "peculiar" and well worthy of being recorded. I think they are called "neighbouring" islands to distinguish them from the *remote* islands in the Bay of Biscay, which are also in a certain sense between Europe and Britain, and mention of them was doubtless suggested to Diodorus's mind by the circumstances of the space between the northern Channel Islands and the Continent *being dry at low water*, like the space between Cornwall and Ictis; and by the other circumstance of the tin being carried past them into Gaul.

135. *Objections answered.* The suggestion of a friend that Diodorus probably alluded to the Scilly Isles, and that Ictis was one of them, is at once upset by the fact that the Scilly Isles are *not* between Europe and Britain. There is also a sounding of as much as forty-eight fathoms between the Land's End and the Scilly Isles; if the intermediate space was once dry land, a greater sinking is implied than I contend for, and Camden's tradition of the Lyonesse country would be realised. Another friend makes the following objections which are given in his own words, he says: "The neighbouring islands lying between Europe and Britain, mean only Mont S. Michel, Portland, and the Isle of Wight," and do not include the Channel Islands, and he relies particularly on the word *γαρ* (for) in the previous sentence* as connecting it with what has previously been said about the Isle of Wight.† He thinks there have been partial sinkings near Mont S. Michel and elsewhere, but not to any considerable extent, and that the fact of the Channel Islands not being sufficiently important accounts for the non-mention of them.

His contention in favour of Portland and Wight being Diodorus's islands have already been answered; and with respect to Mont S. Michel, the space between it and the Continent was the Forest of Scissy, and not sea, until seven centuries and a half after Diodorus's time, as we have already proved.

---

## CHAPTER IX.

### JULIUS CÆSAR, PLINY THE ELDER, PROCOPIUS.

136. It will now be convenient to gather what evidences we can from "Cæsar's Commentaries on the Gallic War," and for the reader's convenience to follow them with an exact translation (in Article 145). It incidentally becomes necessary, in pursuit of our object, to identify, if possible, the localities of his sea fight with the Veneti, and of Sabinus's battle with the Unelli and others. These events, I affirm, took place, the former near Guernsey, Herm, and Sercq., or perhaps Alderney; and the

---

* "For the middle space being dried by the ebb, they carry the tin into this (island) in abundance." † Ictis does not mean the Isle of Wight, as my friend here supposes.

latter not many miles distant from (the present) Coutances. It is well known that Cæsar's skill in concise, correct, and graphic description (of everything occuring under his own personal observation) was all but equal to his transceudent skill as a General, and that his accuracy may be fully relied on. The object of course is, to gather what we can of the geographical state of the localities now under consideration, in his time. He was assassinated in the Senate House at Rome, on the 15th of March, B.C. 44, in the 56th year of his age, twelve years after his victory over the fleet of the Veneti.

137. His friend Aulus Hirtius, who appears to have written the eighth book on the Gallic War says in it: "It is evident amongst all, that nothing has been finished so diligently by others, as not to be surpassed by the elegance of the Commentaries, which are published, lest knowledge of such important events might be wanting to authors, and are so much approved by the judgment of all; that occasion appears to be taken away from, not afforded to authors. At which circumstance my wonder exceeds that of others, for others only know how well and correctly he finished them, but I also "know how easily and quickly." Some remarks will now be given on part of Cæsar's Third Book.

138. There can be no doubt that the country surrounding Dariorigum, which was near but not on the site of Vannes, as well as that city itself did at one time belong to the Veneti. For the custom of calling chief cities after the peoples, as Vannes from the Veneti or Vens, Nantes from the Nannetes, &c., began in the times of the the emperors, But it is not certain that the Dariorigum country belonged to the Veneti at all, in Cæsar's time. For we have seen that Ptolemy (A.D. 117 to 161) leaves a blank for the name of the owners of Dariorigum, which is difficult to understand if it belonged to the Veneti. And at any rate even if it was theirs in Cæsar's time, it is probable that they had much other territory; for Pliny the elder (who probably wrote within a century after the sea-fight with the Veneti), states that they had "almost two hundred islands." It will be convenient to give a literal translation of the passage.* After enumerating the Aquitanian Gauls, he says with respect to, "The seas about the coast; between the Rhine and the Seine is British; between it [the Seine] and the Pyrenees, is Gallic. *Very many islands (almost two hundred)*† belonging to the Veneti. are called Veneticæ, and in the Aquitanian Bay [*i.e.* the Bay of Biscay] Uliarius." These large possessions explain and corroborate the facts mentioned by Cæsar,‡ namely, that the authority of the Veneti was by far more extensive than that of any of the neighbouring states; that they had very many ships; that they surpassed the rest in naval knowledge and experience; that they possessed the whole of the few existing harbours; and that they had nearly all as tributaries who were accustomed to use that sea. I am trying to satisfy the reader in this article, not only that we may not suppose that the sea-fight with the Veneti

* Nat. Hist., Book 4, Section XXXIII (XIX), Valpy's edition.
† The Italics are the present writers.
‡ Book 3, Sec. viii.

took place to the westward of Britanny; but on the contrary, that we must suppose that it took place close to some of the islands Alderney, Guernsey, Herm or Sercq. As they had nearly two hundred islands (some of which are still of considerable extent notwithstanding heavy losses of territory by sinking and washing away), we can understand that their ships, soldiers, and sailors may—indeed, must—have been away at one or more of the most important islands; for how can we suppose so warlike and energetic a people would have left all their islands ungarrisoned and unprotected? And this view is supported by the matters of fact that though Cæsar had his ships built in the Loire,* *at some thirty miles distance only* from Dariorigum, the Veneti neither blockaded him in the Loire, nor destroyed his ships whilst building, or when built. Where, therefore, had they their "three hundred most well-equipped ships" which he mentions in Sec. XIV.? And where had they their soldiers? Doubtless most, if not all their ships, were at some or one of their many islands, namely, in that "Venetia," or portion of Venetian territory where it was evident that Cæsar was first about to carry on war—as he himself tells. in the latter part of Section IX. But the last part of that section is quite conclusive as to the locality of the sea-fight. We will quote it. "The Veneti," he says, "fortify the towns; they bring corn from the fields into the towns; they collect ships as most numerous (quàm plurimas) as they can *into Venetia,* where it was evident that Cæsar was first about to carry on the war. They unite as allies to themselves at that war the the Osismii, Lexobii, *Nannetes,*† Ambiani, Morini, Diablintes, Menapii; they send for auxiliaries from *Britain, which is situated opposite those countries* (eas regiones)." Observe, he distinctly says that Britain was opposite those countries, namely "Venetia," where Cæsar was first about to carry on the war. And clearly Alderney, Guernsey, Sercq, and Herm are "opposite Britain," but no part of the west coast of Britanny is so, nor any others of the two hundred islands. And I believe that it was in the neighbourhood of the three latter islands named, because Guernsey, Herm, and Jethou must have been then united together as one island, and must have been far more extensive, and, therefore, more important, than Alderney, that the sea-fight took place. There is a farther circumstance which appears to count for something. Why did not an author so correct and graphic as Cæsar call the Venetia in question "island, or islands?" The answer appears to be, because his word *countries* or *regions* is especially appropriate; for, as Diodorus tells us, at low water they had the peculiarity of looking *like peninsulas;* and we find Cæsar himself ‡ speaking of them as "*little tongues* and *promontories*."§ They were not clearly and exclusively islands—a more neutral or comprehensive term was preferable; and

---

* Sec. IX.

† Clearly the Nannetes, or people of Nantes, are not opposite Britain, and Cæsar cannot, therefore, have meant that the allies of the Gauls were opposite Britain, but that the countries (regiones), namely "Venetia," where Cæsar was about to carry on the war, were opposite Britain.

‡ Sect. XII.

§ In some editions the word is "linguis," tongues; in others "lingulis," little tongues.

Cæsar, who always used the best words for his purpose, calls them "æs regiones," which words fulfil the requirements of the case exactly.

139. The locality will be farther fixed and confirmed by other statements of Cæsar; while at the same time, in other ways, he throws much light on the present subject of enquiry. He speaks in section ix. of "the nature of the place," and that "they knew the foot-roads to have been cut up by estuaries." Now in restoring the probable ancient coast line in the first map, of course it was necessary to continue the rivers across the territory now lost. This was done by sketching their supposed courses along the deepest soundings, for it is well known that the river bed is the *lowest* ground in every cross section of a valley, except at the mouth or delta, where the level has been raised by deposit of mud brought down by the river itself. The land streams, brooks, and rivers, must, therefore, have run across the long space which, as Diodorus has told us, was dried by the ebb tide: and thus *estuaries appear on the map which necessarily cut up the foot roads.*

140. We learn in Section XII., that their towns were placed on extreme tongues and promontories. Supposing that "hou" means a house, and, therefore, that its plural means a group of houses or a town, we shall then have the various (present) islets or barren rocks, of whose names "hou" or "ou" forms part; identified as the former sites of towns. Captain Richards, R.N., chief of the Admiralty Survey of the Channel Islands' Seas, now in progress, finds that if the sea bottom was lifted 22 fathoms the bottom would be dry at low water all the way from Guernsey to the continent, except one space of about a mile wide, which is two fathoms deeper. Suppose then, for the sake of the present argument, that the sea about and amongst the Channel Islands, as well as the islands themselves, were lifted 22 fathoms higher, we should have a state of things in accordance with Diodorus's description, and Jersey would have become an integral part of the continent. The remark of Cæsar at the end of Section XII. appears to be quite conclusive that the sea-fight, did not take place on the west of Britanny. Because, if the Romans had only had to sail from one part of the west coast to another part of the same west coast, they could not have had "the greatest difficulty in sailing in an immense and open sea." While, on the other hand, they must have had that difficulty, in sailing from the mouth of the Loire to the northern Channel Islands.

141. The "shallows" which Cæsar mentions in Sections XII, XIII., are in perfect harmony with what Diodorus has said, and with the present argument. For if "a long space" was so shallow as to be dried at low water, as the latter assures us was the case, there must have been "shallows" and "great stones and ragged rocks," as stated at the end of Section XIII., and of very great extent too, and of course of a nature to be dreaded by his ships.

142. To the late Mr. Ahier the credit is due for the happy idea that "Cæsar's Promontories" are identical with "Diodorus's Peninsulas."

And his valuable and suggestive work "Tableaux Historiques de la Civilisation de Jersey," and his lending me Abbé Manet's book in connection with the stumps of trees in the sea bottom together, first led me to study this subject. The same hypothesis which restores "Diodorus's Peninsulas," restores also "Cæsar's Promontories," and does a good deal more For example, let us again take Section XIII. We are there informed that the towns "were built on extreme tongues and promontories," and taking the word "hous" as signifying *assemblages of houses*, we shall have towns firstly at *Lihou* and *Jethou*, at the restored Guernsey island; a town at Brec*hou*, another town at restored Sercq island, and another town, Bur*hou*, at restored Alderney island, to say nothing of the Ereh*ous* and Dirouilles. And the people at Jet*hou* town, may have produced Mr. Lukis's shell middings. All these hous, or collections of houses, would find themselves near the coasts of those restored islands, that is to say, "on extreme tongues and promontories," as the first map shows. The "shallows" are thus restored, because the vast tract left dry at low water, must in grea part have been shallow at high water. By means of their many ship the Veneti carried away their effects, up the Estuaries I suppose, to town in the interior, where the advantages they had in defending themselves are obvious. Amongst other reasons, because the Roman ships being in channels which were perhaps narrow, certainly narrow in some parts, the Gauls could attack them from both sides. It is observable that he mentions that the tides were *great*, which can with more propriety be said of the thirty feet tides of Guernsey, than of the tides on the west of Britanny, which are not half as great.

143. In Section XIV Cæsar finding that storming the towns in detail was labour in vain, resolves to wait for his fleet. And as soon as his fleet was seen by the enemy, about three hundred of their exceedingly well equipped ships ranged themselves in order of battle opposite the Roman ships. And the Romans ultimately won the sea-fight, chiefly by the stratagem of cutting the riggings of the Gallic ships with long scythes, which rendered them unmanageable. The affair of the sea-fight "was carried on in the sight of Cæsar and all the army, so that no deed of greater bravery could be concealed; for all the hills and higher places, whence there was a near view to the sea, were held by [Cæsar's] army." I think Cæsar and his army must have viewed this sea-fight from the heights of Guernsey, Herm, Jethou, and Sercq; or some or one of them—rather than from Alderney. Because the four islands named, are now, and must have been then collectively of considerably more importance and greater extent than Alderney, and therefore were more likely to be the chosen centre of the power of the Veneti. Compare the last part of Sec. XI with the last part of Sec. XIV, and it will be evident that Cæsar, his army, and the two fleets, were all assembled in some regions "opposite Britain," which must have been the Northern Channel Islands.

144. In Sec. XV some of the Gallic ships having been boarded by the Romans, the Gauls sought safety by flight, and the Romans ultimately

captured or destroyed nearly every ship of the Veneti before night. In Sec. XVI we learn that the Veneti and the whole of the maritime powers were subdued, and Cæsar took a severe revenge.

In Sec. XI. we learn that Sabinus was sent with three legions to th Unelli, Curiosolitæ and Lexovii (which last people probably occupied the N.W. part of Calvados), to keep those peoples in check. That is to say, to interpose a cordon militaire between those three peoples and the Northern Channel Islands, and prevent help of any kind being sent to the Veneti.

In Sections XVII. to XX. inclusive we learn that Sabinus arrived in the borders of the Unelli, which people, as Ptolemy has established, were seated at and about Coutances, not many miles distant from the site of which city Sabinus must have fought and conquered Viridovix. In Sec. XX. we find that at one and the same time Cæsar was assured of the victory of Sabinus, and Sabinus of the naval battle. This mutual hearing of the two victories at the same time, seems to signify that they took place at no great distance from each other. Which circumstance favours the belief that the sea-fight took place near Sercq or Guernsey, which are only some forty miles distant from Ptolemy's harbour of the Crotiatoni in the territory of the Unelli not far from which Sabinus's battle took place, probably. If the notion of the sea-fight having taken place in the Bay of Biscay opposite Vannes (which some believe), were not already demolished, as I think it is, by the necessity of the locality being "opposite Britain," we have this farther objection to the neighbourhood of Vannes being taken as the locality. Namely, its distance from the Unelli. For the distance from the Unelli to Sercq is only about one sixth as far as the distance from the Unelli to the sea on the west of Vannes. Whence it follows that it would be extremely improbable that Sabinus and Cæsar should mutually hear of each other's victory at one and the same time, because in those days of no steam, a Roman ship could not sail (except by an improbable combination of favourable circumstances) from the Unelli by way of Ushant to the neighbourhood of Vannes—in the *same space of time* which would be required for another ship to sail in the centrary direction. For obviously, the winds and tides favourable to one ship, would be unfavourable to the other. Hence it is very probable that the battles took place *near* each other—as at Sercq and on the west of Coutances, for example. One ship could sail *a short distance* (chiefly along an estuary) in the same space of time which was required for another ship to sail in a contrary direction. This view is corroborative of the theory that the battles took place respectively, about some of the Northern Channel Islands, and near Coutances. To suppose the messengers between Cæsar and Sabinus, to have gone overland, appears to be quite out of the question. Because the distance is more than a hundred geographical miles in a straight line, and would have been through their enemies country. If we accept the Emperor of the French's statement that the battle took place on the east of Avranches, the distance would not have been much less.

We have thus endeavoured to draw fair and reasonable conclusions, from faithful translations.

The Emperor of the French, in vol. 2 of his most interesting "History of Julius Cæsar," page 147, arrives at the following conclusions: That the country of the Veneti *about Vannes*, would be the first attacked. That the Veneti gathered together all their ships, "no doubt, in the vast estuary formed by the river Auray in the Bay of Quiberon," as he represents on Plate 12. And again, page 149, "We may admit that Cæsar started from the neighbourhood of Nantes, and directed his march to the Roche-Bernard, where he crossed the Vilaine, and arrived in the country of the Veneti." And page 150, "He encamped to the south of the Bay of Quiberon, near the coast, on the heights of St. Gildas," with his army. (See Plate 12) And page 156, respecting the scene of Sabinus's contest with the Unelli: "He (Sabinus) established himself on a hill belonging to the line of heights which separates the basin of the sea from the Celune, where we now find the vestiges of a camp called Du Crastellier, at the distance of seven kilomètres to the east of Avranches." (See Plate 13.) In his Plate 1, it is remarkable that along the west coast of Normandy, the Emperor exhibits the then coast line *considerably farther west* than it is at present. Commencing at the Pointe de Cancalle, it runs about midway between the Minquiers and the present west coast, thence about midway between Jersey and the Norman coast, whence it runs out to Cape la Hague, where it tapers to a point. It is called "Côté au temps de César." The present writer thinks it quite possible that the emperor is correct as to the locality of Sabinus's battle. The emperor's other views quoted, do not accord with the reasonings which have been submitted to the reader. His Majesty's volume was entered at the office of the Minister of the Interior so lately as May, 1866—See publisher's announcement, facing title. The present writer showed from Ptolemy, &c., several years before that date, that the land extended much farther westward than the line in the Emperor's map, and frequently insisted on the fact of these extensive sinkings in friendly conversations with M. Edouard le Héricher, who at length admitted that there might have been a little sinking. It is believed that this accomplished philologist took an active part in developing the scenes of Cæsar's achievements in Western Normandy for the Emperor's volume.

TRANSLATION OF PART OF CÆSARS' COMMENTARIES ON THE GALLIC WAR.

145. Book II., s. xxxiv.,—"At the same time he (Cæsar) was informed by Publius Crassus, whom he had sent with one legion to the Veneti, Unelli, Osismii, Curiosolitæ, Sesuvii, Aulerci, Rhedones, which are maritime states, and touch on the ocean, that all those states had been reduced into the authority and power of the Roman people.

Book III., s. vii.,—"* * when Cæsar thought Gaul subdued from all reasons; the Belgæ being overcome, the Germans being expelled, the Seduni being conquered in the Alps; a sudden war arose in Gaul. This was the cause of that war. P. Crassus, a young man, wintered with the seventh legion among the Andes* nearest the ocean sea. He sent off many præfects and tribunes of soldiers into the neighbouring states for the purpose of seeking corn, because there was a scarcity of corn in these places, in which

* Valpy's edition says "people of Anjou, whom Pliny calls Andecavi or Andegavi," Vol. I., p. 114. It is on the Loire.

number T. Terrasidius had been sent to the Eusubii; M. Trebius Gallus to the Curiosolitæ; Q. Velanius with T. Silius to the Veneti.

VIII. The authority of this state is by far the most extensive of all the maritime coast of those regions (regiones); because the Veneti have both very many ships, with which they have been accustomed to sail into Britain; and they excel the rest in the knowledge and use of nautical things; and in the great and open force of the sea, few harbours intervening which they alone hold, they have nearly all tributaries, who have been accustomed to use the same sea. The beginning of the detaining of Silius and Velanius was from them (the Veneti), because through them they thought they would recover their hostages whom they had given to Crassus. The neighbouring (peoples) induced by the authority of these (the Veneti), (as the designs of the Gauls are sudden and immediate) detain Trebius and Terrasidius from the same cause; and ambassadors being quickly sent, they conspire among themselves through their chiefs; that they would do nothing except by common design, and would bear the same issue of all fortune, and they entice the other states, that they would rather remain in that liberty, which they had received from (their) ancestors, than endure the slavery of the Romans. All the maritime coast being brought over quickly to their opinion, they send a general embassy to P. Crassus, "If he wishes to receive his (ambassadors), he may send back to them (their) hostages."

IX. Of which things Cæsar, being well assured by Crassus, orders long ships (ships of war) to be built meanwhile in the river Loire (Liger), which flows into the ocean, rowers to be prepared from the province, sailors to be obtained, because he was too far distant. These things being performed quickly, he hastened to the army as soon as he could through the time of the year. The Veneti and also the other states, the arrival of Cæsar being known, because they at once understood how great a crime they had committed of themselves, that ambassadors—a name which had always been holy and inviolate among all nations—being detained by themselves and cast into chains, resolve to prepare war for the greatness of the danger, and chiefly those things which might belong to the use of ships; with greater hope on this account, because they trusted much in the nature of the place. They knew the foot roads were cut up by estuaries; that navigation was prevented by (our) ignorance of the places and the fewness of the harbours; they trusted that our armies could not delay long among themselves for want of corn. And though at last all things might happen contrary to their expectation, yet that they could effect much with ships; that the Romans had neither any force of ships, nor knew the shallows (vada), harbours, islands, of those places where they were about to carry on the war, and they saw clearly that navigation in an enclosed sea, and in a most immense and open ocean, were far different. These designs being adopted, they fortify the towns, they bring corn from the fields; they collect as many ships as they possibly can into Venetia, where it was evident that Cæsar was first about to carry on the war. They unite to themselves as allies, for that war, the Osismii, Lexovii, Nannetes, Ambiani, Morini, Diablintes, Menapii; they send for auxiliaries from Britain, which is opposite those regions (eas regiones.")

X. He states his difficulties and the many reasons he had for going to war, and resolves to distribute his army more widely.

XI. Therefore he sends his lieutenant Labienus, with the cavalry to the Treviri, who are nearest to the Rhine, and gives him certain directions as to the Belgæ, which are immaterial to the present purpose. He orders P. Crassus, with twelve legionary cohorts and a great number of cavalry, to set out into Aquitania, lest auxiliaries should be sent out of these nations into Gaul, and such great nations should be united. He sends Lieut. Q. Titurius Sabinus with three legions to the Unelli, the Curiosolitæ, and the Lexovii, to take care that that band (of people) should be checked. He appoints D. Brutus, a young man, to the fleet and to the Gallic ships, which he had ordered to assemble from the Pictones and Santoni, and the other subdued countries: and he orders him to set out as soon as he could to the Veneti. Himself hastens thither with the infantry.

XII. The situations of the towns were commonly of this sort, that being placed in extreme tongues (*linguis*, or *lingulis*), and promontories, there was neither access for infantry when the tide rose, which happens always twice in the space of twenty-four hours, nor for ships, because the tide ebbing again the ships might be injured on the shallows. Thus, from each cause an assault of the towns was prevented; and if at any time, perhaps, overcome by the greatness of a work, the sea being shut out by a mound and by piers, and these being raised nearly as high as the walls of the town, they had begun to despair of their fortunes. By many ships, of which they had very great abundance, they carried away all their effects and betook themselves into the nearest towns; there they defended themselves again by the same advantages of the place. They did these things, therefore, more easily for a great part of summer, because our ships were detained by storms, and there was the greatest difficulty in sailing in an immense and open sea, with great tides, with few and almost no harbours."

XIII. He then describes the manner in which the ships of his enemies were built, armed, and rigged. The only advantage his fleet had was, that it was swifter, but his enemies' fleet was better suited to the place, being more strongly built, and able to withstand the violence of storms, so that when the sea began to rage they could trust themselves to it, and they could bear a storm more easily, "and could stop more safely on the shallows and being left by the tide, they feared not the great stones and ragged rocks; the chances of all which things were to be dreaded by our ships.

XIV. Many towns being stormed, when Cæsar understood that so much labour was taken in vain, neither could the flight of the enemies be checked, the towns being taken, nor could they be injured, he resolved to wait for his fleet. When it assembled and was first seen by the enemy, about three hundred of their best equipped ships having set out from port, ranged themselves opposite our (ships)." The Romans won the sea-fight chiefly by the stratagem of cutting the riggings of the Gallic ships with long scythes, which rendered them unmanageable. He proceeds:—"The rest of the contest depended on bravery, in which Cæsar's soldiers easily excelled; and the more so because the affair was carried on in the sight of Cæsar and all the army, so that no deed of greater bravery could be concealed, for all the hills and higher places, whence there was a near view to the sea, were held by the army."

XV. From this Section we gather that, the yards of the Gallic ships being thrown down, some of them were boarded by the Romans, which, when the Gauls saw, they sought safety by flight, and the ships drifting with the wind, so great a calm suddenly came on that they could not move, which was most convenient in respect of the business to be done, for the Romans pursued and stormed each ship, so that very few out of all the number could get to land before the night came on. The battle was fought from the fourth hour until sunset.

"XVI. By which battle the war of the Veneti and of the whole maritime coast was finished," and they surrendered to Cæsar who resolved to be revenged on them, and therefore he put all the senate to death and sold the rest.

"XVI. Whilst these things were carried on, Q. T Sabinus arrived in the borders of the Unelli with the forces he had received from Cæsar. Viridovix commanded them (the Unelli) and had the chief power over all those states which had revolted, from whom he had collected an army and great supplies. And in these few days the Aulerci, Eburovices and Lexovii; their senate being put to death because they were unwilling to be advisers of the war,* shut their gates and joined Viridovix," with a great number of abandoned men and robbers.

"XVIII. Sabinus kept himself in camp convenient for all purposes, while Viridovix encamped opposite him at a distance of two miles." Viridorix daily offered battle, but Sabinus affected to be afraid, and so came into contempt with the Gauls, and, in fact, he did not think he ought to accept battle against so many, Cæsar being absent, who ought to hold the chief command, unless a favourable opportunity offered.

XIX. Sabinus, by the stratagem of sending a Gaul to the enemy, who affected to be a deserter but really was a spy, induces the Gauls to attack him in his fortified camp.

XX. Sabinus's camp was high and gradually steep from the bottom, about a thousand paces. Up this steep the Gauls hastened at great speed, and by reason of the steepness and the great burdens of fascines which they carried, became exhausted and out of breath. Sabinus gives the signal, the Romans charge, and the Gauls immediately turn their backs and are killed in great numbers, and the cavalry having pursued the rest, very few escaped. "Thus at the same time Sabinus was informed of the naval battle, and Cæsar of the victory of Sabinus, and all the states surrendered themselves immediately to Titurius."

By the kindness of a friend I have a copy and translation of part of Lib. iv. of Procopius, *De Bello Gothico*. Procopius is so wild in his statements, and so much at fault in his geography, that it is of no use to quote him.

---

## CHAPTER X.

### On the Significance of some of the Names of Places on the Sailing Charts of the Channel Islands.

146. It is common and notorious that places are often named from some peculiarity of form, position, colour, &c. The Bill of Portland, for example, is so called from its resemblance to the bill or beak of a bird, the northern part of the (so-called) Isle of Portland, forming the head of the bird, and Chesil Bank its neck. In case of any convulsion of nature destroying part of Portland, or of the Bank, it would be known that the head, or the neck, or the bill was missing, and thus *names* become *things*. Again, take Lizard Point, which is so called from the variety of colours of the Serpentine Rock, of which it is formed, resembling the colours of a Lizard,

* Observe that the senate were not put to death by Cæsar *after the two victories* because they had advised the war, but were killed by their own people because they would not advise the war—*during the affair with the Veneti*. We find in s. 20, the spy telling the Gauls that Cæsar himself is pressed with great difficulties by the Veneti, proving that the two battles went on simultaneously.

and the Serpentine Rock is also so called from its variety of colours resembling those of a serpent's back. In this case the latter name helps to an approximate date, for we know that the igneous rock called Serpentine, was only so called within the recent period since geology became a science. For it was called the Damnonium and Ocrinum Promontory in Ptolemy's time. Take another example. The Land's End is so called from being the extremity, or most western point, of England, but there was a period (probably in Ptolemy's time) when the land extended still farther towards the north-west; consequently the present Land's End can only have been so called since the second century. In this way every name on the Channel Islands' chart becomes a history, if we could only interpret it rightly. A few of these have been interpreted chiefly by eminent authorities, and have already been, or will now be, laid before the reader. I mention, as far as I know, what these authorities have done, taking their names in alphabetical order :—

(*a*). M. de Gerville, who studied the antiquities of Normandy, &c., forty years, and copied five or six thousand pages of MSS. and records. He did much in marine dredging.

(*b*). M. Edouard le Héricher, Regent de Rhetorique au College d'Avranches, author of a copious Anglo-Normande and other Glossaires, comprising more than 1,300 octavo pages, and evincing vast research from the very numerous quotations. And also author of "Avranchin Monumental et Historique," consisting of 750 octavo pages, and likewise affording internal evidence of great research.

(*c*). Mr. George Metivier, who has devoted great part of his life to philological studies, and whose accomplishments in that science are such that his countrymen and others are even now engaged in publishing an Anglo-Normande dictionary of his own, as a testimonial in his honour, with his portrait prefixed. I have done what I could to induce this gentleman, with whom I have had (to me) a most interesting correspondence, to pursue his inquiries into the origins of Channel Islands' topographical names. Dr. Hoskins, F.R.S., of Guernsey, is honorary secretary for promoting Mr. Metivier's testimonial.

(*d*). Professor Williams, of Lampeter College. He is Professor of Welsh there, and Britanny having been colonised by a Welsh speaking people, that language is one of the foundations of the Breton language.

Two of my friends who are also quoted, and myself, are amateurs. For my own part, I make no claim to be an expert in philological science, and therefore leave the various interpretations of words to the reader's own judgment.

147. With regard to the question whether any of the names on the charts are likely to have been given by caprice. It has been a custom from time immemorial for the whole agricultural populations of these islands, during certain periods, *which occur several times in every year*, and are called "vraic"-ing seasons, to sally forth almost *en masse*, in carts or boats, as the case requires to cut and bring away seaweed for manure and fuel.

They have names for far more rocks than are named on the charts, which have been, doubtless, handed down from generation to generation. Consequently any *original* name of a rock, or any appropriate name suggested by a special circumstance, may have been adopted from time to time by common consent. But it is submitted that any arbitrary name suggested merely by caprice, without any appropriateness, would scarcely have been adopted by the many, and transferred from generation to generation. Some of the following names have reference to the sinkings, others have not.

### NAMES OF PLACES ON THE CHANNEL ISLANDS CHARTS.

ANNOUET.—Mr. Metivier says (August 4, 1866), "Perhaps I may not have erred in presuming that '*Annouet*' was the Bas Breton '*Annaguet*,' *i.e.*, anathematised, doomed to destruction. Hints in such cases are always more or less useful. When 'le Petit Flambeau de la Mer' was compiled, this reef was very extensive. This confirms your previsions." The present writer has not found Annouet on any of the charts, but future readers will find it.

ALDERNEY.—Mr. Metivier says, speaking of Alderney, "As to Origny, there are several localities of that name in Normandy. In the oldest of our Celtic 'gebicten' (territories) Ireland, and in one of its romantic lakes there is an '*Arinia*' very near the point, a cape not unlike 'la Hague; Rjn (Rign) in Irish means a point." Hence the name Arinia for Alderney.

CASQUET ROCKS.—Again quoting Mr. Metivier: "Concerning *Casquet*, *i.e.*, *Casus rupes* in our Dictionnaire, I have not the slightest qualm." And again, "Casquet is one of the few topographical articles in our Dictionnaire. The termination 'quet' ought not to be noticed. Like *cascade*, casquet comes from the Italian 'cascare,' to fall, Latin 'casicare,' a verb found in Plautus.

If so, I suggest that *casus*, derived from *cado*, signifies "to tumble or fall down headlong"—see Ainsworth's Latin Dictionary—and, therefore, a very appropriate name, if the ground and rocks sunk as I say they did.

DESORMES BANK.—This bank is situated four or five miles north of the north-western angle of Jersey. Does it mean, as the name signifies, that the bank was formerly a "Bank of Elms?" We need not wonder at finding a modern French name attached to the place, because it probably first became sea as lately as 1356.

GRELETS.—May not the large group of rocks so called, situate north-east of the Minquiers, derive their name from *Grêler* to hail, which also means to *spoil*, *destroy*, or *ruin*. Because when the ground sunk the sea would wash away the soil, and *ruin* the tract as land. In Admiral White's "Sailing Directions" the Grelets are mentioned as "extensive shelves of sand, shingle and rocks."

GRUNE.—In addition to what has already been said in Art. 26 on this word, it may be farther observed that the word "Grumo," which only differs from "Grune" by the fraction of a letter—always signifies *some product of dry land.* For instance in Kelham's Dictionary of Norman words, we have "Grume," "Grun," *all sorts of grain.* And in Furetieres Universal Dictionary, "Grume" is said to signify *wood with the bark on*, in contradistiuction to wood squared. In M. le Héricher's "Origines Germaniques," we read:—Grune, du Sax. *Gruna*, que Du Cange définit "locus paludosusus" (a marshy place) existe, avec *Groin*, dans des localités maritimes, telles que la plupart des îlots des Minquiers, entre la Bretagne et la Nord qui sont appelés Grunes," &c. The word Grune does not appear as far as I can discover, on any part of the French coasts except in the Channel Islands Seas, which is of itself a remarkable circumstance.—See M. le Héricher's lucid and copious explantion in his "Origines Germaniques."

Grune has in one instance been applied to a *lofty* marine rock, which is as great a mistake as it would be to call a *mountain* a *valley*. The name has probably only been applied to that particular rock within the recent period since Grune became an obsolete word, understood only by antiquaries. Mr. Metivier understands the word to signify 'a ridge of pebbles, it is a matter of fact also, that the word is frequently applied to a low rock, for pebbles are scarce in these seas. And supposing (for argument's sake) that all the Grunes were once above high water, they would then have been covered with earth as nearly every yard of terra firma is, and they may have been as stated in Art. 26, "Grün" (German) *the Green*; or (as is said in the north of England) "Grund" for *ground.*

HOU.—This word has been treated of in Art. 42 preceding. In the excavations of British Tumuli in the Yorkshire Wolds, where many very ancient human bodies were interred and flint implements and several vases were at the same time found: these ancient sepulchres are thrice called "houe," as if they were *houses* of the dead. See *Times*, Oct. 24, 1866, p. 10. And three other barrows, are each called "houe" again, in the *Times* of Oct. 30, 1866, p. 10. And they are again called "houes" in the Summary as to the excavations, in the *Times* of Nov. 7.

JERSEY.—This island has had several names, and has even been without a name at all, as we have seen. Gibbon gives 409 as the date when Britain and Armorica revolted from the Romans;* Lingard says 411.† At and probably somewhat before that date, it was called in the Roman itinerary, *Cæsarea*. In the year 550 it was called *Augia* or *Augic*; it was also called *Augia* as lately as 757 (Art. 55).‡ During this space of two centuries it was also spoken of as "an island of the shore of Contances," as if it had no name; and it was called also *Brenciana*, vulgo *Brency*. Since when it has been called Gersui, Gersoi, and by Wace, the poet, in the twelfth centur., Gersui and Gersi. Matthew Paris calls it Gersea, and a MS. chronicle in the library at Oxford, Gerzy (Arts. 52, 53). Can this name be derived from *Gercer* (French), to chap, crack, or flaw, *i.e.*, referring to its separation from Normandy? In Art. 59 it has been shown

* Vol. v., p. 348. † Vol. 1., "Hist. of England," p. 88.

‡ *Augia* is derived from *Auge*, a trough, or hollow, and refers I think to the sunken space between Jersey and Normandy.

that *Brecy*, a name of Jersey in 582, means a "remnant," which is very significant of its separation from the main land. We find in Le Héricher's valuable "Histoire et Glossaire," among his Origines Latines, as follows:— "Gerchier, Gercer, en vieux Français *Garcer*, inciser, scarifier, litteralement avoir un eschare, Eschara, d'où Scarificare, découper la peau." In his Origines Celtiques he gives "Jersey appelé *Gersich*, dans les Actes de Saint Helier." The terminal *ey* in Jersey is of course Celtic for *island*." At the end of Art. 59 it was said by the present writer, in consequence of something stated on the authority of Tupper's "History of Guernsey," that the latest sinking between Jersey and Normandy must have taken place since about the year 1000. For 1000 we ought to read 912, if Mr. Mourant, as quoted in Art. 160, is to be depended on, and probably he is. Mr. Métivier thinks Gercer or Garcer too modern to have been the origin of the name Jersey.

MINQUIERS.—This is a very extensive group of rocks south of Jersey, now almost entirely devoid of earth. Mr. Métivier says:—"As to the Minquers, or Minguys, it is not improbable that they were *Minich'is, Minihis*, sanctuaries like that of Great Tugdual, at Treguer, and in the islet of Herm, Eremus."

Professor Williams, of Lampeter, states in a letter to J. Gwyn Jeffreys, Esq., F.R.S., dated August 22, 1866, who kindly handed the letter to me, as follows:—

"MINQUIERS.—The large group of rocks south of Jersey is, I have no doubt, the same word as the Welsh *Meincian* (= meynkyay), which is plural of *maine* (= maynk), which means anything raised, or elevated. The word as found in Gorseddfainc (v.), a throne; *i.e.*, a raised place used as a throne. Gorsedd mainc. It is applied to any kind of seat, especially of stone, and very commonly to a stone bench. In fact, 'bench' is akin to to it. It is applied as a proper name to a rock, rather a high one, on the roadside between this and Pontarddulais, Mainc Ivan Ddu. The plural meinciau is to this day the name of a high group of limestone rocks near Llanelly, on the Carmarthen road."

On this Mr. Métivier remarks:—"Your Celtic friend's suggestion is valuable. The verb *meincio*, to fix benches, is Welsh. Nevertheless, the original term is Teutonic; and *banc*; Kymr, banc, table, bank; Gaelic, *beinc, being*, bench. Having travelled through history, it has always been my wish to confirm etymologies, not by conjecture, but with the help of document and testimony. Let me assure you, notwithstanding that, ere I decide on the signification of *Minquais, Minguis*, I shall reconsider what I thought of that group of rocks being *Minich'is* (*Minihis*), 'lieux de franchise;' Breton *Minic'hi*, Actes de Bretagne, Tome 3, par Dom Hyacinthe Morice, Paris 1746. There are a few such, witness the "Black Book of Landaff" in Wales. Wales is a shocking misnomer. The church of St. Tugdual, contemporary of St. Sampson, the ruins of which I have seen in the islet of Herm, might have been a *minihi*. Its surplice fees were great."

A young friend, who has greatly distinguished himself at Oxford

University, says that "Minquiers" signifies "opening of the rocks," which would be a very appropriate name if correct, under the circumstances of the ground having sunk, for the earth upon and between the rocks would be washed away by the tides, and so leave *openings*. Another friend derives "quiers," the last syllable of Minquiers, from *quays*, or rather, he says, that the two words mean the same thing, the rocks being now like quays.

ORTAC, a remarkable round-topped rock on the north-west of Alderney. Mr. Metivier remarks: "The etymon *Tac*, signum, standard, mast, a conspicuous object, seems to be connected with *or*, limit, border; not only Celtic, but old French, *ore*. We have a great many *Istacs, Etacs*.

POMMIER.—About two miles N.E. of the Casquets, the *Pommier* banks appear on Capt. Richards's and other charts. If I was to say that *apple trees* once grew there, some ingenious gentleman would at once have an answer ready. Oh! no, he would say, the ship *Good Intent*, bound from Jersey to England with a cargo of cider apples, was wrecked there, and the name was in consequence of the quantities of apples which were seen floating about. He would forget for the moment, that *Pommier* means an apple tree, not an apple. I am led to this conclusion by the ingenious interpretations which some of my friends have found for the next name, *Roques aux Bois*. Mr. Métivier thinks Poummier an insular form of pommier, is a misnomer for Paulmier, a pilgrim.

ROQUES-AUX-BOIS.—At 3½ nautical miles in a direction nearly magnetic north-west from Grand Roque on the present westerly coast of Guernsey, and just within the 120ft. line of soundings at low water, mean springs (equinoctial tides fall three feet lower) there is a group of rocks, marked on the chart of Admiral White "Roque au Bois," and on Messrs. Sidney and Richards's chart, "Les Roques aux Bois," or rocks *at the wood*. And between those rocks and Grand Roque, and at two nautical miles from the latter is another rock called "Grune *du Bois*" on the former chart, and "Les Grunes de l'Ouest" on the latter chart, as if the two places had been *Woods*, or at all events low marshy land. A gentleman objects to this interpretation of "Bois," and supposes that when ships became, as it were, entangled among the groups of rocks now bearing the name of Bois, the sailors may have considered themselves according to the proverbial expression "in the woods," that is, in a difficulty how to get out from amongst the rocks. To this I answer: Considering that there are the actual trees of a forest or wood on the west of Guernsey, under the sand, *as far as extreme low water enables us to examine*. And considering that I saw at the farm-house, Fosse-aux-Fèves, near the west coast of Guernsey, many cart-loads of peat which had been dug near extreme low water, several feet below the sand, and abounding in tree roots; and, considering also the many proofs which have been given of sinkings of land in these parts, I think that the gentleman's objection is only an attempt (made, however, in perfect honesty and good faith), to explain away in the sense of getting rid of these remarkable names.

It has also been objected that the names may have been derived from *wreck*, or *drift wood*, having lodged there. To this I answer, that on Messrs. Sidney and Richards's chart, two of the Grunes de l'Ouest, are figured respectively as 10ft. and 6ft. above low water of mean Spring tides and consequently such wreck can only have rested there at most for about two hours, because the rising tide would set it adrift again. I think such brief and rare events can never have had force sufficient to be the origin of the names of these rocks. For wreck wood coming *from distant parts over the Atlantic*, is, I have reason to believe, of rare occurrence on the west of Guernsey.

Sept. 5, 1861.—The present writer saw at the farm-house Fosse-aux-Fèves, near the west coast of Guernsey, many cart loads of gorban, or peat, which had been dug up near extreme low water. It was buried several feet below the sand. This peat abounded with tree roots; a few of the largest were as thick as a man's arm. This circumstances appears to be significant that the peat may extend to an unknown distance below extreme low water. A crucial test would be to take numerous borings in the Channel Islands' Seas, where sinking is believed, for the reasons stated in these papers, to have taken place. This would probably cost not less th[illegible]00—an expense which the writer would not feel justified in incurring.

These are specimens of Channel Islands' sea names. They will serve to enable the reader to judge whether any light can be thrown on our subject by interpreting names. Have we any choice but to believe that there was a "Bois," or wood, at three and a-half miles out into the Atlantic, and to account for its having been so strangely situated in the [illegible]? And is it not utterly incredible that these curious and very significant names should all be the results of mere accident? If the names we have been considering have really any significance at all, then it would follow that such comparatively modern words as Roque au Bois, Pommier, Ormes, &c., would mean that the events they seem to indicate must have occurred within a comparatively recent period. And, in fact, we have already had the year 1356 as the date of the most recent sinkings.

---

## CHAPTER XI.

SINKINGS AT THE SCILLY ISLES. PROBABLE FOUNDATION FOR THE TRADITION OF THE LIONESSE COUNTRY. ON THE IDENTIFICATION OF THE ISLE OF IOTIS. SINKINGS ON THE SOUTH-WEST COASTS OF ENGLAND.

148. If I can succeed in convincing the reader that since the commencement of the Christian era, sinkings have taken place at the Scilly Isles, and between them and Cornwall, and at various places along all the English south-west coast, which lies west of the third meridian of west longitude; taking also into consideration the sinkings on the French coasts previously stated, he will probably be willing to believe that there was a sinking, or sinkings, which extended all the way across the English Channel. If I am right in affirming that no sufficient cause has been suggested for the neutrality in Chapter XIV., except that of the necessary neutrality of the sunken country, we shall, at any rate, have established a sinking for *more than* one-half the distance from Normandy to Cornwall. For the neutral space extended in all directions seaward, according to Poingdestre, for a distance of about 12 leagues (or about 30½ nautical miles) from each of the islands of Jersey, Guernsey, and Alderney. In my opinion the Deeps in the centre of the English Channel are caused by unequal subsidences in the sea-bottom; and no time is so likely for these to have occurred as when subsidences were taking place on the French coasts opposite. On a future occasion I will attempt to prove that this must have been so. These Deeps are, roughly speaking, about fifty per cent. deeper than the sea-bottom adjoining them.

149. We may be sure that the Scilly Isles afford proofs of considerable subsidences since the time of Diodorus. He says:—"Far beyond Lusitania [Portugal] very much tin is dug out of the islands of the ocean nearest to Iberia [Spain], which, from the tin, are named Cassiterides." * Strabo says:—"The Cassiterides are ten in number, and lie near each other in the ocean towards the north from the haven of the Artabri [who lived in the north-west of Spain]. One of them is desert, but the others are inhabited by men in black cloaks, clad in tunics reaching to the feet, girt about the breast, and walking with staves, thus resembling the Furies we see in tragic representations. They subsist by their cattle, leading for the most part a wandering life. Of the metals, they have tin and lead, which, with skins, they barter with the merchants for earthenware, salt, and brazen vessels. Formerly, the Phœnicians alone carried on this traffic from Gades [Cadiz], concealing the passage from every one; and when the Romans followed a certain ship-master, that they also might find the market, the ship-master, of jealousy, purposely ran his vessel upon a shoal, leading on those who followed him into the same destructive disaster. He himself

* Diodorus, Paris edition, Simon Colinæus, 1501, p. 192.

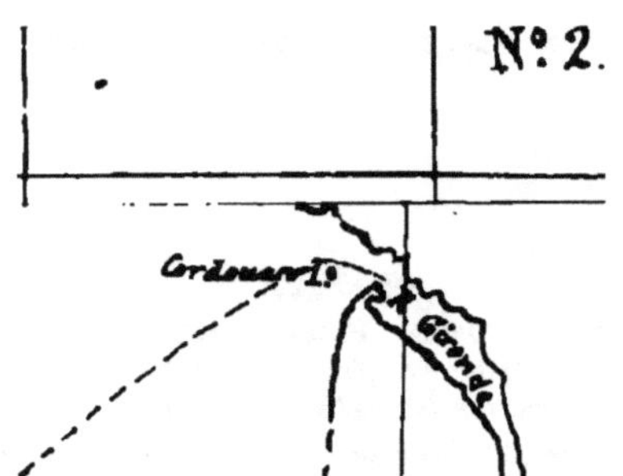
Nº 2.
Gironde

escaped by means of a fragment of the ship, and received from the state the value of the cargo he had lost. The Romans, nevertheless, by frequent efforts, discovered the passage; and as soon as Publius Crassus, passing over to them, perceived that the metals were dug out at a little depth, and that the men were peaceably disposed, he declared it to those who already wished to traffic in this sea for profit, although the passage was longer than that to Britain."* On the contrary, the passage was and is a little *shorter*. Strabo says, also, on the authority of Posidonius, that "tin is not found upon the surface, as authors commonly relate, but that it is dug up; and that it is produced both in places among the barbarians who dwell beyond the Lusitanians, and in the islands Cassiterides; and that from the Britannic islands it is carried to Marseilles."†—which is so far corroborative of Diodorus's passage about extracting tin in Cornwall (Art. 132). Strabo clearly identifies the Cassiterides with the Scilly Isles, by saying:—"Northward and opposite to the Artabri are the islands denominated Cassiterides, situated in the high seas, but under the same latitude as Britain."‡ And D. P. Alexandrinus, who flourished in the time of Augustus, says, in his Geography, line 599, &c.:—"But beyond the sacred promontory [Cape St. Vincent] which they affirm is the extremity of Europe, in the islands Hesperides, where the source of tin is, the rich children of the illustrious Iberi dwell." The Scilly Isles being nearly north of the west coast of Spain, they must have been meant.

150. The Rev. W. Borlase, M.A., F.R.S., clearly proves§ that "the slow advances and depredations of the sea will by no means suffice," to account for the great changes in the Scilly Isles since the times of the Romans. He says the present inhabitants are all new comers, and he nowhere found any remains of the Phœnician, Roman, or Grecian art, all the antiquities are of the rudest Druid times. "All the islands (several of which are now without cattle or inhabitants) by the remains of hedges, walls, foundations of many contiguous houses, and a great number of sepulchral barrows, show that they have been fully cultivated and inhabited. That they were inhabited by Britons is past all doubt, not only from their vicinity to England but from the Druid monuments." There are "several rude stone pillars, circles of stones erect ‖ kist-vaens without number, rock-basins, tolmêns, all monuments common in Cornwall and Wales, and equal evidences of the antiquity, religion, and origin of the old inhabitants. They have also British names for their little islands, tenements, and creeks." He then inquires how the ancient inhabitants came to vanish? And states that two causes occurred to his mind while at Scilly, namely, "The manifest encroachments of the sea, and as manifest a subsidence of the land. . . . The continual advances which the sea makes on the low lands are obvious, and within the last thirty years have been very con-

* Strabo, book iii., chap. 5, sec. 11.
† Strabo, book iii., chap 2, sec. 9.
‡ Strabo, book ii., chap. 5, sec. 15.
§ Phil. Trans. R.S., 1753 Vol. 10, p. 324, &c.
‖ The circles of stones are not necessarily British. Many circles are in the Channel Islands, which were not British until the year 1066.

siderable." The italics in the following passages are by the present writer. "Again, the flats, which stretch from one island to another, are plain evidences of a former union subsisting between many now distinct islands. The flats between Trescau, Brêhar, and Sampson are quite dry at a spring tide, and men easily pass dry-shod from one island to another over sand banks, *where, on the shifting of the sands, walls, and ruins are frequently discovered*, on which at full sea there are 10 or 12 feet of water. But no circumstance can show the great alterations which have happened in the number and extent of these islands, more than this, he says, viz., that the isle of Scilly, from which the little cluster of these cyclades takes its name, is no more at present than a high rock of about a furlong over, whose cliffs hardly anything but "birds can mount, and whose barrenness would never suffer anything but sea birds to inhabit it." Walls and ruins are frequently to be seen on the shores, "foundations which were probably 6ft. above high water mark, now 10ft. under, which together make a difference as to the level of 16ft. *The land between Sampson and Trescau sunk at least 16ft.*, at a moderate computation. This subsidence must have been followed by a sudden inundation, and this inundation is likely not only to have destroyed a great part of the inhabitants, but to have terrified others who survived into a total desertion of their shattered islands. By this means, as I imagine, he says, "That considerable people who were the Aborigines, and carried on the tin trade with the Phœnicians, Greeks, and Romans were extirpated. . . . There are no mines to be seen in any of these islands, but only one lode (so we call our tin veins) in Trescau island, and the workings here are very inconsiderable and *not ancient*. It must therefore be matter "of wonder where the Phœnicians, Greeks, and Romans could have found such a plenty of that useful metal. Whatever resources they had from Cornwall, formerly reckoned probably among the Cassiterides [?] *great part of their tin must doubtless have come from these islands;* but where it was found is uncertain. Nothing now appears *above ground* which can satisfy such an inquiry. . . . The question then is, what is become of these mines? and how shall this question be answered but by confessing that *the land in which these mines were, is now sunk, and buried under the sea.* Tradition seems to confirm this, there being a strong persuasion in the western parts of Cornwall, that formerly there existed a large country between the Land's End and Scilly, now laid many fathoms under water. The particular arguments by which they support this tradition may be seen in Mr. Carew's "Survey of Cornwall," p. 3, and in the last edition of "Camden," p. 11. I have not access to Mr. Carew's work. Camden is quoted at the commencement of Art. 114. Mr. Borlase concludes as follows: "But though there are no evidences to be depended on of any ancient connection of the Land's End and Scilly, yet *that the cause of that inundation*, which destroyed much of these islands, *might reach also to the Cornish shores is extremely probable, there being several evidences of a like subsidence o the lands in Mount's Bay*. [See the abstract of his paper in Art. 113.] The principal anchoring place, called a lake [Guavas lake three miles west of the Mount] is now a haven or open harbour. The Mount, from its Cornish name, signifying a grey rock in the wood, but now at full tide it is half a mile in the sea, and not a tree near it."* The sinkings of the Scilly isles are not necessarily limited to so little as 16ft., because the walls which are now covered 10 or 12ft. at high water may once, before they sunk, have been *many feet* above high water.

151. Dr. Paris, the supposed author of the volume mentioned in the foot note,† says at p. 92, that the Scilly Isles are said to be mentioned by D. Siculus, Strabo, and Solinus. They must, however, have undergone some material revolution since the age of these writers, for we fail in every attempt to reconcile their present state with the description which they have transmitted to us, and what is very unaccountable, not a vestige of any ancient mine can be discovered in the islands, except in one part of Trescau, and these remains are so limited that they rather give an idea of an attempt at discovery than of extensive and permanent mining."

* Dr. Paris, to whom the idea of modern subsidence seems never to have occurred, can only account for the great traffic in tin from the Cassiterides by supposing that under that name St. Just on the main-land must have been included. He proceeds, "We are strongly inclined to believe that the tin of those days came, in part at least, from the opposite coast of St. Just, but of this we shall hereafter speak more fully." And then at p. 141, he says, "St. Just has been considered by Mr. Carne, and not without probability, as having constituted the principal portion of what "was formerly known under the name of the Cassiterides."

152. At p. 92, &c., he says: "In the time of Strabo we learn that the number of these islands did not exceed ten, whereas at present they are upwards of one hundred and forty, but of which the following only are inhabited, viz., St. Mary's, St. Agnes, St. Martin's, Trescou, Bryer, and Sampson. It is curious that the name of the cluster should have been derived from one of the smallest islets (Scilly), whose surface does not exceed an acre." He then says that St. Mary's contains 1,600 acres and nearly a thousand inhabitants, the remaining islets about another thousand inhabitants. From the census of 1851 it appears that the population of Isle St. Mary was then 1,668, Tresco 416, St. Martin 211, St. Agnes 204, Bryher 118, Sampson 10; total 2,627 in the six inhabited islands.

Mr. Carnes' and Dr. Paris's argument, that because there is no mining (worth naming) in the Scilly Isles now, that we must therefore consider part of the main-land at and about St. Just as having been referred to by the ancients under the name of the "Cassiterides," is clearly inadmissible. Strabo's and the Rev. W. Borlase's testimonies, already quoted, distinctly prove that there is no necessity whatever to adopt any such improbable and inaccurate views. It is evident the Isles have sunk, and the ancient mines are lost, and that tin was also got in Cornwall.

154. Camden says‡ the Scilly Isles are called by Antoninus, *Sigdeles;*

* It measures ½ mile on the Ordnance map.
† "Guide to Mount's Bay and the Land's End," by a Physician. 1824.
‡ [illegible]

by Sulpitius Severus (an ecclesiastical and historical writer, who died A.D. 420), *Sillinæ*; by Solinus, *Silures*; by Dionysius Alexandrinus, *Hesperides*; by Festus Avienus (who lived in the latter part of the fourth century), *Ostrymnides*; by several Greek writers, including Diodorus, and by Pliny the elder, *Cassiterides*;* and Strabo has told us† that Publius Crassus "saw that the metals were dug out at a little depth" in the Cassiterides; this was about 57 B.C. So that these Isles were well known to the ancients.

155. In viewing the whole scenery of the stern western coast of Cornwall, "it is impossible," says De Luc, "not to be struck with the idea that the bed of the sea is the effect of a vast subsidence, in which the strata were broken off in the edge of what, by the retreat of the sea towards the sunken part, became a continent; the many small islands, or rocks of granite, appear to be the memorials of the land's abridgment, being evidently parts of the sunken strata remaining more elevated than the rest."‡ That is to say, in De Luc's opinion, the Lionesse country may really have existed.

ON THE IDENTIFICATION OF THE ISLE OF ICTIS.

156. We need only go back about to the time of "Domesday Book" for the origin of the Cornish name of St. Michael's Mount—"Carreg Coedh yn clos," *i e*, Rock of the wood in the enclosure.§ William Camden, who was born in 1550, and died 9th November, 1623, proves that the Cornish language had not become quite extinct even so lately as in his time. He says, speaking of the *Damnonii*, or inhabitants of Devon and Cornwall:—"The old Cornish tongue is almost quite driven out of the country, being spoken only by the vulgar in two or three parishes at the Land's End, and they, too, understand the English. In other parts little or nothing is known of it. 'Tis a good while since that only two men could write it; one of them, no scholar nor grammarian, was blind with age."‖

In the "Penny Encyclopædia," too, edition 1837, heading "Cornwall," we learn that:—"In the reign of Edward VI. a new revolt broke out connected with the religious revolution of that period.¶ The Cornish men took up arms to sustain the Roman Catholic church, and besieged Exeter; but were forced to raise the siege, and at last, though not without difficulty, were subdued. The change of the religious institutions of the country led to the change of the common language of Cornwall; the people, for the most part of British descent, with comparatively few Saxons settled amongst them, had retained a language of their own, a dialect of the Celtic." [Camden gives the Lord's Prayer in Cornish, Welsh, and Armoric respectively, each of which languages resembles the others.**] "The introduction of the English church service paved the way for its gradual deline. When Carew published his 'Survey of Cornwall,' in 1602, it was going fast into disuse. 'The English speech,' says he, 'doth still encroach upon it, and hath driven the same into the uttermost skirts of the shire. Most of the inhabitants can

* From κασσίτερος, tin. † Art. 205.
‡ "Guide to Mount's Bay, &c.," p. 89.
§ See Mr. Métivier's Letter, Aug. 4, 1866.
‖ "Britannia," edition 1722, p. 8.
¶ Edward VI. reigned from 1547 to 1553.
** "Britannia," 1722, p. 8.

speak no word of Cornish, but very few are ignorant of English, and yet some so affect their own, as to a stranger they will not speak English; for if, meeting them by chance, you inquire the way, or any such matter, your answer shall be, *Mee a navidra cousna Sawzneck*, *i.e.*, I can speak no Saxonage. In the reign of Charles I. [1625 to 1649] some aged people near Penryn were quite ignorant of the English language. In the early part of the last century [the eighteenth] Cornish was still spoken by the fisher men and market women near the extreme southern point of the country. At present this ancient tongue is the study of the scholar and antiquary. A few MSS. in it are extant, the most remarkoble of which are some interludes, partly written in the fifteenth century.' "

157. *The Anglo-Saxons in England.*—It will now be convenient for various purposes connected with our subject to give a slight sketch, with dates, of a few of the principal events connected with this people. When the Saxons first began to have a name in the world they lived in the Cimbrica Chersonesus, which we now call Denmark; where they are settled by Ptolemy, who is the first that makes mention of them.* About the middle of the fourth century all the people from the Rhine to the northern extremity of Jutland, were called Saxons. The Jutes or Getes also lived in Jutland, and they with the Angles and Saxons afterwards re-peopled the better portion of Britain.† Camden places the Angles on the north-west of the Rhine in the first century, in Westphalia, &c.; from which Gibbon and Lingard do not differ. In 449, Hengist and Horsa came from Oldenburg, the north-western part of Hanover, and the north of Holland, by request of Vortigern, the most powerful of the several contemporaneous British kings, to assist him to repel the Picts and Scots, and for six years they served him with fidelity. This is the very earliest period at which the Saxon name *Mychel-stop*,‡ or Michael's-place could have been given to Mount St. Michael, but the date of its being first so named is probably later. We find that the third kingdom of the Heptarchy, namely that of the *West Saxons*, which finally swallowed up all the rest, was established by Cedric after a great battle at Charford in 519, and it comprised Hampshire and Berkshire, and, within less than two centuries after all the other counties on their west. Cedric associated his son Kenric with him in the regal dignity, and bestowed upon his nephews the subordinate sovereignty of the Isle of Wight, and died in 534.§ (The Isle of Wight will be referred to again hereafter more than once.) Ina, a subsequent king of the West Saxons, at the head of a resistless army added in 710 several districts to his western provinces, and expelled after long struggles, Geraint, king of Cornwall. King Athelstan also subdued Cornwall at the beginning of the ninth century. *Danegelt*, was a tax collected to defend England against the Danes, or to pay them. Mount St. Michael was called

* "Camd. Brit.," p. clvi.
† Lingard, "Hist. England," vol. 1, p. 86.
‡ "Magna Britannica," vol. 1., p. 309. And Camden's map.
§ See "Lingard's Hist.," vol. 1., p. 96, 124, &c. He quotes Henry of Huntingdon and the *Saxon Chronicle*.

*Dinsol.** (King Edward the Confessor, who reigned from 1042 to January 5th, 1066, when he died and was succeeded by Harold), gave in 1044 to an abbey of Benedictines on St. Michael's Mount, founded previously; † the Mount and all its appendages. And Robert, Earl of Moriton, annexed [the whole or a part of the Mount and its appendages] to God and the Church of St. Michel de periculo maris in Normandy, about the year 1085. It appears very probable that the Cornish Mount was first called Mount Saint Michael, after its chief, the Norman Monastery of Mont St. Michel, at this last date.

158. In the important passage now to be quoted from "Domesday Book" I have translated the words "nunquam geldaverunt" as signifying, 'never paid the Danish tax,' which is their correct signification. Places of worship were exempt from this tax.

"DOMESDAY BOOK."

159. At the end of "Domesday Book," vol. 2, is annexed a cotemporaneous memorandum in abbreviated Latin (in which the book itself is wholly written) as follows:—"In the 1086th year of the Lord's incarnation, being the twentieth year of the kingdom of William, this description was made. Not only through these three counties, ‡ but also through the others," *i.e.*, other counties.

This authentically fixes the date. And I will try to satisfy the reader that at the date named St. Michael's Mount was not yet an island, but was joined to the mainland of Cornwall.

I am fortunate enough to possess a fac-simile photographic copy of the Cornwall part (which calls itself "Cornvalge") of "Domesday Book," printed at the Ordnance Map Office, Southampton, in 1861, from page 2 of which the following is a correct translation:—

"THE LAND OF SAINT MICHAEL.

"Keiwal holds the church of St. Michael. Brismar was holding it in the reign of King Edward § There are 2 hides which never paid the Danish tax. The land is 8 carucates. There is 1 carucate with 1 villan, ‖ and two bordarii, ¶ and 10 acres of pasture. Value, 20 shillings. Of these 2 hides Earl Moriton took away 1 hide, value 20 shillings."

At p. xi. of Domesday Book there appear in the descriptive list of the many estates of Earl Moriton corresponding particulars of the 1 hide which he had taken away.

Now, in the first place, "Domesday Book" gives no reason whatever to suppose that St. Michael's Mount was an *Island* (neither does the Saxon name, Michael's Place, in Art. 157). But there is a good deal of negative evidence to the contrary. Firstly, on page 3, "The land of the Church of Tavestoch" is mentioned exactly in the same way as "The land of Saint Michael" above; though the former is 15 miles from the sea—there being

* "Magna Britannica," vol. i., p. 309.
† "Penny Cyclop.," 1837, Art. Cornwall.
‡ Essex, Norfolk, and Suffolk, which occupy vol. 2.
§ The Confessor. ‖ Villani, inhabitants of villages.
¶ Dwellers near the manor house, or perhaps cottagers.

no mention of "Island" in either case. And in every case while "annoting" those holding possessions ("tenentes") in "Cornvalge," as—"King William, the Bishop of Execestre, the Church of Tanestoch, the Churches of certain Saints, Earl Moriton, Judhail de Totenais, Goscelmus"—there is an entire absence of any mention of Island or Islands on any of the coasts of Cornwall, just as if there had been then no Islands on the coast of Cornwall of sufficient extent to be worthy of mention. Secondly, it is the custom in "Domesday Book," *when a place is an island to call it so*. For example, in vol. 1, folio 75, "Dorsete" (Dorset) we have:—

"The land of the King.

"The King holds the island which is called PORLAND. King Edward held it in his life."

And, again, in Domesday, vol. 1, fol. 396:—

"Hantescire" (Hampshire).

"These lands below written lie in the Isle of Wit" (Wight).

But, thirdly, the Mount could hardly have been an island in 1086, because it then contained at least eight times as much land as it does at present, which probably connected it with the mainland, from which it is even now only ½ mile distant. The truth, Sir Henry Ellis says, seems to be that a hide, a yardland, a knight's fee, &c., contained no certain number of acres, but varied in different places at different times. General Introduction p. 34, there are "four virgates in each hide, and thirty acres to make a virgate." At p. 51, by the Statutum de Admensuratione Terrarum 5½ yards of the Ulna regis or yard of 3 feet, were to make a perch and (p. 50) the elementary acre was 40 perches by 4 perches, as now. At p. 47 it is stated that the hide varied according to different places; but that was afterwards. For we find, at p. 47, Bishop Kennett says, in 1169, "a hide of land at Chesterton contained 64 acres." But, taking the smallest of the following carucates, the 8 carucates would have amounted to 480 acres:—

| | | | | |
|---|---|---|---|---|
| Ibid. | Carucate temp. Richard I. | ...................... | 60 | acres. |
| | Ditto | ...................... | 100 | „ |
| | Ditto Edward I. | ...................... | 180 | „ |
| | Ditto 32 Edward III. (Oxon) | ...... | 112 | „ |
| | Ditto Ditto | Middleton... | 150 | „ |

The hide is generally supposed to have been equal to 120 acres. It was the measure of land in the Confessor's reign, the carucate that to which it was reduced by the Conqueror's new standard. The carucate was as much arable land as could be managed with one plough and the beasts belonging thereto in a year; having meadow, pasture, and houses for the householders, and cattle belonging to it.

Now Sir Charles Lyell gives no less than three views of St. Michael's Mount. Two of them are taken looking south from the coast of Cornwall, one at high and the other at low water. The third view is taken about from Penzance, looking east. He also describes it as consisting chiefly of granite, with some slate rock, and 195ft. high, with precipitous sides,*

* "Principles of Geology," 1867, p. 539-541.

which his three sketches corroborate, as does the shading on the Ordnance Map. And it is quite clear that so far from there being now eight carucates, *i. e.*, several hundred acres of arable land, *there can hardly be a single acre capable of being ploughed, because the ground is too steep.* Taking the hide at 120 acres, the whole area of the mount (two hides) would be 240 acres. At present the whole area is usually stated at 70 acres,* but by the Ordnance Map 1839, which is probably correct, it measures barely 30 acres. So that there are 210 acres missing, how can we account for them except by supposing that the Mount extended further, perhaps in every direction? There can have been no clerical error, for the land of St. Michael is stated to have been two hides, and of each hide particulars are given, and also particulars of the hide taken away by Earl Moriton. Of the first hide we learn details, namely, that there were eight carucates, or as much as eight ploughs could cultivate, one carucate with one villan or villager, two bordarii with their cottages, and probably each a garden, besides ten acres of pasture. The whole of which was worth annually 20 shillings, equal to £30 at the present day. Of the two hides Earl Moriton took the other, which was also worth 20 shillings, or £30 of present money, for the purpose, as we have learnt from another source, of giving it to the Monastery of Mont St. Michel, in Normandy.

160. The great care that was taken to procure correct and authentic information for the survey, precludes the belief that there can have been any material error in the measurement. Sir Henry Ellis informs us in General Introduction, p. 6, that "for the adjusting of this survey, certain commissioners called the King's Justiciaries, were appointed. Those for the Midland Counties at least were the then Bishops of Lincoln, the Earl of Buckingham, Henry de Ferrers, and Adam the brother of Eudo Dapifer, "who probably associated to them some principal person on each shire." And he quotes a curious document showing that the information was given *on oath*. At p. vii., the Inquisitors, it appears, upon the oaths of the Sheriffs, the Lords of each Manor, the Presbyters of every Church, the Reves of every Hundred, the Bailiffs, and six villans of every village, were to inquire into all the necessary particulars. Was not this taking all possible means to obtain correct information? Is it credible that the Mount should have been said to have contained two hides, if it only contained, as at present, one-fourth part of a hide?

We have thus ascertained the fact, that during the last eight centuries, 210 acres, less a small amount, suppose, washed away by the tides, have disappeared, and have to be accounted for. For it would be mere trifling to suppose that the Domesday survey made the Mount eight times as extensive as its real size. If we were to take the largest measure of a carucate our eight carucates of arable land would amount to no less than 1,440 acres. Whereas at present there can hardly be a single acre of land in the whole islet, capable of being ploughed, for it is too steep and rocky!

161. The following accounts of a peculiar and very destructive *inunda-*

---

* See Census, 1851, vol. 1, Div. 5, p. 64, and "Penny Cyclop." 1837.

*tion* (shall we call it?) are not a little remarkable, occurring as it did, thirteen years *after* the Domesday Survey. Florence of Worcester says: "On the third day of the nones of November, 1099, the sea came out upon the shore, and buried towns and men very many, and oxen and sheep innumerable." The still more quaint and equally interesting Saxon Chronicle for that year, corroborates Florence to the very day, for the third day of the nones of November is the 11th, by saying, "On St. Martin's mass day, the 11th of November, sprung up so much of the sea flood, and so myckle harm did, as no man minded that it ever afore did, and *there was the ylk day a new moon*.* This is speaking very much to the purpose. The catastrophes cannot be referred to the great height of the tide, for *the highest spring tides do not occur until several tides after the new moon*, and the 11th of November is several weeks after the Equinox. Have we any choice, therefore, since the average sea-level does not alter, except to believe that the ground sunk, and so enabled the waters to come upon the shore, and to bury very many towns and men, and innumerable oxen and sheep, and to do an unprecedented amount of harm?

162. December, 1866, Mr. Pengelly gave me a printed copy of his paper, of which I am a great admirer, "On the submerged forests of Torbay," and he also lent me his important M.SS., "On the insulation of St. Michael's Mount in Cornwall," and stated that he should feel obliged if I would treat it as freely as if printed, and that I was to use any part of it for any purpose for which it would suit. There was only one way of responding to so much voluntary kindness and liberality, and that was to beg of him to use the same freedom with all publications and M.SS of the present writer, which might come into his hands. This was immediately done, and two numbers of THE ARTIZAN, containing portions of what now appears in this volume, were sent to him, as well as a MS. copy of another portion. And as soon as this chapter shall have been written out, a MS. copy will be made and sent for his acceptance,† since it is obvious that a free intercommunication between gentlemen who have studied the same subject, and who care for nothing but the truth, as in the present case, must be of great advantage.

163. Mr. Pengelly states, in "Submerged Forests of Torbay," that "Florence of Worcester (which he corrects in a letter, to William of Worcester, 1478) expressly asserts that St. Michael's Mount was formerly five or six miles from the sea [the ancient coast line on the map is drawn accordingly], and enclosed with a very thick wood, and, therefore, called in British, 'Carreg lug en Kug,' 'Le Hore Rock, in the Wodd.'" And he gives a reference as in the foot-note.‡ In his MS. (p. 7), he arrives at the following conclusion, in which I entirely agree with him, as to St. Michael's Mount:—"The ancient designation then does betoken a change in the geography of the district—a change not only within the human period, but since Cornwall was occupied by a people who spoke the language which

* Florence and the Chronicle are both quoted from "Milner's Gallery of Nature," 1846, p. 387. See also "Principles of Geology," 1867, p. 387.
† Sent to Mr. Pengelly, Jan. 26, 1867.
‡ "Trans. Roy. Geo. Soc. of Cornwall," vol. ii., p. 134.

was tardily supplanted by the Anglo-Saxon." From his double reason "that nineteen hundred years ago the Mount was not merely insulated, but that it possessed a harbour," I dissent, for the reasons contained in the previous part of this chapter, and elsewhere in the present volume. His two reasons are, first, that a certain rocky ledge, now known by the name "Hogus," which lies parallel and adjacent to the Causeway, leading at low water from Marazion to the Mount," is *old* Scandinavian, and signifies "a rock in or near a wood, adjacent to water, and used for sacrificial purposes." Mr. George Métivier, of Guernsey, who has again and again given me ample reason to believe in his great philological knowledge, and his willingness to communicate it, says, "*Hogus* (in Guernsey *hougue*, French *hogue*, neo-Latin *hoga*) sometimes denotes a stony or quarriable knoll. *Liber Sharburnensis* apud Spelman, says:—'Idem Cannutus* dedit prædicto Edwino Sharburnensi. . . . . quemdam collem et *Hogum* petrosum.'" There is also, in St. Peter's parish, Jersey, a good house called la *Hogue*, near a mass of quarriable crystalline clay-slate. From all which it may be inferred that if "Hogus" is middle aged, it is also modern, which of course only carries us back at most to the middle ages, not to Diodorus's time. Mr. Pengelly's second reason (see his M.S., p. 10, 11), if derived from Diodorus's passage, given in Art. 132, and from Dr. Barham's view, who is said by Sir C. Lyell to have "shown that the Ictis of Diodorus not only answers geographically to St. Michael's Mount, but is just such a promontory as would have been selected by foreign traders as well adapted for defence."† Now, on the other hand, even if the coast had remained unaltered ever since Diodorus's time—a large and unjustifiable supposition—the Roman tin-transporting ships need not by any means have been confined to St. Michael's Mount as a harbour, because, as the Rev. W. Borlase well observes (Art. 150), Guavas Lake is the principal anchoring place. And, consequently, we ought in fairness to believe that the exportation of tin cannot have taken place wholly or even chiefly, from St. Michael's Mount. All these considerations are a heavy blow and a great discouragement to the belief that the Mount is Ictis.

Dr. Barham quotes from the Saxon chronicle the particulars of the inundation of Nov. 11th, 1099; and of another on the same authority, in 1014:—"This year (1014) on Michaelmas eve, Sept. 28th, came the great sea-flood, which spread over this land, and ran up as far as it never did before, overwhelming many towns, and an innumerable multitude of people." Now, astronomers inform us, that about the year 1250 the sun was at its nearest to the earth on the shortest day,‡ and the natural consequences would be (and was historically) that the Swiss glaciers were then exposed to greater heat than any other which they have experienced during the Christian period, and consequently the greatest melting of ice took place then.§

* Canute reigned 1014—1030.
† "Principle of Geology," 1867, p. 542.
‡ "Outlines of Astronomy," 1864, Art. 3695.
§ Principles of Geology, 1867, p. 276.

But this circumstance had nothing to do with the natural height of the tides, and even if it had had to do with them in 1250, that, of course, would not have accounted for unusually high tides on September 28th, 1014, or on November 11th, 1099, nor could there have been equinoctial tides at either of those dates. We cannot get rid of these catastrophes either, by refusing to believe them merely because they do not agree with this or that theory. No other course is open to us I submit, except to explain the immense destruction of towns and people by accepting as a fact, that the ground sunk at those dates. I propose to call it a *sinking* for the future.

He says that an argument for recent changes in the Mount has been found in a charter of King Edward the Confessor, in which St. Michael is spoken of as being *juxta mare*, and that he has seen this translated *near the sea*, but he submits that a more correct rendering would be, *by the sea*, a phrase he thinks sufficiently descriptive of its present situation. Now, on the contrary, I contend that the translation *near the sea* is the correct one; if the Mount had then been insulated, the correct expression would have been *in* or *on* the sea.—See Littleton's Latin Dictionary and White and Riddle's Dictionary.

In order to account for the submarine trees in Mount's Bay, Dr. Barham has recourse to "the low district" theory, but, unfortunately, this district like, that of Guernsey, (Art. 11) would have inevitably filled with water in less than eighteen months, so as to become a lake, which would have rendered it impossible for the trees to grow where they really did grow. "I suppose," he says, "that the lowlands extended about half a mile further towards the sea than they do now, and were there defended from this dangerous neighbour by a ridge of higher land, the situation of which is now indicated by the Long Rocks and others thereabout." Now this mention of the Long Rocks fixes the position of his supposed low district. They are shore rocks between Marazion and Penzance, and the Ordnance map shows that the low district can only have been of trifling extent, namely three quarters of a mile long by half a mile broad; and there is a brook draining 925 acres of land (including the low district itself) which falls into the sea at Long Rocks, which would of course have flowed day and night from year end to year end, into the supposed low district. Let us suppose the average annual rainfall to be 30in., which is little enough, for Cornwall is a rainy country by reason of its hills intercepting the rain clouds as they drift up from the Atlantic. We must, therefore, take about 16in. in depth as the annual "flow" off the land, as explained in Art. 12, both Guernsey and Cornwall consisting of igneous rocks. This would give a supply, in less than eighteen months, which would have filled the low district to overflowing, supposing it to have averaged 7½ft. deep, and then the surplus would have flowed over the lowest part of the "ridge," this lake would, of course, have prevented the trees from ever growing. It is submitted, therefore, that the low district theory must be abandoned. To account for the many other instances of submarine trees, which will be presently proved to exist, on the south-western coasts, I suppose Dr. Barham would have proposed many more low districts, which must now also be abandoned.

Though Dr. Barham admits "encroachments" of the sea, quoting the Rev. W. Borlase's statement (Art. 133), and two submersions in the years 1014 and 1099, he yet uses the following inadmissible argument in the form of a question. "It is admitted," he says, "that the Mount has been pretty much what it is for at least 800 years [No]; what hinders, then, but that it may just as likely have maintained* its ground for 2,000 years, or even a longer period?" I answer, that "Domesday Book" proves that it has *not* maintained its ground for 800 years; and to contend that it did so for the previous 1,100 years, is simply begging the question now debated. In truth, Dr. Barham had not the advantage of considering the effect of Ptolemy's positions of places, nor of "Domesday Book," nor of the many classical, middle age, and modern authorities as to the sinkings of land on the French coasts, which have been laid before the reader. Dr. Barham quotes Morery's Dictionary as to the former existence of a forest round Mont S. Michel, which he disbelieves. This disbelief would have been reasonable enough if the statement as to the existence of the forest had not been, as it is, abundantly corroborated. He did not know that sinkings of land have been the rule, and not the exception, all along the French coasts, and that the like may therefore be true of the Cornish coast opposite. In short, he has not accepted the great axiom that all geological effects, such as elevations and depressions of land, which are known to have often occurred in every part of the world, are due to causes *still in action*.

165. I agree with Mr. Pengelly that the ground cannot have been *washed away* since Diodorus's time (much less can it have been washed away since 1086). He arrives at the conclusion that "twenty thousand years have barely sufficed to carry us back to the 'wood' era, on the hypothesis of washing away (M.S. p. 19).

The ancient block of tin which was dredged up about 1823, in Falmouth harbour,† if we suppose it to have dropped during its transit to the Isle of Ictis (and I know not what else can be inferred from finding it there) would seem to place Ictis opposite Falmouth harbour, and therefore twenty miles east of St. Michael's Mount. Sir Charles Lyell's views, in the new volume of his grand work, as to the identity of the Mount with Ictis, are similar to Mr. Pengelly's, whom he quotes.

166. I have before me *in extenso* Dr. Boase's paper (with section) on sandbanks on the N.W. shore of Mount's Bay,‡ called the Greens. He arrives at the conclusion that "it appears probable that at a remote period these banks filled the greater part, if not the whole of the Bay; and that they have been for ages past, as at the present day, gradually

---

* The word is "obtained" in my MS. copy but I think it must have been "maintained" originally.

† "Lyell's Principles of Geology," 1867, p. 451.

‡ "On the Sand Banks of the N. Shores of Mount's Bay," by H. S. Boase, M.D., vol. ii, p. 136, &c., of "Trans. Roy. Geo. Soc. of Cornwall," read Oct., 1826.

diminishing under the incessant attacks of the waves." He found under a bed of sand ten feet thick, and under a bed of pebbles about sixteen feet thick, on which the sand rested, masses having the appearance of decayed timbers of a ship, perforated by *Pholas Dactylus*. Large trunks and branches of trees were laid along in every direction, in a bed of very dark brown colour. Some portions of the branches were perfect, being covered all round with bark, in a state of great preservation; the trunks are never entire, being split longitudinally, as if they had been crushed. The trees were small, from six to nine inches, rarely a foot in diameter. One piece was fourteen feet long, but not an entire trunk. Far the greatest part of the wood is hazel, with pieces of alder, elm, and oak; these are interspersed with decayed plants and bark, leaves, and twigs of trees, sufficiently perfect to show that they were almost entirely hazel. Hazel nuts were very abundant, the shells in a good state of preservation, but the kernels have entirely disappeared. There were stems and seed vessels of grasses and fragments of insects,* particularly elytra and mandibles of the beetle tribe, still displaying the most beautiful shining colours. On exposure to the air these soon crumbled into dust. He remarked a fœtid odour resembling sulphuretted hydrogen gas. Similar terrestrial remains extended into the marsh beyond high-water mark, as in Guernsey.

The section shows the ligneous bed (not lignite), 3ft. thick and extending 240ft. northwards from high water into the marsh, and upwards of 100yds. southward to low water, where the top of it (covered with a little sand) forms the sea-bed, being continuous all under the beach and the Green, from the marsh to low water. Some parts, as we have seen, had the branches "perfect, covered all round with bark, and in a state of great preservation," plainly signifying that we are not *obliged* to go back to an earlier period than 1099 for their submergence. I think there can be no doubt that within the Christian period the trees must have been alive and flourishing. I can see no reason for attributing them to an earlier date, so far as regards the description and state of preservation of the wood, than similar deposits of about that date on the Norman and Breton coasts. They are only somewhat darker in colour than the submarine wood of the shores of Jersey, which is as recent as 1356, and from which I do not gather that they differ in other respects.

167. Sir Henry de la Beche,† speaking of the whole English coast which lies west of the 3° of west longitude, says "submarine forests are so common that it is difficult not to find traces of them in the district at the mouths of all the numerous valleys which open upon the sea, and are in any manner silted up, so that we may consider they once formed creeks, or the bottoms of estuaries." Sir Henry then gives details as to various submarine forests on the south coasts of Devon and Cornwall, on the

---

* Ogée mentions the prodigious quantity of insects and plants found in Britanny under like circumstances.

† "Report on Cornwall," &c., p. 417, &c.

north-west coasts of Cornwall and Devon, and on the north coast of Somerset as far east as Bridgewater. In some of these pre-historic remains were found, which I attempted to show in the latter part of Art. 133, did not necessarily prove that the very latest sinkings there took place in pre-historic times. And of the others the terrestrial remains are of species still in existence near at hand. The elytra and mandibles of beetles are a parallel case to Ogées fact of the year 709, "when a prodigious quantity of insects and plants of all species died and rotted in the marshes of Dol."* And Mr. Herapath's remarks on the *still fœtid* state of the remains of the Genus Synapta, off Guernsey, perhaps also signify a date not earlier than 709.† If the Rev. W. Borlase (Art. 133), instead of using the round number 1000, had happened to say 1048, it would have fixed his subsidence in 709, which was the year of the great subsidence about Mont S. Michel and the neighbouring coasts of Normandy and Britanny.

We have still Vice-Admiral Thevenard's submersion "of the western extremity of England near the Scilly Isles at the commencement of the ninth century," to account for, see Art. 209. But I do not insist on this. He may have meant the eighth century, when the Rev. W. Borlases's and the great French submergence (709) took place.

168. At Mainporth, between Mawnan and Falmouth, the Rev. Canon Rogers noticed the submarine stump of an oak in the situation in which it grew, the roots, as usual, running amid peat, bearing evidence of having been formed in marshy ground, and containing, he thought, the leaves and roots of *Iris pseudacorus* (the common yellow flag), now growing in the adjoining marsh.‡ He also saw remains of a submarine forest with stumps of oaks and willows where they grew a little above low-water mark, at Porthleven, near Helston.§

"In the Hayle estuary we again have evidence of trees and vegetable accumulations beneath the present level of the sea, and under the Dunbar Sands; at the mouth of the Camel a similar bed has been seen. Traces of submarine forests occur also at Perron Porth, Lower St. Columb Porth, and Mawgan Porth, between these two localities. A similar vegetable bed is stated to be found beneath Braunton Burrows, at the embouchure of the Taw and Torridge, near Barnstaple and Bideford. At Porlock a small submarine forest is well exhibited at very low tides, the stumps of trees, which appear chiefly oaks, standing "in the positions in which they grew. The present action of the sea has bared these trees by removing the silt and sand which once covered them, as can be seen by the continuation of the same bed of vegetable matter inland, beneath sands and silt, behind the present shingle beach that merely reposes, as can easily be seen, upon the inclined plane of the submarine forest."|| The description in the last sentence is exactly true of much of the north-west coast of Guernsey.

* See last part of second paragraph of Art. 76.
† See third paragraph, Art. 131.
‡ "Trans. Geol. Soc. of Cornwall," vol. iv., p. 481.
§ Ibid, vol. i., p. 236, and vol. iv., p. 483
|| Sir H. de la Beche's "Cornwall," &c., p. 112.

Sir Charles Lyell says if we "turn to the Bristol Channel, we find that both on the north and south sides of it there are numerous remains of submerged forests; to one of these. at Porlock Bay, on the coast of Somersetshire, Mr. Godwin-Austen* has lately called particular attention, and has shown that it extends far from the land." ("Principles of Geology," 1867, p. 545.) Sir Charles supposes that a woodland tract once extended all across the Bristol Channel from Somersetshire to Wales, through the middle of which the ancient Severn flowed. If such a tract of land once existed, he well observes, the caves and fissures in the precipitous cliffs on the south coast of Glamorganshire may have been frequented by various animals, all now extinct. In all this there is nothing to prove, that submergences of the forests referred to in this article, may not have taken place within the historical period.

169. Sir Henry proceeds to say, that "another smaller vegetable accumulation is found near Minehead; and among the compressed plants and trees the bones and horns of the red deer have been discovered, a species still wild in the adjoining district of Exmoor. Proceeding eastward along the southern shores of the Bristol Channel, a submarine forest occurs beneath a considerable portion of the Bridgewater levels, and which is well seen to pass beneath the present level of the sea towards Stert Flats. That portion which appears near Stolford has been described in detail by Mr. Leonard Horner,† who notices *Zostera oceanica* among its peat. Professor Buckland and the Rev. W. D. Conybeare consider that the trees at Stolford afford very clear evidence of having grown on the spot where they are now seen, and they have further noticed that trees of large dimensions—fir, oak, and willow—are found in the marshes of the levels at the depth of of 15 or 20ft. from the surface; trunks lying prostrate, and stumps with their roots, in the upright position in which they grew. Intermingled with them are furze-bushes and hazel-trees with their nuts; the whole being, as it were, bound together by a bed of reeds and other palustrine plants.‡

"Part of this vegetable accumulation may be comparatively modern."

170. All the terrestrial relics, now submarine, bear so close a resemblance in their character to the submarine relics on the French coasts, which we *know* have been submerged for the most part within the last dozen centuries,—that, as I believe, we can scarcely avoid coming to the conclusion that the submarine trees and terrestrial vegetation, now below the sea on the English coasts, must be equally modern. On the occasion of my reading a paper on this subject to the Geological Section, at Birmingham, I exhibited part of a submarine tree taken from the sea-bed near St. Helier, where it must have been covered at high tides with from 15 to 20ft. of water. This specimen which I had previously caused to be split along its centre, one of the committee said he thought was "modern," and no one dissented.

171. "It is certain," says Abbé Manet, p. 33, "that the famous Bernard

* Memoir rean Nov., 1865. Geol. Proc.
† "Geol. Trans." vol. III., p. 380.
‡ *Ibid.* second series, vol. I., p. 310.

d'Abbeville who went to live there in the year 1089,"—that is to say, in the then *peninsula* of Chausey, see Art. 58 (second paragraph) "left it about the year 1105." It is *possible* that Chausey may have become what it is now, namely, a large group of rocks six miles distant from the coast, and all bare, except the chief one, which is about a thousand paces long, and covered with a sandy soil, in the year 1099. When we consider the great distance towards Cornwall which the neutral district of the Channel Islands seas extend, it is at least *possible*, as I have said, that the sinking may have extended all across the English Channel to Western Normandy. In the same way the Rev. W. Borlase's date of *about* 757 for the submersion near St. Michael's Mount, may have been at the identical date of the great French submergence in 709. Therefore the sinkings then may also have extended also across the English Channel.

SUMMARY AS TO THE ANCIENT SOUTH-WEST COAST OF BRITAIN.

172. The Rev. W. Borlase has established a sinking of at least 16ft. (perhaps much more) at the Scilly Isles since the time of the Romans,* which accounts for the loss of the ancient tin mines, and Ptolemy has correctly laid down the latitudes and longitudes of places on the north coast of Britanny, with reference to the Isle of Wight and Lizard Point, although the English Channel, a hundred miles wide, intervened. And though some of his figures are either corrupt, or he must have made mistakes in the interior of France, there appears to be no reason for disbelieving his position of the Antœuestæum promontory, though it falls far out in the Bristol Channel; because he could do correct work, and there are the Lionesse tradition and the "inundations" of the 8th century, 1014, and 1099, to support that position. Moreover, we have seen in Art. 48, the truth of the tradition that Mont S. Michel was once ten leagues from the sea, actually established by his position of the mouth of his river Argenis.† All this lends a certain degree of countenance to the corroborative traditions as to supposed lost land at Seven Stones.‡ And this again is supported by Florence of Worcester's statement that St. Michael's Mount was formerly five or six miles from the sea; and again by Ptolemy's position of the Lizard at seven miles seaward of its present place, and as a coping-stone or climax to the whole, we have the actual existence of abundance of submarine forests on the south-west coasts of England. And no violence would be done to probability, if, by reason of the freshness of some of the trees, &c., and their general resemblance to other submarine forests on the French coasts, submerged in 709 and since—we were also to lay it down as a fact, that very extensive submergence of land on the south-west coasts of England must have taken place since Ptolemy's time, and the supposed approximate coast-line, then, is shown on the map in accordance with these reasonings, for they all point to one and the same

---

* Art. 150.

† If the Lionesse country really existed it was probably submerged in the 8th century or 1014, for no such name occurs in Domesday Book.

‡ See commencement of Art. 114.

conclusion. Another highly distinguished man of science ridicules the idea of the former existence of the Lionesse country, by calling it a "romantic tale." He says, "Although there is no authentic evidence for this romantic tale, it probably originated in some former inroads of the Atlantic, accompanying, perhaps, a subsidence of land on this coast." As this eminent gentleman admits that there may have been a subsidence of land and an inroad of the sea on this coast, how can he arbitrarily limit either its length, breadth, or depth; as if he meant to say, "I won't believe in it if you allege that it exceeded (a certain mental number of) acres." Yet the gentleman might have remembered a case, with which he is well acquainted, where a greater tract of land than I contend has sunk on the Cornish coast, namely, 2,000 square miles, were in a few hours converted into an inland sea or lagoon. I refer to the sinking of the Runn of Cutch, so lately as in June, 1819.* To come nearer home. At p. 549 in the 1867 edition of "Principles of Geology," is a map showing the "Line of Coast from Nieuport to the mouth of the Elbe, in which changes have been observed since the historical period." The same map says "The dark tint between Antwerp and Nieuport (about 2,000 square miles in area), represents part of the Netherlands which was land in the time of the Romans, then overflowed by the sea before and during the fifth century, and afterwards reconverted into land." The distance along the coast from the mouth of the Elbe to Nieuport is 350 miles. I ask why anyone doubts that extensive tracts of land have often risen and sunk during the historical period? If these gentlemen will examine Sir Charles Lyell's "Principles of Geology," and Mr. Charles Darwin's "Voyages of the Adventure and the Beagle," with both of which works they are well acquainted, they will find plenty of other proofs both of risings and sinkings of land within the historical period. Moreover, we have the Rev. W. Borlase's distinct testimony (Art. 150), establishing a sinking of at least sixteen feet at the Scilly Isles since the Roman invasion of Britain. And the losses of land caused by the catastrophes in the eighth century, in 1014, and in 1099, have also to be taken into consideration. My friend's argument has dwindled now only to this (for I think everything else which he relied upon has been upset), and it starts with begging the very question which is, in reality, the main point in debate :—"*If there have been no geographical changes on the coasts of Cornwall since Diodorus's time,* then Mount St. Michael must be Diodorus's Isle of Ictis, because there is not now, and (begging the words in italics) there cannot have been then, any other island on the Cornish coasts large enough to be worth mentioning."

Volume II, which will be published when one hundred subscribers at 5s. each are obtained, will contain :—

Farther accounts of submergences, chiefly about Sercq. Also a facsimile of the ancient chart.

What can be gathered from the ancient writers, Nennius and Gildas.

* See Lyell's "Principles of Geology," 1853, p. 461.

On the unique privilege of neutrality of the Channel Islands' seas in all wars, which formerly existed; and its probable origin in sinkings of land.

Two chapters on losses of land on the French coast of the Bay of Biscay. It is not a little remarkable that Pomponius Mela (A.D. 35) says:—"from the mouth of the Garumna (Gironde) that side of the land (of Gaul) runs into the sea, and is opposite the Cantabrian shores." Now, Cantabria means Biscay, which *is not* opposite the mouth of the Gironde, but Ptolemy's ancient mouth of the Garumna *is* opposite to Cantabria or Biscay; and the Isle of Antros may not have been Cordouan, as commonly supposed, but Antros may have been situated as shown by the + on Map 2.

A forged chart. Probable sinkings of land at the mouth of the Somme within the historical period; and on the coast of Belgium, Holland, and Schleswig.

General remarks (not yet written) on sinkings of land in various parts of the world, during the post-tertiary period and down to the present time, with a view of showing that risings and sinkings of land have continued to occur throughout all that geological time. Thus an attempt is being made to trace a small part of the operations of the over-ruling and omnipotent Creator

The sentence immediately preceding the abstract of the contemplated Volume II, commencing with the words *If there have been, &c.*, is entirely attributable to the author of these papers, and it was and is intended to show the reader that the theory of the identity of Diodorus's Isle of Ictis with Saint Michael's Mount, can now only be maintained by begging the question in debate, namely, by assuming in opposition to much evidence to the contrary, that no geographical changes have taken place since Diodorus's time.

It ought not to be supposed that Nennius or Gildas, mentioned in the Abstract, said anything about the neutrality; on the contrary, it did not exist until long after their time.

172*b*. There is a very interesting and suggestive paper in the "Popular Science Review," for April, 1867, entitled "An attempt to approximate the date of the Flint Flakes of Devon and Cornwall, by Spence Bate, Esq., F.R.S." Finally, he contends, "there is no evidence to show that the flint flakes which we find scattered over the surface of Devon and Cornwall may not have been coeval with the history of the period that immediately preceded the introduction of Roman civilisation into this country." That is to say, many flint implements belong to pre-historic periods, and many others are as late as *historic times*. I have already had occasion to show that when tree stumps, with roots, are found in situ *at some fathoms below the level of high water*, the submergence of old forest beds *cannot* (except under very peculiar and exceptional circumstances) be due to the removal of the superficial layer of earth, and the encroachment of the sea. For this obvious reason:—If the tree stumps stand in situ uncovered at a depth of *more than a foot or two below high water*, they will be uprooted by the action of the waves, particularly in storms, and carried away. It is abundantly clear that *all stumps in situ would have been carried off long before the forest ground could have been denuded to the depth of "some fathoms."* Mr. Bate well observes (p. 178-9) that there appears to him "to be some reason for a reconsideration of the subject, whether a subsidence of land around our southern seaboard has taken place or not. The submerged forests on our coasts are numerous, and lands corresponding with these have existed *within the period of history or tradition*, and in some places, as in Torbay and Penzance, *within the memory of the present generation.* These have disappeared and *the sea flows over them some fathoms deep;*" though (he supposes) we know of no sort of change by which we might recognise any subsidence of the land. I have italicised a few passages, from which I think we are once more driven to the conclusion that the ground must have sunk within the historic period.

### The Saxon Chronicles.

172 *c.*—I have before me a valuable octavo volume, entitled, "Two of the Saxon Chronicles parallel,* with Supplementary Extracts from the others; edited, with Introduction, Notes, and a Glossarial Index, by John Earle, M.A., sometime Fellow and Tutor of Oriel College, and Professor of Anglo-Saxon, Rector of Swanswick. Oxford, at the Clarendon Press, 1865." Published by Macmillan and Co. It contains seventy-four pages of well-considered and instructive Introduction, and he encourages us to rely on the truthfulness of the chronicles by saying, at pages lxvi., lxvii., that "the Saxon chronicles which we possess are the guarantees of the truth and fidelity of the subsequent historians, and the changeful mother tongue gives that touch of confidence which the fixed and rigid Latin, much the same everywhere, could never have imparted." It will be desirable to add a few more particulars to enable the general reader to judge for himself *in what degree of estimation these curious ancient records ought to be held.*

There are seven principal Saxon chronicles, which he distinguishes by the seven first letters of the alphabet. They are records of the *most remarkable events which occurred in England*, generally one (sometimes more) in each year, commencing with the numbers of the years themselves in chronological order. They chiefly consist of political events—very rarely a comet or an earthquake is mentioned. "The main features of the anonymous and many-handed chronicle may be seen in a high state of preservation in the Saxon Chronicles. . . . . Towards their close we have historical composition of considerable maturity" (p. ii). The two Chronicles A and E are printed entire. "These two are, in different senses, the most prominent, and challenge the largest amount of notice; the one because it is the highest source, the other because it presents the latest and largest development, and the most composite

* A and E, down to the year 1006 inclusive, after which 1017 is the next year in A (p. 139).

structure of the whole set" (p. iii). "To King Alfred's reign [A.D. 872 to 901] we must assign all the annals down to 449, and many inserted annals down to 731 . . . and here we only have to do with those which are borrowed from Bede" [died 735] (p. viii), of which he gives a considerable list. The annals from 455 to 634 represent the gleanings and reconstruction of the half-lost early history of Wessex, at the time of the first compilation of A in 855 (p. ix). I suppose copies of the chronicles so far were obtained, and the chronicles were then continued more or less independently of each other, at the several places named in the Tabular Statement below.

TABULAR STATEMENT.

(Extracted, except where otherwise stated, from the Rev. Mr. Earle's Introduction.)

A. *The Winchester Chronicle.*—A Saxon chronicle containing annals from before Christ 60 to the year 1070. It is a MS. in Corpus College, Cambridge, called Parker's MS., from Archbishop Parker, who gave it to the college. He ranks it first in the list of Saxon chronicles, and hesitates to judge whether it is really a MS. of the last decade of the ninth century (891). Its internal characteristics connect it with Winchester. B, C and D are similar to A, but not identical with it.

B. *The Chronicle of St. Augustine's, Canterbury.*—A Saxon chronicle from the Incarnation to the year 977. It is one of the Cotton MSS. British Museum. He states some of its peculiarities at pp. xxvii and xxviii.

C. *The Abingdon Chronicle.*—A Saxon chronicle from the invasion of Julius Cæsar to the year 1066. A Cotton MS. The death of Edward the Confessor is narrated with extraordinary solemnity, and the accession of Harold is noticed in terms which imply that the catastrophe of his reign was already known, p. xxxvii. He supposes that in or about the year 1045 the community at Abingdon borrowed books from Canterbury (B) and from Worcester (D), and composed from them (C).

D. *The Worcester Chronicle.*—A Saxon chronicle from the Incarnation to the year 1079. A Cotton MS. Between the years 737 and 806 there is a large influx of material, which appears for the first time in D, and through Florence it became the heritage of all the historians.* In 1066, D goes on to tell the battle of Hastings, in which it is singular, none of the others giving an account of that decisive battle.

E. *The Peterborough Chronicle.*—A Saxon chronicle from the Incarnation to the year 1154. One of the Laud M.S.S. in the Bodleian Library. It gives seventy-five years' history beyond any of the others. In many respects this is the most important of the whole series of chronicles. It is a book of the Abbey of Peterborough, and affords copious proof of its own origin. At p. 218, King William (date 1085) was evidently preparing materials for his Domesday Book :—"Also he let write how much landes his archbishops had, and his lord bishops, and his abbots, and his earls,"

* These materials are perhaps contained in E; if so, they mention no marine inundations.

&c., &c., which countenances the presumed authenticity of the chronicles. Florence and E have each independent materials, yet there is still a common element. We see the contrast between the English language at Worcester and that of Peterborough, p. xlviii. In 1098 and 1102 are examples. In the former of these two the writer feels for the tilth on marsh lands as became a resident in the fens. *The same may be said of the notice in* 1099 *of damage caused by a high flood-tide*, p. xlviii. I now give a translation (where required) and word for word copy in modern English, of the accounts of the inundations of 1014 and 1099 :—

"1014. And on this year on Saint Michael's-mass-even, came that great sea-flood through widely this land, and ran so far up as never before not did, and submerged many towns, and mankind innumerable number."* (p. 151.)

"1099. This year also on St. Martin-mass-day, sprang up to that exceeding sea-flood, and so much to harm did, as no man not remembered that it ever afore did, and was that same day a new moon." (p. 235.)

I have now brought down from the Rev. Mr. Earle's Book—who having been the Professor of Anglo-Saxon in the university of Oxford, considers the chronicles authentic—a historical sketch of the Saxon Chronicles as far as the two important passages just quoted, and the narrative need not be pursued any farther for our present purpose. We have besides the seven chronicles, the Latin chronicle of Ethelweard. Florence of Worcester, the Annalist who was the most vigorous of all the Latin compilers, died in 1118, four years before the compilation of E (p. lix). Two chronicles go by the name of Simeon of Durham, who quotes Northern registers which we have no other trace of. Henry of Huntingdon was an amateur and antiquarian, and had a great fondness for the old Saxon Chronicles. William of Malmesbury aimed at being a historian of a higher order (p. lxiii). We have besides, as Annalists, Matthew Paris and William of Worcester.† It is on record, though I have not personally met with the passage except in writings of the present century, that Mount St. Michael was once five or six miles from the sea and enclosed with a very thick wood. The onus of dis-proving this statement, clearly rests with those who deny it.

Readers can now judge, each for himself, whether or not to accept the Inundations of 1014 and 1099 as sinkings of land partly referred to Cornwall—England being the scene of nearly every individual event chronicled and the chronicles making no mention of the particular localities affected The extraordinary amounts of damages done, plainly as I believe, take them out of the category of simple high tides, there being no mention of storms. The submersion of many towns and innumerable men as well as the loss of 200 acres of land at Mount St. Michael, since 1086, could be satisfactorily accounted for by sinking. On the other hand those who

* The foot notes by giving (unimportant) different readings in D and F, prove that those two chronicles also contain this important record. C gives a complete copy of the record.

† Not mentioned by the Rev. Mr. Earle.

choose (if any) can resist this explanation ; and in that case the *Insulation* of the Mount (the existence of which in 1086, Domesday Book gives no authority for believing) as well as the loss of the 200 acres—remain mysterious and unaccounted for events.

## THE CHANNEL ISLANDS' SEAS.

**172*d*.** A friend of the author's who deservedly enjoys an eminent position amongst scientific men, in his own department of science, argues that the shell *Cerithium vulgatum*, which has been dredged up in a rolled condition (though one specimen was tolerably fresh) in 15 fathoms water on the east of Jersey, and was thrown up on the beach also in a rolled condition at the mouth of the Loire—is now a species proper only to latitudes as warm as the Mediterranean and Adriatic, meaning that, as he supposes, the present conditions of the Channel Islands' seas are unfavourable to its existence, and that the climate has changed. Now, with regard to the latter point, the only change probably is, that there is less cold and ice in the neighbourhood of the Rhine, &c., than there was in Cæsar's time. But this may be accounted for by reason of the greater cultivation of land there, for it is well known that when extensive forests are cleared away, and when the land is drained, and ploughed, and dug, the sun infuses so much more heat into the earth in summer as to render the climate somewhat more temperate in winter; there is no reason for supposing any absolute change, such as the greater or less ellipticity of the earth's orbit, or the greater or less obliquity of the ecliptic, or any alteration of the Gulf stream, or, in short, any change other than what is due to human operations. We have no authority for believing that there has been any appreciable change of temperature in the Channel Islands' seas within the last 2,000 years. If my friend means to affirm that Cerithium could only have flourished as far north as Jersey, so long ago as that geological period when the north of Europe was a warmer climate; in that argument he refutes himself both by quoting Lamarck, who "gave the North Atlantic as a locality" for *Cerithium*, and Professor Sars who "recorded the discovery of a specimen inside a codfish caught off Bergen." It is clear that *Cerithium* has very recently been found much farther north than Jersey. The gentleman also "believed that *C. vulgatum*, which usually inhabits large estuaries and salt marshes, once lived in such situations between Jersey and the mouth of the Loire, and that this tract has since been submerged, and consequently become unsuitable for the continued habitability of the *Cerithium*." Yes certainly, much of the submerged tract has now too great a depth of water for Cerithium. Even if it were quite certain (which it is not) that Cerithium cannot be found alive in the Channel Islands' seas, other peculiarly Southern forms can. If he will refer to an authority whom he highly respects in common with myself, he will find that six of the Mollusca taken in that part of the English Channel which is adjacent to Guernsey, are "peculiarly Southern forms," and that three of these have also been taken on the north coast of Britanny. See introduction to Mr. Gwyn Jeffreys' "British Conchology,"

p. cxi., cxii. So that his argument against sinkings within the Historic period proceeds on the erroneous supposition that the Channel Islands' seas are not warm enough for Southern shellfish; that argument is therefore a nullity both on his own showing and that of Mr. Gwyn Jeffreys' book. It is a nullity, also, because though those former large estuaries and salt marshes which were once shallow waters, are now too deep for Cerithium; yet the whole French coast (with trifling exceptions) consists of shallow water, which again affords a suitable habitat for Cerithium. Besides, let us consider the dredging process for a moment, and we shall soon see how infinitely far short it is of being exhaustive, and consequently how very far the gentleman is, from being able to affirm, that *Cerithium* is not abundant *now in a living state* in the shallow sea of the French coast of the Bay of Biscay, and in the shallow seas of the French coast of the English Channel:—

*a.* In attempting an "exploration of the present sea-bottom, we are only able, at considerable expense, with some personal discomfort, and in such weather as we too frequently meet with in this climate, to scrape up with the dredge a few bagfuls of sand or mud mixed with shells; nor can we hope to examine in this way more than a very few inches in depth. Many deep-burrowing shell-fish altogether escape our observation, or are only procured by chance."*

*b.* "Both sea and land furnish instances (some of which are difficult to explain) of the periodical appearance and disappearance of certain species of mollusca in particular places. Their arrival and departure are often sudden and seemingly capricious. In the case of marine species, this phenomenon is probably the result of changes in the course of tidal and other currents, as well as of the migratory habits of fish. These currents, by accumulating or removing deposits of mud, sand, and gravel, which afford shelter and food to mollusca, conduce greatly to their congregation or dispersal. When such deposits are rapidly formed the shell-bed becomes covered up or silted; and the mollusca are entombed alive for the benefit of future geologists. When their chief enemies, the fish, desert their former quarters and migrate to another feeding ground, the mollusca then increase and multiply, being unthinned except by the tigers of their own kind, or occasionally by the curious conchologist, or by all-devouring death. The destruction of shell-beds by marine currents may account for the prevalent notion that some parts of our sea-coast (as for example South Devon), which used to yield such regular and plentiful harvests of shells to collectors, are now scarcely worth searching,—it being said that the shells have 'deserted' the coast."†

*c.* Taking the tract of sea east of Jersey, and bounded on the north and south by the parallels of the north-east and south-east angles of that island, and calculating from the large scale French Government chart of 1838, it has been ascertained that the tract of sea in question contains

---

* "British Conchology," by J. G. Jeffreys, F.R.S., F.G.S., &c., vol. I., p. lxxxix.
† Ibid, p. xlii.

sixty-seven nautical square miles. And supposing the dredge to be a yard wide, and to have been drawn along the bottom for a distance of four hundred yards, it follows that 400 square yards will have been (superficially) dredged; this would amount to only [illegible] part of the whole area. How utterly far from being exhaustive!

*d.* The reader has already seen that the sands of the Bay of Mont S. Michel have been penetrated in several places to the depth of 50ft. without reaching their bottom, yet the hurricane of 1735 agitated them so much as to bring up vast quantities of trees with roots from the bottom of the sands at whatever depth it is, and, of course, at the same time entombed vast quantities of shell-fish of such species as were present, perhaps *Cerithium vulgatum* among others. It is therefore abundantly clear, for all these four reasons, that quantities of the living *Cerithium* may yet exist on the French coast of the English Channel, if conchologists were only to look for them.

The gentleman continues:—"The presence of submarine peat near the Channel Isles and in the Bay of Mont St. Michel, tends to confirm the supposition; although it is by no means certain that the submergence has occurred within the historical period, as suggested by the Abbé Manet, Mr. Peacock, and others." There are no less than three mistakes in the last half of the sentence. (1.) Abbé Manet had no idea whatever that a submergence in the sense of sinking had taken place, nor of any other cause for the loss of the land than the fatal equinoctial tide of March 709, sustained by a terrible north wind, which he supposed rose to so great an elevation as to "submerge" the land which still maintained its former level. The Abbé forgot to take into consideration, that if that had been so, the waters would have ebbed off again instead of remaining with the land beneath them for 11½ centuries, which is fatal to his theory. The Abbé therefore never supposed at all that a submergence in the sense of sinking had taken place, and this constitutes the gentleman's *first* error. Manet's words are:—"La fatale marée de Mars de l'an 709, l'une des plus considérables qu'on eût jamais vues, et qui, par malheur, fut soutenue d'un vent de nord des plus terribles," page 11.

(2.) Like a celebrated character of old:—

"Castigatque, auditque dolos; subigitque fateri."

That is to say, the gentleman's order of proceeding is, first to intimate doubt which was done in September, 1865, when he could not have known even a tithe of the facts. For though he had the four quarto volumes of MS. in his hands for a few minutes, he only had time to dip into one or two of them here and there. Much less had he any knowledge of the materials which have since been collected. And notably not of one curious fact, which is not even yet (May 1st, 1867), written out, but will be so, immediately. And in short, if he had only even read the four volumes of MS., he would have seen that the changes, whatever their nature, have really occurred within the Christian period. The doubt of 1865 is therefore a mistake, because it was premature, and would be matter for regret if Mr. Peacock should have succeeded in proving his case.

(3). The words "and others" are a mistake. Only *one other* (besides Mr. Peacock) ever even conjectured, so far as appears, that sinkings had taken place. And that other was a friend of the present writer, lately deceased, who only supposed, at haphazard, that the loss of land was caused, either by sinking, or by the melting of the Polar ice.

Thus in one way or other, all the arguments against sinking within the Historic period fail when they come to be closely considered.

172*e*. April 17th, 1867. M. Delalende, of Jersey, 8, Broad-street, St. Helier, a native of Lessay, in western Normandy, and inventor and patentee of a powerful and compact fire-engine, lends me a chart of the Channel Islands and neighbouring French coasts with text, which he says is a cutting from the French newspaper, *Journal de Coutances*, published a few years ago. The gentleman who supplied this curious chart and text to the journal is M. Quenaut, (L.Q.,) of Coutances, Prefect of the Arrondissement of Coutances, and a member of the Archæological Society of Normandy.

M. Quenaut commences his interesting narrative with a detailed account of the action of the high tides on the French shores, which it is not necessary to repeat here. He then proceeds as follows in French, which I translate:—

"I have invited the readers of the "Journal de Coutances" to send me particular information which they might have about the invasions of the sea in the Cotentin;* this appeal has been understood. One has given me to understand that he has seen the traces of a road between Carteret and Jersey, that old Carteret is more than a kilomètre in the sea; another has also seen over all the shore, at low water, the traces of the forest of Sciscy, as I have myself seen at Bricqueville-sur-Mer. It has been proved by a crowd of informations which have reached me that in the disastrous tide of January, 1863, the sea has made no invasion where it met with abrupt downs (dunes). It has been reported to me that some one found near the barque which was discovered at the sluice of Carentan Roman medals and ancient varnished earthenware, signifying that the submersion of this barque was cotemporary with the Roman rule. (See on this subject the excellent work published by M. Pontaumont in the town of Carentan). The persons who by my directions have gone to see the remains of the forest which are to be met with at Bricqueville-sur-Mer, have assured me that one has found the same debris very extensive, and that the trunks of trees are very much larger than on the shore. One has assured me, also, in the English Isles, that there may be seen everywhere on the sandy shores surrounding these isles the traces of the forest of Sciscy. The tradition they represent as having been formerly connected with the continent, and one has assured me that there exists a charter recalling the obligation of a Jersey family to furnish the plank which should serve for the passage of the archdeacon of the Cathedral of Coutances when he proceeded to visit that part of the diocese."

* The N.W. part of Normandy extending southwards to some point between Coutances and Avranches.

### Very Ancient Chart of the Channel Islands and Neighbouring French Coasts.

"Finally," M. Quenaut proceeds, "M. Deschamps-Vadeville has procured me a document extremely curious, which tends to confirm all the traditions and facts stated by M. l'Abbé Lanfranc and the Abbé Manet. It is the reproduction by one of his ancestors—a geographic engineer, bearing the same name—of a chart of ancient Neustria, of the time when it formed part of Gaul-Celtic-Armoric, at the arrival of Julius Cæsar in Gaul. This chart, says the ancestor of M. Deschamps-Vadeville, gives us an idea of the subsequent invasions of the sea since the conquest of Gaul by the Romans. It is a reduced copy which I made in 1714 of an ancient chart, in tatters, creased by lines and damp, which was presented to me at Mont S. Michel by the holy Father de St. Amand. It was of 1406, *and one had used for it the letters of the 13th century, which proves that it was itself the copy of a more ancient chart.** This chart, which we reproduce with the greatest part of the legend which accompanies it, is perfectly in accordance for the coasts of la Manche, with the first memoir which we have published; and for the coasts of Calvados, with the uncovered aqueducts conducting to the hamlets or towns invaded; the waters come from the cliffs of Port and Arromanches. The shores of the islands of Alderney and Guernsey, on which the invasions of the sea have overcome much land, are at this day represented by the islets, the banks, and the reefs. The plateau of the Minquiers, which has replaced the island of Selsouef, destroyed by the sea, has, according to the very exact chart of M. Beautemps-Beaupré, the form of this island. The ancient Regneville, designated anew on the chart on the west, by the sign °, would be, according to this chart, in the middle of the reefs of Ranquet, where I myself have seen the traces of carriage roads. This chart, the most ancient in existence, and by consequence the nearest approximation to the invasions of the sea, is therefore very probably near the truth, by its antiquity, by its agreement with the historic documents which we possess, and with the suppositions which the recent discoveries of debris of habitations and forests on our sandy shores have permitted to be made.

"The reduction of the chart which we publish was designed by M. Gosselin, acting surveyor of highways, which he has reproduced with great exactness."

M. Quenaut then gives a copy of the memorandum of M. Deschamps-Vadeville, the elder, which he calls a "Legende." I reproduce it in the original French, authenticated as it is by M. Quenaut's initials (L.Q.) at foot.

### Legende.

"Cette carte qui représente les costes de l'ancienne Neustrie (province de Normandie), aux temps qu'elle faisoit partie de la Gaule-Celtique-Armorique à l'arrivée de Jules César dans les Gaules, et qui nous donne une idée des envahissements subséquents de la mer, depuis la conqueste

* These italics are M. Quenaut's.

des Gaules par les Romains, est une copie raisonnée, que j'ai prise en 1714 sur une vieille carte en lambeaux, trouée par les vers et l'humidité, qui me fut présentée au Mont St. Michel, par le Père religieux de St. Amand; elle estoit de 1406, et l'on avoit pour elle employé des lettres du XIII.e siècle, ce qui prouve qu'elle avoit esté elle-mesme la copie d'une carte plus ancienne. Elle offre à la vue d'antiquaire le nom et la position de chaque ville et monument celtique, dont la connaisance a pu arriver jusqu'à nous. Et comme j'ay eu l'avantage de bien estudier l'antiquité de mon pais, par mon savoir en langue celtique, et que j'ay fait par toute la mer qui avoisine notre belle Normandie et enveloppe de ses eaux houleuses les isles Angloises et Françoises de ces parages, des estudes de sondage et parcouru son fond dans les grandes marées, comme ingénieur-geographe pour le roy, je me suis assuré par ces nombreuses opérations, qu'il y avait utilité pour le science de la reproduire, en aiant toutefois d'en corriger les défauts qui existent grandement dans le plan géographique, l'auteur n'aiant pas, à beaucoup près, comme moi, observé les degrés de longitude et de latitude de tous les points de sa carte.—L.Q."

VARIOUS PARTICULARS OBTAINED FROM M. DESCHAMPS VADEVILLE'S ANCIENT CHART, BY MEANS OF A SCALE OF ENGLISH STATUTE MILES.*

The chart contains a scale of myriametres, and it appears from the Table at the end of Herschel's "Outlines of Astronomy," and also from another Table in Beardmore's "Hydraulic and other Tables," that a myriametre = 6.2138 statute miles, and the scale for the measurements has been drawn accordingly.

The continental land is represented as commencing three miles west of the present western extremity of Alderney, and the whole breadth of land from north to south measured across the present centre of the isle is six miles. Alderney, however, is joined to the continent by a neck of land which is nowhere less than three and a-half miles broad. And northern Normandy is shown as extending from three to four miles farther into the English Channel than it does at present, all the way from Cape la Hague to the meridian of Caen, which is the eastern limit of the chart. A Roman road is shown from the east end of Alderney to the town of "Corbillo," on the east of Cape la Hague.

Guernsey, Herm, Jethou, and Sercq are all shown as one island extending much farther into the sea in all directions than the present coasts, its extreme length is 23½ miles, and its extreme breadth 14 miles. It extends 4½ miles into the Atlantic from the south-western present extremity of Guernsey, and 3½ miles into the Atlantic from the present north-west coast of that island. It extends 5 miles north-east from the most north-eastern extremity of Guernsey, and 3 miles east of Herm, and 2½ miles east of Sercq. It extends 4 miles south-east from the southern extremity of Sercq, from which point the former north-western extremity of Jersey is shown as only 8½ miles distant. The land also extends 2½ miles south of

* All the French Government charts bear this gentleman's name.

the present south-coast of Guernsey. The whole of this large island is called "Sarnia Fanaff."

Jersey (called "Augia Fanaff") is united to the continent by a tract of land four times the breadth of its present eastern end, and at 4½ miles east of its north-eastern angle the position of the traditional plank for the archdeacon is shown. The land extends 4 miles west from the present coast in the centre of St. Ouen's Bay, about 3½ miles north of the present north coast, and about 5½ miles south of the present south coast of Jersey. A Roman road extends from about the centre of Jersey by the south end of St. Catherine's Bay to Portbail. On this road the plank is shown, and called "la Planche."

An island called "Selsveff," co-extensive with the Minquiers rocks, is shown. The eastern extremity of this island is 5½ miles distant from Chausey, which forms part of the continent. An estuary extends from Avranches to a place at 12½ miles east of that town, where it is joined by another estuary, extending thence to Pontorson, all between the two estuaries being dry lands. The land extended in breadth 4½ miles north of St. Malo, and a tract of land has been lost of from 2 to 5 miles wide, all the way from S. Malo to the meridian of St. Brienc (called Bidovs an Traovyow), which is the western extremity of the chart. The land between Portbail and Cape la Hague extended from three to six miles farther into the sea than it does at present. Western Normandy is shown as abounding with Roman roads, and the ancient coasts are everywhere cut up by estuaries, as Cæsar says they were.

The chart measures 8.83 inches from E. to W., and 7.87 inches from N. to S. The scale is 2.02 inches to 25 English miles.

This chart substantially confirms my restoration in the first map, which, as the reader knows, was produced independently, from information gathered from Cæsar, Diodorus, Ptolemy, and other ancient writers, assisted by the hypothesis that there had been a general sinking of about 22 fathoms. If the chart is to be depended on, the sinking must have been greater than that. The reader is now in possession of all the information I possess about this curious chart, and can form his own judgment upon it.

## Conclusion.

If I had been advancing some *strange* doctrine which was possibly heretical, the opposition offered in two or three quarters would have been intelligible, and laudably cautious. But I have done no such thing; quite the contrary. That "*all geological changes are due to causes still in active operation*," is so thoroughly true that it is established as a geological axiom, and the opposition is utterly astonishing. For it would be a retrograde step, not suited to the advanced state of geological science and contrary to truth, to contend that natural elevations and depressions of land, have not occurred at all periods and all over the earth during the whole historic period. A very few geologists object to this axiom in practice, though they cannot but accept it in theory. I can only lament what I believe to be the judicial blindness of these gentlemen, if they continue to oppose the reception of so large a mass of evidence, all pointing in one and the same direction; namely, to establish that vast sinkings of land have taken place as stated, and within the Christian period. Those who reject the theory of sinking in this matter, will, as I believe, however great their scientific reputations, find themselves in the dilemma of having rejected the only possible mode of accounting for the facts.

After this supposed Conclusion, it was found necessary in order to finish the subject to add the following pages:

### Mount Saint Michael on the Cornish Coast; and Mont S. Michel and its sister Islet, Tombeléne, on the French Coast.

It will be convenient for us all to remember the present areas, measured horizontally, of these three Islets, namely; (1) Mount Saint Michael, Cornwall, which measures 30 English acres. (2) Mont S. Michel on the French Coast, which measures 20 English acres. And (3) Islet Tombeléne situated two English miles north of Mont S. Michel, which measures between 20 and 30 acres. With Tombeléne we have nothing to do, except to remember that its name, derived from *Tumba Beleni* or the tomb of Belenus—never belonged to the Cornish Mount Saint Michael. We will for the future call the three Islets each by its own name, namely, Mount Saint Michael, Mont S. Michel, and Tombeléne.

Mount Saint Michael has been stated by some to contain as much as 70 acres, while others call it as little as 7 acres. Both these are incorrect. Measuring on the Ordnance Map (the beauty and minute accuracy of which are well known) with the assistance of a microscope, the dimensions are found to average 22 chains by 14 chains, the area therefore is 30.8 acres; but say in round numbers 30 acres. And its circumference is about three-quarters of a mile, measuring along the north side of the Harbour, and including the small plain occupied by the village. Mr. J. P. St. Aubyn has kindly sent me a plan on a large scale by which it appears there are 21 acres, measuring only to the edges of the cliffs. There are three perspective views of the Mount in the new edition of Sir C. Lyell's *Principles of Geology* from which it is evident that the slopes of the cliff include a considerable horizontal space. And I have not the least doubt that the correct measure of the Island within high water mark, is about 30 acres.

Geoffrey of Monmouth, made Bishop of St. Asaph in 1152, in his *British History*, which has been characterised by my friendly opponent as "so very romantic"*— cannot of course be relied on as to the state of the Cornish coast so long before his own time as the year 492. But his statement as to the distance between Tintagel Castle and the shore of the north coast of Cornwall in his own time—which no doubt accords with its present proximity to the shore—is doubtless true. And the statement is also perfectly consistent with the subsidences which I say took place previously to Geoffrey's time, namely, in the years 1014 and 1099. We ought not to be surprised at his non-mention of the catastrophes which happened at the latter dates, because these papers have proved that the Chroniclers very often omitted to record the actual disappearances of lands, (see Art. 86 and 87) and he apparently did the like in the present instance.

As it is not contended that *every* part of the coasts on the south-west of England have sunk within the Historical period, it is quite possible that an

* *The Antiquity of Man in the south-west of England*, by W. Pengelly, F.R.S., F.G.S., &c. Trans. of Devonshire Assn., 1867. The present writer frequently quotes Historical statements from this interesting paper.

exceptional case of stability may exist on the North Devon coast. There are however, on the other hand, special reasons for believing that on the North Devon coast as well as on the N. Cornwall coast, Sinkings may have taken place much within the Historical period—over and above what is stated in Art. 167 on the authority of Sir Henry de la Beche. Custom, founded on common sense, has established that churches shall be built as nearly as may be, in the centres of the parishes; being the most convenient situations. And when we see a handsome and very ancient church standing *close to the sea-coast*—far larger than the present scanty population require, with houses of a much superior class to those required now. Those circumstances suggest at all events, the possibility, that the Parishes may once have extended farther seaward, and consequently that the population must have been both of a superior class and more numerous than now; and that must have been within the Historical period, for the Churches must have been built since the country was Christianized. And not much of the loss of territory can be attributed to the washing away of land, because the north coast of Devon is so rocky that the sea could make but little impression on it. A very interesting volume informs us as follows:*—"The view of Bideford Bay is unusually fine from Clovelly........Leaving behind us the rich woods and grand features of Leigh Court, we emerged on that bare and open country, which is characteristic [also] of Northern Cornwall........Yet bleak as this country appears it bears the marks of having been in olden time of considerable importance. The churches are particularly fine, and of very ancient date. Hartland [N. Devon], in this neighbourhood, is even said to have been founded by Githa, wife of Earl Godwin†. On our road we turned aside to visit the church of Morwenstow, *a very fine structure, standing on the sea coast*........The situation of the church on the high bleak coast of the sounding sea, unsurrounded by the little groups of dwellings usually clustered about a village tower, appeared desolate in the extreme, and caused us to be more surprised at the grand proportions and antique beauty which the interior presented. *That wide area* [namely the interior of the Church] *could never have been intended for the sparse population at present existing.*" He gives a Legend of Morwenstow, fixing the date of the Church, A.D. 850, (p. 26—29).—"About four miles further on we entered the village of Kilkhampton. It is not very striking in appearance, being composed principally of low mud cabins. A few houses of a better sort have been lately built, and to judge from the Church, *there must have been many such in former times.* This fine structure stands now as a solitary memorial to the departed grandeur of the neighbourhood. Hard by stood in ancient days the mansion, or rather castle, of Stow—a structure dating from almost mythic ages, " (p. 33, 34). He says at p. 97, and I give my friendly opponent the benefit of his opinion: "We cannot dismiss this subject without noticing that this isle [Saint Michael's Mount] is supposed, and no doubt justly, to have been the Iktis mentioned by Diodorus."

I accept the statements that the retrogression by washing away, of the south coast of Cornwall, is so very slow that Mount Saint Michael cannot have become an Island by such retrogression of the cliffs within so long a period as 16,800 years; and that its insulation is therefore due to subsidence or sinking of the ground. Whatever depths of fresh-water, sand and gravel, mixed with sea-sand and silt—may exist below the bed of the river Fal, so far inland as at Falmouth or Penryn; we can infer nothing therefrom as to the age of the submarine trees *off the coast*, and the introduction of such statements only tends to confusion. We have had abundance of proof in this

* *Yachting round the west of England*, by the Rev. A. G. L'Estrange, B.A., of Exeter College, Oxford, R.T.Y.C., 1865.

† He died in the year 1053.

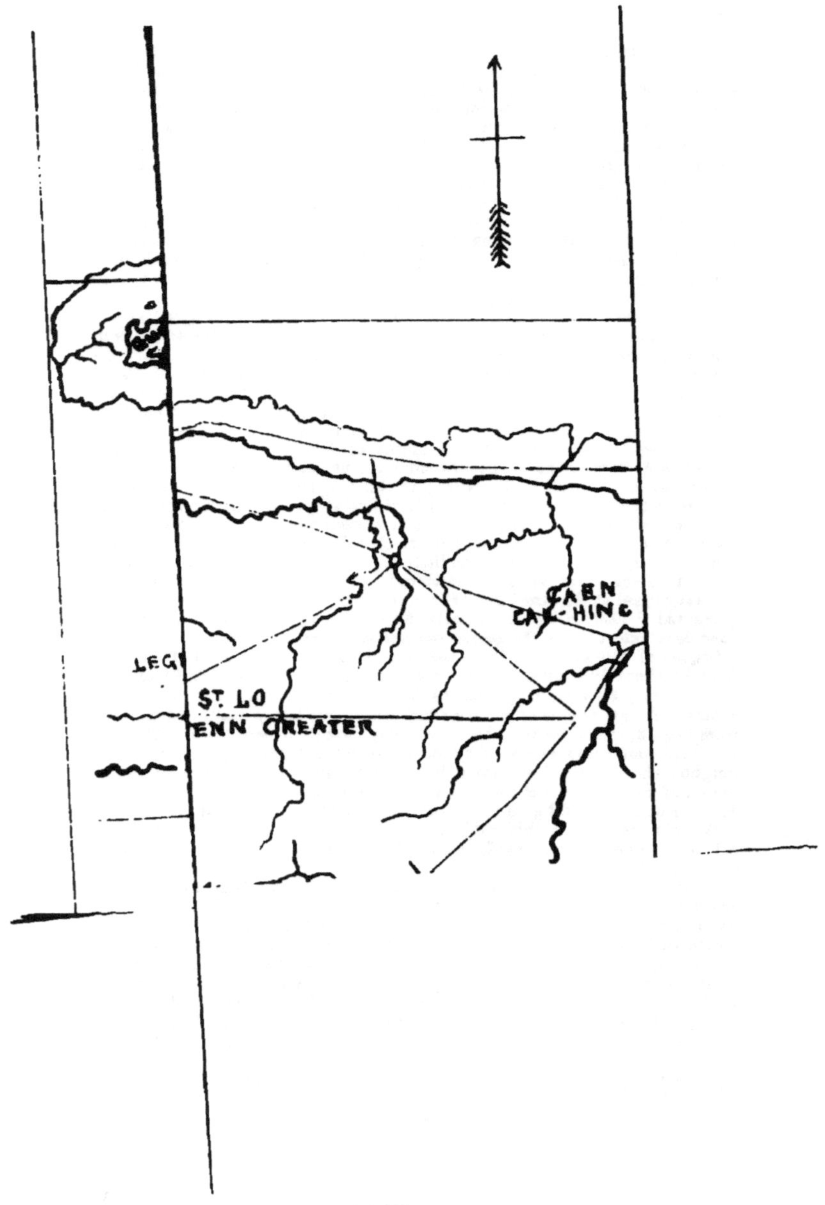


* Art. 161.

* *Yachting round the west of England*, by the Rev. [illegible] College, Oxford, R.T.Y.C., 1865.

† He died in the year 1053.

volume, that the submarine trees on the coasts, like those on the French and Channel Islands' coasts, are often covered to so slight a depth that the action of the tides frequently exposes them to open daylight. And the latest subsidences of the forests need not by any means be referred back to the Prehistoric Mammoth era, merely from the circumstance of bones and other relics of extinct animals having been found; for the obvious reason that those relics may have Risen and Sunk again and again with the ground on which they were deposited. The three high tides which occurred on the south coast of England in 1817, 1824, and 1859—at a considerable distance of time from either equinox—were evidently totally inadequate to the effects caused by the catastrophes of 1014 and 1099, and ought not to have been compared to them. If otherwise, why does not my friendly opponent enter boldly into details of the *burying* of "towns and men very many, and oxen and sheep innumerable" by his recent high tides, similarly to the catastrophe of 1099 from which I quote?* Evidently because no similar destruction has taken place within the present century, else it would be matter of notoriety, and is not so.

Saint Michael's Mount was called Dinsol until it was given to the Monastery of Mont S. Michel not many years before 1086, the date of Domesday Book. And even if we are to be so complaisant to the Historian, as to believe that Saint Michael has ever been seen there by human eyes—we are at any rate not bound to believe that the Saint would go there so early as 490 or 495 which was more than 500 years before the Mount was given to him. Whatever else the two pilgrims St. Keyna and St. Cadoc, did or did not see when they met on the Mount in 490; we have at any rate no reason whatever to believe that they saw the Mount was then an Island. And the Mount is by no means referred to *as an Island*, even at so comparatively recent a time as the year 1044, by the expression "juxta mare"—quite the contrary.

## WHAT IS MEANT, AND WHAT IS NOT MEANT, BY THE MOUNT HAVING BEEN *JUXTA MARE*, IN THE YEAR 1044?

Edward the Confessor in 1044 granted a Charter to a body of Monks already established in the Mount, in which charter the said Mount is described as being "juxta mare." It is of great importance to the question whether the Mount was, or was not, then insulated that we should settle what is the correct English of Juxta. Any Latin-English Dictionary will inform us. In Littleton's Latine Dictionary, editions 1678 and 1684; Juxta is Englished "*Nigh, by, near to, toward, hard by, next after, all along*": in White and Riddle's Latin-English Dictionary, 1862; in reference to Space, Juxta signifies (1) "*Close together, adjoining one another.*" (2) Juxta signifies especially "*Close, close beside, hard by, close or very near at hand.*" also (3) "*in the immediate neighbourhood, at no great distance, not far off.*" The Mount therefore was in 1044 *near the sea*, exactly in the same sense as the towns Marazion and Penzance are now near the sea, but not *in* it. If the Mount had been insulated, the Charter, to be correct, must have said, "in mari" *in* the sea, not "juxta mare," *near* the sea. Or otherwise the Mount would have been called "Insula Sancti Michaelis" the Island of Saint Michael, at once. Saint Michael's Mount and Mont S. Michel, were both of them, properly and necessarily designated "Mount" before they were insulated—it was the only way of briefly describing them; and it appears the distinctive name of Mount, was continued by custom *after* their Insulation, when it would have been sufficient to call them "Island of Saint Michael" and "Ile de S. Michel." If the Charter had been intended to

* Art. 161.

say the Mount was "next" * the sea, the expression would have been "Mons proximus mari," and even then it would only have proved that the Mount was very *near* the sea as Marazion now is. "By" the sea in the sense of "near," is a perfectly correct translation of *juxta*. In Virgil and Ovid, Juxta and its equivalent Prope, are repeatedly used to signify *nigh*, or *near to*. I am under the necessity of meeting the allegation (p. 21) that *near*, *next*, or *by* the sea; are correct descriptions of the present Mount—with a direct negative. The Mount is *in* the sea which entitles it to the name of Island. On the other hand Marazion and Penzance are *near* the sea just as the Mount no doubt was in 1044, before it became an Island. To affirm otherwise would be doing violence to language, just as it would be to say when we are only *near* the Mount, that we are *in* it. Also when we are only *near* a ship at sea, we might find at the cost of drowning that we were not *in* it. Again, if we were *near* a house on fire, we should be glad and fully convinced that we were not *in* it. In point of correctness and candour therefore, we are all bound to admit that the Mount was only *near* the sea, NOT Insulated, in the year 1044.

It has also been proved in Articles 159, 160—from Domesday Book; that the Mount had not been insulated in 1086.

The Record following, contains two mistakes, but is probably in the main correct. It appears that *Alexander II.* was and *Gregory* was not, Pope in 1070. It is also a mistake of William of Worcester to call the Mount, "Saint Michael in Tumba," because the name Tumba, as we have seen, belongs to Tombelêne on the French Coast. The Record is as follows :†—"Pope Gregory, in the year 1070, granted to the Church in the Mount of St. Michael in Tumba in the county of Cornwall . . . . . . that all the faithful who enriched that church with their benefactions and alms, or visited it, should be forgiven a third part of their penances."—The important point in all these statements is, that we have not seen even the faintest spark of reason to believe that the Mount was Insulated in 1044, 1070, or 1086; it was in fact, so far as we have any evidence, not Insulated until the year 1099.—This Record and Art. 159 on Domesday Book, both corroborate the statement at the end of Art. 157, that the Mount really was the identical territory which was given to Mont S. Michel which had no other territory in Cornwall. We have valuable evidence in the *Antiquity of Man, &c.*, that the geographical condition of the Mount in the 15th and 16th centuries—namely subsequent to the year 1099—must have been nearly what it is at present.

The alleged apparition (see William of Worcester's *Itineraria*) of Saint Michael, in the Cornish Mount in 710, is evidently a confused account of the alleged appearance of the Saint on Mont S. Michel in 709. See Art. 78, in which I have given all the essential part, omitting only the figment of the apparition.

Diodorus's important passage translated in Art. 132, causes no material difference of opinion, so far as correct translation is concerned. My friendly opponent's translation is practically the same as mine. He gives in a parenthesis as I do, the vital sentence about the "peculiar thing" down to the word "peninsula." My translation is rigidly literal, his exhibits more freedom. And there is fortunately no question as to the original text of Diodorus. The Lecturer himself named no less than four rivals‡ in opposition to the Mount for the honor of being Ictis—on the supposition that (as he states at p. 7) "at present the Mount measures about seven acres only." The same measure of seven acres is given in *Antiquity of Man*, p. 21.

* *Antiquity of Man in the south-west of England*, p. 21.

† As quoted in *Antiquity of Man in the south-west of England*, p. 13.

‡ *See Report of Mr. Pengelly's Lecture at the Royal Institution*, p. 7.

The measure really and truly is about 30 acres as we have seen. But passing over this difference, and accepting the seven acre measure (for the moment), we are told at p. 7 of the Royal Institution Lecture:—"The Mount is by no means a solitary rock of its kind. Within seventy miles east of it, there are certainly four that actually are, or probably were within the last 1900 years, precisely similar though slightly larger Islands—Looe Island, St. Nicholas Island, the Mewstone, and Borough Island." At p. 10 the point under discussion is begged as follows:—"It [namely the Mount] possesses all the characters, and occupies the position of the Iktis (?) of Diodorus, and no other existing island has any claim to the distinction; nineteen centuries ago it possessed a safe harbour (?) so that its insulation must have been effected long before (?)." Now, accepting the four islands with their attributes as stated, (for the sake of argument), we may add to the number a fifth island, namely St. Clement's on the west of Mount's Bay—making together five rivals to the Mount for the honor of being Ictis. And supposing it were true that the five are, or were within 1900 years, as alleged, precisely similar to though slightly larger than the Mount; we have as much right to give any one of them credit for possessing a safe harbour as the Mount itself, also any one of the five may equally so far as we can know, have occupied the position of Ictis! We have therefore arrived at the conclusion that Looe, St. Nicholas, Mewstone, Borough, St. Clement's and the Mount—have each an equal claim to be considered the ancient Ictis. Who shall decide among the six?—But this is not the only difficulty. If we must needs suppose that the four first-named islands probably were within the last 1900 years, precisely similar to *though slightly larger* than the Mount *really* is, namely 30 acres—we must also admit that there has been a far greater loss of land than was caused by the wearing away by the action of the sea, which it is agreed has been only trifling. That is to say, there must have been a Subsidence, or Sinking, since the time of Diodorus; WHICH IS THE THING THAT WAS TO BE DEMONSTRATED.

We have now arrived at the conclusions, *firstly*:—that taking the seven acre measure, Ictis cannot now be identified; and *secondly*:—that taking the thirty acre measure, one or more Sinkings must have taken place since the time of Diodorus.

We are not at liberty to suppose as is done on p. 6 of the Royal Institution Lecture, that so careful and correct a writer as Diodorus, would (improperly) refer to the trifling two or three feet tides of the Mediterranean, when he was writing about things "between Europe and Britain," where the tides are far greater and in some places twenty times as great, see Art. 103. Nor would that Historian have remarked that a space so narrow as 1680 feet, which is less than one-third of a mile, was peculiar for its largeness; when in fact the space covered and uncovered by high tides on the shores of the English Channel often exceeds a mile wide. I have submitted to the reader in Art. 134, that Diodorus must have referred to the Channel Islands. It is quite clear that his expression "a large space being dried" cannot have referred to so small a space as the distance between Mount St. Michael and the present coast of Cornwall, which measures only 1680 feet.—The following is an illustration of the general accuracy and discrimination of Diodorus, and it is connected with our general subject. It justifies us in having confidence generally, in his descriptions of Physical facts then open to inspection. Immediately after his passage of which Art. 132 is a translation, he proceeds to say (I translate from p. 209 of Henry Stephens's *edito princeps* of his History, date 1559) as follows:—"We will now relate concerning the substance called amber [electros]. There is near the Ocean a marine island opposite Scythia beyond Gaul which is known by the name Basileia: on this the tide casts up abundance of the substance called amber, which appears in no other part of the habitable world. But concerning it many of the ancients have written very extraordinary and incredible fables and whose imaginative stories have been refuted." Scythia is well known to have comprised a large tract of northern Europe and Asia, including Prussia proper and the marine lakes Curische Haff and Frische Haff, both in the neighbourhood of Königsberg and Memel. And we ought not to be too sure, considering the many physical changes which have taken place in other localities since, that there may not actually have been an "island" there when Diodorus wrote.* Now let us compare Diodorus's statement above given, with the statement in *The Times* of September 18, 1867, of which the following are extracts; and we shall at once be convinced of the fidelity of Diodorus's narrative:—"*The amber trade.*—The trade in this mineral is becoming more extensive every year at Memel. The diggings in the Samland, the district between Königsberg and the Baltic, recently yielded 5300lb. of amber in one year. Amber is found on the sea coast of Eastern Prussia, and on the shores and at the bottom of the Fresh and Curish Haffs. It is fished for in the surf with nets, or dug up out of the sands, but the most successful method is to dredge for it at the bottom of the water. In former times amber was only procured by picking it up on the sea shore, but it has since been discovered that large amber fields exist from 16 to 30 feet below the surface of the sea, in a tertiary stratum......The diggings up to 1862 had yielded very fair profits, but by the system of dredging, a Memel firm in one year obtained 17,500lb. of amber, at a cost of about 50,000 Prussian dollars. In 1863 the quantity collected by this method was nearly twice as large; in 1865 more dredging machines were in operation, and 53,000lb. of amber were raised. In 1866 the quantity had increasd to 73,000lb. At present about 14 machines and above 400 workmen, work day and night when the harbour is not frozen up."

It is very handsome of my friendly opponent to quote the following passages from Leland, Carew, and Harrison, making as they do, against his own argument. I quote them from p. 24, &c., of "*The Antiquity of man in the south-west of England*," not having access to the original works. "Leland (1533 to 1540) says, 'Ther hath been much land devourid betwixt *Pensandes* and *Mousehole*.† Ther is an old legend........a Tounlet in this Part (now defaced and) lying under the water.'‡ He subsequently states that 'In the Bay betwyxt the *Mont* and *Pensants* be found near the Lowe Water Marke, Rootes of Tress yn dyvers places, as a token of the Grounde wasted; and thus furnishes the earliest known mention of the submerged forest, as well as of evidence of loss of area.' Carew (1602) having stated the Cornish name of the Mount, adds in a note (which the reader will please observe):— 'Tradition tells us that in former ages the Mount was part of the insular continent in Britain, and disjoined from it by an inundation, or incroachment of the sea, some earthquake or terrestrial concussion."—"The tradition of the loss of area on the west of Lands End, is thus mentioned by Harrison (which is a remarkable corroboration of Ptolemy's positions of the Promontories, *Belerium* and *Ocrinum*):‖—'It doth appéere yet by good record, that whereas now there is a great distance betweene the Syllan Isles and point of the Land's End, there was of late years to speke of scarslie a brooke or drain of one fadam water betwéene them, if so much, as by these euidences appeereth and are yet to be séene in the hands of the lord and chiefe owner of those Isles'." The evidences are however not *now* forthcoming.

* Amber is partly dug out of a bed of bituminous wood, and is probably a resin.—*Chambers's Cyclop.*

† 2 miles south of Pensance on the west side of Mount's Bay.

‡ *Leland's Itinerary*, Vol. 3, p. 17, 1768

‖ *An Historical description of the Island of Britaine*, by W. Harrison, prefixed to Holinshed's Chronicles, 1586, Vol. 1, Third Booke, chap. x, page 397.

There is another circumstance which ought also to count for something. *Magna Britannia*, published anonymously in 1722, is evidently the work of a judicious and well-informed Archæologist. And it states as follows, speaking of Mounts Bay (Vol. 1, p. 308) :—"'Tis a tradition among the people here, that the Ocean breaking in violently, drowned that part of the country which now is the Bay." Now traditions are not necessarily myths, on the contrary they may fairly be taken as corroborative of the circumstance to which they refer, if that circumstance shall have been previously substantiated on reasonably good evidence, as in the present case. If it should be objected, that traditions as to former irruptions of the sea are current in many places, I answer—Sinkings have occured in many places also, within the Historic period; and the traditions consequently are very likely to be correct. We cannot reasonably insist on their being pure fictions invented from an abstract love of deceit, for the sole purpose of deluding posterity without hope of advantage of any sort! These traditions instead of being in excess of the truth, do not even go as far as Ptolemy in establishing the former great extent of land towards the south and north-west of Cornwall. I conjecture that Wolf rock is Ictis, but believe the identification of that ancient Island is both impossible and unimportant.

My friendly opponent is well entitled to respect and consideration for his very able Reports which have done much to establish the vast antiquity of man ; and also for his several valuable papers on various subjects connected with the Geology of the south-west of England—even if the reader should conclude, as I do, that it is incorrect to refer the latest Sinkings on the Cornish and neighbouring coasts to *pre-historic* times. He has (unintentionally) largely helped me to materials for proving my case, and I offer him my best thanks, in the interest of what I believe to be scientific truth.

Not an atom of evidence has been produced either proving or tending to prove, that Mount St. Michael can have been insulated previous to the year 1099. While on the contrary, many proofs and probabilities have been given that Cornwall extended much farther seaward. It is also clear that the insulation when it did occur, was due to one or more Sinkings of Land.

## CHAPTER XII.

### Further evidences of Sinkings, among the Channel Islands.

173. Sept. 1866. I have received a small specimen of oak wood from Mr. Lukis who also kindly informs me that it was dug up last winter, about half tide mark, in Cobo Bay (on the west of Guernsey) where much peat is extracted.* The tree he says was nearly twenty feet long, and its roots were beneath the trunk, embedded fast in the clayey soil.—I think the Guernsey Sinkings must have occurred perhaps in the year 709, the wood being much darker than similar specimens found near Jersey, where the Chief Sinkings are certainly much more recent.

174. M. de Gerville mentions at p. 22 in his pamphlet, that amongst the possessions of the Vernons in the Isle of Sercq in the 12th century, were the lands of Hannière and Fosses and a salt-work called Beveland, of which not a trace remains. He had no notion of the Sinking, but thought the land had been washed away. He says:—"J'ai trouvé que les Vernon y possedaient encore une terre de la Hannière (de Hanneria), et une terre des Fossés (de Fossetis), avec une saline de Bevelande (Salinam de Bevelanda) dont il ne reste aujourd'hui aucune trace, parce que l'action de la mer est dévorante dans une île où elle est incessamment en lutte contre les rochers

* Mean Spring Rise is 26 feet, see Messrs. Sidney and Richards' Chart.

inaccessibles qui l'entourent." And Mr. Métivier mentions that in the Charters respecting Sercq, there are proofs that there were lands round it (with Franco-Dutch names); that the sea has swallowed up. La Gevaude, or Givaude is a wreck of Sercq; and Paul Warnefrid, Deacon of Aquileia a contemporary and friend of Charlemagne, called it Eviodia; it is a reef of rocks S.W. of Brecqhou (which is near Sercq) and has been the scene of many a shipwreck.

175. Mr. Gwyn Jeffreys, F.R.S., in his 1865 Report on Dredging among the Channel Isles, p. 2, mentions certain circumstances connected with the subject now under consideration. On considering the account given in Lyell's *Principles of Geology*, 1853, pp. 326 to 331 both inclusive; I agree with Mr. Jeffreys that the Sinkings in the Channel Islands' Seas were on the whole anterior (though still as I believe completely within the Historical period) to the Sinkings of the submarine forests on the shores of the North of Europe. And Mr. Godwin-Austen* finds that "the Polder formation indicates a change of level, or of relative elevation of the land, of small amount, but of remarkable uniformity, from Ostend to the coast of Hanover," of which more in Art. 233. This is a distance of 260 English miles. Sir Charles's dates and those given in the present volume, completely fix the periods of the Sinkings on the north of Europe and French coasts.

Mr. Jeffreys also dredged up, among the Channel Isles, Eocene fossil shells, near Guernsey.† Does not this signify that the sea between Guernsey and Normandy which in Cæsar's time was 'shallow,' and which Diodorus says was 'dry at low water'—may have been (possibly not very long before) *dry land?*

## CHAPTER XIII.

### Nennius and Gildas, the Historians.

176. Watt's *Bibliotheca Brittannica* says that Nennius, an ancient British Historian was Abbot of Bangor, and flourished about the year 620. He was author of *Eulogium Britannicæ*, otherwise called *Historia Britonum*.

In the edition of Nennius and Gildas published for the English Historical Society in 1838, it is stated as follows on the authority of Nennius, the presumed author of the Latin MS. "Historia Britonum" which bears his name. He probably wrote a little later than the middle of the 9th century. The earlier MSS. give dates varying from A.D. 796 to 994, and some of them assign the authorship to another. However these things may be, the edition in question states as follows at p. 20:—Maximian‡ was the seventh emperor who reigned in Britain. He marched forth with all his British soldiers from Britain, and slew Gratian the King of the Romans‖ and held the Empire of all Europe, and he was unwilling to dismiss his soldiers who had marched with him; to Britain to their wives and sons and possessions; but he gave them many countries from the pool which is above the top of Mount Jove as far as the city which "is called Cantguic and as far as the western Heap (Cumulum) that is, 'Cruc Ochidient.'§ These are the Armoric Bretons, and never returned hither [*i.e.* to Britain] to this day. On this account Britain has been occupied by foreign peoples and its citizens expelled, until God has given them help. According to the ancient tradi-

* Pro. Geol. Soc., Jan. 1869, p. 252.

† See Brit. Assn. Report, 1865; Trans. of Sections, p. 62, 63.

‡ ? Maximus. ‖ Aug. 25, A.D. 383, according to Gibbon.

§ That is "A mount to the West."

tion of our seniors there were seven Roman Emperors in Britain; but the Romans say there were nine."

Mount Jove is well known to have been an early name of Mont S. Michel which is at the north-eastern boundary of Britanny, and it appears to be meant; and not the Great St. Bernard as the editor of Nennius supposes in a foot note, on the strength of a passage which he states that "Usher quotes from the life of Oudoceus, in the register of Landaff, which states, that in his time the kingdom of Armorica extended as far as the Alps. *Primord*, p. 561." Cantguic, the same editor says means "Quoentavic, situated upon the river Quenta (now Carche,) near the monastery of St. Josse and Estaples. It is mentioned by Heddius (Vit. Wilf. c. xxiv.), Beda (Hist. Eccl. iv. 1), and by various other writers." This cannot be so. Estaples is in Picardy and 200 English miles to the north-east of Mont S. Michel which is on the eastern boundary of Britanny. Cantguic and the Western Heap must have been, and may perhaps be still under other names, on the *west* of Britanny. It is observable that this ancient author, whoever he was, mentions "verticem Montis Jovis," with capital letters as if it was a Mountain of importance. A notion which is not inapplicable to Mont S. Michel in its ancient extent and height, seeing that it was the only thing at all like a mountain which was to be found in the neighbourhood. Maximus certainly did not give to the Bretons, all the vast tract of country extending from the Straits of Dover to the Alps. The "Western Heap" may perhaps mean the Isle of Ushant, which is a steep and craggy island like a heap almost all round. Or it may possibly mean the Heights of St. Gildas, which are on the west of Britanny, on the south of the Gulf of Morbihan. Or it may perhaps mean, the west end of the Montagnes Noires on the south of Brest, as if Nennius had said "as far as the western heap extends [westwardly]."

177. On the south of the Gulf of Morbihan which is the marine lake to the west of Vannes—is the peninsula of Ruis, Ruys, or Rhuis, to which Gildas who "was born A.D. 425; in the thirteenth year of his age passed over from Scotland, of which he was a native, into France, at that time under the rule of Childeric the son of Merovius, where he founded the monastery of Ruys."* ...... "he came to a certain island, which is situated in the sight of the village of Ruys."† The island must either have been Belle Isle, or one of the two small islands between it and the main land, *if* they then existed as at present. We have no information whether or not the Gulf of Morbihan then existed.

ON THE UNIQUE PRIVILEGE OF NEUTRALITY OF THE CHANNEL ISLANDS' SEAS DURING ALL WARS, WHICH FORMERLY EXISTED; AND ITS PROBABLE ORIGIN IN SINKINGS OF TERRITORY IN THOSE SEAS.

## CHAPTER XIV.

178. This singular privilege formerly existed, most undoubtedly, and even so lately (according to Poingdestre) as the year 1628. He suggests something as to "ye beginning or antiquity of this neutrality"—which is simply begging a reason, not accounting for the fact—as we shall see presently. It is clear that the peculiarity cannot be attributed to Political causes; for the two chief parties to the Neutrality, the English and French, were on more than one occasion at war with each other, while at the same time both of them not only respected but also enforced the observance of the Neutrality in the most decided manner against their own and each other's

* Preface to Gildas, p. vii. † Acts of the Saints i 16.

subjects. Besides if the cause had been Political, either in time or in circumstance, we should have known how it originated. For we hear nothing of its existence until so lately as after the middle of the 15th century—an origin so very recent that if it had its rise in Politics, History must have recorded what the causes were. Whereas Poingdestre correctly says that "it hides its origin in the clouds," that is in total darkness. But on the contrary, if it had its origin in some Physical event in which the English, the French, the Normans, the Bretons and the Channel Islanders, had all the common interest of being fellow-sufferers. Misfortunes suffered in common would be a bond of union. Then we may at once understand that the Sunken country would not be part of the "High Seas," but would remain private property and be, *ipso facto*, Neutral. And it can be understood from the non-mention of Sinkings about Guernsey,—why there should be so little record of these catastrophes.* We will quote two important public Documents to establish the actual existence of the Neutrality, before arguing further upon it.

179. In Falle's History of Jersey, 1734, p. 354: commences a copy of "The Bull of Pope Sixtus IV. touching the Privilege of Neutrality, contained in an Inspeximus of King Henry VIII." It is dated "12th May, in the fourth year of our Reign," that is A.D. 1513. This Bull denounces as Pirates, Thieves, Malefactors, &c., and threatens with the greater Anathema (to which it subjects them *ipso facto*) all who infringe the Neutrality, which it applies to all the Isles of the Diocese of Coutances, namely to the whole of the Channel Islands. The Bull is of course in Latin.

180. At p. 374 in the same volume, is a copy of a letter of the Count de Laval, Governor of Bretagne, under Francis I. King of France; to the Magistrates of Morlaix, relating to a prize-ship taken contrary to the privilege of Neutrality, and ordering restitution to be made of the ship, goods and merchandise. The letter is dated June 20, 1523, and fills about six octavo pages of print.—We will now lay before the reader various Historical statements as to the Neutrality.

### JOHN SELDEN.

181. There is in the public Library of St. Helier,† a work entitled *Joannis Seldeni Mare Clausum sev de dominio maris, Libri Duo*, 1636. That is "The closed sea of John Selden or concerning the dominion of the sea, two books, 1636." 8-vo.—Watts's Dictionary says:—"John Selden one of the most learned men of the 17th century, was born near Terring in Sussex, 1584; died 1654."—On the fly leaf of Selden's volume (the "two books" are bound together) in the St. Helier's Library, is the following MS. note in French:—"See Bibliothèque Anc. & Mod. de M. le Clerc, tom. XXV. page 396.—King James I. gave an order "in 1626 to *Selden* to collect everything he could which might serve to make it appear that the empire of the sea belonged to the Crown of Great Britain. Charles I. undertook to revise the work and publish it; in 1636 it was printed in folio. The King [Charles I.] ordered on the 26th May that a copy should be placed in the coffer of the Privy Council, another in the Court of Exchequer, and a third at the Admiralty, as a certain memorial of the Empire of the Sea. In the meantime an edition in 8-vo. was printed in Holland having the same title as the one printed in London. This edition was forbidden by the King because other matter had been added in Holland. These additions were nevertheless not made in the name of Selden, but of a Professor of Leyden, named Marc

* The indifference of the Indians to the Sinking at the Runn of Cutch in 1819, is a parallel case of indifference.

† No. 14, Ga. 11.

Zuer Boxhorn, who prefixed a Preface wherein he defends the navigation of the Hollanders, against the Flemish. This defence which is very meagre is the consequence of a very remarkable event, which is that of a treaty of *Intercourse*, as one may call it, that is to say of mutual commerce concluded at London in the year 1495, between Henry VII., King of England, and Philip, Archduke of Austria, Burgundy, &c. The treaty was concluded at London the 24th of February, 1495, and ratified the 26th day of March, in the year 1496. This treaty may be found in the XII volume of the Acts of England of year 1496. Those who would read let them turn to what is a treaty between equals; at the place which Selden has pretended that only the Kings of England have the right of Navigation and Commerce in the Ocean, and that when they have accorded it to others, that it was begged by favour; that they were endowed sole Lords, who held the keys of the Sea to close it or open it as they found convenient." *

182. The title page of Selden's work bears in print at foot, "*Londini*" (at London), but this is corrected in the margin, in the same handwriting as the long note which we have just translated, as follows (in Latin):— "*Not so but in Holland.*"

To proceed with our account of the Volume:—

Selden in his Dedication to King Charles, stands out stoutly as follows:— "That in brief space it would be seen that the most thoroughly investigated right, by which, through all time, the British Ocean has been esteemed as the Sacred Patrimony of thy British" [Sovereignty].—This is followed by a Latin Preface, containing many quotations from Marcellus, Justinian, Seneca, Valerius, Vegetius, Cicero, Lucan, Virgil's Æneid, Propertius, Pliny, and others, but throwing as I think, no light on the subject. The Dedication is dated "Inner Temple, November 4, 1635." Next comes the Syllabus of Selden's 26 chapters, forming his first Book, and the Syllabus of the 32 chapters forming his second Book of which, the 19th and part of the 22nd chapters are underlined with pen and ink. Then follows Boxhorn's Apology for the Navigations of the Hollanders, against the Neutral (Hevterum) sea. In which the Navigations of preceding ages, their laws, and institutions, are especially vindicated from public records."—Next comes "A treaty of peace, mutual and commercial, or intercourse of navigations. Confirmed at London in the year 1495, between Henry VII. King of England, and Philip, Archduke of Austria, Burgundy, &c. From the Library of Marc Zuer Boxhorn." Then follows Selden's two Books as aforesaid.—The present writer will lay before the reader a brief report, of his own, of the drift and substance, of the Apology, the Treaty, and of the two Books. And will then let the several Historians speak for themselves.

183. In the Apology, Boxhorn, by reference to History and Treaties, contends for the rights of the Hollanders in the narrow seas. The Treaty, as the anonymous writer in MS., on the fly leaf, well observes; is a treaty "between equals," and King Henry who signs and seals it at Westminster on March 26, 1496, certainly makes no sort of claim to exclusive rights in any seas, such as Selden afterwards claims for his successor.

184. Selden in his first book ranges through all History, Sacred and Profane; treats of Divine Rights, the Israelites, the Greeks, the Syrian, Egyptian, Pamphylian, Lydian and Ægean Seas: and many other things Abstract and Material, which appear to have nothing to do with the present question. At the commencement of his second Book, he says:—"It having been shown in the former Book that the Sea and Land are equally capable of private dominion, and that by every sort of right, whether Divine, Natural or according to the Law of "Nations;" it remains, he says, to show the Rights of the King of Britain in the surrounding Ocean. He

* See Camden's Britannia, edition 1722, p. 1518.

insists that the Ocean surrounding Britain, which he affirms we call universally "British," is divided into four parts. All of which, he says or supposes, that several ancient authors whom he names have called *British* and the like he thinks is true of the Gallic and Biscayan Seas. And he gives a Map and quotes an *Arab* Geographer in that language (of all knowledge of which language the present writer is innocent) in support of his argument. The heading of his second Chapter is the assertion, "That the *British* not yet reduced under the power of the Romans, occupied as lords with the Island of that name, the Ocean having that surname, chiefly that which is on the South and East." Now on the other hand, we have Cæsar himself telling us the contrary in Art. 145 preceding, § viii. Cæsar there says, that the Veneti had very many ships with which they have been accustomed to sail into Britain, and that they had nearly all as tributaries who have been accustomed to use that sea. This clearly proves that the Veneti both possessed and exercised extensive rights in the English Channel. And Pliny the elder proves the same thing in the following passage, where he says that between it, namely the Seine, and the Pyrenees is Gallic property. For he says (*Nat. Hist.*, book 4, Sec. 33) after enumerating the Aquitanian Gauls :—"The seas about the coast [of Gaul]. At the Rhine is the Northern Ocean. British between the Rhine and the Seine. Between it [namely the Seine] and the Pyrenees is Gallic." He then tells us that there are, "Very many islands (almost two hundred) of the Veneti, which are called Veneticæ, and in the Aquitanian Bay, Uliarius." But we need not follow Mr Selden any further into the thirty-two chapters of his vain attempt to establish the right of the Kings of England to the Dominion of the Narrow Seas. For it is matter of notoriety that the rights of the Kings of England in Normandy and the Channel Islands and their Seas, originated precisely on the 14th October, 1066, when William, previously only Duke of Normandy and of the Channel Islands, conquered Harold, King of England, in the battle of Hastings, and became King of England himself, retaining still his Duchy of Normandy with all its appurtenances. Of these appurtenances the Channel Islands have continued to belong to the English Sovereigns down to the present day. These are the facts of the case.

185. It will however, notwithstanding the statement of facts which has just been given, in the latter part of Art. 184, be the most convenient course to allow the Historians to speak (with brevity) for themselves.

In the Appendix to Falle's History of Jersey (1734) is a letter by Abraham Morant, dated London, October 27, 1733, containing remarks on the 19th Chapter of the second Book of Mr. Selden's *Mare Clausum*, that letter having been addressed to Mr. Falle himself. In it Morant quotes Selden as saying :—"That the Kings of England have always (perpetuè) been in possession of the Islands near the French shore; that is (as he explains himself) of the Islands of Jersey, Garnesey, and others on the coast of Normandy and Bretagne, and consequently have been Masters of the Sea, in which these Islands lie." To which Morant replies in his letter (p. 442) as follows :—"These Islands were part of the ancient province of Neustria, and subject to the Kings of France of the first and second Race, till the year 912, when Charles IV. King of France, harassed by the repeated invasions of the Norman Free-Booters, was, in order to quiet them, forced to grant Rollo and his followers these Islands, with the whole rich Province of Normandy." And :—"When the Normans became possessed of Neustria, and with it of these Isles, they were by them withdrawn from the Jurisdiction of the Archbishop of Dol, and annexed to the See of Coutances."

186. The aforesaid date of 912 is interesting for our purpose for another reason, independent of the question of Neutrality. It was stated in the latter part of Art. 59 (on the authority of Tupper's *History of Guernsey*) that

the Channel Islands were transferred from the Diocese of Dol to that of Coutances, a full century later than Morant's date. If the correct date of the transfer is 912, than it must have been *(if ever)* at some time between 912 and 1356 (the year of the last Sinking about Jersey) that the Diocesan crossed the only water between Nomandy and Jersey, on a plank.

## FIVE THEORIES OF THE CAUSE OF THE NEUTRALITY, ALL DIFFERENT FROM EACH OTHER.

## DEFINITION OF THE NEUTRALITY.

### SELDEN'S THEORY: See his Book 2, p. 412, &c.

187. "'Nor indeed is it easily to be conjectured whence was derived that singular and perpetual right of Truce which the inhabitants of Cæsarea, Sarnia and the other islands lying before the Norman shore and in the sea itself, enjoy, wherever war rages amongst the surrounding nations, unless it be derived from this marine Dominion of the Kings of England. Concerning that right William Camden, most learned in the evidences of the ancients, speaks thus briefly:—' For by an ancient privilege of the Kings of England, there is here a kind of perpetual Truce, and how hot soever the war be, the French and others have liberty to come hither to Trade, and to depart again without molestation.'* But the same thing occurs more at length in some regal letters patent, where it is thus explained concerning Cæsarea:— ' that in time of war the Merchants of all nations and others as well strangers as natives, enemies as well as friends, freely, lawfully and with impunity can and may approach the said islands and maritime places with their ships, merchandise and goods, as well to escape storms, as to transact other their lawful affairs in the place and in that same place transact free commerce of traffickings, and the business of merchants, and remain there safely and securely, and pass from thence and return as many times as they please without harm, molestation or hostility whatsoever in their matters, merchandise and goods or their persons, and that, not only beneath the island and the maritime places aforesaid and the precinct of them, but also within the spaces everywhere distant from them as far as the sight of man, that is so far as the sight of the eye can follow.' "—And he asks whence this privilege can have been derived, if not from the Kings of England? You see that it extended as far as the acuteness of the eyes can be spread abroad (possit diffundi) from the shore. If not from the Kings of England, as they are both lords of the Sea and Islands (and it has been mentioned before, by what right the Islands themselves belong to them) has this privilege emanated, it cannot with reason be pointed out, whence it has arisen. This privilege is not extended to other Princes (so far as we know).† But only to the Kings of England; who unless they were lords everywhere of the circumambient ocean, by what title, have they prescribed truces of this sort in that matter throughout such large spaces applying to those islands amongst nations of every sort? Not only indeed in bays, as we have said, but also through the spaces thence, at will extended through their marine territory."

Such a peculiar privilege certainly requires a special explanation.

* This Treaty is not found in Mr. Rawdon Brown's *Venetian state Papers*, which will be referred to, towards the end of this chapter.

† We shall soon see that the Kings of France had the same privilege, and what is more they rigorously enforced it.

### MR. POINGDESTRE.

188. The following is Mr. Poingdestre's statement on the Neutrality. It is given entire (divided only into articles by numbers for convenience) because his is the best and most complete description of this remarkable privilege.

" Of the priviledge of Neutrality.

*(Harleian MSS. No. 5417, Chapter XI.)*

" I come nowe to a priviledge of all the Islands together soe singular that the like is not to be parallel'd elsewhere in any age, That a Tract of Islands should have and enjoye by the acknowlegment of all bordering naīons the benefitt of a perpetuall peace, not onely in theire Ports, but alsoe in y$^{e}$ seas about them, soe farre as the best eye of man cañ discover in the cleerest day; where the greatest enemyes, who any where else would pray upon one another, within y$^{e}$ compasse of that Priviledge become good friends and trade one with another as if they were not in warre. This priviledge howsoever strange it may appeare, is most certaine and hath been observed and acknowledged not onely by some particular men for theire private gaine, but by the Kings & Princes themselves; who have enjoyned the due observation of it to their subjects. But forasmuch as of late it is become something obscure, through the carelesnesse or neglect of some who ought to have cherished it, the Reader will pardon me if I dwell somewhat longer upon it. That there is such a thing as I havo sayd, may easily be shewed by testimony of writers, not onely of y$^{e}$ English nation, but others alsoe. Every body knows what Cambden says of it in his Britannia Cap. Insulæ minores many alsoe have scene Mr. Seldens booke de Dominio maris Cap. 19 & 21. where they acknowledge that in these Islands are perpetual Induciæ. they might have sayed Perpetua Pax; for it is rather a perpetuall peace, where there can be noe warre at all, then a Truce. But lett them give unto it the name of Truce or Neutrality or Refuge Place; it matters litle, soe the thing be acknowledged. Mr. Selden will have this priviledge to be derived from the onely grace & favour Beneficio Regum Angliæ; because he had seene it in k$^{g}$ Ed. 6 his charter, & perhaps he knewe noe other ground for it, then that. Indeed it is most true that without their speciall grace & most abundant favour wee could never have had it, much less have kept it. But yet if it be true that other Princes and nations are likewise concerned therein, it must alsoe be true that their concurrence & consent must have been had aforehand to make it effectuall; and this consent by long use and practice must have growne into an inveterate Custome; which hath y$^{e}$ force of Lawe, even among those who otherwise have no dependance from each other. Doctor Heylin in his survaye, sayes out of Selden that, That by ancient priviledge of the Kings of England there is in these Isles in a manner a continuall truce, & y$^{t}$ it is lawfull both for Frenchmen and others, howe hot soever the warre be followed in other parts, to repair thither without danger and there trade in all security. But it is a great mistake in him to add that this priviledge is founded upon a Bull of Pope Sixtus. It is true that there is such a Bull & a very thundering one.* But that the sayed priviledge could be sett up by any Pope; or that any instance be given that the like was ever don, it is not to be beleeved: For that is as if the Pope should against the right of all nacons take into his protection the subjects of any Prince in the time of open warre, and hinder his lawfull enemy from warring

* In Falle's History of Jersey, edition 1734, p. 334, is a copy of " The Bull of Pope Sixtus IV. touching the Privilege of Neutrality, contained in an inspeximus of K. Henry VIII." It is dated " 12th May in the fourth year of our reign." That is A.D. 1513. It denounces as Pirates, Thieves, Malefactors, &c., all who shall have infringed the Neutrality and declares that they are, ipso facto, subjected to the greater Anathema, and it fills more than eight closely printed 8-vo. pages. All the Islands of the Diocese of Coutances are included by it.

against them. As if he should excommunicate the Kg of France for assaulting any of y^e King of Spaine his Provinces in time of open warre. which being absurd to beleeve. wee may conclude that y^e sayd Bull was not the ground of y^e sayd Neutrality, but rather that y^e sayd Neutrality was y^e ground of the Bull. It is likewise true what he further adds, that this Bull was verified in the Parliam^t of Paris; & (he might have added) by the consent of Kg Lewis the Eleventh & confirmed by his sonne and successor Charles the Eight, and by his spall order proclaimed in all y^e Port towns of Normandy, as it had ben all Britany over before that, by y^e comand of Francis the last Duke of that Province; But it doth not follow that the said verification was merely in obedience to the Pope; who cannot excomunicate any one person for doing what the Lawe of nations & comon reason permitts, much lesse such an Assembly as that Parlement is knownne to have allwayes ben: but rather because they were assured that the Pope intended thereby to represse y^e insolencyes of those who went about to breake a Priviledge agreed to by all nacons, even by those who did violate it. for otherwise it had ben no iniustice in a free nacon not to submitt to an agreem^t made by others & not consented to by it selfe. The true cause then of this Neutrality must be an universall concurrence, either expresse or tacit of y^e Princes & States concerned therein, knowne to all their subjects, at least those having to doe with the Sea, & soe inured by continued use, that none could pretend ignorance of it, or have any just pretence to breake it. And such is this priviledge even in y^e judgment of strangers. The Booke called les Us et Coustumes de la mer, printed at Rouen by authority Ano 1671. Dabondant (sayth he) si la Prise a estr' faite en lieu d'Asyle ou de Refuge, come sont les Isles & mers de Jersey & Grenezay en la coste de Normandie, ausquelles les François & Anglois, poz. quelqs guerre qu'il y ait entre les deux Couronnes, ne doivent insulter ou courre l'ung sur l'autre, tant & si loing que s'estend l'aspect ou la veüe des dites Iles &c. Wee have here in Jersey the Patent of Henry the Seventh exemplifyed by his sonne Henry the 8th. conteining verbatim the foresayed Bull, & comanding y^e same to be notifyed and obay'd in all their Dominions. As for the Bull it selfe, it was obtained at the request of King Edouard y^e 4th presented to that Pope by his Ambassad^rs as it is express'd in the body of the Bull. It is somewhat long and tedious. but the Importance of the Priviledge requireth that it should be produced and inserted here at lenght." Mr. Poingdestre then quotes the Bull at full length. It does not give the date when it was issued, but it must have been between 1471 and 1483, that being the whole of the time during which Sixtus IV. and Edward IV. were contemporaries while Sixtus was Pope, and Edward, King. So that the Neutrality was in force then."

### MR. POINGDESTRE GIVES THE SUBSTANCE OF THE BULL.

189. "The sume of all is, that King Ed. 4. being sensible of the violation of this neutrality by some Roavers at Sea, thought good to seeke for a remedy by the Censures of the Church, which were in those times much redoubted which he obtained by his Ambassad^rs at Rome. This terrible Bull containes first a severe monitory, & then upon refusall to submitt, an Excommunication, Anathematization & Curse implying no lesse than eternall damnation, with confiscation of goods and chattells, & such Lands as the offend^rs held of the Church, dishabilitation to have or hold any Ecclesiasticall dignity, to dispose of goods by Testament, to make any valable Instrum^t, if they were Notaryes. The like against Abetters, favourers Receptors & buyers of goods taken contrary to y^e tenor of y^e Bull, allthough they were Comonaltyes; without sparing any of what dignity soever, Earles, Dukes, Princes, yea Kinges & Queenes alsoe. And to make

it more effectuall yᵉ. Archbishop of Cant. yᵉ. Bishop of Sarum & yᵉ. Dean of St. Peter, yᵗ. is Westmʳ. impowrd to pronounce it with Interdiction of all Acts & exercise of Religion, where it should be violated in publiqe & to see it duly executed &c."

190. "I would faine know whether in any reasonable mans opinion it be likely: first that Edward yᵉ. 4th. would have become a Suitor to yᵉ. Pope for such a strange Bull, to vindicate a Priviledge airy and doubtfull? or secondly, In case he had been soe weake as to doe it, whither we may suppose that the Pope reported for a prudent person, would have yeelded to his desire in a Request importing yᵉ. damnation of many Christian soules, soe much trouble to their persons & losse of goods & Estates? or if both they had ben soe grossely mistaken, yet may wee beleeve that Henry the 7th beleeved generally to have ben very cautious, & by King James in a Ltrè to yᵉ. Baillif and Jurats of this Islands styled an Excellent Prince, would unavisedly swallowed the sayd mistake; & his sonne Henry yᵉ. 8th. a very acute Prince have followed him therein, & have guyded his sonne Edward the 6 into yᵉ. same error, & after him his daughter Queene Elizabeth?"

191. "But forasmuch as I have heard it doubted by some, whither such a Priviledge in a frontier place, where the King keepes a perpetuall Garrison in pay, can be soe practicable as not to endanger yᵉ. security of it, in regard of Designes which, by meanes of such free accesse, might be framed underhand preiudiciall to his Maᵗⁱᵉˢ Right: I might in answeare to that doubt offer this Question; whither they thinke that soe many wise & warlick Princes who have allowed of it, were not prudent enough to see any Inconvenience following the same: But I will aske them further Whither they thinke it practicable in time of peace? If they say noe Then farewell all comerce. for all Townes of any considerable trading, are in some sort fortifyed, & may be surprised. But if they say yes, my Replye will be, That in these Islands it is allways time of Peace, espally for merchants & such like who come in a peaceable waye; But for others, it is yᵉ. part of such as Comand there, to see there be nothing don in preiudice of their Trust. But after all, why should the practicablenesse of it be called in question? when experience of soe many ages hath sufficiently shewed that it is soe. Wee have a Judgment in Parchment of very ancient writing, given at Morlaix, concerning a ship of Guernezey taken in yᵉ. Channel by a vessell of warre belonging to Britany, in the time of warre between England and France; which ship was released by virtue of yᵉ. sayd priviledge: yᵉ. true Coppy of which shall be given in its due place, after this Booke. In yᵉ. sayd Parchment is found a faire acknowledgmᵗ. both of yᵉ. priviledge & of yᵉ. practice of it during yᵉ. greatest hostility, wherein it is declared That allthough these Islands are of yᵉ. Kg. of England's obedience, neverthelesse they are neuters of all antiquity,* as well by reason of their sayd priviledge as by vertue of the agreemᵗˢ. made betweene yᵉ. Princes, & by Apostolicall Censures; as alsoe because it hath pleased the King our Soveraigne Lord (saythe the Governor of Britany who was at that time Francis the first King of France) to declare his will and intencon to be not to warre against them nor to doe them harm in body or goods, noe more than if they were of his obedience; And that likewise by Declaracon of yᵉ. King of England (viz Hen. 8.) yᵉ. Subjects of yᵉ. French King nor his Confederates were not to be hurt or molested in body or goods, soe long as they were within yᵉ. liberty of these Isles; soe as the subjects and Allyes of both Princes might with safety repaire and traffick therein, & in yᵉ. limitts

* Duncan's and Tupper's Histories of Guernsey will be quoted, presently. Duncan only traces the Neutrality up to 1472, Tupper thinks it did not exist in the 14th century, and Poingdestre gives no proof that it did. It certainly did not exist in Cæsar's time, for I think it has been proved that his sea-fight with the Veneti took place near some of the northern Channel Islands.

thereof as in a Country Neuter, not doing any act of warre one against another, under great penaltyes &c."

192. "The French Kings Declaracon therein mentioned concerning y^e. sayd neutrality, agrees to a Ltre. patent under seale, directed by Charles the 8th. to Mons^r. de Gravelle Admirall of France, published in all Port tounes of his Dominions A son de Trompe; whereof y^e. Coppy shall be placed hereafter, for y^e. very originall is with us, as likewise y^t. of Francis Duke of Britany, who before made y^e. like for his Dukedome: of which Ltres. because they were to serve in many places, they caused divers authenticall Copyes to be sealed and sent some to one port & some to another. There might be found divers more evidences for this priviledge, which are in particular hands. As for our public Records they were long time consumed by fire with y^e. Cohue: whereof one hath escaped very notable it happened in the Duke of Somersett's time, when y^e. warre was very hot with France. Some French vessells were then in the Port at St. Albin's laden and ready to sett sayle. It happened that some English Privateeres with three hundred men aboard them arrived theither, and offered to seize on them as Enemyes. which Henry Cornish then Deputy Gov^r. for the sayd Duke being informed of, caused the strenght of y^e. Island to be gathered together, & had layed them by y^e. heeles, had they not prevented him by departing thence. Moreover wee have an Act of the year 1524 made in y^e. Assembly of y^e. 3 Estates of this Isle the then Governor & y^e. Comissioners sent over hither from y^e. King being present, howe that a Prize made by one Denys Pointy within the precinct of these Isles, contrary to y^e. neutrality was judged tortionary and illegall, and y^e. sayd Pointy condemned to make restitution, with costs. which was accordingly don.

This neutrality was acknowledged long after, that is in 1614, in a plea for 3 Jersey merchants before y^e. Parlement of Britany, which is in Print, in which it is sayd, that these Islands had y^e. priviledge de rester neutres pendant les guerres d'entre les deux Royaumes.

Lastly in y^e. yeare 1628 when a Barke laden with goods from St. Malos & address^d. to Mr. Baillehache an Inhabitant, was sett upon by one Capt. Barker in the Port of S^t. Aubin lying at anchor there, the Court ordained that it should be released, for many reasons, & especially for this of neutrality, forasmuch (sayd y^e. Act) as it is not lawfull by our Priviledges confirmed by our most bountifull King, for any of his Captaines or other his subjects to take any one whether frend or foe about these Isles as farre as mans sight can extend it selfe, as they will answeare it at their perills & be severely punished &c. unto which Judgm^t. Capt. Barker did submitt. And during y^e. warre about y^e. Isle of Rhee and Rochel y^e. marchant Hosiers came from as farre as Rouan and Paris to Jersey & Guernezey and there bought & openly conveyed awaye a greate number of Bayles of Stockings, without any hinderance; and y^t. not once but many times: and y^e. same Liberty hath been taken at other times by those of Coutance & Carteret, who were connived at by the then Govern^r. though noe great freind to y^e. sayd neutrality."

### POINGDESTRE STATES THE BOUNDS OR EXTENT OF THE NEUTRALITY.

193. "There remaine yet two points to be cleered: the one concerning Bounds and Extent, y^e. other of the beginning or antiquity of this neutrality. The Judgm^t. of Morlaix above menconed says that the Guernezay ship in question was taken en la Grande Mer entre le pays d'Angletre & l'Isle de Guernezay, betweene Engld & Guernezay, belike in y^e mid-channell.* The

* At p. 374, &c., of the 1734 edition of Falle's *History of Jersey*, is a copy of "A letter of the Count de Laval, Governor of Bretagne; under Francis I., King of France, to the Magistrates of Morlaix, relating to a Prize taken contrary to the Privilege of Neutrality." It orders restitution to be made of the Barque, Goods and Merchandise. The date is June 20, 1523. It fills about six 8-vo. pages.

precinct of it y^e. Popes Bull & by y^e. Charter of y^e. two Henryes 7th & 8th expresses it per visum oculi. that of Queene Eliz. King James, King Charles y^e. first & second, quatenùs visus oculi posset assequi. nowe an ordinarye eye in a cleere sumer day will easily discover Le cap dettelles 3 leagues from S^t. Maloes which is about twelve* from Jersey; and in that proportion it will comprehend such a circuit of Sea as will take in all y^e coast of Normandy as farre as Cap de la Hague, above halfe waye to the coast of Britany towards Brehat and y^e. Seven Isles all y^e sea room betweene Jersey, Guernezey Sercke & Aureney; from y^e. North of Guernezey twelve or fourteen leagues towards y^e. ocean, and from Aureney neere halfe waye over the English Channell: within those bounds is y^e. Precinct of y^e. sayd neutrality to be limited; which may for that reason be called Mare Pacificum."

It will be well for the reader to bear in mind, in case he should ultimately come to the conclusion that the Neutrality originated from, & was consequently co-extensive with, the Sinking; that then it would follow that the Sinking must have extended from Alderney fully half way across the English Channel! The Boundary taken at 12 leagues from the nearest parts of the respective chief Islands, is marked on the general Map "Limit of the Neutrality."

### POINGDESTRE'S THEORY AS TO THE ORIGIN OF THE NEUTRALITY.

194. "The last point concerning y^e. begining or antiquity of this neutrality, is as obscure as the thing itselfe is certaine: the body of it is now in full viewe, as I think; but Caput inter nubila condit.† It is by some argum^ts. probable that y^e. first Inhabitants of these Isles came from the Coast of Britany. but that the Princes of y^t Provinse had to doe with the islands themselves in point of Dominion may appeare by what D'Armentre‡ reports in his Hist. viz. that Childebert King of France & Hoel styled by him King of Britany bestowed these Isles upon Sampson Bishop of Dol as an augmentation of Diocese, y^e. one as Imediate, the other as Paramount Lord thereof; & soe they continued long after in union with y^e. sayd province, from which they after received theire Christianisme; till being separated from it by y^e. Norman Invasion, they were forced to change their masters, & soe began to depend from that Coast, & were made part of y^e. Diocese of Coutance; yet not soe as to forgett theire old relacon to the Britons, with whom it is probable that they continued in amity, not entermedling with y^e. quarells which afterwards fell out betweene the Dukes of both Provinces. And it is as likely that when in King Johns dayes the Dukedom of Normandy revolted from him, y^e. sayd Islands felt very little or nothing of that change; except that some gentlemen of Normandy who possesst lands there were deprived of them for not coming to the King's peace; yet with this Caution, that they should be restored to them, cum terræ Angloru & Normannoru fuerunt comunes that is when Normandy should be reduced. In all other things the relation they had with Normandy remained entire as before y^e. several Religious Houses of that Dukedome who had lands or Tythes belonging to them in y^e. sayd Isles were suffered to enjoye them peaceably and quietly; & y^e. Bip of Coutance continued his care & Jurisdiction over them, without molestacon or intermission for

* 12 leagues by 2400 toises of 6.394593 feet each, give 30.3 nautical miles. By this measure the Neutrality is marked on the Map.

† "It hides its head among the clouds."

‡ D'Argentre, *Hist. Bret.* fol. 114B. "A cest Archeuesque [S. Magloire] Childebert donna quelques Isles & terres en Normandie, de Rimoul, Augia, Sargia & Vesargia, qui estoient Isles en la coste; car le trouue cela aux vielles lettres."

any warres yᵗ followed afterwards, downe allmost to our times; which could not be don, without a tacit agreement & correspondence between us & them, as it had ben afore betweene yᵉ Britons & us. And soe you may see here yᵉ spring and rising of these perpetuæ Induciæ in this Triple knott of the Islanders with yᵉ Brittons and Normans; which yᵉ Kings of France have hitherto connived at; and the Kings of England found soe necessary for us & soe litle prejudiciall to them; that they have don what I have declared heretofore to tye it faster. This entercourse & liberty of comerce with these Islands in time of warre being observed by other bordering nacons on these seas, they were easily induced to come into it by imitacon, & finding yᵉ good of it to continue and maintain it. And soe I have don with this notable Priviledge."

#### REMARKS ON POINGDESTRE'S THEORY OF THE NEUTRALITY.

195. Mr. Poingdestre simply begs the question. The Kings of France did far more than "connive" at the Neutrality. We have seen in the latter part of Art. 191 that King Francis I. of France declared his will and intention not to war against the Channel Islanders nor do them harm in body or goods, any more than if they were his own subjects. And in Art. 192 we have the Admiral of France by command of his Sovereign, proceeding under the authority of a Letter Patent to proclaim the Neutrality by sound of Trumpet in all the Port towns of France—a proceeding as solemn and official as possible, and extending far beyond *connivance*. The Duke of Brittany had previously done the like in his Dukedom. And both the King and Duke evidently did their utmost to establish the Neutrality in the most effectual manner, by causing authentic copies of the Declaration in favour of it, to be sealed and sent some to one port and some to another. Moreover, as we have seen, the Neutrality was carried into practical effect more than once, by compelling the restitution of Ships, Goods, &c., which had been seized in violation of it. There must have been something else in the back-ground which Mr. Poingdestre's theory does not reach. We shall see immediately that Duncan, Tupper, Camden and Falle—four commentators—are all dissatisfied with Poingdestre's theory, as proved by each of them publishing a new one of his own. And that Duncan and Tupper nearly agree with each other, but differ from Camden and Falle.

#### THEORY AND STATEMENTS IN DUNCAN'S HISTORY OF GUERNSEY.

196. It appears in Art. 188 that according to *Les Us et Coustumes de la mer*, the Neutrality only existed as between the French and the English. Poingdestre alleges (but gives no proof) that the Channel Islands are "neuters of all antiquity" which appears to be sufficiently disproved, especially by Pliny the elder's statement that the sea was *Gallic* from the Seine to the Pyrenees. It is stated in Duncan's valuable History, p. 223, that the privilege of Neutrality remained in force from the reign of Edward III. to the reign of William and Mary. The author of that work thinks that "Edward the third when in profound peace with all the powers of Europe, took into his gracious consideration the unhappy fate to which the Channel Islands had been exposed for many preceding centuries from the horrors of war, chiefly caused by their proximity to the French coast. To prevent the occurrence of these calamities, and to ensure peace and tranquillity for the future, the privilege of neutrality was conceded."—This cannot be the reason of the neutrality; for as we have seen, the French Monarch and the Duke of Britanny so far from having considered it a movement pointed against themselves, were as energetic and as willing to have it established

and put in force as the King of England or the Channel Islanders themselves. Duncan's allegation that it dates only from the time of Edward III., seems only to be founded on the fact which he states as follows:—"The first instance of this convention is a safe conduct from Louis, the bastard of Bourbon, then admiral of France, in the name of the King his master, dated Valognes, Feb. 25, 1472, applicable only to the inhabitants of Guernsey and the islets depending upon it, such as Serc, Herm and others which it is practicable to reach at low water,* excluding all others except the Parish of the Vale, and the isles of Lihou and Castle Cornet; and this order was to be in force till the 15th of April following, when a general safe conduct was promised."

But there must have been some cause for this safe conduct of an *earlier* date. Because it is to the last degree improbable that the King of France would have issued a safe conduct at that particular time, ex mero motu, and without any reason at all other than what had always existed. Why should he have taken any more interest in the Channel Islands, than in any other territory which did not belong to him? Duncan's History assigns no reason for the Neutrality except a conjecture that it was to prevent a recurrence of calamities. A reason which is equally applicable to every other part of the world, but which has nowhere else led to Neutrality. Therefore it cannot be the reason of the Neutrality.

197. Duncan says that in 1482, Charles King of France, ordered the release of a Guernsey barque and 25 to 30 traders and their effects, the same having been seized and detained at the port of Lantriguer. Several other similar cases of the enforcement of the Neutrality are recorded by Duncan.

198. At p. 121 of Tupper's important and interesting *History of Guernsey*, it is stated that Pero Nino afterwards Conde de Buelna, a Spaniard, persuaded the Breton lords to join him in an expedition against Jersey. And at least 1000 men, Spaniards, Normans and Bretons, landed and had a sanguinary battle with the Islanders in 1406. The transaction appears to have been lawless, but it does not prove either that the Neutrality did, or did not, exist as early as 1406, nor does it even prove that the attack was an infringement of the Neutrality. For we have seen (at the commencement of Art. 188) that the tract of Islands had and enjoyed by acknowledgment of all bordering nations the privilege that: "Soe far as the best eye of man can discover in the clearest day" the greatest enemies should become good friends and trade one with another, and by the printed and authorised Law in *Les Us et Coustumes de la mer* of 1671, we find that—if a prize was taken in an Asylum or place of Refuge, such as are the Isles and Seas of Jersey and Guernsey on the coast of Normandy (as between the French and English) in any war which may be between the two Crowns, they must not insult or chase one another so much and so far as the aspect or view from the said Isles extends itself. Ships and cargoes were evidently the objects in favour of which the Neutrality existed. Not military operations on land, nor the protection of life or property on land. Must we not therefore conclude that the Neutrality was connected with something specially belonging to the Sea, and do not the vast Sinkings which changed so much Land into Sea, exactly supply an adequate cause? Was not the land which had sunk and become sea still private property and not part of the High Seas, and was it not therefore necessarily Neutral?

* It is not practicable to go *on foot* from any one of these islands to any other at low water, at present.

### THEORY STATED IN TUPPER'S HISTORY OF GUERNSEY.

199. This History says, p. 127, "Moved by the calamities to which the Islanders were subjected from their proximity to France, and which he* had probably witnessed in Guernsey, that monarch conceded this Neutrality to them, and solicited the Pope to enforce it with the anathemas of the church."—These words signify protection against France; but on the contrary, France was a party to the Neutrality and a strenuous supporter of it, as we have already seen, and Mr. Tupper himself tells us at p. 129, where it is stated that:—"In the year 1523, temp. Henry VIII., during the war between England and France, a Guernsey vessel taken in the Channel by a privateer of Morlaix, was, by order of Count de Laval governor of Britanny, released in consequence of this privilege." And as the French carried the Neutrality into effect quite as strenuously as the English, it is impossible that King Edward *alone*, can have originated the Neutrality.

### CAMDEN'S THEORY.

200. Camden calls the Neutrality "An ancient privilege of the Kings of England," which allegation as made by Selden has, it is submitted, been signally disproved. Besides, grants from the Kings of England could obviously bind no one but themselves and their subjects. We do not appear to have advanced one single step towards accounting for this singular privilege, unless we accept the theory that the Neutral country was the Sunken country.

The Neutrality was finally extinguished by the arbitrary act of King William III, about the beginning of the 18th century.† Or according to another authority, the Neutrality ceased in 1689.‡ Selden's and Camden's theories are identical, the one with the other.

### FALLE'S THEORY.

201. Mr. Falle the Historian of Jersey, thinks that "the strongest reason for the concession of this Neutrality is to be sought principally in the very limited commerce of those times, and that it excited little or no attention, or jealousy among the contending powers." Now on the contrary, we have seen by the Pope's Bull, and the repeated restorations of vessels and goods captured in violation of the Neutrality—both on the part of England, France and Britanny: that infringements of the Neutrality did excite a great deal of attention, and were strenuously resisted on all hands.

202. The present writer has carefully examined Mr. Rawdon Brown's Calendar of Venetian State papers, but though the latter gives many papers relating to international transactions between France and England in the 15th century, the papers throw no light whatever on the subject of the Neutrality, which is never alluded to.

### SUMMARY OF OPINIONS AS TO THE CAUSE OF THE NEUTRALITY.

203. Selden and Camden think it was an ancient privilege of the Kings of England.

Poingdestre thinks it arose from what he calls a Triple Knott of the Islanders with the Brittons and Normans.

Duncan thinks it originated from King Edward Third's pity for the losses

* King Edward IV., 1461 to 1483.

† Duncan's *Hist. of Guernsey*, page 231. ‡ Tupper's *Hist. of Guernsey*, p. 138.

the Islanders had sustained during many centuries from the French. Tupper thinks with Duncan, referring however to Edward the Fourth.

Falle thinks it arose from the commerce being limited, and (he alleges) captures excited little or no attention.

Lastly, the present writer thinks Neutrality was co-extensive with the Sinking in the Channel Island's Seas, and that the former originated in consequence of the latter. But he distinctly says that by far the largest part of the sunken land namely on the west and north, has always been subaqueous since Cæsar's time. His allegation only is, that the soundings on the west and north within the limit of the Neutrality, are probably deeper than they were in Cæsar's time.

204. The last Sinking (which was near S. Malo) appears to have happened in 1437, or not long after. And in Art. 196, we first find the Neutrality in operation, *after* that date, viz.: on Feb. 25, 1472; which was no doubt after the farm of Césembre had disappeared, as explained in Art. 92. We have seen in Art. 100, that a French league is equal to 5,116⅜ yards, and that Poingdestre supposes the Neutrality to have extended about 12 leagues* from each of the islands Jersey, Guernsey and Alderney. This distance is equal to about 30½ Nautical miles, and the limits of the Neutrality are marked accordingly on the general Map. If the limits of the Sinking and the Neutrality be identical the former appears to have extended above half way across the Channel, and in that case the Deeps would of course indicate the lines of Deepest Sinkings.

*Note.*—Chapters xv. and xvi., which refer to the French coast of the Bay of Biscay, are not ready for publication. Especially as when my leisure serves, through the kindness of my friend, Henry Witcomb, Esq., I am assured that Mr. Cortambert, of the Imperial Library of Paris, will be happy to render me every assistance in his power, and he says he shall be able to place at my disposal many works that will give me some very valuable information on the subject of my work. I will however quote a remarkable passage from the Geography of Pomponius Mela (A.D. 45), which is as follows:—"A Garumnæ exitu, latus illud terræ procurrentis in pelagus† et ora Cantabricis objecta littoribus." That is to say 'From the mouth of the Gironde that side of the land [of Gaul which he is describing] running into the sea, and the coasts are *opposite to* the Cantabrian shores.' Now Cantabri and Cantabria, mean respectively the people and the province of *Biscay*, in Spain. But Cordouan isle and the present mouth of the river Gironde, are *not* opposite Biscay; but if Ptolemy is correct in exhibiting them as having been in his time, much farther out into the Bay of Biscay; then, and in that case they may have been *opposite* Biscay. And Ptolemy and Mela may have been both correct, instead of concurring in an error. See Map 2.

## CHAPTER XVII.

230. The following is an extract from the Jersey Magazine for the year 1809, p. 153. Published by J. Stead, not now published.

### A FORGED CHART.

*Encroachments of the Sea.*—On this subject the following particulars have been related by a person whose veracity cannot be questioned, however he may have been imposed upon in some points by the Dutch skipper who gave him the information. At every event the facts as they are reported are interesting and worthy of further inquiry.

'About the year 1799, the captain of a Dutch Surinam ship belonging

* Art. 193. † ? Pelagum.

to Amsterdam, saw at Calais in the possession of a respectable individual who had been mayor of that place, a chart of the British Channel and of a part of the North Sea, delineated on parchment; this chart which was 850 years old, extended on the east to Heligoland ; on the north to Orfordness ; and on the west to the present site of the Isle of Wight, which then formed part of the main land of England [?]. The principal headlands as they now exist were correctly laid down. Between Dover and the opposite side of the coast of France, there was a space of three miles only [?]. Calais must therefore have then been situated in the interior. Not any entrance was described either into Dunkirk, Flushing, or Beerhaven, the Island of Goree being attached to the main land, of which it formed a part. There was not any passage to Rotterdam. Not any Flemish banks were laid down; the space occupied by them, and immediately between them and the coast opposite, likewise constituting a portion of the main land. But in the North Sea, the depth of water in this chart corresponded with the present depth. The Vlie or Fly Island, as it is now called, was connected with the main land .... The island of Jersey was once so near the coast of France, that the small brook separating it from the main land, required nothing more than a plank for the passengers to cross ; and it is not many centuries since the house in Jersey, which anciently supplied the plank, still paid a small fine in lieu of that service. 'S'.

231. Now the Isle of Wight was an Island in A.D. 43 or 44. We read in Suetonius that Claudius "compelled two very powerful nations, and above twenty towns, and lastly the Isle Vectis of Britain to surrender partly under the command of Aulus Plautius the consular lieutenant, and partly under that of Claudius himself." Claudius reigned from A.D. 41 to 54.—It may be seen in the *Appendix* to p. 91 (see after), that Pliny (died A.D. 79) includes the Isle Vectis (by which name the Isle of Wight was well known to the Romans) amongst a number of other islands which he names. Erroneously saying that Vectis was between Ireland and Britain. We have also seen in Art. 157 that Cedric after a great battle in 519, bestowed upon his nephews the subordinate sovereignty of the Isle of Wight, and died in 534.—And we have seen in Art. 159, on the authority of Domesday Book, that the Isle of 'Wit' or Wight, was an island in 1086 ; and of course it has been an island ever since. The chart therefore was a forgery in showing the Isle of Wight as not an island in the middle of the tenth century.

232. *With regard to the width of the Straits of Dover.*—Cæsar "orders all to assemble at the harbour Itius ; from which harbour he knew the passage into Britain was the most convenient, about 30,000 paces from the continent."* Doubtless the distance across was about the same as at present, though the form of both the English and French coasts have altered so much as to have caused the well-known difficulty in identifying the places whence Cæsar sailed from Gaul and where he landed in Britain. He is not likely to have made a passage of 30 Roman miles in length (= 27½ English miles) if the narrowest passage was only 1-9 or 1-10 of that distance, as it must have been if our famous chart had been correct. The late Admiral White assured the present writer, that in taking soundings on the Varne and the Ridge, two shallows in the Straits of Dover, he often brought up with the sounding lead pieces of fossil ferns. And in January, 1861, the present writer also obtained from John Slater, an Oyster Fisherman living at Gorey, a fossil fern which he said he had dredged up in the Straits of Dover, between Dover and Calais. England has probably not been joined to the continent since the Glacial period.

* *Cæsar de Bell. Gall.*, Book v., sec. 2.

SUBMERGENCES ON THE DUTCH AND BELGIAN COASTS.

233. Sir Charles Lyell* speaks of the contests of the ocean on one hand, and the river Rhine at its mouth on the other hand, for ascendancy. He states that there was a period when the river had the advantage in the struggle, and "perhaps the relative level of the coast" and set of the tides were very different: but for the last two thousand years the result has been in favour of the ocean. He speaks however of natural and artificial barriers having given way and admitted very destructive inroads of the sea. And quotes M. E. de Beaumont as having "suggested that there has in all probability been a general depression or sinking of the land below its former level over a wide area." He also mentions that one of the most memorable inroads of the sea in Holland occurred in 1421, when the tide burst through a dam and overflowed seventy-two villages and formed a large sheet of water called the Dies Bosch. "Thirty-five of the villages were irretrievably lost, and no vestige, even of their ruins, was afterwards seen." It is difficult to account for the entire and permanent disappearance of every vestige of these thirty-five villages, unless we suppose (what is very probable) that the alluvial ground has sunk and been silted over with sand, as in the Bay of Mont S. Michel. If it did not sink, there would have remained some ruin or gable, or at the very least heaps of bricks and stones, or of ships which had sunk; as also of wrecked ships and bones of hundreds of drowned sailors in Haarlem Lake,† but nothing of the kind has ever been discovered. A careful examination of ancient Records, still probably obtainable, would decide as to the formation of the Zuyder Zee and Straits of Staveren inundated in the 13th century, also as to the series of Islands from the Texel to the mouth of the Weser, of which much has been lost since Pliny's time, also as to the losses of the Isle of Heligoland since the year 800, *whether they are due to Sinkings or not*. And the same with respect to that which is now a Bay called the Dollart, and was it appears an alluvial plain of great fertility in the time of the Romans. We have testimony that changes of level of land have taken place on the coast of Holland. Mr. Godwin-Austen says:—"The Polder formation indicates a change of level, or of relative elevation of the land, of small amount, but of remarkable uniformity, from Ostend to the coast of Hanover.... from specimens in the Antwerp Museum it would appear that when a breach is made in the Polder mud, a terrestrial surface with large trees is exposed. The like was met with in the excavations for the new docks, consisting of rich peat. This old land surface is to be seen at low water, beneath the Polder mud. In like manner it underlies the Zeeklei of Holland; and much probably of the surface of the peat or old fen of Belgium and Holland (Hooge Veenen), above the level of the Polders, is merely an upward and inland extension of the same surface of plant-growth."‡

Again, in Sir C. Lyell's *Principles of Geology*, 1867, p. 549, is a Map exhibiting by dark tint, that the land all the way from Antwerp to beyond Nieuport, 100 miles in length by perhaps 20 miles in breadth—was land in the time of the Romans. That it was then overflowed by the sea before and during the 5th century, and afterwards reconverted into land. Whether this reconversion was caused by artificial embankments, or whether the land itself rose in height, we are not informed. These changes were of course, *within the Historical period*.

* *Principles of Geology*, 1853, chap. xx.

† *Antiquity of Man*, p. 147.

‡ Godwin-Austen, on the Belgian Tertiaries, Pro. Geol. Soc., Jany., 1866, p. 252.

### SUNKEN TRACTS GENERALLY BECOME SILTED OVER AND CONCEALED.

234.—I have previously expressed hopes that dredging on the sunken tracts would form a crucial test as to the actuality of the Sinkings. My hopes of proofs of that kind are now small for some time to come. Mr. Jeffreys says "in exploring the present sea bottom, we can only hope to examine a very few inches in depth.* And we find in the published reports of Forbes and M'Andrew and other experienced dredgers, that "while they failed utterly in drawing up from the deep, a single human bone, they declared that they scarcely ever met with a work of art even after counting tens of thousands of shells and zoophytes. These were collected on a coast line of several hundred of miles in extent, where they approached within less than half a mile of a land peopled by millions of human beings."† And in draining the lake of Haarlem, Sir Charles says that in the whole 45,000 acres, human bones were sought for in vain.‡

### LAND SHELLS FOUND ON SEA BOTTOM MAY POSSIBLY BE INDICATIONS OF A SUNKEN COUNTRY.

Mr. Jeffreys, having taken by the trawl, a land shell, *Helix rupestris*, in 20 to 30 fathoms seaward of Plymouth, explains it, not as a relic of a sunken country, but as having been probably washed down by a river or freshwater stream and transported a long way before it sunk to the bottom :|| his opinion on this point may, or may not, be correct. He also says the like of a *Trochus Helicinus*, also a land shell, dredged by him about 25 miles north of Unst the most northerly of the Shetland Islands. He thinks the shell must have been dropped there by some animal.§ He however in consequence of havingdredged up shallow water shells, mentions that they afford another confirmatory proof of his hypothesis that "the Shetland sea-bed has sunk considerably during a comparatively recent period."** History is against the supposition that this change can have taken place during the Historical period. Cæsar describes Britain as triangular, and assigns respectively to its south, west, and east coasts; the lengths of 500, 700, and 800 Roman miles.†† This is roughly its present shape, and though the losses of land on its coasts by Sinking and Washing away have greatly exceeded its gains‡‡ since Cæsar's time, we may not suppose there have been any considerable submergences during that period. Neither does the occurrence of dead littoral shells in the bed of the German Ocean, forty miles from the coast of Aberdeen,|||| refer us to anything so recent as the Historical period. Because if there had been an island or promontory so far out in the German Ocean, Cæsar or Ptolemy or some other of the ancient Historians or Geographers would have mentioned it. The like remarks apply to the circumstance of shallow water shells having been brought up from the bottom of the Atlantic, between Malta and Jamaica. But all these circumstances afford a new source of interest to Conchologists and Geologists, namely that they may look to this as an established fact which their labours may be expected to corroborate from time to time—namely that extensive Submergences have taken place, not only during the

* *British Conchology*, Introduction, p. lxxxix. † *Antiquity of Man*, p. 146.

‡ I hope the day is near at hand when Dredging will be conducted on Scientific and Exhaustive principles. Namely, by using steam-vessels drawing a heavy Dredge 15 or 20 feet wide on each side.

|| *British Conchology*, vol. 1, p. 222. § *Brit. Conch.*, vol. 3, p. 297.

** See his *Report to Brit. Assn.*, 1864, p. 329. †† *Bell. Gall.*, lib. v., sec 10.

‡‡ See Lyell's *Principles of Geology*, 1867, chap. xx.

|||| See Mr. Robert Dawson's paper, *Pro. Geol. Soc.*, Feb., 1866, p. 260.

Primary, Secondary, and Tertiary periods—but also throughout the Post Tertiary period, and down to the present day.

235.—Mr. Geikies' interesting papers* show that there must have been an elevation of a large tract of low land at the mouth of the Clyde within the last sixteen or seventeen centuries.

OTHER SINKINGS ON THE COASTS OF THE ENGLISH CHANNEL.

236.—But to return to the English Channel. Sir C. Lyell states that "at the mouth of the river Canche, which joins the sea near the embouchure of the river Somme, yew trees, firs, oaks, and hazels have been dug out of peat which is there worked for fuel, and is about three feet thick. During great storms, large masses of compact peat, enclosing trunks of flattened trees, have been thrown up on the coast of the mouth of the Somme; seeming to indicate that there has been a subsidence of the land and a consequent submergence of what was once a westward continuation of the valley of the Somme, into what is now a part of the English Channel."† The tendency of Sir Charles's views is hardly to attribute these trees to a period so recent as the Historical, yet he does not actually controvert such a supposition. For he says (p. 110) that the workmen deny that the peat grows. "This, as M. Boucher de Perthes observes, is a mistake; but it implies that the increase in one generation is not very appreciable by the unscientific." We are not therefore precluded even by adopting all these views from believing, that so small a thickness of peat as three feet, may have accrued, and consequently that a subsidence may have taken place, within the Historical period at the mouth of the Somme. In fact at p. 111 Sir Charles says "we have already seen what changes in the relative level of sea and land have occurred in Scotland since the time of the Romans, and are therefore prepared to meet with proofs of similar movements in Picardy." And if analology may count for anything, we have had still farther and stronger reasons for believing in the subsidence at the mouth of the Somme, from the many Sinkings which have been proved to have taken place on neighbouring parts of the French coasts.

237.—With respect to Ptolemy's position of the city of *Juliobona*, Which would have been only a slender foundation, if it had stood alone: We have a support to his statement in a degree at least; namely by Quenaut's ancient Chart, and the alleged fact already stated, that the Marcou Islands once formed part of the continent.

THEORY AS TO THE DEEPS IN THE ENGLISH CHANNEL.

238.—With regard to the "Deeps" on the Map No. 2; they are (speaking roughly) about 50 per cent deeper than the sea immediately adjoining them. And it appears very probable that they are due to unequal subsidences of the sea-bottom, and no period is so likely for such subsidences to have occurred, as the times when subsidences were taking place on both sides of the English Channel, namely within the Historical period. Without stepping aside into the great question now debated in the scientific world, *how have the Lake basins been formed?*—farther than is necessary for the present purpose: the present writer may be permitted to observe, that he is quite disposed to believe the theory of M. Guyot, as the only reasonable solution of the present positions of the erratic blocks and drift in the great valley of Switzerland.‡ The various species of Igneous

* Geikie, Geol. Quart. Journ., vol. xviii. † *Antiquity of Man*, p. 109.

‡ See Sir C. Lyell's *Antiquity of Man*, p. 297 et seq.

erratics have evidently been supplied from the masses of rock *in situ* and of corresponding species, which are still to be seen on both sides of the Rhone. And which after debouching from the mouth of the Rhone valley at the east end of the lake of Geneva, must have been carried straight across the great Swiss valley, by an enormous glacier in the glacial period, as moraines; partly to Chasseron near the S.W. end of lake Neuchatel, where their maximum height is 2,015 feet above the surface of the lake. Part of the erratics derived from the same parent rocks on the right bank of the Rhone, after debouching at the east end of Geneva lake, have turned along by Berne to Soleure, where their maximum height not being so great by 1,600 feet as the height of those at Chasseron—that great declivity sufficiently accounts for the erratics having been carried by glacier action to Soleure. In like manner, other erratics derived from parent rocks of other Igneous species on the left bank of the Rhone, have been carried along the present course of the lake of Geneva, to the town of that name, near which some of them are now found, also at about 1,500 feet lower than those at Chasseron. The Igneous erratics supplied by the valley of the Rhone can easily be distinguished from the limestones, sandstones and clays which crop out on the sides of the great Swiss valley, and on which those Igneous erratics now lie. Now some eminent Geologists suppose that the enormous glaciers of the glacial period, may themselves have scooped out the great lakes of Switzerland and Italy—a theory to which Sir Charles and others object. The present writer believes that the question whether the lake basins are due to glacial action, or to unequal subsidence—will ultimately be settled by a compromise. That is to say, the question as to any given lake will have to be settled by whatever evidence can be gathered as to its own individual history. For example, Sir Charles well observes that if such scooping out by the glacier had really taken place, there ought to have been a great lake extending from the east end of lake Geneva across the great valley to the S.W. end of lake Neuchatel; because the glacier would have had greater thickness, *i.e.*, greater power; between the two points named, than it could have had along the actual lake of Geneva. But there is in fact no lake extending from the east end of Geneva lake to Chasseron, as there ought to have been by the *glacial* theory. He also points out similar weak points in the scooping-out-by-glaciers theory, in the Italian valleys. We can well understand that glaciers may, and do, plane and groove rocks, and that they also plough up the earth to at least a moderate depth. But it is impossible to suppose that they can ever have hollowed out one of the great lakes. Let us take for example Lago Maggiore which Sir Charles says (p. 312) is more than 2,600 feet deep—say half an English mile, or 2,640 feet. How impossibly stupendous must have been the magnitude of the glacier, for it to have scooped out solid rocks and earth to that great depth! Farther, suppose we take one-fourth of the extreme depth as a rough approximation to the average depth, and take also the lake as 38 miles long by an average of two miles wide, which length and breadth are about correct, according to Mr. Keith Johnston's Atlas. This would give a capacity to the lake of no less than 9½ cubic miles. The *Athenæum* of December 28, 1867, in a Review of Mr. Morell's *Scientific Guide to Switzerland*, quotes him as stating that the length of Lago Maggiore is 40 miles, its breadth 1½ to 3 miles, and its depth 2,465 feet; which by the same method of calculation give its content as 10½ cubic miles. The reviewer also quotes Professor Ansted's *Physical Geography*, as stating the length at 54 miles, the breadth 3 to 8 miles, and depth only 1,100 feet; which give the content on the same hypothesis, 15⅔ cubic miles. The three sets of data give results more nearly concurring than the wide differences of the dimensions rendered probable.

Not to overstate the case, I take the *smallest* cubic content of the Lake. And lakes Geneva and Constance, and Wener and Wetter, as well as the lakes of Central Africa and the great American lakes are still more capacious. If these were all excavated by glaciers, what became of all the prodigious masses of rocks and earth after they were excavated? The advocates of the excavation theory, to be consistent, ought to go a step farther, and contend for the Baltic, the Adriatic, and the Black and Caspian seas having been also excavated by glaciers: a development of their theory which they probably would not venture to support. How can there ever have been glaciers on the very Equator itself, so inconceivably great as to have hollowed out the immense lakes of Africa? Yet on the other hand, if we examine the rest of the Maps of Switzerland, of Southern Norway, and of Northern and Central Sweden*—I do not see how we can avoid the conclusion, that the small lakes there are due, in part at least, to the ploughing up by glaciers—if we give proper consideration to their elongated forms stretching along the valleys in the directions which the glaciers must have taken.

239. It is worth while to pursue the glaciers excavation theory a step farther, not for its own sake, but out of respect to the few eminent men of Science who are supporters of it. The 9½ cubic miles of solid material would more than equal the content of a frustrum of a square pyramid, equal in height to the height of Mont Blanc above the sea, *i.e.*, 3 miles; each of the four sides of the bottom measuring 2½ miles, and the top being a mile square. In other words, 9½ cubic miles are equal to 18,645 times the cubic content of the great pyramid in Egypt.† Where is the vast mass of solid materials now, and where is the similar mass which, according to the glacier excavation theory, must have been excavated from lake Como? Assuredly these masses are not to be found on the banks, or in the beds, of the small tributary rivers which convey the surplus waters of those lakes to the Po! We at once get rid of these great difficulties by supposing with Sir Charles Lyell, that the ground subsided, or was upheaved, unequally; and so produced cavities for the great lakes and Seas. Probably therefore, the bottom of the English Channel subsided unequally, and produced the "Deeps." And there is no time so likely for its latest subsidences to have occurred, as the time, or times. when large tracts were subsiding along its coasts within the Historic period.

240. In order to admit of such subsidences, I have endeavoured to show in a tract on Steam, &c., that there *must* be cavities in the Earth's crust: because of the Eleven reasons (or some of them) which are stated in the said Tract.

### CAVITIES IN THE EARTH'S CRUST.

It cannot be supposed that the excavations forming the beds of the great lakes and inland seas, are due to accidental floods, such as that which occurred in the valley of Bagnes in 1818;‡ when "this flood left behind it, on the plains of Martigny, thousands of trees torn up by the roots, together with the ruins of buildings. Some of the houses in that town were filled with mud up to the second story." This small excavation of a few feet in depth of

* See an interesting paper in the *Quarterly Journal of Science*, January, 1867, p. 44.

† See *Antiquity of Man*, p. 40, where the pyramid is said to contain 75 millions of cubic feet.

‡ *Principles of Geology*, 1853, p. 210.

alluvion, is utterly inadequate to account for lakes and seas whose depth can be reckoned by thousands of feet.

241. It is not contended that the phenomena treated of in this tract, were directly due either to volcanic action, or to earthquakes, or to violent action of any kind. They appear to have been simple settlings down almost without noise, and from unknown causes, of large tracts of dry land and sea bottom, into cavities which must necessarily have pre-existed, else no subsidences could have taken place; and the roofs of which gave way at the several dates stated, for reasons which are not understood. There is no ground for believing that any of the Sinkings are continuous as in the South of Sweden. The Steam Tract referred to, attempts to show in what way volcanoes, earthquakes, and such cavities, are all connected together.—I think we cannot avoid the conclusion that within the Christian period there have been extensive and deep subsidences of land along the north-coasts of Europe (with few intervals) from the mouth of the Weser and north of Holland, to the Pyrenees; the French coasts having subsided to a greater depth than the Dutch and Belgian. There is considerable reason to believe that within the same period, the subsidences may have extended all across the English Channel from the north coast of Britanny and west coast of Normandy, to Cornwall.

## MR. LAMONT ON SPITZBERGEN.

242. Mr. Lamont's paper on *Risings* of land at Spitzbergen, read before the Geological Society in 1859, is very interesting. It is relevant to our present purpose because it helps to prove that changes in the level of Land have taken place within the Historic period and are not confined to Prehistoric times. Drift wood and bones of whales being found 30 feet above present high water, plainly prove that a change of level must have taken place much within the Historic period:—

Mr. Lamont cruised about Spitzbergen in his yacht in the summer of 1858, and went up the Stour Fiord, which he remarks is a Sound dividing the island, not a Gulf. The first thirty miles of coast along which he sailed on this Fiord, consisted almost entirely of the faces of two or three enormous glaciers: the water is shallow, seldom as much as 16 fathoms, and such appears to be the case all around Spitzbergen; and hence icebergs of very large size are not found. The shores are mostly formed of a muddy flat, from ½ mile to 3 miles broad ...Protruding trap rocks appear on these flats ....The upper part of the Sound has much drift wood, chiefly small pine trees weatherworn and waterlogged, and some wreck wood. Bones and skeletons of whales are numerous. Drift wood and bones of whales were observed several miles inland, and high above highwater mark—at least 30 feet. Whales skeletons were also seen high up on the 'Thousand Islands.' These circumstances connected with the fact that seal fishers and whalers state their belief in the shallowing of these seas, lead the author to think that Spitzbergen and the adjacent islands are emerging from the sea at a rate even more rapid than that at which some parts of Norway have been shown to be rising.—*Anthenæum*, June 25, 1859, p. 845.

## PERPETUAL RISINGS AND SINKINGS OF LAND HAVE OCCURRED AT ALL PERIODS AND IN ALL PLACES.

One of the most eminent Geologists of the present day, well observes:—"To those whose attention has never been called to the former changes in the earth's surface which geology reveals to us, the position of land and sea appears fixed and stable. It may not seem to have undergone any material alterations since the earliest times of history; but when we enquire into the subject more closely, we become convinced that there is annually some small variation in the geography of the globe. In every century the land is in some parts raised, and in others depressed in level, and so likewise is the bed of the sea." *Lyell's Principles of Geology*, 1867; Vol. 1 p. 248.—And again, Sir C Lyell says:—"in our own times, as for example in Chili, in 1822, the volcanic force has overcome the resistance, and permanently uplifted a country of such vast extent that the weight and volume of the Andes must be insignificant in comparison; even if we indulge the most moderate conjectures as to the thickness of the earth's crust above the volcanic foci." —*Ibid.* p. 133.

# APPENDIX AND VOUCHERS.

(*See p.* 1, 31, *ante.*)

## ON THE LENGTH OF TIME DURING WHICH BRITAIN WAS POSSESSED BY THE ROMANS.

Mr. Lewin, on reading a paper "On the Castra of the Saxonicum littus," at the Society of Antiquaries, began by fixing the limits of the Roman rule in Britain from A.D. 42 when A. Plautius arrived, to A.D. 409, when the Romans, according to Zosimus the cotemporary historian, were finally expelled, so that their domination lasted for just 367 years — *Athenæum*, June 29, 1867, p. 857.

Gibbon says (vol. 1, p. 5): "The only accession which the Roman empire received, during the first century of the Christian Æra, was the province of Britain... After a war of about forty years undertaken by the most stupid, [Claudius, who reigned A.D. 41—54] maintained by the most dissolute, [Nero, who reigned A.D. 54—61] and terminated by the most timid, of all the emperors, [Domitian who reigned A.D. 81—96] the far greater part of the island submitted to the Roman yoke"... Vol. V, p. 346. Britain and Armorica revolted from the Romans A.D. 409.

## THE ROMAN ITINERARY, SO-CALLED, OF ANTONINUS.

The following are a few facts gathered chiefly from Wesseling's Preface to the Itinerary. This Preface, while it contains a large mass of very valuable comments on the authorship of the Itinerary, by about seventy learned men—is the most crabbed and complicated piece of latinity I ever encountered. The several dates I have added.

Alexander the Great had his *Bæmatistæ* or measurers of his journeys. And it is not likely that such data would either be destroyed or allowed to sink into oblivion. No doubt they formed a basis for the Itinerary. B.C. 355—323.

Some other materials for an Itinerary, existed as early as Polybius's time, 124 B.C.

Strabo who died A.D. 25, Pomponius Mela who flourished about A.D. 45, and Pliny the elder who lived A.D. 23—79; laboured very diligently in this business.

Metius Pomposianus who lived A.D. 81—96, represented the whole world on parchment.

Marinus the Tyrian and Claudius Ptolemy, laboured hard in preparing materials that were suitable for an Itinerary.

The Romans penetrated the whole of Britain in the first century after Christ and probably collected materials suitable for an Itinerary.

Ælius Aristides, about A.D. 176; mentions bridges, measurings, roads and inns—which could hardly have come into existence without the distances from one to another being known. Ammianus Marcellinus is believed to have used the Itinerary in the 4th century. Ælius or Actius Lampridius, in the 4th century, says that two months before the then emperor set forth on a journey, he put forth an edict stating that he would stop at the inns in their order, then in the camps, then at the granaries, until the borders of the Barbarians were reached.

This being so, it is probable the distances from station to station were known.

Hieronymus Surita well remarks, that he cannot get to an earlier date than about A.D. 200 to 330 for the Itinerary. Vegetius in the 4th century expressly mentions Itineraries.

## REMARKABLE ANGULARITY OF SUBMARINE ROCKS, *page 7 antè, &c.*

On Sept. 2, 1867, I visited the chief or most westerly, of the Chausey Isles. And on sailing up the channel on the eastern side of it, the remarkable angularity of the rocks covered and uncovered by the tides was very conspicuous. This is perfectly intelligible. The ground having sunk within a few centuries to within reach of the tides, the water has washed away the soil, leaving the angular faces of the rocks exposed. On the other hand where the rocks on the surface of the islet are high and dry, they are well rounded, having no doubt been exposed to the weather for hundreds of thousands of years.

(See *page 14 antè.*)

[COPY.] "Jersey, 24 April 1866. My dear Mr. Peacock, I

have been this morning told by the master of one of the Littlehampton steamers that when visiting St. Brelade's Bay a few days ago, he was shown by an old man whom he accidentally met, three or four trees (one of large size) lying in the sand, near the centre of the bay, and at about half tide mark:—the heavy storms of this winter having washed off the sand covering. I mention this thinking you may perhaps be inclined to ride out as far as St. Aubin at an early day, and walk down to the bay at low water, to confirm by actual inspection and evidence your theory of the submersion of the coasts at that part of the island. Yours &c.

(Signed) T. W. CLARKE."

I did not go, the testimony above is sufficient.—R. A. P.

(*See page 24 ante.*)

THE ISLE OF ECREHOU WAS INHABITED, SO NUMEROUSLY AS TO REQUIRE DAILY MASS, SO LATELY AS 1337.

Copy, *Ex Gallia Christiana, t.* xi., *inter Instrum. Ecc. Bajoc, col.* 94, quoted from M. Gerville's Tract, p. 35, &c.

"Universis sanctæ matris ecclesiæ filiis ad quos præsens scriptum pervenerit, Petrus de Pratel in Domino salutem. Noverit universitas vestra me divinæ pietatis intuitu concessisse et dedisse, et præsenti charta mea confirmasse Deo et ecclesiæ sanctæ Mariæ de Valle-Richerii, et monachis ibidem Deo servientibus, pro salute animæ Johannis illustris regis Angliæ, qui insulas mihi dedit, et pro salute animæ meæ, et patris et matris meæ, et omnium antecessorum meorum, insulam de Escrehou integre, ad ædificandum ibidem basilicam in honore Dei et beatæ Mariæ, ita ut divina ibidem celebrentur mysteria singulis diebus, habendam et possidendam libere et quiete, plenarie et honorifice, in liberam et puram et perpetuam eleemosynam, et quidquid in eadem insula poterunt augmentare et ædificare. Item concessi prædictis monachis quidquid, ab hominibus meis de Gersy, et de Gernese, et de Aurene, eis caritatis intuitu rationabiliter datum fuerit, salvo jure meo. Ut autem hæc mea donatio ratam futuris temporibus obtineat firmitatem, cam præsenti scripto et sigilli mei munimine confirmavi, his testibus, Engerano de Pratel fratre meo, Roberto de Freschen, Hugone Croc, Gilleberto de Ovill, militibus, Villelmo Capellano, Richardo clerico, Nicolao de Mara, Will. Cornuele, Villelmo clerico de Camera, et pluribus aliis, anno Verbi Incarnati 1203.*

*(Ibid., col. 447, inter abbates Vallis-Richerii.)*

Gabriel...... abbas Vallis-Richerii, duos monachos misit anno 1337 die Jovis ante Dominicam Palmarum, ad conservandam et regendam capellam beatæ Mariæ d'Ecrehou.

La carte du diocèse de Coutances, publiée par Mariette, en 1687, représente, parmi les rochers d'Ecrehou, la Maître Isle, sur laquelle il marque une chapelle ruinée. On peut bien croire que, depuis 150 ans, la mer n'a pas cessé son action sur les côtes de cette petite île.

## (CHANGES IN HERM.)

Au moment où nous nous occupons des plus petites îles, je crois pouvoir donner ce qui a rapport au Couvent des Cordeliers dans celle de Herm, quand ils la quittèrent pour s'établir en Guernesey, où ils restèrent jusqu'au temps de la reine Elizabeth. Cette charte est tirée du cartulaire de Cherbourg, et l'archiviste m'en a depuis communiqué l'original.

Noverint universi quod nos fratres ordinis minorum, in insula de Hern Constantiensis diocesis prope Guerneseum, sub decreto sacri concilii Constantiensis, degentes, renunciavimus renunciamusque omnino juri possessionis, proprietatis vel perpetuitatis dictæ insulæ, nec intendimus in præjudicium seu damnum venerabilium dominorum abbatis et conventus de Cherbourc ordinis S. Augustini ibidem manere, salvis tamen ædificiis per nos seu fratres nostros inibi factis, si contigeret nos ab illa insula quovis modo repelli seu amoveri. Datum sub sigillo quo utimur, et sub manu præsidentis ejusdem loci,

---

* It is stated in the *Calendarium Rotulorum Chartarum*, in the reign of King John, as follows:

1° anno John (p. 9), NOTE. King Richard I. died April 1109, when John succeeded.

"28. PETRUS DE PRATELLIS 128.

Gerse }<br>
Gernese } Insulæ.<br>
Aurene }<br>
Esterlinges<br>
Altena etc. tenend' quousq, etc."

"29. PETRUS DE PRATELLIS 150 (p. 14)

Geresey }<br>
Gernese } insul' . . . . . Gersey.<br>
Averne }

de consilio pariter et assensu omnium fratrum in dicta insula nunc temporis commorantium, die Veneris post festum B. Mariæ, scilicet, assumptionis, anno Domini millesimo quadringentesimo quadragesimo. Constat de interlinea *nostros.*—Datum ut supra.

F. J. Doube. Verum est.

(See *page* 74 *antè.*)

J'ai conservé l'approbation du mot *nostros* en interligne, parce que la plupart de mes lecteurs n'ont probablement pas l'habitude de ces sortes de rectifications dans les chartes latines.

Au moment où les Cordeliers allaient quitter l'île de Herm, ceux du Cotentin abandonnaient les îlots de Saint Marcouf pour se fixer à Valognes; * ceux de l'île de Chausey y restèrent plus longtemps, avant de transférer leur maison dans le voisinage de Granville."

LECANU'S HISTORY.

(*See p.* 25, 28, *&c., antè.*)

From Lecanu's *Histoire des Evêques de Coutances*, 1839; I have gathered a few important testimonies, as may be seen by consulting the Text and this Appendix. The number of his authorities is extraordinary, and he is well entitled to the best thanks of all lovers of Historic truth. He gives the following as the sources from which he obtained his information:

His friends M. de Gerville (who placed at his disposal the treasures of his rich library.†) MM. Taforel, Lebrédonchel, curés. Lebrec, head of the great seminary. Ybert, canon of Coutances. Bubot, professor at the seminary. Letertre, librarian of the city of Coutances. Quenault, Lebreton, Hervieu, Destouches, Rapilly, Olivier, curés. Dolbet and Lenoël, landowners. M. Dechoiseul's library.—The Livre Noir of Coutances cathedral, in which events have been written day by day since 1278.—Registers, charters and memoirs of this and neighbouring dioceses.—Acts of synods, mandates, episcopal ordinances, registers of churches, genealogies, histories of families, parishes, &c.—*Ecclesiastic* writings, including acts of the metropolitan church, registers of the Court of Rome,

* It appears probable that the sinking of the Islets of Marcouf may have been the cause of the Cordeliers abandoning them to settle at Valognes. If so, that sinking must have occurred *since* 1440, when the Cordeliers of Herm yet lived in that island.

† Of 5 or 6,000 pages of MSS.

acts of provincial, national and general councils. The Chronicles of Orderic Vitalis, Guillaume-de-Jumièges, Guillaume-de-Poitiers, Robert-du-Mont, Reginon, Flodoard, Wace and many others. Of Annals, the ample collection published by Marten, Lucas d'Achery and other compilers.—*Secular* writings, which consist of Acts of Parliament, councils of the King, researches of the nobility, registers of different chancelleries, and the history of everything of which the bishops took part.—The traditions near the present period are from recollections of old men; and for times long past *The Acts of the Saints*, certain legends and popular beliefs.—He studied monuments, churches, altars, edifices, repositaries of families, pictures, sculptures, &c.—Thirty-four authors whom he names.—An anonymous MS. at the abbey of S. Victor at Paris, and another MS. belonging to M. d'Herouval, both well known to the learned. —Ben Thomas Demons's "Recherches sur Coutances."—Toustain de Billy's Memoirs of the Cotentin.—"The lives of the Bishops of Coutances," by Rouault; and notes upon it by Bisson.—The voluminous memoirs of M. Lefranc.—Bisson in the Almanacks of Coutances.—Piton in his new-year's-gifts of Coutances.—Divers authors in the Annals of la Manche, and especially in private histories of the Isles of la Manche [Channel Islands], of Cherbourg, S. Marie-du-Mont, de Nebon, &c.—Besides these he has studied many other books and MSS. which he names and describes.

These vast researches and M. Lecanu's excellent method of treating his materials, evidently entitle the *Histoire des Evêques de Coutances*, to great respect and authority. And it is matter for regret that certain eminent men of science—who ought to have known better—have attempted to throw ridicule on Lecanu's very valuable history. For no better reason so far as I can discover, than because its statements disagree with their own preconceived ideas.

At p. 70 it is evident that he had no notion of anything beyond violent invasions of the sea, (chiefly in 709) on the W. coast of Normandy and N. coast of Britanny. Which, so far as he can perceive—by reason only of a S. W. wind having blown for many months with great violence—overturned many trees, and accumulated so much water on the coasts (!) that the March tides over-ran a great extent of country. It was not until 860 that the forest was totally submerged, &c., &c.

From *Lecanu's Hist. des Evêques de Coutances*, 1839, p. 14: —

"Trois superbes routes militaires joignaient Cosedia [Coutances] à Coriallum [Tourlaville near Cherbourg], l'une était directe, la seconde se rapprochait du rivage, pour passer à Grannonum [Gouey near Portbail], la troisième se dirigeait par Alauna, [Alleaume near Valognes]. Quatre autres partaient de la première de ces villes dans les directions de Rennes, en passant par Fanum-Martis, de Vire, Rouen et Avranches; une autre traversait la presqu'île, pour joindre Grannonum à Cruciatonum [which falls according to Ptolemy about 3 English miles south of Lessay]. Une autre encore se dirigeait d'Alauna par Portus-Cruciatonum et Augustodurum, ou Torigny. Voir, pour plus de détails, deux Mémoires de M. de Gerville, sur les villes et les voies Romaines."

The following are extracts from the *Histoire des Evêques de Coutances*, par M. Lecanu, 1839:

"Une vaste marais appelé Chesey *Scissiacum*, couvert de forêts, remplissait tout l'espace maintenant occupé par l'Océan, depuis la côte de Bretagne jusque vers Cherbourg, ou le Val-de-Saire, en s'élargissant du côté de Chausey et Jersey, sur une profondeur maintenant inconnue." p. 14.

He informs us also that "le prêtre Aroaste...... fut l'ami et le collaborateur de Leontien," third bishop of Coutances and "l'on pourrait peut-être lui attribuer la fondation du monastère *de Sciscy*. Nous placerons ensuite S Gaud: ce saint évêque d'Evreux se démit de son siége en faveur de Maurution, son disciple, et vint, en 480, achever de se sanctifier *à Sciscy*, il y mourut en 491. Vers ce temps ou peu après, Pair (or Paterne) et Escouvillon (or Escupilio), originaires de Poitou, épris de l'amour de la vie cénobitique, vinrent faire leur noviciat dans le même monastère, et s'y élevèrent à une si grande sainteté qu'ils furent choisis, Pair pour évêque d'Avranches,* et Escouvillon pour abbé du monastère de Mandane, (Mandanense monasterium) en un diocèse voisin." p. 27.

"En langue Germanique les mots de Sci, Scé ou Sée veulent dire amas d'eau, notre pays fournit un grand nombre de Sci et de Pont-cé, beaucoup même de nos rivières n'ont pas un autre nom; témoin, la *Sei*-ne, la *Scie*, la *Sie*-enne, la *Se*-rre, ou *Sai* re, la *Sée*, la *See*-lune, etc. Que veut donc dire le mot de Sci répété, comme dans Sciscy, à moins qu'un pays de rivières, un marais? C'est ce même nom de marais qu'une constitution de Louis le Débonnaire, de l'an 817, donne à ces lieux; aux environs de Granville, les sables du bord de l'ocean portent encore le nom de marais; et à Barneville, les paroisses du rivage s'appellent paroisses des rivières, ou pays de rivières.

---

* Il souscrivit en cette qualité au concile de Paris, de l'an 557. Le monastère de Sciscy était à Saint-Pair, près Granville." *Lecanu* p. 27.

Les dimensions de ce terrain marécageux ne sauraient être assignées: voici ce que nous en connaissons: 1° nous nous sommes assuré que depuis Saint-Pair jusqu'à la pointe de la Hague il existe de très-nombreux pieds d'arbres enracinés dans les glaises du rivage; 2° c'est une tradition constante que Jersey n'était éloigné du continent que de la longueur d'une planche; cette tradition est plus étendue que le diocèse de Coutances, car Hermant l'a consignée dans son Histoire des Evêques de Bayeux; 3° c'est une autre tradition que le Mont-Saint-Michel était éloigné de plusieurs lieues de la mer [!], Thomas Leroi l'a inscrite dans ses *Curieuses Recherches*, et les faits viennent à l'appui; en effet la route de *Fanum Martis* à *Condate* (Rennes) passait au moins deux lieues en de-çà de cette montagne, et en outre, la constitution dont nous venons de parler la place, non dans la mer, mais dans un marais: *Monasterium marisii primi;* * 4° il existe en pleine mer, sous Cancale, un banc à fleur d'eau fort bien connu des pêcheurs d'huîtres, nommé le Fort-Romain: ce nom semble très-significativ; 5° le nom latin de Chausey est *Scisciacum;* 6° il y a sous Bréville un banc appelé Banc-de-la-Haie, ou *Haya*, qui en est la traduction, veut dire un fourré d'épines; et un rocher du nom de Pont-ès-Rogues, *Rogus* signifie buisson; 7° à moitié route de Carteret à Jersey l'on trouve des rochers du nom d'Ecrehous, cette terminaison signifie habitation.

Cette grande étendue de terrain, couverte d'eaux et de forêts, n'a pas été toute d'une fois envahie par la mer, mais elle l'a été par portions et à diverses époques, ainsi que nous l'apprennent l'histoire, les traditions et des faits récens: suivant les aveux de la terre de Bretteville, à monsieur le comte Armand de Bricqueville, l'Ile-Pelée† .... faisait encore partie du continent au treizième siècle. L'ancien *Grannonum*, auprès du *Portus-Ballii*, est presque tout entière, nommée Isemberville, et dont la chapelle Notre-Dame-de-Grâce, maintenant sur Quettehou, était l'église paroissiale, a dû être submergée pareillement." *Lecanu*, p. 21, 22.

"Le monastère de Mandane était séparé de celui de Sciscy par un bras de mer, et en était distant de plus de trois milles." p. 30.

"En l'an 566, les saints fondateurs de Nanteuil, Marcou, Criou et Domard sortirent du nombre des vivans; Laut se rendit au monastère et présida à leur sépulture." p. 37.

---

* Cette charte est la donation à l'abbaye du Mont-St.-Michel d'un monastère situé très-près du mont, et appelé Monastère-du-Premier-Marais (*in latere montis*). Lecanu p. 22.

† Near Cherbourg, it is now 2950 yards, or more than 1½ mile distant from the coast.

AUTHORITIES FOR BELIEVING THAT JERSEY WAS ONCE WITHOUT A NAME, WHICH WOULD BE INCREDIBLE, IF IT HAD ALWAYS BEEN AN ISLAND.

(*See p.* 32 *antè.*)

Robert Gaguin, a French Historian who died in 1501, relates under the heading King "Chilperic," who reigned from 570 to 584: "atque ita Prætextatus consilio extrusus est. Quem apprehensum rex ergastulo servari mandat. Inde cum liberatus ferme noctu evaderet; contumelia vulneribusque affectus tandem in insula Constantinæ dyocesis relegant."
See Gaguin's *Hist. Franc.* fol. xxii B.

Mr. George-S. Syvret, editor of the MS. *Chroniques de Jersey* gives at p. 237 of his printed edition the tradition about the plank as follows:—"On dit aussi qu'une maison doit fournir à un Seigneur, une planche pour traverser le ruisseau qui separoit Jersey de la France."

In *Massoniuss's Annals*, p. 55; We read "Is in insulam Constantini littoris relegatur," signifying that "He [a bishop] is banished into an island of the shore of Coutances:"—meaning no doubt the Isle of Jersey. This was about A.D. 574.

From *Neustria Pia*, p. 67. (See antè p. 35.)
"Sisciacum.

"Illic postea relegatus est S. Prætextatus. Rothomagensis, 17 Archiepiscopus, jussu Chilperici regis, ad instantiam Fredegundis Reginæ: in insulam maris (scribit S. Gregorius Turonensis) *quæ adjacet civitati Constantinæ, in exilium est detrusus.** Ea autem insula vocabatur *Brenciana*, vulgo *Brency*; in mari Oceano sita, prope littus civitatis Constantiensis, in Neustria inferiore, si Tillio credimus.† At in antiquititibus MSS. Normaniæ, nuncupatur *Gergia*, seu *Gersayum*, and *Sisciacum*, Gallicè, Gerzay, and Chesay: Juxta Cœnalem, in eo S. Prætextato.‡ A fratribus Franciscanis postea inhabitata, sed exindè ab hæreticis, profligatis, Macropolim juxta è prospectu, consedere sunt coacti; quamquidem insulam opinatus est, & rectius, præfatus episcopus Cœnalis, illam esse, ubi illis priscis temporibus *Sisciacum*, S. Paterni nobile extabat Asceterium, nunc omnino dirutum, & complanatum."

---

* Lib. 1. Histor. Franc. cap. 18.

† Tillius in *Chronico de Regib. Franc.* ad ann. 582.—See also *Neustria Pia*, p. 712.

‡ Tom. 3 *Hierarchiæ Eccles. Neustriæ*, MS.

In "*Vita S.Samsonis act. SS. Bened. Sæc.* 1 p. 171" we read:—"Erat autem non longè ab hoc Monasterio insula quædam nuper fundata à quodam egregio viro ac sancto Presbytero Pyro nomine, in quâ insulâ et ego fui, apud quem, inquam, Samson cohabitare volebat."

In *Aimoini Monachi, Hist. Franc.*, Paris, 1567, p. 183, we read:—"Prætextatus episcopus Rothomagensis accusatur"... and at p. 190 we also read that the same Prætextatus "in insula quadam maris quæ civitati adjacet Constantiæ, in exilium relegatur."

—It is obvious that Jersey had only LATELY become an island; all these authorities refer to it as *an island without a name*; how otherwise could so considerable an island have been NAMELESS?

### RECORDS AS TO THE FORMER CONDITION OF MONT-S. MICHEL.

*(See antè p. 37 &c.)*

"Les manuscrits du Mont S. Michel, écrits avant le Xe siècle, ajoutent que le Mont de Jupiter s'elevait au milieu d'un forêt replie de bêtes fauves, et qu'alors, comme aujourd'hui, la mer en était éloignée d'environ deux lieues et demi. *Milibus distans sex*, MS. No. 24.—*Milibus distans sex*, MS. No. 80.—*Milibus distans sex*, M.S. No. 34; seconde Chronique abregèe, à la fin du Manuscrit......"
See *Hist du Mont S. Michel*, par l'abbé Desroches, 1838 p. 72.

(The following is from *Neustria Pia* p. 371.)

"Mons S. Michaelis, Gallicè, Le Mont S. Michel. Ann. 709.
Caput I.

Hæc rupes antiquitus Mons* erat, cintus Syluis & saltibus, ad sex milliaria in longum, ad quatuor in latum, productus, hinc solo, indè mari Oceano contiguus, quatuor leucis ab Arboretana urbe dissitus, in confinio Normanniæ, et Britanniæ Armoricæ: dictus, *Mons in procella Maris*, vel, *in periculo Maris*, aut *Mons in Tumba;* in cujus radice sedem fixerant eremitæ nonnulli, animo pietati et Deo maximè addicto. Cibos, & alimenta *ilis* mittere solebat Paræchus de Beauuoir." &c.

And at p. 372 of *Neustria Pia*, may be read as follows:—

"Dum igitur dicti nuntij, itinere perficiendo, annum impenderent: Deo permittente, mare Syllam, quantacunque esset

---

* The ancient author Nennius, also mentions "verticem Montis Jovis," in capital letters as if it was a mountain of importance.

superauit ac prostrauit; repleuitque arena locos Monti Tombelini adjacentes. Nuntij autem reversi 16 Octobris, Saltus arena refertos adeò mirati sunt, vt nouum orbem se ingressos putuaverint."

Dr. Hairby gives a list of some of the MSS. in the Library of Avranches, or in possession of the Archæological Society of that city.

The following, from the *Acts of the Saints*, are corroborative of *Neustria Pia* as to the large tract of land which has been lost around Mont-S.-Michel; namely part of the forest of Sciscy:—

"Acta Sanctorum ordinis S. Benedicti,* Collegit Dominus Lucas Archery, & Joannes Mabillon, Paris 1662, 9 vols. folio:—

An. Chr. Seculum I. p. 152, 163.—Ex codd Manuscriptis.
565 1. Sacratissimus igitur Paternus Episcopus
Ap. 16. Pictavis......

4. Igitur cùm tertio decimo anno vir Dei ageret in Pontificatu, statim altera die Paschæ cum fratres Sesciaco visitare cuperet, in infirmitatem irruit. Pariter autem sanctus Scubilius in Mandanense monasterio in infirmitatem incidit. (Arturus de Monstier in Neustria Pia p. 68 suspicatur Mandanense monasterium non aliud esse à Maduinensis diæc. Constantiensis, cujus cœnobii jamdudum extincti Abbas fuit sæculo IX. S. Odobertus, ut suo loco videbimus). Tunc missi se obviantes Beatum Scubilionem in itinere commonent ut fratri occurreret, sed brachio maris opposito non valuit nocturno tempore transfretare. Attamen cùm à se Sancti fere tria millia spatia interessent, eadem nocte Beatus Paternus unà cum sancto fratre suo glorioso proposito nobili in triumpho, felici viatico cùm Choro Angelico in cœlesti senatu de terrenis pias animas emiserunt ad Christum, quem Lauto Episcopus qui ibidem antè dies octo ad visitandum advenerat, cùm ad Basilicam Scesciaco Beatum Paternum deduceret, impendens exequias...... Ex schedis à V. C. D. d'Heronval communicatis."

"Anno Christ. 708
Oct. 16. Seculum III. pars I p. 86, Cap. 1 de situ loci † [Mont S. Michel]...... sed et mare recessu suo devotis populis bis inde desideratum inter præbet beati petentibus limina Archangeli Michaëlis, qui pri-

* Scripta ab Auctore anonymo ante sæculum X. Ex. MSS Codd. nostro Germanensi et Chesniano.

† Scripta ab Auctore anonymo antè Seculum X. Ex MSS. Codd. nostro Germanensi et Chesniano.

mùm locis, sicut è veracibus cognoscere potuimus narratoribus, opacissimâ silvâ claudebatur longè ab Oceano (Codex Chesnianus habet: *ab Oceano* (ut æstimatur) octo millibus distantibus) æstu milibus distans sex, altissima præbens latibula ferarum. Et quia secretiora cœli per contemplationem subtilitatis rimari volentibus gratissima esse solent remotiori eremi loca, inibi olim habitâsse comperimus Monachos, ubì etiàm usque nunc duæ extant Ecclesiæ priscorum manu constructæ: Nempè una in honorem S. Stephani, alia in honorem S. Symphoriani, quæ ampliùs non extant. Nam ipsi Monachi ibidem Domino servientes dispensatione cuncta regentis Dei sustentabantur, Presbytero quodam de villa quæ dicitur Asteriacus* taliter eis ferenti auxilio. Non *Cameraci*, ut putavit Baronius cognominis Autberti longè antè Cameracensis. Episcopi vocabulo deceptus. Nam ut illi sine quo humana nòn potest exegi vita, deerat victus, fumo signifero discurrente altaque cœli petenti, onerabat asellum dapibus dilectione vera farcitis; sicque duce invisibili prævio, per loca ibat invia, ac redibat ferens domini jussu illisque necessaria. Sed quia hic locus Dei nutu futuro parabatur miraculo sanctique sui Archangeli venerationi, mare quod longè distabat paullatim adsurgens, omnem silvæ magnitudinem suâ virtute complanavit, & in arenæ suæ, formam cuncta redegit, præbens iter populo terræ ut enarrentur mirabilia Dei. Princeps spiritum angelica revelatione dedicaverit prædictum locum."

.....................

"Ann. Christ. 708 Oct. 16. IV. De adventu Reliquiarum.

Summi interea nuntii repedantes, post multi itineris spatia, ad locum quo digressi fuerant, ipso die quo fabrica completa est in monte jam dicto in occiduis partibus, quasi novum ingressi sunt orbem, quem primùm veprium relinquerent plenum" &c.

In Dr. Hairby's *History of Mont S. Michel*, 1841; the vegetation of Mont Tombelène, which is situated two miles north of Mont-S.-Michel, is consistent enough with the "briars" just mentioned. He says at p. 157, &c., that Mont Tombelène, is a rugged uninhabited rock, dreary and desolate. Its vegetation consists of thorns, brambles and nettles. Its former habitations are ruins almost level with the surface, its elevation is not more than 120 feet above the level of the sands, but its area is larger than that of Mont-S.-Michel.

---

* Nuno Beavoir.

The following are from *Acta Sanctorum* on the Forest of Scissy:

P. 1102 "Itaque in *Sesciaco* quadem die Aroastes Presbyter offert..."

*Ibid.* "Item cum de *Sessiaco* accessisset Abrincas..."

P. 1103 "In cellula sua quam primum ædificaverat *Sessiaci* quiesceret"..... &c. &c. &c.

—I have considered Sigebert, but it is not necessary to quote him.

It is said in *Neustria Pia* p. 66 under date "Ann. 548 & 550." Sesciacum or Sisiacum, Gallicè Chesay: an old monastery: of which the founder and first abbot, was S. Paterne, afterwards bishop of Avranches.

We learn from Manet (p. 60) that S. Pére or Paterne died in the desert of Scissy on his return from inspecting the monasteries of *Menden at* 1600 *toises N.N.E. of the isle of Aaron* (on which isle S. Malo stands); and Maudan or Maudun, at one league from Chausey. The positions of these and of other monasteries are fixed according to these and other forthcoming dimensions on Map No. 1.

The following is quoted from Manet's book p. 95, 96, being his note No. 49:—

"(49) *Territoire qui fut épargné en* 709 *sur la côte de Normandie.*—On assure, dit M. Rouault (Vie de Saint Gand, préf.) que, tout le long de ces hauteurs, la forêt de Sciscy conserva encore long-temps à peu près une demie-lieue de large. —Un anonyme prétend même que ce ne fut qu'-au mois de mars 1153, que la mer acheva totalement ses ravages vers Pont-Orson, le Pont-Aubaut, et le Gué de l'Épine, sous Avranches.—Ce qu'il y a de certain, c'est que nous avons une constitution de Louis-le-Débonnaire, de l'an 817, où, parlant des couvens de son royaume qui ne devaient à son ost ou armée que des dons en argent, sans milices, il met en tête de ce dénombrement le monastère de Saint-Michel du premier marais *(monasterium sancti Michaelis maresci primi)*: expressions qui semblent indiquer qu'alors proche ce mont subsistait encore un de ces marécages entremêlés de bois, dont Ninnius, abbé de Bencor * en Angleterre, a parlé au sixième ou septième siècle. *(Usserius*, Brit. Eccl. Antiq., p. 107; et Deric, t. v., p. 21.)—Ce ne peut donc guère être que depuis cette année 817 au plus tôt, que les choses, dans le fond de cette baie, ont

* ? Bangor.

achevé d'être entièrement réduites à l'aspect qu'elles présentent maintenant."

Ancient and Modern Heights of Mont S. Michel, from Manet's note 33 at p. 60 of his book :—

"*Le mont Saint-Michel et tout ce qui le concerne.* Ce bloc énorme de granit, singulier en toutes manières, n'a pas moins de 200 pieds de hauteur,* sans compter ce qu'y ont ajouté les ouvrages de l'art.—Il n'a qu'environ un quart de lieue de circonférence par la base, et il est coupé presque à pic de tous les côtés.—De loin, il ne paraît que comme une grosse tour isolée au milieu d'une gréve blanche et unie de 8 à 10 lieues carées de surface, où l'on ne voit pas la moindre petite pierre, excepté Tombelène, dont nous parlerons ci-après.—Du haut de ce panorama, dont tout l'ensemble, *dans son état primitif, avait* 565 *pieds d'élévation*, les personnes qui sont en bas ne peuvent être reconnues, et semblent autant de pygmées qui rampent à l'entour."

Dr. Hairby's plan of Mont-S.-Michel, from which I find that the present horizontal area of the Mont is 20¼ acres, is carefully drawn to a scale of 1·4000th of the natural size, and is to all appearance, correct. This scale is about five statute chains to an inch. He mentions (p. 144) that the entrance of the arched gateway is 140 feet above the level of the sand, and very correctly states that the turrets on each side of the entrance, are of exquisite workmanship. He says (p. 128) that the whole height to the top of the towers is 378 feet: And that a large dyke before the entrance gate to the island, traced by the sea in 1822, exposed the end of a causeway paved with large stones, ten feet below the surface. This causeway led to the entrance gate.

*Mém. de l'Acad. Celtique.* tom. IV. p. 384, 8vo. Paris, 1809 :—

"En effet, les grèves actuelles du Mont-Saint-Michel, étaient une portion du continent, couverte de bois. Le Coesnon traversait cette grande forêt, également arrosée par l'Ardée et la Sée, qui se débordaient en marais. Ninnius, auteur anglais, parle de l'Etang, qui de son temps, existait *supra Montem*

---

* Les geomètres qui, en 1775, dressèrent le plan de ce mont, lui donnèrent 450 toises de tour sur le grévage, 180 pieds seulement d'élévation jusqu'au sommet du roc, et en totalité 400 pieds depuis le niveau de la grève jusqu'à la lanterne du clocher ; mais nous avons d'autres bonnes autorités pour les mesures que nous avons déterminées. *See Abbé Manet's Work.*

*Jovis*,* dans le neuvième siècle une charte de Louis le Débonnaire, de 817, fait mention de marisci primi, et suppose par conséquent plusieurs marécages ; et l'anonyme, dont Mabillon a recueilli l'ouvrage, assure que ce terrain, couvert de bois, fut, peu à peu, noyé par la mer."

DAILY SINKINGS OF LAND IN BRITANNY, NARRATED BY D'ARGENTRE.

His Histoire de Bretagne, 1611— fol 41 F &c. describes the course of the river Couësnon, the boundary between Normandy and Britanny, from Foulgeres down to Mont S. Michel, which some, he says, have thought is the promontory Ocrinum. In thinking so, however, they have been mistaken, the Ocrinum promontory being the Lizard, on the south coast of Cornwall. The mistake evidently arose from confusing Mount Saint Michael near the south coast of Cornwall with Mont-S.-Michel in the angle of France where Normandy joins Britanny. I have underlined in the following quotation, the remarkable passages in which he describes the Sinkings of land :

" Passant outre on va à S. Michel du Mont de Tumbe, que quelques uns pensent que ce soit Ocrinum promontorium in periculo maris, comme ils disent, edifice admirable & presque surmontant nature, qui a esté quelquefois en l'obéissance des Ducs de Bretagne, duquels les Abbez & religieux dudit lieu, tiennement bonne part de leur foundation, lesquels Ducs pour enseigne de ce, feirent passer quelque temps la riviere de Couësnon pardeuers la Normandie, où il en disent encore un proverbe, qui deflors prist son origine,

Si Couësnon a faict folie,
Si est le mont en Normandie.

Pour mettre la place deuers eux, jusques a ce que par le temps la riviere s'est respandue, & repris cours sur le terrouer de deça au dessus le pont au Bault, là où ladite riviere rencontrant le reflus de la mer, quande elle remonte deux fois de jour, elle est contrainte de le quitter au plus fort, & s'escoulant sur *la terre, qu'elle trouve au dessoubs, elle est tellement respandue, qu'elle a donné une ou deux lieues du pays de Bretaigne de bons et gras pasturages, au Normands, & submergé un grand canton de pays, du meilleur de Bretaigne ; ce qu'encores fait, &*

* The text in Nennius's *Historia Britonum*, published by the English Historical Society in 1838, is "sed dedit illis multas regiones, a stagno quod est super verticem Montis Jovis usque ad civitatem quæ vocatur Cantguic, et usque ad Cumulum occidentalem, id est, Cruc Ochidient." p. 20.

*fera de jour en jour*, s'il ny est pourueu, tellement que sur la plainte des habitans, ayant eu par deux fois commission du Roy, pour faire obvier par œuvre de main à cest inconvenient, & contraindre les habitans à contribution, apres y avoir faict ce qu'on a peu par assemblée d'hommes & de conseils, il ne s'est jusques à icy peu trouuer beaucoup de moyen, de refrener ce furieux element, qu'il n'ait ruiné édifices, villages, & enfoncé la terre, faisant un dommage inestimable, duquel l'inconuenient *prend chacun jour accroissement, pour un jour manifestement ruiner plus de quatre lieues de très bon pays, & plus de cent mil livres de revenu aux propriétaires.* Par ceste borne de Pontorson deuale la riviere de Couësnon, prenant sa source de Foulgeres, et va tomber au lieu susdit au dessus de Dol, et la pert son nom, s'en allant rendre avec la mer au port de Cancalle."

CANCALLE AND BAY OF MONT S. MICHEL AND THE POSITION OF ITS MONASTERIES AND TOWN. *See Manet, p.* 59, *&c.*

"Dans la partie de cette même forêt qui était en Bretagne, et que les riverains appelaient forêt de Cancaven ou Cancavre (aujourd'hui Cancale), on remarquait principalement trois monastères fameux par les saints pénitens qui s'étaient consacrés à la vie érémetique (Deric, t. I. p. 29 etc.; t. III, p. 136, 376, etc., Butler, t. x, p. 207, etc.): savoir celui de Dol, que saint Sampson II illustra par ces vertus en 554, et qui était précédemment du diocése d'Aleth, comme nous avons amplement prouvé dans nos grandes Recherches; celui de S. Moack, à pres de cinq lieues de Dol en tirant vers Chausey, et à une lieue de distance vers le nord-nord-ouest du bourg de Lhan-Kafruth, que la mer a dévoré ainsi qui lui. Le terme *lhan, llan*, on *lan*, signifiait en vieux langage celtique temple, église, ou plutôt *area templi*, l'*aire*, le *sol*, la *place*, et même *le territoire voisin d'un temple*. Ainsi *Lhan-Kafruth* équivalait à *église* ou *bourg de Lhan-Kafruth*.—Rivallon, frère de saint Judicaïl * roi de Bretagne, avait en ce lieu une de ses maisons de chasse. Violent comme il l'était, ce prince, dans un accès d'humeur, avait fait brûler le monastère de saint Moack; mais bientôt après, heureux pénitent, il y rétablit toutes choses en meilleur état, à l'instigation de saint Thurien ou Thuriave, évêque de Dol, (Gallet, Mém. sur l'orig. des Bret. Armor, ch.

* Morery's Dictionary says Judicael succeeded Alain, le Long, who died 690. This is quite consistent with the sinking of 709, of which we have had so much proof. Judicael we see was living shortly *before* the sinking in the Bay.

6, n. 18).—Enfin celui de Taurac ou Caurac, à 1700 toises à l'orient de la pointe actuelle de la chaîne en Cancale, ou brillèrent saint Similien, qui en fut le premier supérieur, saint Ethbin ou Egbin, et un saint Guignolé ou Guinolé qu'il ne faut pas confondre avec le pieux abbé de Landevenech, porteur du même nom.* Ce dernier monastère fut rebâti quelque temps après avoir été ruiné par les troupes du roi Clotaire Ier, lorsqu'elles vinrent, en 560, punir Canao, comte de Bretagne, de la protection qu'il avait accordée à Chramne, révolté contre son père et son souverain.

La plupart de ces interessans asiles, et autres dont le nom seul est resté dans la mémoire des siècles, étaient en son temps sous la discipline de saint Scubilion, qui les visitait souvent, et qui avait fondé en outre, à 1600 toises au nord-nord-est de l'île d'Aaron [S. Malo], celui de Menden, qu'on doit soigneusement distinguer de celui de Maudan ou Maudun, à une lieue de Chausey, où ce vénérable vieillard faisait ordinairement sa résidence."

(*Trigan*, t. I. p. 129 ; *Deric*, t. VI. p. 310 &c )

I have had the pamphlet of M. Bonissent, Membre de la Société géologique de France, &c., &c., 1860, under consideration. It does not call for any remark at present.

## SAINT MALO AND NEIGHBOURHOOD.

The following is from D'Argentré's *Hist. Bret.* Folio 62A, &c.

"Il se trouve qu'au passé la ville de S. Malo n'estoit pas de toutes partes environées de mer, laquelle toutefois depuis a gagné bien loin au deça, en sorte que le pays qui est entre la ville & Sesembre, qui est une île distant de deux lieuës en laquelle y a un couvent de Cordeliers, estoit terre ferme, & void on par les comptes des revenus de l'Evesché du chapitre de ceste Eglise, que le receueurs faisoient charge et descharge du revenu des marests d'entre la ville & le Couvent de Cesembre, & encore à present les receueurs ent font chapitre en deniers comptez & non receus. Et se trouve aux registres de la Senechaussee de Rennes, qu'autrefois il y eut procez entre le Duc et les Évêques pour le pasturage desdits marests, où le Duc pretendoit que ses hommes avaient droit de mener leur bestail en commun."—Manet proceeds (p. 105) :—

Ce que l'historien de Bretagne avance ici s'être pratiqué

* Ethbin, after the destruction of Taurac retired into Ireland, Guignolé died at Taurac monastery.

long-temps, pour conserver la possession de ce terrain au cas que la mer s'en fû retirée, est de la plus grande vérité, et parfaitement conforme aux pièces originales dont nous allons citer quelques extraits.—Un regître capitulaire en effet, commencé en 1415, porte formellement qu'ün particulier fût condamné, pour avoir laissé échapper ses bêtes dans le Prez de Césambre. —Sous la date de 1425, ce même regître contient un compte rendu l'année précédente au chapitre par le nommé Jean Billart, receveur de la manse capitulaire, lequel s'y charge d'avoir reçu 21 livres 8 sols de Colas Gochard, fermier des Prés de Césambre.—Il conste d'ün autre état signé par Dom Pierre Billart en 1437, qu'à cette époque, la dernière probablement de ces prairies était encore affermée trente sols à un appelé Charles Cauchart.—Enfin, en 1486, ce même Pierre Billart, ou un autre de même nom, 'ne compte et ne se charge de la ferme de Césambre, parce que ledit recepveur n'en a point jouy.'

*Farther proofs of losses of land are to be found in the fact that the chain of rocks and islets sea-ward of S. Malo, are considered to belong to the lordship of S. Malo; and* NOT *to the Ducal or Royal Domain like other islets situate in the Sea and the Rivers;* as Manet will now inform us:—Manet proceeds p. 106:

"On pourrait, s'il en était besoin, ajouter à toutes ces démonstrations historiques et physiques, que, dans les différens aveux rendus aux ducs et aux rois par nos évêques jusqu'au 29 décembre 1689, tout le rang des rochers nommés les Portes, les îles de Césambre, Harbour, Grand et Petit-Bés, les Marais, Talards, etc., sont désignés comme étant des dépendances de la seigneurie ecclésiastique de St. Malo, et non des appartenances du domaine ducal ou royal comme les autres îles situées dans la mer et les rivières; et que ces aveux ont toujours été reçus par la chambre des comptes sans blâme ni contestation: ce qui n'aurait certainement pas eu lieu, si les prétentions de nos prélats n'eussent reposé sur un fait notoire, savoir, que ce squelette d'un continent dévoré avait, de toute antiquité, fait partie du territoire des églises d'Aleth et de Saint-Malo."

### EARTHQUAKES.

(See *page* 14 *antè.*)

It is obvious that there must have been sinkings of the Earth, in other words Earthquakes, when these changes of level took place. But were they such as are popularly called earthquakes, that is to say *were they accompanied with great violence?*—I think not, there being no reason to suppose so. We have no reason to suppose anything more than a *quiet* settling down of the ground from day to day, sometimes. And at other times *quiet* settlings down at certain periods named.

Commencing with Tacitus A.D. 17 and proceeding in order to Pliny the elder, Baronius, Labbe, Aimoin, Gibbon, Lecanu, Lobineau, Dr. Mallet's Report to the Brit. Assn.—which is exceedingly comprehensive—down to 1397. I do not find any reason to believe that Earthquakes, properly so called, have caused any of the Sinkings of Land which we now have under consideration.

### PLINY THE ELDER.

(*See page 92 ante.*)

In his *Nat. Hist.* Lib. IV. Sec. XXX. Pliny enumerates the islands neighbouring to Britain as follows, erroneously stating that Vectis, the present Isle of Wight is between Ireland and Britain:

"Sunt autem XL Orcades, modicis inter se discretæ spatiis. Septem Acmodæ,* et XXX Hebudes: et inter Hiberniam ac Britanniam, Mona, Monapia, Ricina, Vectis, Limnus, Andros. Infra vero Siambis, et Axantos. Et ab adverso in Germanicum mare sparsæ Glessariæ, quas Electridas Græci recentiores appellavere, quod ibi electrum nasceretur. Ultima omnium, quæ memorantur Thule."

Also in the Book IV of his said Natural History, Sec. XXXIII Pliny, after enumerating the Aquitanian Gauls, says:—

"Maria circa oram †: ad Rhenum septentrionalis oceanus, inter Rhenum et Sequanam Britannicus, inter *eum et Pyrenæum Gallicus. Insulæ complures* ‡ *Venetorum*, et Veneticæ appellantur, et in Aqutanico sinu Uliarius."

The two passages I have underlined clearly prove that the sea between the mouth of the Seine and the Pyrenees was the property of the Gauls, and that one of the Gallic peoples namely the Veneti must have had great rights in that sea. In fact Cæsar tells us that the Veneti received tribute from all who used that sea. We can scarcely doubt that the whole of the sea from the mouth of the Seine to the Pyrenees belonged to the Veneti, how else could their number of almost 200

* Supposed to mean the Shetland Isles.

† He is speaking of the coast of Gaul.

‡ Almost 200 Valpy says.

islands have been made up? And if all the islands were theirs, the neighbouring seas must have been theirs also.

(See *page* 102 *antè*.)

In Allen's illustrated Hand Book of Charnwood Forest, p 19:—"*Guern*, (British) an alder." Can this be the origin of the name Guernsey? *Ey* being Celtic for Island.—Gale is given as the authority for Guern, "Quoted in Gough's Camden, Vol. 2, p. 212."

(*See p.* 127 *antè*.)

The inundations of 1014 and 1099 cannot fairly be limited (as has been supposed) to the Banks of the river Thames. The former "sea-flood" ran "*through* WIDELY *this land*" we are told.—We may not limit such an expression *merely* to the Banks of the Thames. And in 1099, we are told that on a certain day named, that exceeding sea-flood sprang up and did so much harm as no man remembered that it ever did before. And there was the *same* day a new moon. Now the extreme height of spring tides in Cornwall does not happen until two or three days *after* new (or full) moon.—A sinking (or sinkings) of the ground, is the only way to explain these matters and the loss of a large tract of land.

(*See antè p.* 137.)

*Eulogium Historiarum*, Vol. 3 p. 49.—A.D. 1089.

"Secundo anno regni sui* terræ motus ingens totam Angliam exterruit, III idus Augusti, horrendo miraculo, ut ædificia omnia eminus resilirent et mox pristino modo residerent. Secuta est inopia omnium fructuum, tarda maturitas frugum, ut vix ad festum Sancti Andreæ messe reconderentur."

That is to say "a mighty earthquake affrighted all England, on 30 August, 1089, being a terrible wonder, so that all buildings at a distance sprung back and presently settled down in their former places. A dearth followed In 1091 there were severe thunderstorms and whirlwinds, several houses thrown down in London. In 1091 by the violence of the thunder the tower of Sarum (that is Salisbury) Cathedral, was unroofed.

At p. 51 we are told that in the year 1099 a sea wave ascends the river Thames and immerses many country houses and inhabitants.

---

* William Rufus.

"Duodecimo anno fluctus marinus per Tamensim fluvium ascendit et villas multas cum hominibus mersit."

It is to be observed that the Earthquake of 1089 affected *all England*, and may have been the cause of the changes at Mount Saint Michael. And it is very possible that the sinking about the Mount took place not in 1099 as stated at p. 187, but in 1089.

## A MILL, THE LAND OF FOSSES AND HENNERIA, AND THE SALT WORK OF BEVELANDE, LOST TO SERCQ.

The following, down to the words "voisinage de Granville" inclusive, are copied from M. de Gerville's pamphlet, p. 32—37.

(*See page* 143 *ante.*)

### CARTA RICARDI DE VERNONE.

Notum sit omnibus præsentibus et futuris quod ego Ricardus de Vernone concessi, et præsenti charta confirmavi, abbatiæ sanctæ Mariæ Montisburgi locum S. Maglorii qui est in Serco insula, cum omni clauso, et sedem molendini, quod fuit S. Maglorii, ubicunque poterit convenientius et commodious poni in dominico meo, cum exclusis et stramen unius bladii, videlicet avenæ ad focum monachi qui ibi habitabit. Dedi præterea eidem loco S. Maglorii, et monacho Montisburgi in eodem Deo servienti, in perpetuam elemosinam, pro amore Dei, et salute animæ meæ, triginta solidos andegavenses; et insuper ad luminare S. Eustachii, decem solidos andigavenses, ita ut monachus prædicti loci annuatim illos denarios ad festum S. Christophori in eadem insula per manum ministri mei omnes simul recipiat, de quatuor libris andigavensibus, quas in eadem insula de redditu habebam, et insuper terram de Fossetis, et de Hennaria, quam homines mei mihi juraverunt esse de dominico meo, et obschar de omnibus partagiis segetum mearum Deo et S. Eustachio et S. Maglorio in perpetuam elemosinam dedi. Actum fuit hoc anno incarnati verbi millesimo centesimo nonagesimo sexto, in eadem insula, in capella S. Maglorii, coram me. Ut autem ista elemosina in perpetuam fideliter teneatur præsentem cartam sigillo meo confirmavi. Testibus istis, Petro de Oglandris, Ricardo de Osouvilla, Willelmo clerico et pluribus aliis.

A cette charte est appendu un sceau. Il représente un cavalier portant un écu chargé d'un sautoir. L'on sait que ce sont les armes de la famille Vernon, à laquelle appartenait Mathilde, femme du fondateur de Blanchelande.

Notre sceau a pour légende; *Sigil. V. Ricardi de .. none.*

Ce qui concerne la saline de Bevelande est indiquée dans une charte de Robert de Barneville qui donne à l'Abbaye de Montebourg: *Viginti solidos de centum solidis quos habeo a domino Willelmo de Vernone in Serco insula in feudum, et unam salinam in Bevelanda.*

(*See p.* 148, *ante.*)

The following is from the *Mare Clausum* of John Selden' 1636, p. 412—414:

"Neque sane facilè conjectandum est, undenam originem habuerit jus illud induciarum singulare ac perpetuum quo Cæsareæ, Sarniæ, ceterarumque insularum Normannico littori præjacentium incolæ etiam in ipso mari fruuntur, flagrante utcunq; inter circumvicinas gentes bello, nisi ab Angliæ Regum Dominio hoc Marino derivetur. De jure illo, ad hunc modum brevitur ex veterum testimoniis edoctus, Gulielmus Camdenus. Veteri Regum Angliæ privilegio perpetuæ * hîc sunt quasi induciæ, & Gallis aliisque, quamvis bellum exardescat, ultrò citròque huc sine periculo venire & commercia securè exercere licet. Fusius autem in diplomatis aliquot regius idem occurrit,† sic de Cæsarea explicatum, quod tempore belli omnium nationum Mercatores & alii tam alienigenæ quàm indigenæ, tam hostes quam amici, liberè, licitè et impunè queant et possint dictæ insulæ & locis maritimis cum navibus, mercibus, & bonis suis, tam pro evitandis tempestatibus quàm pro aliis licitis suis negotiis inibi peragendis adire, accedere, commeare, ac frequentare, ac libera commercia negotiationum ac rem mercatorum ibidem exercere ac tuto ac securè commorari, indèque commeare ac redire toties quoties absque damno, molestiâ, seu hostilitate quâcunque, in rebus, mercibus, bonis, aut corporibus suis, idque non solum infra insulam & locos maritimos prædictos ac præcinctum eorum, vèrum etiam infra spatia undiquo ab eisdem distantia usque ad visum hominis, id est quatenus visus oculi possit assequi." And then he argues stoutly that the Neutrality is a privilege of the kings of England, which argument I think I have refuted.

## SINKING OF LAND IN FLORIDA.

"A despatch from Lake city, Florida, states that a few days

---

* ?

† "Rot. pat. 2 Ed. 6 part. Rot. pat. 2 Elizab. part 6. & Rot. pat. à Jac. regis part 19." The *Calendarium Rotulorum Patentium* in St. Helier's Library only comes down to the 23rd year of Edward IV.

ago nearly two acres on a farm in Hamilton county suddenly sunk to the depth of fifty feet from the surface of the surrounding land. It immediately filled with water, and submerged the tops of the tallest trees. The ground is still sinking and now covers four acres. The streams and creeks lose themselves in the surrounding country which forced the outlet in this way. The sinks occur occasionally, but this is the largest and deepest ever known."—*Supplement to Record newspaper*, June 19, 1868.

## GRADUAL ELEVATION AND DEPRESSION OF LAND IN CHINA AND JAPAN, NOW IN PROGRESS.

"The 'American Journal of Science and Arts' for March contains two papers on recent geological changes in China and Japan, namely, one by Mr. Albert S. Bickmore, and one by Mr. Raphael Pumpelly. Both authors describe the gradual rise of the land in eastern China, and give more or less precise descriptions of the extraordinary changes that have recently taken place in the courses of some of the rivers, notably the Yellow River. Mr. Bickmore, however, believes that at Foochow and about the mouth of the river Min, there is an area which has for some time been slowly subsiding, presenting a remarkable exception to the general rule."—*Quarterly Journal of Science*, July 1868, p. 408.

## A TWELFTH REASON WHY THERE MUST BE CAVITIES IN THE CRUST OF PHE EARTH.

In the *Steam Tract* pages 46 to 53 I have suggested Eleven reasons why there must be cavities in the crust of the Earth. I now suggest a Twelfth reason of a very striking and comprehensive character:

It is well known that the surface of the earth can be divided into two equal hemispheres in such a manner that one hemisphere shall contain nearly all the dry land and the other nearly all the oceans and seas. Sir Charles Lyell takes as the centre of the land-hemisphere, a point in St. George's Channel about midway between Pembroke and Wexford: * Sir John Herschel fixes on Falmouth as the centre.† The difference, about 125 miles, is unimportant. The latter also gives ‡ the mean height

---

* *Principles of Geology*, 1867. Vol. 1, p. 257.

† *Outlines of Astronomy*, 1864, p. 186.

‡ *Outlines*, p. 189.

of the continent of Europe above the sea as 1342 English feet, that of Asia 2274 feet, of North America 1496, and of South America 2302 feet. Now the land-hemisphere comprehends the whole of Europe, Asia, Africa and N. & S. America—excepting only small portions of the southern ends of Asia, Africa, and South America. Consequently making proper allowance for the respective areas, there is a protuberance of the land-hemisphere in excess of the height of the sea-hemisphere of about 2000 feet. Moreover rocks are about 2½ times as heavy as sea water, and common earth and clay nearly twice as heavy: we may therefore safely take the protuberance of 2000 feet as having *twice as great* a specific gravity as sea-water. But farther, the sea of (suppose) an average depth of 3 miles, or 15840 feet has *only half* the specific gravity of an equal depth of land, and 15840 must therefore be added to the 2000 feet. Making a thickness of 17,840 feet, where one hemisphere has *only half* the sp. gr. of the other. This would make our earth very LOP-SIDED, and it could by no means revolve on its axis and in its orbit in the equable manner in which astronomers assure us it actually does revolve. Sir John well observes * that "considering the whole mass of land and water as in a state of *equilibrium*, it is evident that the half which protrudes must of necessity be *buoyant;* not, of course, that we mean to assert it to be lighter than *water*, but, as compared with the whole globe, *in a less degree heavier* than that fluid. We leave geologists to draw from these premises their own conclusions (and we think them obvious enough) as to the internal constitution of the globe, and the immediate nature of the forces which sustain its continents at their actual elevation; but in any future investigations which may have for their object to explain the local deviations of the intensity of gravity, from what the hypothesis of an exact elliptic figure would require, this, as a general fact, ought not to be lost sight of."—Every geologist will of course judge for himself how the vast compensation is effected so as to bring the vast mass of more than 3⅓ miles thick, which has *twice* the specific gravity of sea-water—into equilibrium with the sea-hemisphere. For my own part, I can conceive no theory adequate to account for the phenomenon, unless we are to believe that very extensive cavities almost everywhere exist in the crust of the earth. I endeavoured to prove (see *Steam Tract* p. 51) that the vast masses of materials ejected by volcanoes, must have left cavities beneath; and that cavities must also have been caused by the solidifying and consequent contraction of melted stone.

---

* *Outlines*, p. 186.

These things being so, we can well understand that sinkings (to say nothing of elevations) of land, must constantly occur.

### SUMMARY.

I think there can be no doubt that within the last nineteen centuries, and even in some cases since the commencement of the eighth, twelfth and fifteenth centuries, a vast tract of land and sea-bottom have sunk; in many cases more than a hundred feet. That such sunken tract extends from the Scilly Isles along the coasts (both north and south) of Cornwall and Devon and along part at least of the Bristol Channel on the coast of Somerset. That the Sinking probably extended from the south coasts of Devon and Cornwall all across the English Channel, to and amongst the Channel Islands, and to the mouth of the Seine, and thence along the coasts of Normandy and Britanny as far as Portrieux (the ancient Staliocanus Portus) where it ran out to nothing. That such Sinking extended into Britanny as far as Pontorson, Dol and Suliac.

That another tract has also sunk within the Christian period. That such tract extends along the coasts of Belgium, Holland and western Prussia; about from Nieuport to the mouth of the Elbe.

There is also reason to believe, if we may trust to Ptolemy's positions of places on the former French coast of the Bay of Biscay—corroborated as they are by each other, and in one instance by Pomponius Mela. That a vast tract of land, sometimes upwards of 70 miles wide, has been lost along great part of the French coast since the middle of the second century. Chapters XV and XVI (which not being matured have not been printed) give reason to believe that a comparatively small tract of land, called the Aunis, on which the city of Rochelle stands, and some thirty miles square, has Risen a few feet since the commencement of the twelfth century.

There has also been within the Christian period a Sinking on the north coast of Britanny, extending about from Lannion to the N. W. angle of Britanny. And Sena insula or the Isle of Sein on the W. of Britanny was within the same period 8 or 9 miles long, instead of only one mile as at present.

The intrepid and persevering African traveller Sir Samuel Baker relates that a wild naked savage whom he names, pressed him with questions—"If a large river flows from the great lake what is the good of it *" I have been several times pressed with similar questions as to the Sinkings, and also with

* Baker's *Great Basin of the Nile*, Vol. 1 p, 251.

the remark—"It must have taken you a deal of time!" And these pressures were not from naked savages, but strange to say—well dressed and well educated gentlemen thus attempted to throw cold water on scientific researches!

I am well aware that lakes and arms of the sea must occasionally be the receptacles of drift peat and trees, and that such facts by no means prove that the bottoms of such lakes and arms of the sea have sunk within the Historical period. And also that trunks of trees apparently *in situ* below the level of the sea have been found on the coast of Hampshire and elsewhere, occasioned however solely by sand and pebbles having been washed out from beneath the surface soil which thus became depressed: and not by such subsidences as are the present subjects of consideration.*—But on the other hand, during the short period since South America has been colonised by Europeans, we have proof of alterations of level at the three principal ports on the western shores Callao, Valparaiso and Conception—which are far distant from each other.† And Sir Charles and Mr. Darwin having satisfied themselves that the vast and numerous coral Islands of the Pacific have slowly and gradually sunk 3 or 4 thousands of feet and are sinking still.—We need have no hesitation then in believing in Historical Sinkings. Dr. Dawson also has proved a very general sinking down of the land on the coast of the Bay of Fundy.

This little treatise was intended to have been in the hands of readers a year ago, but great and unnecessary delay has taken place in the printing through no fault of mine. The two principal maps have been Engraved, but the impressions proved to be unfit for the reader's use, and it was found to be impossible to rectify the plates. I therefore recopied them on lithographic transfer paper which is difficult to draw upon. The impressions though coarse are pretty accurate.

R. A. P., Jersey, July 1868.

---

* Lyell's *Principles of Geology*, 1868, Chapter 46.
† Ibid. Chap. 47.

# ON STEAM,

AS THE

# MOTIVE POWER IN EARTHQUAKES

# AND VOLCANOES,

AND ON

# CAVITIES IN THE EARTH'S CRUST;

BY

R. A. PEACOCK, Esq., C. E.

JERSEY, JUNE 1866.

*Single copies of this Pamphlet sent free by post to any address on receipt of 1s. 6d. in stamps, or a dozen copies for 15s. by Post Office order.*

JERSEY:

LE LIEVRE, BROTHERS, MACHINE PRINTERS & BOOKSELLERS,

13, HALKETT PLACE.

# PREFACE.

(October, 1867.)

*Opinions of several eminent men of Science, on this Steam tract, or on the Nature of the Motive Power.*

THE ASTRONOMER ROYAL, M.A., D.C.L., F.R.S. &c.

" Royal Observatory, Greenwich,

" August 16, 1866.

" SIR,

" I have to acknowledge receipt of your Tract on Steam and Volcanoes, following your letter of August 10. I scarcely doubt the correctness of your general idea that the explosions of volcanoes are caused by steam. When I was at the summit of Vesuvius, in a quiet time, there were two great jets of vapour. One was sulphurous, most poisonous; the other was perfectly pure steam. The vapour on the head of Etna had the same appearance, but I did not go into it. I have examined the extinct volcanoes of the Vivarais in France (Dept. de l'Ardeche). The quantity of basaltic matter which has flowed out—at Jaugeac for instance—is many times greater than that of the volcano. I am sorry that I have not a copy of my paper in the Philosophical Magazine 1863 November, on the destructive energy of heated water. I have shown there that when water is heated under a pressure of 60 lbs. to the square inch, every cubic foot of water has a destructive energy (when permitted to expand into steam) equal to that of 2 lbs. of gunpowder.* With the intense

* It will have a total force on the superficies of the cubic foot of 23 tons 320 lbs.—*Editor.*

heat of volcanoes the destructive energy must be enormously greater.

R. A. Peacock, Esq. (Signed) G. B. Airy."

D. T. Ansted, Esq., M.A., F.R.S., &c. &c., states in a letter to the author, written in 1866, now unfortunately mislaid, that he has been a believer for 25 years that Steam is the cause of Earthquakes and Volcanoes.

Sir David Brewster, K.H., F.R.S., &c. &c.

The author having seen it stated in print that Sir David in addressing the University of Edinburgh in 1862, speaking of the Earth, said as follows:—"Imprisoning under its elastic crust fire and water, and other elements of danger, their explosive forces are exhausted in the earthquake, and find vent in the volcano—the safety valve of that great caldron which boils beneath our feet."* This passage having been quoted in a letter to Sir David (which was accompanied by a copy of the Tract) produced the following answer:—"Sir I beg to thank you for your interesting pamphlet 'On Steam, Volcanoes and Earthquakes,' and I am glad to find that the opinion of mine you refer to is coincident with yours, founded on so many well established facts. I am, Sir, ever most truly yours. (Signed) D. Brewster."

"Allerly, Melrose, April 30th 1867."

Edward Gibbon, Esq., author of the History of the Decline and Fall of the Roman Empire, speaking of the Earthquakes which raged with uncommon violence during the reign of the emperor Justinian, expresses himself as follows:—"The nature of the soil may indicate the countries most exposed to these formidable concussions, since they are caused by

* See Dr. Cumming's *Moses right and Bishop Colenso wrong*, p. 151.

subterraneous fires, and such fires are kindled by the union and fermentation of iron and sulphur [?]. But their times and effects appear to lie beyond the reach of human curiosity; and the philosopher will discreetly abstain from the prediction of earthquakes till he has counted the drops of water that suddenly filtrate on the inflammable mineral, and measured the caverns which increase by resistance the explosion of the imprisoned air."*

The Rev. John Michell, M.A., then Woodwardian Professor of Mineralogy at Cambridge, published in 1760, in the *Phil. Trans. R.S.* (Vol. 11, p. 448, &c.) a paper entitled "Conjectures concerning the Cause, and Observations on the Phenomena of Earthquakes;" particularly of that great earthquake of November 1, 1755, which proved so fatal to the city of Lisbon, and whose effects were felt as far as Africa, and more or less throughout Europe. These effects he attributes to steam. And he also thinks (p. 458) that steam is the cause of volcanic explosions.

Drs. Hutton, Shaw and Pearson, who abridged the Philosophical Transactions from their commencement in 1665, to the year 1800; appear to have thought so much of the paper, that though they have abridged it somewhat, they yet give it a space of about twenty-five quarto pages, which the present writer ventures to say it well deserves; it is quoted several times in the Tract.

Sir R. I. Murchison, Bart., K.C.B., F.R.S., &c., President of the Geological Section of the Birmingham Meeting of the British Association for the Advancement of Science, said on the occasion of the author's reading a paper, that he had not the least

* *Decline and Fall*, Chapter xliii, Sec. ii.

doubt that steam escaped from the earth when it got vent, and that when it did not get vent it caused undulation.

September 9, 1865.

H. C. Sorby, Esq., F.R.S., F.G.S., &c., &c.

" Broomfield, Sheffield, Sept. 17, 1866.

" My dear Sir, I am much obliged to you for a copy of your paper on Steam, &c. A large part of it very well agrees with my own views on the subject. I herewith have pleasure in sending a copy of my paper on Crystals, &c.

(Signed) H. C. Sorby."

## ANSWERS TO OBJECTIONS.

The following are the author's reasons for objecting to the seven various theories undermentioned; the first of which is, that an eminent Geological Chemist contends that steam is only the active agent in the fourth, or most feeble phase of earthquakes and volcanoes :—

(1). It is an ascertained fact that, within known limits at least, the force of saturated steam increases about as the 4½ *power* of the temperature, and conversely the temperature increases about as the 4½ *root* of the force; being an enormously rapid ratio of increase.

The following table illustrates the immense degree in which quantities, i.e. forces, are increased by raising them to the 4½ power. Take for example the number 10 and compare its various powers in the following list and it will then be seen how vastly it is increased, namely up to 31623 nearly :—

The number ........................ 10

| | |
|---|---|
| Its square or second power............ | 100 |
| Its cube or third power .............. | 1000 |
| Its biquadrate or fourth power ........ | 10000 |
| Its four and-a half power... | 31622 $\frac{78}{100}$ |

Upwards of seventy cases are cited in the Tract, where either steam, or its constituents fire, and water, were actually present in great quantities in earthquakes, in volcanoes, and in geysers; and the total quantities of fire, and water existing *in* and *on* the earth are known to be extremely great, therefore the supply of steam may reasonably be supposed to be extremely large.* Case No. 57, proves that steam and hot water were at all events *present* in the two intensely powerful volcanic explosions accompanied by a violent earthquake, of mountain Galangoon, Java, in 1822; † when ashes and lapilli were propelled to the great distance of forty miles from the mountain, and great blocks of basalt were thrown to the distance of seven miles.

"Cotopaxi was ascertained by the French Academicians to have hurled a rock calculated to weigh 200 tons, to the distance of 3 leagues." See article on Physical Geography, in *Cyclop. Brit.*—This rock supposing it to have been of granite or basalt, must have contained about 100 cubic yards, equal nearly to a cube each of whose sides measures 14 feet. In *Chambers's Cyclop.*, the rock is said to have measured 300 cubic feet and to have been thrown more than 8 miles from the crater; 300 feet give a cube with sides of 6 ft. 8 ins. There are no means of calculating the initial force employed, in the absence of all knowledge of the form of the rock, the angle of projection, and the depth at which it started.

* When fire and water meet, steam forms with great facility both in air, and in gases, and in mixtures of the two. It forms with even greater facility *in vacuo*, according to M. Regnault's experiments. Large quantities of sulphuric acid impede its formation.

† See Sir C. Lyell's *Principles of Geology*, 1853, p. 460.

When sea-water gets down to heated matter, as it certainly does, because hot water and steam are largely ejected from submarine volcanoes, it follows that steam of greater or less force, according to the greater or less degree of heat, will be produced. And consequently, action of greater or less violence according to the greater or less degree of heat, will take place. That sea-water must actually have been present previous to certain violent volcanic explosions, is proved by the following facts:—A hundred parts of sea-water contain 96½ parts of pure water, and 2½ parts of chloride of sodium or common salt, the remaining one part consisting of various other substances. And the fumes which escape from Vesuvian lava have been observed to deposit common salt.* And sea-salt was, in fact, extracted by Gay Lussac by simple washing, from the Vesuvian lava of 1822, in the proportion of 9 per cent.†^ It is evident that when sea-water is converted into steam by the heated matter, the salts will either be expelled or remain behind as the case may be, alike whether the intensity of the action is great, or only moderate. The explosion of Vesuvius in October, 1822, (when salt was found in the lava) must have been one of great violence, for Sir C. Lyell mentions that the great crater of that mountain had been gradually filled during twenty-two years by lava and scoriæ so as to be no longer a cavity, yet the whole of the vast mass was blown out and more than 800 feet of the cone were carried away by the violent explosions of 1822.‡

De Luc in his "Lettres Physiques et Morales sur l'Histoire de la Terre et de l'Homme," speaking of volcanic action in the Lipari Isles in 1757, says distinctly that, *it is the sea-water itself which the heat forces out again.* The following is a translation of

* Sir H. Davy, *Phil. Trans.* 1828, p. 244.

† *Ann. de Chim. et de Phys.*, t. 22. ‡ *Principles of Geology*, p. 375.

^ And on Feb. 8, 1868, during a series of volcanic explosions

his words, quoted from the *Universal Magazine* for April, 1783, p. 176:—"From the base of the volcano, a few inches above the calm surface of the sea, a number of little boiling springs are observed to ooze. The water of these springs is salt, which proves that it is the sea-water itself, filtered through the crevices of the mountain, and which the heat forces out again."

*Spectroscope of Volcanic Flames.*—"At a late meeting of the French Academy of Sciences, M. St. Claire Deville described the analytic results obtained by M. Janssen, who had been sent over to Santerino by the Minister of Public Instruction to examine the flames of the volcano there with the spectroscope. *Hydrogen* was found to be the chief component of these flames; but *sodium*, copper, *chlorine* and carbon were also discovered in them."—*Illustrated London News*, July 27, 1867, p. 91.

Hydrogen constitutes *one-ninth* part by *weight*, and *two-thirds* by *volume* of pure water. And the chlorine and sodium are equivalent to chloride of sodium, or common salt. That is to say, once more, the sea-water got down to the melted lava. And in fact, the eminent chemist previously referred to says, that "in an eruption of maximum intensity, the predominant volatile product is *chloride of sodium*." (See *Quarterly Journal of the Geological Society*, No. 87, p. 320.) Proving the conversion of sea-water into steam, as much in volcanoes of the greatest, as of the least intensity.

Other forces, such as (2), (4) and (5), possibly cooperate with steam, where no help is required.

*Metallic-bases-of-the-earths-and-alkalies Theory, and Theory of liquid gases.*—(2). The following three-fold difficulty presents itself in opposition to the acceptance of the theory that volcanic eruptions are caused, either by the contact of the metallic bases of the earths and alkalies with water and air, or by gases condensed into liquids :—

*a.* Is there reasonable ground for believing that the bases, or the liquid gases are always present in earthquakes and volcanoes in sufficient quantities?

*b.* If yes, then have the bases or the gases, sufficient force to produce the greatest effects of earthquakes and volcanoes, say not less than 500 tons per square inch ?*

*c.* Does steam do nothing?

These three queries were sent to an eminent gentleman (with a Tract) who is a supporter of the metallic-bases-of-the-alkaloids Theory, which produced the following letter :—

" —— October 6, 1866.

" Sir,—No doubt steam has much to do with the phenomena of volcanoes, but what is the cause of the evolution of steam? Chemical processes production of heat, which by so taking place would account for it, and this has led me to speculate upon the effects of water coming into contact with the unoxidised nucleus of the globe as seeming to solve the problem." In answer to which the author of the Tract replied as follows :—" Dear Sir, I think you believe with me that Steam is the cause both of Earthquakes and Volcanoes." This closed the correspondence.

*Simple Heat Theory.*

(3). Simple heat can exercise no explosive force. When it does not melt rocks it can only expand their bulk. Alone, it could only have increased the diameter and height of mountain Galangoon; it could not have propelled solids at all, much less to a distance of many miles. What a peaceable thing is the hottest fire!

* See Steam Tract, p. 24.

*Attraction of the Sun and Moon Theory.*

(4). It is a well ascertained and curious fact, that more earthquakes have taken place in autumn and winter, than in spring and summer. And the Moon being nearer the earth, from the middle of October to the early part of the following April, and the Sun being nearer the earth also during the same period —it follows that the united attractions of those luminaries on the surface of the earth will be greater then than during the rest of the year. And it has been supposed that this was the cause of the greater frequency of earthquakes in autumn and winter. The united attractions of the sun and moon under the most favourable circumstances, though great as a whole, are however infinitesimally small in amount per square inch in comparison with the volcanic force, as can easily be proved. For example:—a cubic foot of sea-water weighs about 64¼ lbs., whence it follows that a column of sea-water one inch square must be nearly 27 inches in height, in order to weigh 1 lb. And that being about the height of spring tides in the open Pacific Ocean, it follows that the united attractions of the sun and moon on the surface of the earth under the most favourable circumstances, only amount to about 1 lb. per square inch, a force so trifling as to be of no importance in the present question, though in the aggregate its amount is very considerable.

*Electricity.*

(5). The play of lightning about the summits of volcanoes when in action, has often been observed. But the electricity is only a consequence, not the cause, of the volcanic force. "The development of electricity by the evaporation of water has recently been submitted to more special examination, in consequence of its having been found that when vapour so formed, issues in a strong stream from a narrow aperture, as from the escape pipe of a high pressure steam boiler, the steam passes off intensely charged with positive electricity, and the boiler if insulated becomes so strongly excited with the negative electricity, as to afford the most powerful source of statical electric force that is now known. The phenomenon was first observed on this great scale by Mr. (now Sir William) Armstrong of Newcastle, but Faraday has shown that the great development of electricity does not arise from the change in the state of aggregation of the water, but from the strong friction of the issuing jet of steam against the pipe through which it passes."* The activity of the lightning about the top of the crater, is therefore a proof that steam is operating with great violence from within. See Steam Tract, p. 27, article 8.

(6). A gentleman who has distinguished himself by experimental investigations, and by numerous publications on the present subject, assumes that volcanoes, and the centres of earthquake disturbances, are near the sea, or other large supplies of water; (which is true) and he says that when an *irruption* of igneous matter takes place beneath the sea-bottom, the first action must be to open up large fissures in its material, and he enters at some length into details as to the supposed *modus operandi* of Steam, first formed in the spheroidal state. Now the difficulty opposed to this method of accounting for Earthquakes and Volcanoes, appears to lie in the word "irruption" which the present writer has italicised. What is the nature of the force which causes the first irruption of igneous matter? It cannot be simple heat, even if that be as great as the heat of melted lava, 3000° Fahr. See (3). We ought not to beg the force which we are attempting to explain and account for!

* *Elements of Chemistry*, by Sir R. Kane, M.D., M.R.I.A., 2d edition, 1849, p. 162.

(7). Another theory attributes great earthquakes to "an actual pulsation in the fluid matter beneath the earth's crust, propagated in the manner of great waves of translation from enormous ruptures occasioned by the tension of elastic matter." Here again the enormous ruptures if conceded, would by no means account for the tremendous *projectile* forces described on page v: which as this Tract proves (see Nos. 57, 58, 59, 66 on pp. 37, 38)—are only modifications of Earthquake force. Besides, the further question must be asked, does Steam do nothing?

### *Lunar Volcanoes.*

It is not at all impossible that these may also be owing to steam. We are told on high authority:—"It by no means follows, then, from the absence of visible indications of water or air on this side of the moon, that the other is equally destitute of them."*

The following is quoted from the Record newspaper of June 3, 1867, and appears to prove the present volcanic activity in the moon:

"*Changes on the surface of the Moon.*—M. Flammarion has sent to the Academy of Sciences a paper on the crater of Linnæus in the moon. This crater appears lately to have undergone great changes. Instead of the appearance which the lunar craters usually present, there is nothing left but a sort of whitish cloud attached to the top. M. Flammarion is of opinion that the crater has disappeared by sinking, or that the neighbouring plain has risen to its level. M. Chacornac, in a paper on the same subject, appears to entertain a similar opinion."

"On every hand we receive confirmation of Dr. Schmidt's discovery of the disappearance of the lunar crater Linné. After a careful discussion of

* Herschel's Outlines of Astronomy, 1864, p. 289.

the evidence, Schmidt comes to the conclusion that the change which has actually taken place corresponds—only on a greatly magnified scale—to the changes produced by mud volcanoes on our own earth. He conceives that the whole of the internal part of the crater has been filled up by erupted matter, which has further overflowed, so as to obliterate under gently-sloping declivities the once steep outer walls of this vast crater. The matter within the crater seems to have cooled; since Schmidt, Secchi, and other observers have detected a minute depression nearly in the middle of the light spot which now marks the place of the crater. If we remember that the crater was described by Lohrman, Beer and Mädler, and others, as 'very large' (nearly six miles across) and 'very deep,' we must recognize the fact that lunar volcanic activity is far from being extinguished." *Quarterly Journal of Science*, July, 1867, p. 383.

Supposing water to exist in one or more of the moon's deep cavities on that side which is never seen from the earth, and fire in her interior, then steam may be produced; and the pressure of her atmosphere would be practically nothing on the very elevated parts of the side which we see. In that case the height to which solids might be hurled from her mountains by her volcanic action, would be very great indeed, because we should have the resistance of the lunar air, nothing; and gravity only one-sixth of what it is on the earth's surface.* The writer forbears to calculate or speculate on the possibility of solids being projected to within reach of the earth's attraction.

It is submitted that the various matters stated in the Tract and in this Preface, leave Steam "master of the situation;" and that it ought to be accepted as the cause of Earthquakes and Volcanoes.

* See Steam Tract, p. 24

⁂ *A sufficient perusal of each of the following Tables may be accomplished with very little trouble. The preliminary text explains the method of making the calculations and their object, and then by reading the headings of the columns of figures, and next by passing the eye and the finger down the Columns of Differences* per cent., *the reader will see (what is the chief object of the Tables) how very small the Differences between the best Experiments and the Calculations—always are, and can test intermediately, by repeating the calculations, as many quantities as he thinks necessary.*

*Every calculation has been proved, and the print has been corrected by comparing every individual quantity with the original Calculated Tables.*

*The facts quoted and the reasonings speak for themselves.*

which was duly transmitted to him.

## NEW FORMULA FOR CALCULATING THE TEMPERATURE, OF HIGH-PRESSURE STEAM FOR ANY PRESSURE EXCEEDING 25 lbs. PER SQUARE INCH; AND TABLE CALCULATED THEREBY.

I HAVE had the following very simple formula in use, for more than two years past, whilst making certain calculations in connection with a small volume now preparing for publication; and it occurs to me that, as some time must necessarily elapse before the book is ready, it may be as well to publish it at once, for the convenience of scientific and practical men. I therefore beg a corner for this communication in your widely-circulated and valuable publication.

*Rule.*—Divide the logarithm of the given number of lbs. pressure by $4\frac{1}{2}$, and to the quotient, which is a logarithm, add the constant logarithm 2·07, and the sum is the logarithm of the number of degrees Fahrenheit required.

*Example.*—What is the thermometric temperature, Fahrenheit, of steam, giving a pressure of 300 lbs. to the square inch ?

$$\text{Logarithm of } 300 = \frac{2.4771213}{4\cdot5} = \cdot550471 +$$

$$2.07 = \text{log. } 2\cdot620471 = 417\cdot32^\circ = \text{temperature required.}$$

At the latter end of last year the second series of " Useful Information for Engineers " was published by Dr. William Fairbairn, F. R. S. At page 313 he gives 13 experiments on the pressure of steam of various temperatures, of 242·90° and upwards, of which a copy is given in the annexed table, with his own numbers.* It will be found that the constant 2·07 gives results very closely approximating to Dr. Fairbairn's experiments, the greatest difference being only as 1 in 517, or ·47 of a degree of Fahrenheit ; whilst the least difference is only as 1 in 9575, or ·03 of a degree of Fahrenheit : the differences being sometimes + and sometimes — ; that is to say, sometimes the calculations are *greater*, and sometimes they are *less* than experiments, which is for obvious reasons more satisfactory than if they were always + or always —. Another mode of making the comparison is as follows, and also gives very satisfactory results:—Adding together Dr. Fairbairn's column of temperatures, we get the sum of 3492·78°, and the sum of the corresponding calculations is 3494·03°, difference 1·25°, which divided by 13 (the number of the experiments), gives less than 1-10th of a degree of Fahrenheit for the average difference between experiment and calculation, the former being the greater.

He gives also at p. 313, a set of nine experiments on the pressure, with temperatures of less than 200°. But pressures below boiling point follow a different law of increase, and it was also foreign to my purpose to consider them. He informs us (at p. 312), that the experiments are being extended to higher pressures than 290° Fahrenheit. I venture to predict that those results will not be materially different from the following calculations. I say this with confidence, because the experiments of the French Academicians, Messrs, Arago and Dulong, follow the same law of increase, making only a very slight difference in the constant, namely, 2·07125 (instead of 2·07), the differences again

* See p. 7.

being sometimes *plus*, and sometimes *minus*. The experiments of the Academicians were not direct. They were carried up to 439·34°, which gave a pressure of 375 lbs., and my calculations only once differ from them as much as 1°. When the two series of experiments are respectively averaged by the formula as above, it appears the difference is only as 1 in 347 (about ·288 per cent.), between the two columns of calculations, which is a difference quite immaterial for all practical purposes. Of course Dr. Fairbairn's experiments are preferahle because they were *direct*.

Well might the jacket of the funnel of the Great Eastern burst, when it is seen by the table that 1,141°, the temperature of a common fire, is capable of giving a (hypothetical) pressure of more than twelve tons to the square inch. This pressure would soon be arrived at (if the boiler were capable of sustaining it) if the engine-man were to allow the whole of the water to become steam by neglecting to replenish the boiler with water.

The reason why the constant is not the same in both cases is obvious. *The experiments themselves differ*. The reader can use which constant he pleases, or split the difference: either of them is near enough for any practical purpose.

The *pressure of steam expressed in lbs. per square inch increases nearly as the* 4·5 *power of the temperature, and vice versâ.* And the use of the constants is only the same thing stated in another form, to save figures and diminish labour. Thus let it be assumed (for the sake of illustration only) that the temperature required to give a pressure of 300 lbs. to the square inch is *exactly* 418·96° Fahrenheit, neither more nor less; and let it be required what is the temperature necessary to give a ton (2,240 lbs.) pressure on the square inch, assuming as aforesaid that the pressure increases exactly as the 4·5 power of the temperature.

Here we have

300 lbs. = log. $\frac{2{\cdot}4771213}{4{\cdot}5}$ = ·5504714

: 418·96 = log. ... ... ... 2·6221726

: : 2240 lbs. = log. $\frac{3{\cdot}350248}{4.5}$ = ·7444995

3·3666721

Deduct first term ·5504714

The temperature required 654·94° = 2·8162007

But to shorten the process, we have only to take again the 4·5 root of 2240 lbs. ... ... ... = ·7444995 log.

And add the constant... ... 2·0717012

654·94° = 2·8162007

being nearly the same as the two constants used in the table, namely 2·07 and 2·07125, and we then have 654·94° as before, being nearly the same as in the table; clearly showing, as affirmed, that *the pressure of steam is about as the* 4·5 *power of its temperature*, perhaps exactly the same in reality.

R. A. P.

*St. Helier, Jersey.*

---

On January 3, 1862—a date fixed by a memorandum made on the same day—in conversation with three other gentlemen at the home of one of the party, the author expressed himself (according to a note in writing by one of the gentlemen which is substantially correct) as follows: "I have a distinct recollection, among other things, of your stating your opinion, that Steam generated in the interior of the earth and seeking a vent was the most likely cause of Earthquakes, and had apparently been employed as a principal agent in former convulsions, and probable collapses of the Earth's surface."

On August 28, 1863, during the Meeting of the Association at Newcastle-upon-Tyne the author handed a small MS. book to one of the local Secretaries, (who stated that he placed it on the desk of the Assistant-General Secretary) the contents of which are now printed the intention having been that it should be submitted to the proper Section, in accordance with the invitations given in the daily Journals. But in consequence, he supposes, of the late period of the presentation of the book to the Secretary, it was not brought before any Section, and the author ultimately obtained it back again, and it is now before him.

There could evidently be no harm in showing (by way of hypothesis) what amounts of pressure would be arrived at by various very high temperatures, on the supposition that the same law continued to prevail, which might, or might not, be true. Because it had become evident that if that law, or anything like it, did really obtain at the heat of melted lava, the force of steam at that high temperature would be amply sufficient to account for the greatest effects of Earthquakes and Volcanoes.

The following is a copy of the contents of the small book in question, which is labelled "Steam formula."

## TEMPERATURE OF STEAM AND ITS CORRESPONDING PRESSURE, WHEN SUCH PRESSURE IS NOT LESS THAN 25lbs. PER SQUARE INCH.

R. A. Peacock, Jersey.

The formula by means of which the following calculations were obtained will be given *presently*.* Because it would appear

* It has already been given.

to be the most convenient course to exhibit in the first instance how nearly the calculations agree with Dr. Fairbairn's and M. Regnault's experiments, respectively.

The following series of experiments are quoted from "Useful information for Engineers." Second series, 1860, p. 313, the third column consisting of calculations by the Formula for corresponding pressures. The difference never amounts to half a degree Fahr.

| lbs. pressure of Steam per square inch. | Temp. Fahr. by Dr. Fairbairn's experiments. | Calculation. | Difference. |
|---|---|---|---|
| lbs. | ° dec. | ° dec. | |
| 26·5 | 242·90 | 243·37 | —·47 |
| 27·4 | 244·82 | 245·19 | —·37 |
| 27·6 | 245·22 | 245·59 | —·37 |
| 33·1 | 255·50 | 255·71 | —·21 |
| 37·8 | 263·14 | 263·36 | —·22 |
| 40·3 | 267·21 | 267·14 | +·07 |
| 41·7 | 269·20 | 269·17 | +·03 |
| 45·7 | 274·76 | 274·70 | +·06 |
| 49·4 | 279·42 | 279·50 | —·08 |
| 51·7 | 282·58 | 282·34 | +·24 |
| 55·9 | 287·25 | 287·28 | —·03 |
| 56·7 | 288·25 | 288·20 | +·05 |
| 60·6 | 292·53 | 292·48 | +·05 |
| | 3492·78 | 3494·03 | |

As the formula sometimes gives *greater* and sometimes *less* results than Dr. Fairbairn's experiments, it may be said to a certain extent to average the experiments.

### M. Regnault's Experiments.

M. Regnault found that one law of increase of pressure prevailed from—86° to + 32° Fahr., another law from 32° Fahr. to 212° Fahr., and that a third law obtained between about 212° Fahr. and 432° Fahr., beyond which his experiments did not extend. We shall consequently see that the results given by the formula for 14.7 lbs. are 1°.50 too great, but that this excess gradually diminishes until for 29 lbs. pressure M. Regnault and the formula give precisely equal temperatures. Afterwards the formula up to 80 lbs. pressure gives results less and less than those produced by him, but the difference never amounts to quite so much as a degree of Fahrenheit. Afterwards the difference between the formula and M. Regnault gradually diminishes until for 300 lbs. pressure, there is only a difference of ·18 Fahr.

The figures given in the column headed Regnault, are obtained from "Mills and Millwork by Dr. W. Fairbairn," p. 202. They are copied from his

"Table V. Of the pressure and corresponding temperature "of saturated Steam, obtained from the Tables of M. Regnault "by interpolation and reduction to English measures."

*Note.* There appears to be an inaccuracy in the column headed Regnault, opposite 51 lbs. pressure, as the following Table shows :

| lbs. | Regnault. ° | Difference. |
|---|---|---|
| 48 | 278·30 | |
| 49 | 279·59 | 1·29 |
| 50 | 280·85 | 1·26 |
| 51 | 282·09 | 1·24 |
| 52 | 283·32 | 1·23 |
| 53 | 284·53 | 1·21 |
| 54 | 285·73 | 1·20 |

When the Temperature 282.09 is substituted as corrected above, for what stands in the Table in "Mills and Millwork" namely 282.60, the Differences follow in a proper decreasing order. And the correction has been made accordingly in the following Table :

| Pressure in lbs. per square inch. | Regnault. Fahr. | Calculation. | Difference. |
|---|---|---|---|
| | ° dec. | ° dec. | |
| 14·7 | 212· | 213·50 | —1·50 |
| 15 | 213·02 | 214·46 | —1·44 |
| 16 | 216·29 | 217·56 | —1·27 |
| 17 | 219·42 | 220·51 | —1·09 |
| 18 | 222·37 | 223·33 | —·96 |
| 19 | 225·19 | 226·03 | —·84 |
| 20 | 227·91 | 228·62 | —·71 |
| 21 | 230·54 | 231·11 | —·57 |
| 22 | 233·08 | 233·51 | —·43 |
| 23 | 235·43 | 235·83 | —·40 |
| 24 | 237·75 | 238·07 | —·32 |
| 25 | 240· | 240·24 | —·24 |
| 26 | 242·16 | 242·34 | —·18 |
| 27 | 244·16 | 244·39 | —·13 |
| 28 | 246·32 | 246·37 | —·05 |
| 29 | 248·30 | 248·30 | equal |
| 30 | 250·23 | 250·17 | +.06 |
| 31 | 252·09 | 252·01 | +·08 |
| 32 | 253·94 | 253·81 | +·13 |
| 33 | 255·70 | 255·53 | +·17 |
| 34 | 257·47 | 257·23 | +·24 |
| 35 | 259·15 | 258·90 | +·25 |
| 36 | 260·83 | 260·52 | +·31 |
| 37 | 262·44 | 262·11 | +·33 |
| 38 | 264·04 | 263·67 | +·37 |
| 39 | 265·58 | 265·20 | +·38 |
| 40 | 267·12 | 266·70 | +·42 |
| 41 | 268·60 | 268·16 | +·44 |
| 42 | 270·07 | 269·60 | +·47 |
| 43 | 271·50 | 271·02 | +·48 |
| 44 | 272·91 | 272·40 | +·51 |
| 45 | 274·30 | 273·77 | +·53 |
| 46 | 275·65 | 275·11 | +·54 |
| 47 | 276·99 | 276·42 | +·57 |
| 48 | 278·30 | 277·72 | +·58 |
| 49 | 279·59 | 279·— | +·59 |
| 50 | 280·85 | 280·25 | +·60 |
| 51 | 282·09 | 281·49 | +·60 |

| Pressure in lbs. per square inch. | Regnault. Fahr. | Caln. | Difference. |
|---|---|---|---|
| | ° deo. | ° deo. | + |
| 52 | 283·32 | 282·70 | ·62 |
| 53 | 284·53 | 283·90 | ·63 |
| 54 | 285·73 | 285·08 | ·65 |
| 55 | 286·90 | 286·25 | ·65 |
| 56 | 288·05 | 287·40 | ·65 |
| 57 | 289·19 | 288·53 | ·66 |
| 58 | 290·31 | 289·65 | ·66 |
| 59 | 291·42 | 290·75 | ·67 |
| 60 | 292·51 | 291·84 | ·67 |
| 65 | 297·77 | 297·08 | ·69 |
| 70 | 302·71 | 302·01 | ·70 |
| 75 | 307·38 | 306·67 | ·71 |
| 80 | 311·83 | 311·10 | ·73 |
| 85 | 316·— | 315·32 | ·68 |
| 90 | 320·03 | 319·35 | ·68 |
| 95 | 323·87 | 323·22 | ·65 |
| 100 | 327·56 | 326·92 | ·64 |
| 105 | 331·10 | 330·49 | ·61 |
| 110 | 334·51 | 333·92 | ·59 |
| 115 | 337·84 | 337·24 | ·60 |
| 120 | 340·99 | 340·44 | ·55 |
| 125 | 344·06 | 343·54 | ·52 |
| 130 | 347·05 | 346·55 | ·50 |
| 135 | 349·93 | 349·47 | ·46 |
| 140 | 352·76 | 352·30 | ·46 |
| 145 | 355·60 | 355·06 | ·54 |
| 150 | 358·30 | 357·75 | ·55 |
| 160 | 363.40 | 362·91 | ·49 |
| 170 | 368·20 | 367·84 | ·36 |
| 180 | 372·90 | 372·54 | ·36 |
| 190 | 377·50 | 377·04 | ·46 |
| 200 | 381·80 | 381·37 | ·43 |
| 210 | 386·00 | 385·52 | ·48 |
| 220 | 389·90 | 389·52 | ·38 |
| 230 | 393·80 | 393·39 | ·41 |
| 240 | 397·50 | 397·13 | ·37 |
| 250 | 401·10 | 400·75 | ·35 |
| 260 | 404·50 | 404·26 | ·24 |
| 270 | 407·90 | 407.67 | ·23 |
| 280 | 411·20 | 410·97 | ·23 |
| 290 | 414·40 | 414·19 | ·21 |
| 300 | 417·50 | 417·32 | ·18 |

**Assuming the same ratio of increase to obtain up to 1141°, we shall have for various temperatures as follows :**

| Pressure in lbs. per square inch. | Calculation. |
|---|---|
| | ° deo. |
| 360 | 434.58 |
| 400 | 444·87 |
| 450 | 456·67 |
| 500 | 467·49 |
| 560 (½ ton.) | 479·41 |
| 600 | 486·82 |
| 650 | 495·56 |
| 700 | 503·78 |
| 800 | 518·96 |
| 900 | 532·71 |
| 1000 | 545·34 |

| | Pressure in lbs. per square inch. | Caln. |
|---|---|---|
| | | ° deg. |
| | 1120 (½ ton.) | 559·25 |
| 576° Lead melts ............................ | 1279·09 | 576·— |
| | 1680 (¾ ton.) | 611·98 |
| | 2000 | 636·15 |
| 640° Linseed Oil boils ..................... | 2055 | 640·— |
| | 2240 (a ton.) | 652·37 |
| 662° Mercury boils (Professor Daniell). | 1 ton 152 lbs½. | 662·— |
| | 2 tons. | 761·02 |
| 802° Charcoal burns ....................... | 2½ tons 73 lbs. | 802·— |
| | 3 tons. | 832·77 |
| | 4 | 887·75 |
| | 5 | 932·88 |
| | 6 | 971·45 |
| 980° Dull red heat (Daniell) ............ | 6¼ | 980·30 |
| | 7 | 1005·31 |
| | 8 | 1035·58 |
| | 9 | 1063·05 |
| | 10 | 1088·23 |
| | 11 | 1111·53 |
| | 12 | 1133·23 |
| 1141° Highest temperature of common fires. (Daniell). | 12 tons 839 lbs. | 1141· |
| | 14¾ tons. | 1186·40 |

A sufficient number of calculations for the present purpose appears now to have been given.

[Here followed explanations and examples of the method of making the calculations, which being similar to those already given on p. 4, 5, need not be reprinted.]

By the use of the constant Log. 2·07 the previous tables have been calculated.

Aug. 28, 1863.

---

## ON THE PRESSURE OF STEAM AT HIGH TEMPERATURES.

BY R. A. PEACOCK, C. E.

[Extract from the *Artizan* of Jan. 1, 1864.]

It may, perhaps, be of interest to some to see the calculations by this formula placed side by side with the results of some of the best known experiments and formulæ.

The following table gives a copy of the "more trustworthy of Arago and Dulong's experiments after all necessary corrections," copied from "A Treatise on Heat," by the Rev. R. V. Dixon, A.M., Dublin, 1849, p. 173, and copied by him from "Ann. de Chim. et de Phys.," tome xliii, p. 108, reduced, however, from Cent. degrees to Fahr., and from elastic force in atmospheres, to pressure in pounds per square inch by the present writer, an atmosphere being taken at 14·7lb. It will be seen that the formula does not agree with MM. Arago and Dulong's experiments, but that it does agree nearly with other well-known experiments specified afterwards.

The American Commissioners' experiments which are not now given, differ as much from the formula as MM. Arago and Dulong's, but in a different way.

*MM. Arago and Dulong's Experiments.*

| Pressure. | Temp. Fahr. Observed. | Temp. Fahr. Cal. | |
|---|---|---|---|
| lbs. per sq. in. | Deg. | Deg. | Diff: + |
| 31·458 | 254·66 | 252·83 | 1·83 |
| 42·196 | 271·94 | 269·88 | 2·06 |
| 67·23 | 301·46 | 299·31 | 2·15 |
| 95·516 | 326·12 | 323·61 | 2·51 |
| 108·4198 | 335·30 | 332·84 | 2·46 |
| 170·99 | 371·30 | 368·31 | 2·99 |
| 252·619 | 404·24 | 401·68 | 2·56 |
| 254·089 | 405·32 | 402·20 | 3.12 |
| 272·008 | 410·90 | 408·33 | 2·57 |
| 316·858 | 425·12 | 422·42 | 2·70 |
| 351·8298 | 435·47 | 432·36 | 3·11 |

The following are the experiments of Dr. Wm. Fairbairn F.R.S., given at p. 313 of "Useful Information for Engineers," second series. The formula, it will be seen, never differs as much as half a degree Fahr. from experiment ; and the calculations being sometimes less and sometimes greater than the corresponding experiments, indicate that the experiments are averaged by the formula, and some of the differences are quite insignificant.

[This Table has already been printed at p. 7 antè.]

The following are M. Regnault's experiments from 23lbs. to 300 lbs. per square inch, from which the formula never differs as much as three-quarters of a degree Fahr., and at 300lb. pressure it very nearly coincides with experiment.

Regnault's experiments, as now given, are copied from Dr. W. Fairbairn's "Mills and Millwork," vol. 1, p. 202, obtained from the tables of M. Regnault, by interpolation and reduction to English measures.

[This Table has already been printed at p. 8 and 9 antè.)

The following table is given in THE ARTIZAN for October, 1863, p. 219, the third and fourth columns being calculated by the present writer as before.

| Press. | Mr. Birckel's Temp. | Temp. Cal. | |
|---|---|---|---|
| lbs. per sq. in. | Deg. | Deg. | Diff. |
| 24·54 | 239 | 239·255 | —·255 |
| 28·83 | 248 | 247·976 | +.024 |
| 33·71 | 257 | 256·745 | —·255 |

| Press. | Mr. Birckel's Tem. | Temp. Cal. | |
|---|---|---|---|
| lbs. per sq. in. | Deg. | Deg. | Diff. |
| 39·25 | 266 | 265·574 | + ·426 |
| 46·49 | 275 | 274·426 | + ·574 |
| 52·52 | 284 | 283·33 | + ·67 |
| 60·40 | 293 | 292·27 | + ·73 |
| 69·21 | 302 | 301·25 | + ·75 |
| 79·03 | 311 | 310·264 | + ·736 |
| 89·86 | 320 | 319·24 | + ·76 |
| 101·90 | 329 | 328·285 | + ·715 |
| 115·10 | 338 | 337·3 | + ·7 |
| 129·80 | 347 | 346·43 | + ·57 |
| 145·80 | 356 | 355·5 | + ·5 |
| 163·30 | 365 | 364.564 | + ·436 |
| 182·40 | 374 | 373·63 | + ·37 |
| 203·3 | 383 | 382·75 | + ·25 |
| 225·9 | 392 | 391·82 | + ·18 |

This table, by Mr. J. J. Birckel, agrees very nearly with Mr. Regnault's.

In the November number of The Artizan, Dr. Macquorn Rankine, F.R.S., publishes a paper "On the Expansive Energy of Heated Water," in which he gives a table, which we quote from; and which, in its first part, consists of some of the identical figures just given under the name of Mr. J. J. Birckel.

The following is Dr. Macquorn Rankine's table—the last two columns being added in the usual manner by the present writer.

| Initial Absolute Pressure. | Initial Temp. Fahr. | Initial Temp. Fahr. Calculated. | |
|---|---|---|---|
| lbs. per sq. in. | Deg. | Deg. | Diff. |
| 23·83 | 248 | 247·976 | + ·024 |
| 52·52 | 284 | 283·33 | + ·67 |
| 89 86 | 320 | 319·24 | + ·76 |
| 145·8 | 356 | 355·5 | + ·5 |
| 225 9 | 392 | 391·82 | + ·18 |
| 336·3 | 428 | 428·05 | —·05 |
| | { about 2360 | { 729,632lbs. or 325·7 tons. | |

[Here some small matters of detail, of no importance now, are omitted. The following is extracted from The Artizan of Feb. 1, 1864.]

For the purpose of exhibiting in the following table that the temperature gradually increases with the pressure, which ought clearly to be the case if the calculations are correct, the whole of the calculations are given. This also will enable any one to make a comparison between the best known experiments and the calculations. For a reason which will presently be explained, ·543 per cent. ought to be added to each of the following calculations of temperatures, in order to produce the respective pressures stated opposite to them.

**Table of Pressures and corresponding Temperatures of Saturated Steam, the calculating being on the theory that the temperature increases as the 4½ *root* of the pressure and conversely that the pressure increases as the 4½ *power* of the temperature.**

| Press. lbs. pr. sq. in. | Calcns. Tem. Fahr. deg. | Press. lbs. pr. sq. in. | Calcns. Tem. Fahr. deg. | Press. lbs. pr. sq. in. | Calcns. Tem. Fahr. deg. |
|---|---|---|---|---|---|
| 25 | 240·24 | 49·4 | 279·50 | 110 | 333·92 |
| 26 | 242·34 | 50 | 280·25 | 110·25 | 334·08 |
| 26·5 | 243·37 | 51 | 281·49 | 115 | 337·24 |
| 27 | 244·39 | 51.45 | 282·02 | 115·1 | 337·30 |
| 27·4 | 245·19 | 51·7 | 282·34 | 120 | 340·44 |
| 27·6 | 245·59 | 52 | 282·70 | 124·95 | 343·51 |
| 28 | 246·37 | 52·52 | 283·33 | 125 | 343·54 |
| 28·83 | 247·98 | 52 | 233·90 | 129·8 | 346·43 |
| 29 | 248·30 | 54 | 285·08 | 130 | 346·55 |
| 29·4 | 249·05 | 55 | 286·25 | 132·3 | 347·90 |
| 30 | 250·17 | 55·9 | 287·28 | 135 | 349·47 |
| 31 | 252·01 | 56 | 237·40 | 139·65 | 352·11 |
| 31·458 | 252·83 | 56·7 | 288·20 | 140 | 352·30 |
| 32 | 253·81 | 57 | 288·53 | 145 | 355·06 |
| 33 | 255·53 | 58 | 289·65 | 145·8 | 355·50 |
| 33·1 | 255·71 | 58·8 | 290·53 | 147 | 356·14 |
| 33·71 | 256·74 | 59 | 290·75 | 150 | 357·75 |
| 34 | 257·23 | 60 | 291·84 | 154·3 | 360 (1) |
| 35 | 258·90 | 60·4 | 292·27 | 160 | 362·91 |
| 36 | 260·52 | 60·6 | 292·48 | 163·3 | 364·56 |
| 36·75 | 261·70 | 65 | 297·08 | 165 | 365·40 |
| 37 | 262·11 | 66·15 | 298·23 | 170 | 367·84 |
| 37·8 | 263.36 | 67·23 | 299·31 | 170·99 | 368·31 |
| 38 | 263·67 | 69·21 | 301·25 | 180 | 372·54 |
| 39 | 265·20 | 70 | 302.01 | 182·4 | 373·63 |
| 39·25 | 265·57 | 73·5 | 305·30 | 190 | 377·04 |
| 40 | 266·70 | 75 | 306·67 | 195 | 379·22 |
| 40·3 | 267·14 | 79·03 | 310·26 | 200 | 381·37 |
| 41 | 268·16 | 80 | 311·10 | 203·3 | 382·75 |
| 41·7 | 269·17 | 80·85 | 311·83 | 210 | 385·52 |
| 42 | 269·60 | 85 | 315·32 | 220 | 389·52 |
| 42·196 | 269·88 | 88·2 | 317.92 | 225 | 391·48 |
| 43 | 271·02 | 80·86 | 319·24 | 225·9 | 391·82 |
| 44 | 272·40 | 90 | 319·35 | 230 | 393·39 |
| 44·1 | 272·54 | 95 | 323·22 | 240 | 397·13 |
| 45 | 273·77 | 95·516 | 323·61 | 250 | 400·75 |
| 45·49 | 274·43 | 95·55 | 323·63 | 252·619 | 401·68 |
| 45·7 | 274·70 | 100 | 326·92 | 254·089 | 402·20 |
| 46 | 275·11 | 101·9 | 328·28 | 255 | 402·52 |
| 47 | 276·42 | 102·9 | 329·01 | 260 | 404·26 |
| 48 | 277·72 | 105 | 330·49 | 270 | 407·67 |
| 49 | 279· | 108·4198 | 332·84 | 272·008 | 408·33 |

(1) Soft solder, two parts tin and one part lead, melts at 360°.

| Pressure. lbs. pr. sq. in. | Calons. Tem. Fahr. deg. | Press. lbs. pr. sq. in. | Calons. Temp. Fahr. deg. | Press. per sq. in. tons lbs. | Calons. Tem. Fahr. deg. |
|---|---|---|---|---|---|
| 280 | 410·97 | 980 | 542·90 | 6¾ | 997·21 |
| 285 | 412·60 | 1000 | 545·34 | 7 | 1005·31 |
| 290 | 414·19 | 1050 | 551·28 | 7¼ | 1013·17 |
| 300 | 417·32 | 1100 | 557·01 | 7½ | 1020·84 |
| 315 | 421·87 | 1120, ½ ton. | 559·25 | 7¾ | 1028·30 |
| 316·858 | 422·42 | 1200 | 567·89 | 8 | 1035·58 |
| 330 | 426·25 | 1279·09 | 576· (2) | 8¼ | 1042·69 |
| 336·3 | 428·05 | 1300 | 578·08 | 8½ | 1049·63 |
| 345 | 430·48 | 1400 | 587·68 | 8¾ | 1056·41 |
| 351·8298 | 432·36 | 1500 | 596·76 | 9 | 1063·05 |
| 360 | 434·58 | 1600 | 605·38 | 9¼ | 1069·54 |
| 375 | 438·54 | 1680, ¾ ton. | 611·98 | 9½ | 1075·90 |
| 400 | 444·87 | 1700 | 613·59 | 9¾ | 1082·13 |
| 420 | 449·72 | 1800 | 621·43 | 10 | 1088·23 |
| 440 | 454·40 | 1900 | 628·94 | 10¼ | 1094·22 |
| 450 | 456·67 | 1984 | 635 (3) | 10½ | 1100·10 |
| 460 | 458·91 | 2000 | 636·15 | 10¾ | 1105·86 |
| 480 | 463·27 | 2055 | 640 (4) | 11 | 1111·53 |
| 500 | 467·49 | 2100 | 643.09 | 11¼ | 1117.09 |
| 520 | 471·58 (1) | 2200 | 649·77 | 11½ | 1122·56 |
| 540 | 475·55 | 2240, a ton. | 652·37 | 11¾ | 1127·94 |
| 550 | 477·49 | Tons. lbs. | | 12 | 1133·23 |
| 560, ¼ ton. | 479·41 | 1 152 | 662 (5) | 12¼ | 1138·43 |
| 580 | 483·16 | 1¼ | 685·54 | 12 839 | 1141 (9) |
| 600 | 486·82 | 1½ | 713·89 | 12½ | 1143·50 |
| 620 | 490·38 | 1¾ | 738·77 | 12¾ | 1148·60 |
| 635 | 492·99 | 2 | 761·02 | 13 | 1153·56 |
| 650 | 495·56 | 2¼ | 781·20 | 13¼ | 1158·46 |
| 660 | 497·24 | 2½ | 799·71 | 13½ | 1163·28 |
| 680 | 500·55 | 2½ 73 | 802 (6) | 13¾ | 1168·03 |
| 700 | 503·78 | 2½ 332 | 810 (7) | 14 | 1172·72 |
| 720 | 506·95 | 2¾ | 816·82 | 14¼ | 1177·34 |
| 740 | 510·04 | 3 | 832·77 | 14½ | 1181·90 |
| 750 | 511·57 | 3¼ | 847·72 | 14¾ | 1186·40 |
| 760 | 513·08 | 3½ | 861·80 | 15 | 1190·84 |
| 780 | 516·04 | 3¾ | 875·11 | 15¼ | 1195·22 |
| 800 | 518·96 | 4 | 887·75 | 15½ | 1199·54 |
| 820 | 521·81 | 4¼ | 899·79 | 15¾ | 1203·82 |
| 840 | 524·61 | 4½ | 925·37 | 16 | 1208·04 |
| 850 | 526 | 4¾ | 922·30 | 17 | 1224·42 |
| 860 | 527·36 | 5 | 932·88 | 18 | 1240·07 |
| 880 | 530·06 | 5¼ | 943·05 | 19 | 1255·06 |
| 900 | 532·71 | 5½ | 952·85 | 20 | 1269.45 |
| 920 | 535·33 | 5¾ | 962·31 | 25 | 1334 |
| 940 | 537·89 | 6 | 971·45 | 30 | 1389·15 |
| 950 | 539·16 | 6¼ | 980·30 (8) | 50 | 1556·14 |
| 960 | 540·41 | 6½ | 988·88 | 100 | 1815·28 |

(1) **Bismuth melts, 471·6°. (Dixon on heat.)**
(2) **Leads melts, 576°.**
(3) **Iron, read heat in the dark, 635°.**
(4) **Linseed oil boils, 640°.**
(5) **Mercury boils, 662°.**
(6) **Charcoal burns, 802°**
(7) **Antimony melts, 810°.**
(8) **Iron, dull read heat, 980°.**
(9) **Heat of a common fire, 1141°.**

*Hydrogen burning in oxygen 5478°*

The following are the several melting heats of some of the more refractory metals, with the hypothetical pressures of steam of equal temperatures calculated by the formula:

| Calculations of Pressure in Tons per square inch. | | | |
|---|---|---|---|
| 114 | ...... Brass melts at | ...... 1869° (11) | Fahr. |
| 115 | ...... Silver ,, | ...... 1873° (12) | ,, |
| 153 | ...... Copper ,, | ...... 1996° (13) | ,, |
| 237 | ...... Gold ,, | ...... 2200° (14) | ,, |
| 326 | ................................ | 2360° (15) | ,, |
| 687 | ...... Cast iron ,, | ...... 2786° (16) | ,, |
| 959 | ...... Subterranean fusion.. | 3000° (17) | ,, |

The temperatures marked [6,8,9,10,11,12,13,14,16], are on the authority of Professor Daniell, F.R.S., the temperature 2360, is stated by Dr. Macquorn Rankine, F.R.S., to be that about at which the water in an engine boiler would be totally evaporated. (Artizan, Nov. 1863, p. 252.) In Sir W. G. Armstrong's address to the British Association, at Newcastle (p. 9.), he assumes the temperature of subterranean fusion to be 3000° Fahr. The other melting points, &c., have been obtained from a small volume on steam, published by the late Mr. Weale.

*Earthquakes, Volcanic Explosions, and Upheavals of Strata.*—There is another point of view in which this formula may possibly be not without interest to a class of scientific men, other than engineers. More than a century ago, the Rev. John Michell, M.A.. "conjectured" that steam might be the cause of earthquakes, and he reasons very ably at considerable length on the subject.* His idea, however, seems to have been dropped, except by a very few, by whom it is entertained only as one out of several conjectural causes. Now if, as must now and then happen, fissures open in the bed of the sea, by the action of earthquakes and close again after a few seconds or minutes, it follows that a large body of water will rush down and be imprisoned, and come in contact with the fused matter below. This water will necessarily be converted into steam, which will only remain quiescent as long as it is everywhere surrounded by a resistance greater than its own expansive force. If the formula approximates towards the truth, unless the resistance amounts to a thousand tons per square inch or thereabouts on every side, in certain cases an explosion will take place of sufficient force to account for an earthquake or volcanic eruption, as the case may be. In reading accounts of volcanoes and earthquakes, it will frequently be observed that *hot water* and *steam* are ejected, to say nothing of the *hot water* and *steam* which notoriously issue from boiling springs and geysers. The writer has made a consi-

* Phil. Trans. R.S. 1760. Vol. 51, p. 447, &c.

derable collection of such cases. There is then plenty of direct proof of the existence of steam in the bowels of the earth, and steam will not be idle if it can find any point of less resistance than its own expansive force. Therefore, in considering the cause or causes of earthquakes, volcanic explosions, and upheavals of strata, you cannot get rid of steam. For let us look from whatever point of view we will, the pressure of saturated steam must be enormous long before it reaches the temperature of 3,000 degrees.

At the Bath meeting, Sept. 1864, in the mechanical section, (see Report, p. 19,) the author read a paper on Steam, Volcanoes, &c.

Fifty or sixty copies of the following table were distributed in the Geological Section at Birmingham September 9, 1865.

## TEMPERATURES AND PRESSURES OF HIGH PRESSURE STEAM.

By R. A. Peacock, C.E., Jersey.

| Pressure per square inch. | Regnault's Exp'ments | Dr. Fairbairn's Experiments. | As 4½ Roots of Pressures. | Diffs. | Differences per cent. |
|---|---|---|---|---|---|
| | Temp. F. | Temp. F. | Temp. F. | | |
| lbs. | deg. | deg. | deg. | deg. | deg. |
| 24·998 | 240 | ... | 240·244 | —·244 | —·102 |
| 26·5 | ... | 242·90 | 243·375 | —·475 | —·195 |
| 27·3518 | 245 | ... | 245·093 | —.093 | —·038 |
| 27·4 | ... | 244·82 | 245·188 | —·368 | —·150 |
| 27·6 | ... | 245·22 | 245·585 | —·365 | —·149 |
| 29·8753 | 250 | ... | 249·946 | +.054 | +·022 |
| 32·5899 | 255 | ... | 254·824 | +·176 | +·069 |
| 33·1 | ... | 255·50 | 255·705 | —·205 | —·080 |
| 35·5005 | 260 | ... | 259·715 | +·285 | +·110 |
| 37·8 | ... | 263·14 | 263·362 | —·222 | —·084 |
| 38·6169 | 265 | ... | 264·617 | +·383 | +·145 |
| 40·3 | ... | 267·21 | 267·137 | +·073 | +·027 |
| 41·7 | ... | 269·20 | 269·17 | +·03 | +·011 |
| 41·9587 | 270 | ... | 269·543 | +·457 | +·170 |
| 45·5259 | 275 | ... | 274·474 | +·526 | +·192 |
| 45·7 | ... | 274·76 | 274·71 | +·05 | +·018 |
| 49·3332 | 280 | ... | 279·417 | +·583 | +·209 |
| 49·4 | ... | 279·42 | 279·50 | —.08 | —·029 |
| 51·7 | ... | 282·58 | 282·34 | +·24 | +·085 |
| 53·3953 | 285 | ... | 284·374 | +·626 | +·220 |
| 55·9 | ... | 287·25 | 287·29 | —·04 | —·014 |
| 56·7 | ... | 288·25 | 288·20 | +·05 | +·017 |
| 57·722 | 290 | ... | 289·34 | +·66 | +·228 |
| 60·6 | ... | 292·53 | 292·48 | +·05 | +·017=1/[illegible] |
| 62·328 | 295 | ... | 294 319 | +·681 | +·231 |
| 67·2231 | 300 | ... | 299·306 | +·694 | +·232=1/[illegible] |
| 72·422 | 305 | ... | 304·302 | +·698 | +·229 |

An atmosphere is taken at 14·7 lbs. per square inch.

| Pressure per square inch. | Regnault's Exp'ments | As $4\frac{1}{2}$ Roots of Pressures. | Differences. | Differences per cent. |
|---|---|---|---|---|
| | Temp. F. | Temp. F. | | |
| lbs. | deg. | deg. | deg. | deg. |
| 77·9345 | 310 | 309·303 | +·697 | +·225 |
| 83·7802 | 315 | 314·315 | +·685 | +·218 |
| 89·9689 | 320 | 319·332 | +.668 | +·209 |
| 96·5104 | 325 | 324·352 | +·648 | +·200 |
| 103·4292 | 330 | 329·381 | +·619 | +·188 |
| 110·7302 | 335 | 334·412 | +·588 | +·176 |
| 118·433 | 340 | 339·446 | +·554 | +·168 |
| 126·5523 | 345 | 344·486 | +·514 | +·149 |
| 135·1028 | 350 | 349·527 | +·473 | +·135 |
| 144·0992 | 355 | 354·565 | +·435 | +·123 |
| 153·5562 | 360 | 359·614 | +·386 | +·107 |
| 163·4934 | 365 | 364·660 | +·340 | +·093 = $\frac{1}{1075}$ |
| 173·9206 | 370 | 369·705 | +·295 | +·079 |
| 184·8574 | 375 | 374·750 | +·250 | +·067 |
| 196·3234 | 380 | 379·795 | +·205 | +·054 |
| 208·3284 | 385 | 384·838 | +·162 | +·042 |
| 220·8871 | 390 | 389·876 | +·124 | +·032 |
| 234·024 | 395 | 394·918 | +·082 | +·021 |
| 247·7538 | 400 | 399·949 | +·051 | +·013 |
| 262·0912 | 405 | 404·980 | +·020 | +·005 |
| 277·0509 | 410 | 410·007 | —·007 | —·002 = 1/[illegible] |
| 292·6525 | 415 | 415·029 | —·029 | —·007 |
| 308·9156 | 420 | 420·047 | —·047 | —·011 |
| 325·85 | 425 | 425·058 | —·058 | —·014 |
| 343·4753 | 430 | 430·063 | —·063 | —·015 |
| 350·7224 | 432 | 432·063 | —·063 | —·015 |
| 411·6* | 447 [illegible]† | 447·71 | —·71 | —·159 = 1/[illegible] |

* = 28 atmospheres, and † = 230·56 centigrade. See Rev. R. V. Dixon's "Treatise on Heat," p. 183.

---

At the Birmingham Meeting, on Sept. 9, after distributing the copies to the President and Committee, and amongst the members present—the author called attention to the enormously rapid ratio in which Steam Pressure increases in proportion to the increase of Temperature. It does not increase merely as the square or second power, nor as the cube or third power, nor as the square of the square or fourth power—it increases still more rapidly than any of these, namely, *as the $4\frac{1}{2}$ power of the Temperature.** The pressures of greatest amount in the Table and the Temperatures corresponding therewith, are the highest present limit of our exact knowledge. But fortunately we are not without practical proof of the enormous amount of Steam pressure even at the temperature of melted brass, which is only 1869°, whilst the heat of melted lava is probably not less than 3000°. The Rev. John Michell wrote a very valuable paper *(Phil. Trans. R. S.,* 1760 Vol. xi. p. 458, &c.) in which he contended that earthquakes were caused by steam. But the paper has scarcely, if at all, been believed in. He says that in casting two brass

* The Author has since seen occasion very slightly to modify this law, as will appear presently.

cannon "the heat of the metal of the first gun drove so much damp into the mould of the second, which was near it, that as soon as the metal was let into it, it blew up with the greatest violence, tearing up the ground some feet deep, breaking down the furnace, untiling the house, killing many spectators on the spot with the streams of melted metal, and scalding others in the most miserable manner." These effects were evidently produced by the steam of a few ounces of water only, for it is called merely "damp," and it must therefore have been very powerful steam. Now, according to the late Professor Daniell, F.R.S., brass melts at 1869° F.; and supposing (for the sake of argument) that the empirical law continued to prevail, the pressure of the steam would be 114 tons per square inch. The author then offered to read some accounts of the ejection of Steam from Volcanoes, Earthquakes, &c., which the President of the Section thought was unnecessary, because they were so well known.

The President then remarked that he had not the least doubt that Mr. Peacock's conclusion was a right one. He had not the least doubt that steam escaped from the earth when it got vent, and that when it did not get vent it caused undulation.

No one of the Committee or Members present signified anything like dissent from these opinions.

An account on the subject will appear in the forthcoming volume of the British Association in due course, to which the Author refers; he has not kept a copy and therefore cannot reprint it.

The table (distributed at Birmingham), so far as relates to M. Regnault's experiments was quoted from a table at p. 259,260 of the Rev. R. V. Dixon's *Treatise on Heat.** His column of "force in inches of mercury" being reduced to lbs. per square inch, on the principle of taking 14·7lbs. to an atmosphere. The last line of the table is obtained from p. 183, where he says the pressure of about 28 atmospheres has a corresponding steam temperature of 230·56° Centigrade or 447° Fahr. The following are

*Extracts from an unpublished M.S.*

But it was right to go to the fountain head, and accordingly Vol. XXI of *Mèmoires de l'Institut* has been referred to, where M. Regnault gives a full account of his steam experiments for the French Government, and many tables of results. His experiments are as nearly perfect as anything merely human could be expected to be. In fact, more nearly so than could a priori have been expected, when we consider the many difficulties and dangers which he had to encounter and overcome. He gives the pressure in millemètres of mercury, taking 760 millemètres to an atmosphere. And he takes as his standard

* Hodges and Smith. Dublin, 1849.

the Observatory of Paris in latitude 48° 50′ at 60 mètres (196ft. 10in.) above the level of the sea. Sir John Herschel gives* mean barometric pressure at sea level on 1 square inch in lbs. 14·7304." But the pressure would be less than that at the Paris Observatory, nearly 200ft. above the sea.

*Data used in calculating the three following tables.*

| | |
|---|---|
| Specific gravity of mercury at 32° Fhr. (water at 40°)* ........................................ | 13·596 |
| Hence a cubic foot of mercury weighs lbs.... | 849·75 |
| And a column of mercury a mètre high (39·37079 English inches)* and one inch square, weighs lbs............................ | 19·360678 |
| And an atmosphere of 760 millemètres therefore weighs lbs. ................................ | 14·714132 |
| And it follows that an atmosphere will be equal to a column of mercury of the height, inches.................................. | 29·9218 |

At p.p. 625-6 M. Regnault gives a table "des forces élastiques de la vapeur aqueuse" from which may be gathered by comparison with his table at p. 608, that the latter was calculated by his formula H. Table II. now given is calculated from data obtained from his table at pp. 625-6, and it will be seen that his formula gives results all but identical with the $4\frac{1}{2}$ roots of the pressures, the Differences being quite insignificant, for they range only from $+\frac{1}{4891}$ to $-\frac{1}{2703}$. There is therefore *practically no difference between his formula and that used by the present writer :—*

Table II. Being extracts from M. Regnault's table calculated by his formula H., and given by him in Mem. de l'Institut, vol. 21, p. 625-6. Reduced by the present writer to English denominations, and compared with his own calculations, made as $4\frac{1}{2}$ roots of pressures.

* Outlines of Astronomy, 1864, p. 716.

## Table II.

| M. Regnault's millemetres, reduced to lbs. pressure per sq. inch. | Mean temperatures centigrade, reduced to Fahr. | | Calculated as $4\frac{1}{2}$ roots of pressures. Temperatures | Differences. + or — | Differences. per cent. + or — | |
|---|---|---|---|---|---|---|
| lbs. dec. | Cent. Deg. | Fahr. Deg. | Fahr. Deg. | | | |
| 24·5767 | 115 | 239 | 239·3344 | —·3344 | —·140 | |
| 28·8722 | 120 | 248 | 248·0568 | —·0568 | —·023 | |
| 33·7627 | 125 | 257 | 256·8341 | +·1659 | +·065 | |
| 39·3076 | 130 | 266 | 265·661 | +·339 | +·127 | |
| 45·5699 | 135 | 275 | 274·5333 | +·4667 | +·170 | |
| 52·6152 | 140 | 284 | 283·4452 | +·5548 | +·195 | |
| 60·5128 | 145 | 293 | 292·3924 | +·6076 | +·207 | |
| 69·3351 | 150 | 302 | 301·3705 | +·6295 | +·208 | $=+\frac{1}{481}$ |
| 79·1574 | 155 | 311 | 310·3752 | +·6248 | +·201 | |
| 90·0586 | 160 | 320 | 319·403 | +·597 | +·187 | |
| 102·1188 | 165 | 329 | 328·449 | +·551 | +·167 | |
| 115·422 | 170 | 338 | 337·51 | +·49 | +·145 | |
| 130·054 | 175 | 347 | 346·58 | +·42 | +·122 | |
| 146·1034 | 180 | 356 | 355·6605 | +·3395 | +·095 | |
| 163·6604 | 185 | 365 | 364·7433 | +·2567 | +·070 | |
| 182·8170 | 190 | 374 | 373·827 | +·173 | +·046 | |
| 203·6670 | 195 | 383 | 382·9072 | +·0928 | +·024 | |
| 226·3065 | 200 | 392 | 391·982 | +·018 | +·005 | |
| 250·8307 | 205 | 401 | 401·0473 | —·3473 | —·012 | |
| 277·3381 | 210 | 410 | 410·101 | —·101 | —·025 | |
| 305·925 | 215 | 419 | 419·13 | —·13 | —·031 | |
| 336·689 | 220 | 428 | 428·16 | —·16 | —·037 | $=-\frac{1}{2703}$ |
| 369·732 | 225 | 437 | 437·161 | —·161 | —·037 | |
| 405·15 | 230 | 446 | 446·139 | —·139 | —·031 | |

Tables III. and IV. give the highest temperatures used by M. Regnault in his experiments. Where two or more of his Nos. are mentioned in the same line, the mean results have been taken.

*Note.* It will be observed by comparison of columns 4 and 5 with each other, both in Table III. and Table IV., that the temperatures are reduced a little too much by taking them as $4\frac{1}{2}$ roots of the pressure given in columns 2. And a small supplementary quantity viz. 0·543° F. *per cent.*, has been added in column 6, which makes them nearly equal to the experimental temperatures given in column 4, the mean difference *per cent.* averaging only 1 in 714 in Table III.; and being also insignificant in table IV., as will be seen by examination :—

Table III. Being a selection of gradually increasing temperatures and pressures taken from Serie *y* of M. Regnault's experiments. See. Mem. de l'Inst. Vol. 21, p. 565-7.

| M. Regnault's millemetres, reduced to lbs. press. per sq. in. | Mean mercurial temperatures centigrade, reduced to Fahrenheit. | | Calculated as $4\frac{1}{2}$ roots of pressures. Temperatures. | $4\frac{1}{2}$ roots of pressures + 0·543 F. *per cent.* on col. 4. | Differences between Col. 4 and Col. 6. | Differences *per cent.* between Col. 4 and Col. 6. | M. Regnaults' experiments. |
|---|---|---|---|---|---|---|---|
| lbs. dec. | Cent. Deg. | Fahr. Deg. | Fahr. Deg. | Fahr. Deg. | | | His Nos. |
| 91·0665 | 161·17 | 322·106 | 320·194 | 321·943 | +·163 | +·050 | 3, 4, 5. |
| 106·597 | 167·58 | 333·644 | 331·597 | 333·409 | +·235 | +·070 | 6, 7. |
| 130·979 | 176·32 | 349·376 | 347·128 | 349·025 | +·351 | +·100 | 8, 9. |
| 146·39 | 181'17 | 358·106 | 355·816 | 357·761 | +·345 | +·096 | 10, 11, |
| 167·748 | 187·33 | 369·194 | 366·749 | 368·754 | +·440 | +·119 | 13. |
| 193·392 | 193·82 | 380·876 | 378.528 | 380·596 | +·280 | +·073 | 19. |
| 200·595 | 195·57 | 384·026 | 381·616 | 383·701 | +·325 | +·085 | 27, 28, 29. |
| 240·71 | 204·48 | 400·064 | 397·394 | 399·566 | +·498 | +·124 | 30, 31, 32. |
| 266·874 | 209·60 | 409·28 | 406·611 | 408·833 | +·447 | +·109 | 35. |
| 287·818 | 213·685 | 416·633 | 413·495 | 415·757 | +·876 | +·210 | 36, 37. |
| 314·336 | 218·24 | 424·832 | 421·674 | 423.981 | +·851 | +·200 | 42, 43, |
| 321·834 | 219·46 | 427·028 | 423·89 | 426·209 | +·819 | +·192 | 45, 46. |
| 316·738 | 218·675 | 425·615 | 422·387 | 424·698 | +·917 | +·215 | 48, 49. |
| | | | | | | +·126 | = mean difference or 1 in 714. |
| 2 | 3 | 4 | 5 | 6 | 7 | 8 | |

Table IV. gives similar results.

It is clear, therefore, that the formula ought to stand as follows, (with the exception only that the two first and three last quantities in Table IV., column 8, are a little above the average, the intermediate twenty-four quantities giving only infinitesimal differences).

*Corrected formula.* Temperature calculated as $4\frac{1}{2}$ roots of pressures + about 0·543° F. *per cent.* on column 6 = approximately the mean actual temperatures *

M. Regnault says, p. 619, that the graphic curve by which he represents his pressures and temperatures in his large plate, " présente un point d'inflexion " at 627·2° C, (1160·96.° Fahr.) " Enfin " says he, " la courbe qui tournait sa *convexité* vers l'axe des températures " up to the temperature named, " tourne sa *concavité* vers ce même axe, à partir du point d'inflexion, l'ordonnée tend vers un maximum, et la courbe a pour asymptote, une ligne parallèle à l'axe des températures, dont l'ordonnée est ... 121,617 atmosphères" which amount to about 800 tons pressure per square inch. " Ce serait donc là la limite supérieure de la force élastique de la vapeur." As far as he can judge ; but he very properly adds :—" Mais il serait à mon avis tout à fait déraisonnable d'attacher une signification réelle à ces points singuliers de la courbe, qui sont si loin en dehors des limites où nos observations peuvent atteindre." Supposing he is correct in saying that steam pressure may continue to increase up to about 800 tons per square inch and *no higher*, that force would still ac-

* The 0·543° F. per cent. has in reality been calculated on column 4, inadvertently ; but the greatest difference, namely, for the last quantity, is only diminished thereby 0·193 per cent. (1 in 5,026), which is an insignificant difference.

count for the greatest effects of earthquakes and volcanoes. Fig. 1, is from his plate.* Will the curve if continued, ever become a vertical line? Treating the temperature 3,000° by the corrected formula for the moment, the quantity obtained is 935¾ tons. But the question of main importance is not whether the highest steam pressure continues to increase as far as 800 tons, or 900 tons per square inch; but whether the pressure continues to increase *up to one of those or in some other enormously rapid ratio or ratios, so as to account for the most powerful forces of earthquakes and volcanoes?* M. Regnault's views plainly tend towards an affirmative conclusion, And he is evidently an impartial witness, for he had no thought that his achievements and opinions had any bearing on the cause of earthquakes and volcanoes, because he never mentions either the one or the other; as it was no part of his object to enter into any considerations other than the phenomena connected with "Des Machines à Vapeur."

Table IV. Being a selection of gradually increasing temperatures and pressures, taken from Série *z* of M. Regnault's experiments. See Mem. de l'Institut, Vol. 21, p. 568, &c.

| M. Regnault's millemetres, reduced to lbs. pressure per sq. inch. | Mean mercurial temperatures Centigrade reduced to Fahrenheit. | | As 4½ roots of Pressures. | 4½ roots of press. +0·543° F. *per cent.* on experiml. temp. in col. 4. | Differences between Cols. 4 and 6. | Differences *per cent.* between Cols. 4 and 6. | M. Regnault's Experiments. |
|---|---|---|---|---|---|---|---|
| lbs. dec. | Cent. | Fahr. | Fahr. | Fahr. | | | His Nos. |
| 25·6456 | 116·40 | 241·52 | 241·609 | 242·920 | +1·400 | —·580 | 3 |
| 33·6925 | 125·15 | 257·27 | 256·7153 | 258·112 | — ·842 | —·327 | 6 |
| 41·322 | 132·00 | 269·60 | 268·628 | 270·092 | — ·492 | —·182 | 8 |
| 50·4629 | 138·91 | 282·038 | 280·827 | 282·358 | — ·320 | —·113 | 10 |
| 61·9105 | 146·31 | 295·358 | 293·88 | 295·484 | — ·126 | —·042 | 13 |
| 67·3625 | 149·45 | 301·01 | 299·444 | 301.078 | — ·068 | —·022 | 16 |
| 71·7964 | 151·86 | 305·348 | 303·716 | 305·374 | — ·026 | —·008 | 18, 19 |
| 79·4936 | 155·79 | 312·422 | 310·669 | 312·365 | + ·057 | +·018 | 21 |
| 84·4232 | 158·14 | 316·652 | 314·85 | 316·569 | + ·083 | +·026 | 24 |
| 89·8585 | 160·47 | 320·846 | 319·245 | 320·987 | — ·141 | —·044 | 25, 26 |
| 94·7687 | 162·65 | 324·77 | 323·042 | 324·805 | — ·035 | —·011 | 27, 28, 29 |
| 100·8593 | 165.24 | 329·432 | 327·544 | 322·333 | + ·099 | +·030 | 33 |
| 111·493 | 169·365 | 336·857 | 334·922 | 336·751 | + ·106 | +·031 | 34, 35 |
| 120.947 | 172·80 | 343·04 | 341·035 | 342·898 | + ·142 | +·041 | 36 |
| 134·4498 | 177·39 | 351·302 | 349·179 | 351·087 | + ·215 | +·061 | 38, 39 |
| 144·463 | 180·50 | 356·9 | 354·769 | 356·707 | + ·193 | +·054 | 41, 42 |
| 156·638 | 184·13 | 363·434 | 361·206 | 363·179 | + ·255 | +·070 | 46 |
| 166·972 | 187·05 | 368·69 | 366·372 | 368·374 | + ·316 | +·086 | 48 |
| 183·701 | 191·44 | 376·592 | 374·228 | 376·273 | + ·319 | +·085 | 49, 50 |
| 194·701 | 194·18 | 381·524 | 379·095 | 381·167 | + ·357 | +·093 | 52 |
| 208·748 | 197·475 | 387·455 | 385·009 | 387·113 | + ·342 | +·088 | 53, 54 |
| 234·836 | 203·16 | 397·688 | 395·218 | 397·377 | + ·311 | +·078 | 57, 58 |
| 279·276 | 211·94 | 413·492 | 410·736 | 412·981 | + ·511 | +·123 | 59, 60 |
| 305·05 | 216·51 | 421·718 | 418·873 | 421.163 | + ·555 | +·131 | 62 |
| 326·338 | 220·15 | 428·27 | 425·2 | 427·525 | + ·745 | +·174 | 65 |
| 352·997 | 224·31 | 435·758 | 432·685 | 435·051 | + ·707 | +·162 | 67 |
| 382·9 | 228·89 | 444· | 440·574 | 442.985 | +1·015 | +·229 | 76 |
| 409·034 | 232·56 | 450·608 | 447·086 | 449·533 | +1·075 | +·238 | 81 |
| 409·223 | 232·605 | 450·689 | 447·1317 | 449·5789 | +1·1101 | +·246 | 78,79,80,81 |
| 2 | 3 | 4 | 5 | 6 | 7 | 8 | |

* The vertical line is divided into degrees Centigrade; and the horizontal divisions show one atmosphere of pressure, divided into 100 parts.

*Fig. 1.*

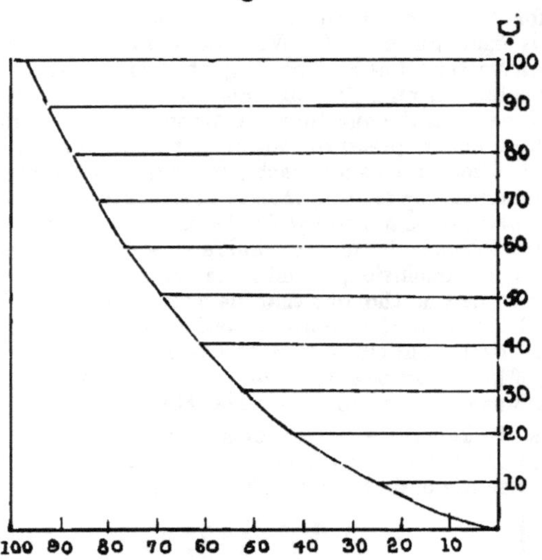


*Fig. 2.*

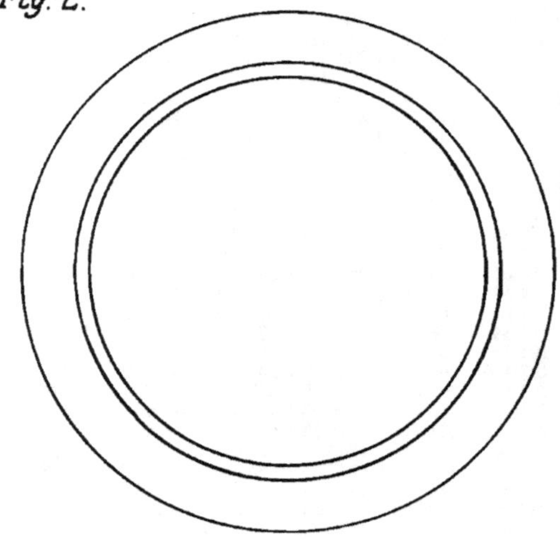

If we were to hear a loud explosion and to see the fragments of a building flying in the air, and a cloud of smoke spreading itself among the ruins, and on entering the smoke to perceive the well-known smell of gunpowder, we should naturally conclude that gunpowder was the cause of the catastrophe. So also in the late explosion at Erith, even if we had known that there was a portion of gun-cotton in each magazine, we should still call the accident a *gunpowder* explosion. Ought we not, then, to attribute the various species of natural disturbances of the earth's crust chiefly or even entirely to steam, when it or its constituents are proved to have been present, as we shall now see in at least seventy cases, even if metallic bases of alkaloids were present also? Because amongst other reasons, we shall find in these evidences, Humboldt and Sir Humphrey Davy condemning the alkaloid theory as *co-operative* only. Whilst he would have a difficult task, who undertook to prove, that metallic bases of the alkaloids were always present in *sufficient quantity* to cause the greatest explosions. No such difficulty exists with regard to steam; indeed, it is self-evident that it may be present in all but unlimited quantity, the amount of oceanic and fresh water, and of subterranean fire being so inconceivably great. We shall see in evidence No. 40, that the Kaimeni submarine volcano has been active for 2,000 years. That is to say the Mediterranean has not been able to quench the fire, which must therefore be very vast. The like is true of the volcanoes under the Pacific Ocean, for its average depth is but as an exceedingly thin film when compared with the mass of the earth.

We know that "the terremotos of South America, indicate violent horizontal oscillations similar to the wave movements of the sea; or perpendicular upliftings, as if a power was operating on the roof of a cavern from the interior, struggling to force it open, and dash it away in fragments with everything upon it."* Very powerful steam might clearly do either of these things, according to whether the sides or the tops of the caverns offered the least resistance. We purpose on a future occasion to prove that there must *necessarily* be caverns. The very powerful steam, when it increased in volume without increase of temperature, might lift a weight which it had not power to explode (just as every one can lift a weight which is too great for him to throw) and thus *slowly and gradually elevate a country*, Spitzbergen and northern Norway for example. On the other hand if steam ceased to be produced from any cause in a given cavity, the steam already contained therein would gradually cool by the natural conducting away of heat by the surrounding cooler ground, and allow the roof to settle; and so cause a *gradual continuous depression*, as in the south of Sweden.

* Milner's Gallery of Nature, p. 430.

In extensive reading on the subject of all kinds of natural disturbances of the earth's crust, the present writer has found no reason to believe, nor any allegation, that steam or its constituents are ever absent.

An initial force of 243.2 tons per square inch may be taken as a fair representation of the average effects of volcanoes. That is to say, it would propel a mass of granite 9ft. thick from a supposed focus at three miles below sea level up to one mile above sea level—total, four miles of vertical height. Of this force considerably more than one-half would be expended in overcoming the resistance of the atmosphere, as will now be shown :

FALLING OR ASCENDING BODIES.

The velocity generated by Gravity in vacuo is given by Sir John Herschel in Outlines of Astronomy (1864, p. 716) as 32.18169 feet in a second of time, in latitude 35° 16′. It is well known that a body propelled vertically upwards ascends 32·18169 feet in each second, less than it did during the previous second. And it follows that (avoiding any fractions of a second) a body must ascend for 36 seconds to attain a vertical height of 21,433 feet which are equal to 4 miles and 313 feet, and it must ascend 1158.54 feet during the first second.

*Force required to overcome the gravity of a mass of granite 9 feet thick.*—The specific gravity of granite being taken at 2651, the weight of a column of granite one inch square and 9 feet high will be 10.355 lbs :, and the total resistance of the column of granite in vacuo would be foot-pounds, or equal to the weight 10.355 lbs : × 21433 = 99.08 *tons*.

*The resistance of the air.*—Say atmospheric pressure at 45 miles above sea level = 0, the pressure at sea level at average temperature is 14.7304 lbs : per square inch *(see Herschel ibid :)* and the average resistance of the air viz : at one mile below sea level, to be overcome by the column of granite, would therefore be 15.057742 lbs : per square inch × 21433 feet = 144.12 *tons*.

And 99.08 tons + 144.12 = 243.2 tons.

*Note.* The heated air in the Volcano would have less pressure than 15.057742 lbs :, but on the other hand we may suppose the propelled mass of rock has to be fractured off, or at least to overcome the friction of contact, which would require additional force,

The temperature of Steam by the corrected empirical formula at p. 21 to overcome 243.2 tons per square inch, must be 2223.56° F. And by the same empirical formula, to overcome twice the pressure, or 486.4 tons, would only require saturated steam of a temperature of 2594.8° Fahr.— And in like manner a pressure of 935¾ tons would be produced by saturated steam of 3000°, which temperature therefore gives a pressure about 48 per cent. greater then the pressure due to a temperature of 2593.8° Fahr.

Now perhaps the results given by the formula are not widely different from the truth, but even if they were widely different, and in the most unfavorable sense, namely, in that sense which gives much less power to steam of very high temperature, it still appears that saturated steam of 3000°, even after deducting about 48 per cent. from its power as calculated, would have *twice the power* required to propel a mass of granite 9 feet thick to a height of four miles. Hence it follows that Steam power reduced to this great extent, would yet have force sufficient to account for the greatest effects of Earthquakes and Volcanoes.

Can there really be any reasonable doubt that steam is capable of exerting a much greater force than this after the perusal of these papers?

Every reader will, of course, judge for himself; but, for my own part, I long ago arrived at the conclusion that steam has amply sufficient power to cause the greatest effects observable, and that OTHER FORCES CO-OPERATE WHERE NO HELP IS REQUIRED. This was illustrated last month by showing that the late accident at Erith would still have been a *gunpowder* explosion, even if there had been a little gun-cotton in each magazine. There is no risk of attempting to prove too much in these papers, because the greatest amount of steam power contended for, as it happens, is only about enough to account for the tremendous convulsions of the coal period.—See *Siluria*, 1859, p. 529, &c. Evidence No. 57 following would seem to have required nearly the maximum force of steam for which these papers contend.

## The Contact of the Metalloid Bases with Water and Air may be a co-operating cause in Earthquakes and Volcanoes.

" The nucleus of our planet is supposed to consist of unoxidised masses, the metalloids of alkalies and earths. Volcanic activity is excited in the nucleus by the access of water and air. *Volcanoes certainly pour forth a great quantity of aqueous vapour into the atmosphere*, but the assumption of the penetration of water into the volcanic focus is attended with much difficulty, considering the opposing pressure of the external column of water and of the internal lava; and the deficiency, or, at all events, very rare occurrence of burning hydrogen gas during the eruption (which the formation of hydrochloric acid, ammonia, and sulphuretted hydrogen certainly does not sufficiently replace) has led the celebrated originator of this hypothesis (Sir Humphry Davy) to abandon it of his own accord."—*Bohn's Cosmos*, vol. v., pp. 169, 170.

" Whilst Davy in the most distinct manner gave up the opinion that volcanic eruptions are a consequence of the contact of the metalloid bases with water and air, he still asserted that the presence of oxidisable metalloids in the interior of the earth, might be a co-operating cause in volcanic processes already commenced."—*Bohn's Cosmos*, vol. i., p. 234, and p. 170, vol. v.

Gay Lussac thinks that "the penetration of sea water does not appear to him to be improbable under certain conditions."—Foot note to *Bohn's Cosmos*, vol. v., p. 169.

It is well known that the late Baron Humboldt examined more volcanoes than perhaps any other man ever did, and that he experienced some earthquakes in South America and in the east. His "difficulty" aforesaid, besides being answered by himself in the same sentence, is also answered by him in No. [illegible] following, by what he aptly calls "a very striking proof" of water having got down to a volcanic focus. Water *must* get down to a volcanic focus, because we shall often find steam and hot water coming out again.

EJECTIONS OF STEAM OR AQUEOUS VAPOUR FROM VOLCANOES.

1. Sir Humphry Davy says, the volcanoes of Central America give out *aqueous vapour in very large quantity*, as well as certain gases.—*Lyell's Principles of Geology*, 1853, p. 549.

2. In the explosion of the volcanic mountain Cosiguina in Central America, there was a noise of as many cannon from various parts of the Gulf of Fonseca. An enormous coal black cloud of smoke rolled high above the summit of the volcano. This cloud was fine ashes so abundant as to produce darkness. There was a tremendous subterranean report as of a thousand cannon, heard at several hundred miles distance.* The eruption was most violent for three days. *Clouds of steam* continued to rise from the volcano for months after. The eruption commenced January 20, 1835.—*Travels in Central America*, by Dr. Carl Scherzer, vol. ii, p. 224, &c.

The four following evidences are from Sir Charles Lyell:—

3. At the great eruption of Skaptàr Jokul in 1783, in some places where the *steam could not get vent*, it blew up the rock, throwing fragments to the height of more than 150ft. About a month previous to the eruption on the main land, a submarine volcano burst forth in the sea, and a new island was thrown up (which volcano must *necessarily have produced steam*); the island was named by the King of Denmark, Nyöe, or the New Island, consisting of high cliffs, but before the end of a year nothing was left but a reef of rocks from 5 fathoms to 30 fathoms under water. (This is similar to what took place at Graham Island, see post No. 51.) Earthquakes, which had long been felt in Iceland, became violent on the 11th of June, 1783, when Skaptàr Jokul on the mainland, distant nearly two hundred miles from Nyöe, threw out a torrent of lava.—*Principles*, p. 425.

* Humboldt says at nearly 560 geographical miles distance.—*Bohn's Cosmos*, Vol. v. p. 275.

Besides proving the existence of steam, this proves two other things, namely, that the *same* causes operate both in earthquakes and volcanoes. And secondly, that there may be cavities, or at all events, fissures or communications continued through the great distance of two hundred miles. The like may be gathered as to distant communications underground from Nos. 24 and 59.

4. " *Aqueous vapour* constitutes the most abundant of the aëriform products of volcanoes in eruption."—*Principles*, p. 553.

5. " We know that volcanoes in eruption not only emit fluid lava, but *give off steam* and other heated gases, which rush out in enormous volume, for days, weeks, or years, continuously, and are even disengaged from lava during its consolidation."—*Lyell's Manual*, p. 601. (Ed. 1855.)

I believe in the soundness of the following, which Sir Charles Lyell suggets as a speculation; it is quoted from his *Principles of Geology*, p. 558. He says: " In speculating on the mechanism of an ordinary volcanic eruption, we may suppose that large subterranean cavities exist at the depth of some miles below the surface of the earth, in which melted lava accumulates; and when water containing the usual mixture of air penetrates into these, the *steam* thus generated may press upon the lava and force it up the duct of a volcano, in the same manner as a column of water is driven up the pipe of a geyser."

6. Sir Charles quotes Sir H. Davy as stating that the subterranean cavities of Vesuvius *threw out large volumes of steam* during an eruption.—*Principles*, p. 550.

7. Schmidt saw clouds of volcanic smoke and *steam*, which encompassed his observatory on Vesuvius during the great eruption of 1855.—*Intellectual Observer*, vol. i, p. 149.

8. Whoever has seen the blowing off steam from a boiler will probably recognise Sir William Hamilton's " mass of smoke like whitest cotton," in the following abstract, as steam. This opinion is corroborated by the latter part of No. 50, following. 1

Sir William says that for two years previous to the eruption of Vesuvius in 1779, its top had never been free from smoke. On August 5th he saw *a mass of smoke like whitest cotton* issue, four times as large as the mountain itself, which is 3,700ft. high; stones, scoriæ, and ashes shot up at the same time 2,000ft.; at times heavy liquid lava poured forth over the sides of the crater. On August 8th there was a loud report, and instantly a column of liquid transparent fire rose as high as the mountain itself; puffs of very black smoke accompanied, and at the same moment could be seen bright electrical fire playing briskly in zig-zag lines.* On August 9th there was a *subterraneous boiling noise*, and smoke of two sorts, *white as snow* and black as jet, the black being scoriæ and minute ashes. Very large stones mounted to an immense height, forming parabolas, leaving a trace of white smoke. Some burst like bombs, others burst into a thousand pieces soon after

*"Sir W. mentions this circumstance to prove, that the electrical matter so manifest during this eruption actually proceeded

emission. On August 11th the last explosion came, and gradually increased, being louder than any before. *A mountain of white cotton-like clouds* rose to an extraordinary height, and formed a colossal mass indescribably great.—*Phil. Trans. R. S.*, 1780, v. xiv, p. 163, &c.

May we not conclude that on this last day Vesuvius was blowing off its steam, its business being finished for the time? Sir William made his observations from Pausilippo through a good telescope. He was not on the spot so as to ascertain whether the "white smoke" was steam or not.

9. Mr. William Smith, C.E., F.G.S., proprietor of THE ARTIZAN, has lately visited Vesuvius and Etna, and says, in answer to a question in a letter dated June 23, 1865, "he thinks steam *is* generated during volcanic action, and is a material agent in the production of those explosive effects which are observable both at Etna and Vesuvius."

10. Mr. J. J. Jeans, British Vice-Consul at Catania, says, in a letter dated Feb. 4, 1865, "A deplorable accident has happened at Etna by an explosion caused by the contact of *burning lava with some cistern or watercourse*, by the effects of which a number of Sappers have lost their lives, but the particulars are not known."—*Illustrated London News*, Feb. 25, 1865.

Here we have a distinct proof of lava converting water into steam, and causing a destructive explosion.

11. M. Fouqué has communicated to the Academy of Sciences an account of his recent ascent of Mount Etna. He states that the eruption of February, 1865, has not materially changed the configuration of the great crater . . . . It is only towards the south that he found fissures from which were issuing torrents of suffocating fumes *composed of steam* charged with sulphuric and hydrochloric acid, the latter predominating. He found a "fumerolle" with a temperature of 203° centigrade, which is equal to 397·4° Fahr.

12. From *Art and Nature under an Italian Sky*, 1850, p. 110, published anonymously, we gather that just as the author reached the base of the cone of Vesuvius a magnificent explosion took place. The sound has often been compared to the firing of artillery, but he thought a much more apt comparison was the *bursting of an immense steam boiler.* A vast quantity of red-hot stones was projected, some of them to the height of 300 feet. *The projecting force is evidently steam*, he says, *from the appearance of the vapour and the shower of hot water which falls around.*

13. In a recent eruption of Mount Vesuvius, *aqueous vapour* and storms of ashes issued. At Torre del Greco a sea whirlpool of 360ft. diameter was boiling violently and emitted a strong sulphurous odour: the sounding was 23 fathoms. The principal development was carbonic acid gas.—*Morning Advertiser*, Dec. 28, 1861.

Was the water descending by the whirlpool to the volcanic focus?

14. Von Buch found that in a crater in the Canary Islands, were open fissures out of which hot vapours rose which in 1815 were 145° F., and were probably at boiling point lower down. The exhalations appeared to be *aqueous vapour*, but they could not be pure steam, for the crevices were incrusted with siliceous sinter.—*Principles*, p. 438.

15. From near the centre of the volcanic mountain Bromo in Java (see Voyage of H.M.S. *Fly*, vol. ii., p. 68), rises a rough conical mound, 600ft. or 800ft. high, having on one side a number of subordinate craters. One of these had been frequently active in 1845 when Mr. Jukes visited it, and was then belching out *much smoke and steam*, with a great rumbling noise proceeding from the depths of the great funnel-like crater.—*Jukes's Manual of Geology*, 1857, p. 290.

16. James D. Dana, the geologist of the United States exploring expedition, says vol. x., p. 368, " That the ordinary eruption and usual action of a volcano proceed principally *from water gaining access* to a branch or branchlets belonging to a particular vent, and not to a common channel below : *the fresh waters of the island are the principal source of the vapour* (evidently steam*) of Kilauea." This is one of several deliberate conclusions which Mr. Dana arrived at.

17. Mr. Coan was present in December, 1864, at the eruption of the volcano of Kilauea in one of the Sandwich Islands. He spent a night near a beautiful pit crater called Napau, nearly circular, about 300ft. deep, a mile perhaps in diameter, and with a bottom of sand so smooth and hard that a regiment of cavalry might be reviewed there. One eighth of a mile from this crater fissures are opened in the earth, *out of which scalding steam and smoke have issued from time immemorial*, and affording heat enough to cook for an army.— *American Journal of Science*, quoted in *Illustrated London News*, Oct. 28, 1865, p. 415.

18. The island of Hawaii, formerly called Owhyhee, is an immense volcano of 4,000 square miles, its summit Mowna Roa being 16,000ft. high. *Volumes of smoke and steam* were ascending from the vents, but as the evening closed, fire after fire appeared glimmering through the vapour; *some of the cones were ejecting fragments of rock*: others ashes, lava, and *boiling water*.— *Gallery of Nature* p. 210. *Mantell's Wonders of Geology*, p. 724, &c.

19. " Chimborazo throws out *masses of mud* and elastic fluids." —*Cosmos* vol. v., p. 336.

*Note.*—Mud implies the presence of water.

* The words "evidently steam" have been inserted by the present writer, not by Mr. Dana.

### Earthquakes are actually fed by Water.

20. In a paper read by M. Pissis before the French Academy, see *Comptes Rendus*, Jan. 27, 1862, he says, "it is generally believed in the districts of S. America which are most subject to earthquakes, that *those disturbances occur during the rainy season*, and up to the period of drought." During twelve years of his own residence on the spot this theory held good; and *the years of most violent rain* were *distinguished by a great number of earthquakes.*

### Active Volcanoes are actually fed by Water.

21. Mr. Dana and Dr. Junghuhn say that the volcanoes of the Pacific Islands, however large, *however much exposed to heavy rains, support no rivers*, so long as they are in the process of growth, or *whilst the highest crater emits showers of scoriæ and floods of lava.* The ejected matters are very porous. — *Lyell's Manual*, 1855, p. 497.

22. The like is true of Etna, for we read as follows: — "An unusual silence prevails on the Val del Bove, Etna; for there are not torrents dashing from the rocks, nor any movement of running water in this valley such as may be almost invariably heard in mountainous regions. *Every drop of water that falls from the heavens, or from the melting ice or snow, is instantly absorbed by the porous lava.*"—*Principles*, p. 405.

"Running water in general exerts no power on Etna, *the rain which falls being immediately imbibed by the porous lava*, so that vast as is the extent of the mountain, it feeds only a few small rivulets, and even these are dry during the greater portion of the year."—*Principles*, p. 411.

23. It often happens that a *lake which has endured for centuries* in a volcanic crater, *disappears suddenly on the approach of a new eruption.*—*Principles*, p. 389.

24. It is well known that on the shores of the island of Cephalonia there is *a cavity in the rock into which the sea has been flowing for ages*, and many others doubtless exist in the leaky bottom of the ocean. The water, perhaps, being *converted into steam and escaping upwards.*—*Principles*, p. 389.

*Note.*—Cephalonia is 300 miles distant in a direct line from Etna, and from the stufas of the Lipari Isles, and 360 miles from Vesuvius, which appear to be the nearest vents. There may, therefore, be a cavity or cavities extending for either of these distances.

### Rocks ejected from a Volcano by Steam.

25. Speaking of the angular masses of the agglomerate of the Caldera of Palma, Sir Charles Lyell says that "the only cause he knows capable of dispersing heavy fragments of 3ft., 4ft.. or 6ft. in diameter, without blunting their edges, *is the power of steam;*

unless, indeed, we could suppose that ice had co-operated with water in motion, and the interference of ice cannot be suspected in this latitude (28° 40′ N.), especially as he looked in vain for signs of glacial action here and in the other mountainous regions of the Canary Islands.—*Manual*, 1855, p. 503.

DEPOSITS OF WATER, AND OF ICE AND SNOW, READY TO DESCEND INTO VOLCANOES BY GRAVITATION THROUGH THE POROUS STRATA.

26. " At Volcan d'Ansango are *two chasms filled with water.*"—*Cosmos*, vol v., p. 336.

27. There are *several marshes* and *two small lakes* in the long and broad ridge which unites the volcanic mountains Cotopaxi and the Nevado de Quelandana.—*Cosmos*, vol. v, p. 339.

28. In the crater of the Volcano of the Island of S. Lucia are *several small basins periodically filled with boiling water.*—*Cosmos*, vol. v, p. 422.

29. The thirty-eight considerable volcanoes of the Isle of Java are remarkable for the quantity of sulphur and sulphurous vapours discharged. They rarely emit lava, but *rivers of mud issue from them.* The crater of Taschem contains *a lake* $\frac{1}{4}$ *mile long* strongly impregnated with sulphuric acid.—*Principles*, p. 353.

30. The Persian volcano, Demavend, *is covered with perpetual snow.*—*Cosmos*, vol. v, p. 361.

31. Two volcanic mountains, Petschan and Hotshen, of Turfan (Asia), are separated by a gigantic block of mountains 420 miles long, *crowned with eternal snow and ice.*—*Cosmos*, vol. v, p. 360.

32. The most extensive, and, probably, the latest pre-historical eruptions of Ararat, *have all issued below the limit of perpetual snow.*—*Cosmos*, vol. v, p, 361.

It is obvious that in the many other cases where volcanoes have their tops higher than the limit of perpetual snow, there is a means of producing steam ready to descend. And it ought not to be forgotten that nearly all the volcanoes in the world, are either in the bed of the Pacific Ocean, or in its islands, or not far distant from its shores, and they are doubtless fed by its waters directly, or by its rains indirectly.

EJECTIONS OF STEAM FROM GEYSERS.

33. " *Steam is exclusively the moving power* in the geysers of Iceland."—Lyell's *Principles of Geology*, p. 553.

34. It has more than once happened *after earthquakes* (in Iceland that *some of the boiling fountains* have increased or diminished in violence or volume, or entirely ceased, or that new ones have made their appearance."—*Ibid.*

*Note.*—Does not this prove the connection of geysers and earthquakes ? "

35. "*Steam of high temperature* has continued for more than twenty centuries to issue from the 'stufas' of Italy," and "many craters emit hot vapours in the intervals between eruptions, and solfataras evolve incessantly the same gases as volcanoes," proving them to have one common origin."—*Ibid*, p. 546.

36. At the foot of Sulphur Mountain, in Iceland, *steam issued from all parts*. There was a caldron of boiling mud fifteen feet in diameter; near this was an irregular space filled with water boiling briskly, and at the foot of the hill *steam rushed with great force from* among the loose fragments of rocks.—Sir George Mackenzie's *Travels in Iceland.*

37. Such is the *explosive force of steam of the Great Geyser* of Iceland, that very hard rocks are sometimes shivered by it into very small pieces.—*Principles*, p. 554.

38. At the geysers near San Francisco Bay, California, the air is strongly flavoured with sulphur, and the water is strongly ferruginous. There is an alkaline spring surrounded with jets of sulphur, and deposits of magnesia, Epsom salts, and various alkaline mixtures. You hear boiling springs, and are *half choked with steam.* A horrible mouth in the black rock belches forth tremendous volumes of sulphurous vapour. The waters boil in mad fury, the temperature is about 500°. An egg dipped in is taken out boiled. *The steam rushes from the largest vent hole with such force, and heated to such a degree, that it first becomes visible only at the distance of 6ft. from the earth.* It rises to the height of 80 feet.—*Home and Abroad*, second series, by Bayard Taylor, p. 81, &c.

39. It is said of a mud volcano, about 150 miles from the head of the Gulf of California, that those only who are familiar with the *wild rush of steam* can realise the rude sounds of the mud explosions. *The steam jets issue* from conical mounds of mud of from 3 to 15ft. high: from some *the steam rushes in a continuous stream;* in others, the action is intermittent, *each rush of steam* being accompanied by a shower of hot mud, sometimes thrown to a height of 100ft. These discharges take place every few minutes. The volcanic action has been more violent at a former period, as is proved by the traces of former eruptions, and fragments of pumice stone scattered about the plain.—*John A. Veatch, M. D., Titan*, April, 1859, p. 465, &c.

I endeavoured, in citing these evidences, to classify volcanoes, earthquakes, geysers, hot springs, &c., each under different headings. But they *would* commingle with each other, especially in what follows, and they *thereby prove that they have all one common origin, namely, steam.*

## Active Volcanoes beneath the Sea must necessarily produce both Steam and Earthquakes.

40. The Gulf of Santorin in the Grecian Archipelago has been for 2,000 *years a scene of active volcanic operations.* The Gulf contains three volcanic islands, namely, Old, New, and Little Kaimeni. Pliny informs us that Old Kaimeni rose above the water 186 before Christ. It was increased in size by other eruptions in A.D. 19, 726, and 1427. In 1573 another eruption produced Little Kaimeni. In 1650 a submarine outbreak gave rise to a shoal, which was surveyed in 1848 by Captain Graves, and found to have 10 fathoms of water over it, the sea deepening around it in all directions. This eruption lasted three months, covering the sea with floating pumice. *At the same time an earthquake destroyed many houses* in Thera.—*Principles*, p. 441.

It is well known that Santorin has been for some time, and is now in active operation; sending forth clouds of steam and flames, and giving earthquake shocks.

## Submarine Eruptions in very deep Water.

41. "In the 'Nautical Magazine' (says Sir Charles Lyell) for 1835, p. 642, and for 1838, p. 361, and in the 'Comptes Rendus,' April 1838, accounts are given of a series of volcanic phenomena, earthquakes, troubled water, floating scoriæ, and columns of smoke, which have been observed at intervals since the middle of last century, in a space of open sea between longitudes 20° and 22° west, and about ½° south of the equator."—*Principles*, p. 436.

*Note.*—I find this situation is more than 600 miles from the nearest land, which is the small island of Ascension, and the sounding is 2,800 fathoms, according to Lieut. Maury's chart. The hydrostatic pressure would be 7,496lbs., or about 3⅓ tons per square inch on the bottom. Steam, however, overcame this pressure, and in addition gave shocks to ships on the surface, as will be seen in the two next evidences. And the mass of fire must be very great not to have been extinguished by the vast volume and pressure of water.

42. "Submarine volcanic action near the equator has been for some years going on. We have now two accounts of it observed by ships, but a few miles apart from each other—the *Dallas*, Captain Wikander, and the *Melbourne*, Captain Cowie—on March 20th, 1861. The latter says:—'We were startled by a heavy and loud rumbling noise, and at the same time felt the ship tremble from stem to stern, which lasted four or five minutes. The noise resembled more the low grumble of distant thunder than the harsh, grating noise produced by the ships taking ground. The *Dallas* lost her false keel by the collision." *Illustrated London News*, Aug. 17, 1861, p. 157.

43. "Feb. 9th, 1835, at 10 hrs. 45 min., on board the barque *La Couronne*, of Liverpool, a shock was felt at sea in 0° 57′ south latitude, and 23° 19′ west of Greenwich." See "Comptes Rendus," t. 6, p. 514, as quoted by Lieut. Maury in "Physical Geography of the Sea."

*Note.*—From Lieut. Maury's chart the sounding would be about 3,000 fathoms, and the inertia of the water 8,031lbs, or more than $3\frac{1}{2}$ tons per square inch.

44. *A Volcano in the Ocean.*—The ship *Orient*, 1032 tons, Capt. John Harris, the arrival of which with a cargo of wool, &c., has already been announced, and which sailed from Adelaide Nov. 10, brings the report that on Friday, Nov. 17, at 7.15 a.m., when in lat. 51°, 44′ S. and long. 160°, 49′, * with a moderate wind from N.N.W., and a clear sky, the ship commenced ringing the bells and trembling violently, as if she were passing over a rough bottom in shallow water. In an instant all was confusion on board, as the crew and passengers thought she was settling down. The violent trembling lasted two or three minutes, with nothing visible. Sounded the pump well and found no water; and sounded over the ship's side with the deep sea lead, but found no bottom. The conclusion arrived at by all on board was, that the ship had experienced the effects of a submarine volcano.—*Morning Advertiser*, Feb. 16, 1866.

### Submarine Eruptions at less depth.

45. *An earthquake at sea.*—Capt. P. E Lawson, of the barque *Viking*, of Sunderland reports that on the 16th ult., at 2 p. m., while in latitude 36° 18′ north, and longitude 2° 32′ west, (which position is in the Mediterranean 165 nautical miles east of Gibraltar, opposite the Bay of Almeria) he experienced a severe shock of an earthquake, as though the ship had taken a shoal of rocks; and so severe was it that the vessel was shaken with great violence, and everything on board was similarly affected. This lasted above five minutes, when the shock subsided, and the vessel resumed her course, nothing the worse for the severe shaking she had undergone. The weather at the time was beautifully fine, and the water remarkably clear.—*Record Newspaper*, Aug. 21, 1865.

46. "On the 20th Nov., 1720, a burning island was raised out of the sea near Tercera, one of the Azores, at which place several houses were shaken down by an earthquake which attended the eruption. This island was about three leagues in diameter and nearly round; whence it is manifest that the quantity of pumice stones and melted matter requisite to form it, must have been amazingly great."—Rev. John Michell, *Phil. Trans. R.S.*, 1760, p. 452.

* Some 1,400 miles east from the nearest land, which is the south island of New Zealand.

47. Another example of the same kind happened at Manilla in 1750. This, also, was attended with violent earthquakes, to which that island, as well as the rest of the Philippines, is very much subject.—*Ibid.*

48. Barren island in the Bay of Bengal, east of the Andaman Isles, in lat. 14° 15′, when seen from the ocean presents on almost all sides a surface of bare rocks rising with a moderate acclivity towards the interior; but at one point there is a cleft by which we can penetrate into the centre, and there discover that it is occupied by a great circular *basin filled with the waters of the sea*, and bordered all round by steep rocks, in the midst of which rises a *volcanic cone very frequently in eruption.*—*Principles*, p. 466.

49. In 1835, a submarine *volcano* broke out near Bacalao Head, Isle of Juan Fernandez, about a mile from the shore, in *sixty-nine fathoms water*, and *illuminated the whole island* during the night.—*Principles*, p. 454.

50. In the Aleutian Archipelago eruptions are frequent, and about thirty miles north of Unalaska, near the Isle of Umnack, a new island was formed in 1796. It was first observed at a *point in the sea from which smoke had risen. Flames* then issued from the new island which illuminated the country for ten miles round; a *frightful earthquake* shook the new formed cone, and showers of *stones* were *thrown as far as Umnack.*—*Principles*, p. 352.

*Note.*—The *flames in the water* in the two last evidences cannot have failed to produce *steam.*

In 1806 another, and in 1814 a third, submarine island arose among the Aleutian Islands.—*Principles*, p. 468.

*Note.*—There are vast tracts of submarine volcanoes. (See *Lyell's Principles of Geology*, p. 350, &c).

51. Graham Island, off the south-west coast of Sicily thirty miles, rose in July, 1831, in 100 fathoms water, *steam playing an important part*, and disappeared again in three months. The following are a few details:—

About a fortnight after the eruption was first visible, Sir Pulteney Malcolm passed over the spot in his ship and felt the shock of an earthquake, and the same shocks were felt on the west coast of Sicily—direction, S.W. to N.E. About July 10, John Corrao passed in his ship near the place, and saw a column of water 60ft. high and 800 yards in circumference, rising from the sea, and soon after *a dense steam in its place* rose to the height of 1,800ft. On his return from Girgenti on July 18, he found a small island, 12ft. high, with a crater in its centre, ejecting volcanic matter and immense *columns of vapour.* In August, there was a violent ebullition and agitation of the sea on the south-west side of the island, indicating a second vent not far from the surface.—*Principles*, pp. 432, 434.

There is a similar account in Milner's "Gallery of Nature," p. 376, &c., which says, in addition, that Admiral Sir H. Hotham sent an officer to report, whose account confirms the preceding statement. This officer particularly mentions the *vast volumes of pure white steam*, which tends to corroborate the opinion expressed in No. 8, that Sir William Hamilton's white cotton-like vapour was *steam*. We have had, and shall have, abundance of proof that Vesuvius ejects vast quantities of steam and boiling water.

### Ejections of Steam from Earthquakes.

Are not the two following cases proofs that steam must be the cause of earthquakes?

52. At Deception Island, in Tierra del Fuego, where earthquake shocks are of most constant occurrence, there are no less than 150 *chasms* or fissures, *from which steam pours forth with a loud hissing noise.—Chamber's Edinburgh Journal*, Aug. 17th, 1861, p157. .

53. Baron Humboldt says that *hot steam was ejected* during an earthquake in 1812, at New Madrid, in the valley of the Mississippi.—*Cosmos*, vol. 1, 209.

### Ejections of Water and of Mud (which implies the Presence of Water) from Volcanoes. Also Sinkings of Rivers and other Waters.

Following are some additional evidences that steam issues from Vesuvius, and necessarily in vast quantity, for it becomes condensed into torrents of water, which descended the cone, and are as destructive as lava itself. Lava is generally ejected from volcanoes during eruptions, but is not always mentioned in these evidences, because the object now is to exhibit aqueous products, not molten matter.

54. "Not long before the eruption of Vesuvius in 1631, in one part of the plain (at the foot of the cone) covered with ashes, were three small pools, one filled with hot and bitter water, another salter than the sea, and a third hot but tasteless. In December, 1631, *great floods of mud were as destructive as the lava itself;* no uncommon occurrence during these catastrophes; for *such is the violence of rains produced by the evolutions of aqueous vapour*, that torrents of water descend the cone, and become charged with impalpable volcanic dust, and rolling along loose ashes, acquire sufficient consistency to deserve their ordinary appellation of *aqueous lavas*."—*Principles*, p. 374.

55. From *Gallery of Nature*, p. 781, we learn that:—"Among the peculiarities of Vesuvius the *emission of boiling water from its flanks*, has often been remarked; this is not uncommon with translantic volcanoes, together with torrents of mud—a compost of water and ashes—forming a fetid clay."

56. It is stated in the *Encyclop. Brit.*, vol. xvii., in an article attributed to Sir John Herschel, Bart., F.R.S., that "an *earthquake* happened in 1631 at Mount Vesuvius, which covered with lava most of the villages at its foot, and *sent forth torrents of boiling water.*"

57. The following is so important and so full of significant facts, that it is quoted almost entire from *Principles*, p. 430. At Galangoon in Java in 1822 there was a volcanic eruption. "In July, 1822, the waters of the river Kunir, one of those which flowed from its flanks, became for a time hot and turbid. On the 8th October following, a loud explosion was heard; the earth shook, and *immense columns of hot water and boiling mud*, mixed with burning brimstone, ashes, and lapilli of the size of nuts, were projected from the mountain like a water spout, with such prodigious violence that large quantities fell beyond the River Tandoi, 40 *miles* distant (sic)*. . . . . It was remarked that the *boiling mud and cinders were projected with such violence* from the mountain, that while many remote villages were utterly destroyed and buried, others much nearer the volcano were scarcely injured. The first eruption lasted nearly five hours, and on the following days the *rain fell in torrents*, and the *rivers* densely charged with mud *deluged the country far and wide.* At the end of four days (Oct. 12), a second eruption occurred more violent than the first, in which *hot water and mud were again vomited*, and great blocks of basalt were thrown to the distance of seven miles from the volcano. *There was at the same time a violent earthquake*. . . . . and in the night of October 12th, 2,000 people were killed."

58. In Quito, on July 19th, 1698, *during an earthquake*, a great part of the crater and summit of the volcano of Carguirazo fell in, and *a stream of mud and water issued* from the broken sides of the hill.—*Principles*, p. 503.

59. The following is a remarkable case of the connection of a volcano with another mountain, and with an earthquake at great distances, and of the ejection of water. It is from the "Encyclop Brit.," vol. xvii., p. 511. In 1797 *it was proved that the volcano of Pasto was connected with the volcanoes of Quito.* Black smoke had issued from Pasto for months, but *suddenly disappeared at the moment when the city of Riobamba*, 65 *leagues distant, was destroyed by a terrific earthquake.* The country round, namely 40 leagues from south to north, and 20 leagues from east to west, undulated with extreme violence for four minutes. Round the mountain every town was thrown down, and two cities buried underneath impending mountains. The base of Mount Tunguragua, near Riobamba, was riven asunder, and *poured out streams of water and mud which filled valleys 600ft.*

* At a guess, there must have been some such a force as 800 tons per square inch at work on this occasion.

*deep.* Suffocating exhalations were emitted from Lake Quilotoa, and, it is said, flames also. Violent shocks were felt for three months over a district 170 leagues from north to south, and 140 from east to west. The curious fishes (pimelodes cyclopum) were found in the ejected water of the volcano.

*Note.*—Much more than what we have called the "average" effects of volcanoes and earthquakes appears to have been in operation in this case.

60. From the same volume we learn that, on March 26th, 1812, subterraneous thunderings were heard, the ground undulated, and at one shock the fine city of Caraccas was destroyed with 10,000 of its people. By this earthquake *the great Lake of Maracaibo had its level lowered,* and the *riven earth* at Valencia and Puerto Cabello *poured forth enormous torrents of water.*

61. "*Mud,* black smoke, and even flames were ejected at Messina in 1781."—*Cosmos,* vol. i., p. 209.

62. On May 7th, 1860, *several earth shocks* were felt at Myrdalen, a village in the southern district of volcano Kotlugia, after a rest of thirty-nine years. *Next day the volcano threw up an immense quantity of water.* There was a pretty heavy shower of ashes, accompanied by subterranean thunder.—*Athenæum,* July, 1860, p. 94.

63. Boussingault says, Chimborazo has ejected *masses of mud,* elastic fluids, and trachytic blocks.—*Cosmos,* vol. v., p. 335.

64. Next morning after the formation of Monte Nuovo, in 1538, an eye-witness says, the inhabitants of Puzzuoli were covered with a *muddy and black shower,* which continued all day. —*Principles,* p. 367.

Another account says, jets of red hot lava, large rocks, and sometimes *mud composed of a mixture of pumice, tuff, and water,* were hurled into the air.—*Principles,* p. 370.

### Ejections of Water, often Hot, from Earthquakes and from Risings and Sinkings of Strata, and from Earthquakes combined with Volcanoes.

65. "*Hot water* was ejected *from an earthquake* in Catania in 1818."—*Cosmos,* vol. i., p. 209.

66. There was a *tremendous earthquake* in Peru in 1746, 200 shocks in twenty-four hours. A *volcano* in Lucanas *burst forth the same night* and *so much water descended* from the cone *that the whole country was overflowed;* and in a mountain near Pataz three other volcanoes burst out, and frightful torrents of water swept down their sides,—*Principles,* p. 501.

67. In 1692, Port Royal, in Jamaica, with about 1,000 acres adjoining, sunk in one minute into the deep. In Clarendon precinct the earth gaped, and *spouted up* with prodigious force *great quantities of water* at twelve miles from the sea. In 1746

the ocean burst in upon the land, when the barrier of land sank into the sea; Lima was overwhelmed, and the present port of Callao formed. These convulsions were accompanied by *eruptions of water and mud from several volcanoes* among the Andes, many hundreds of miles distant.—*Phil. Trans.*, *R.S.*, 1760, vol. xi., p. 469, and *Encyclop. Brit.*

68. The earthquake by which Jeddo was destroyed, in 1783, destroyed also twenty-seven other towns and villages, totally. *Boiling rivers overflowed their banks*, and at least 180,000 people are said to have perished.—*Quarterly Review*, Oct. 1863, p. 461.

Sir Rutherford Alcock, vol. 1. p. 186, says of the same earthquake :—" Twenty-seven towns and villages were destroyed; *the rivers boiling and overflowing*, inundated the whole country to complete the work of destruction."

69. Humboldt says, a very striking proof of the origin of *hot springs* by the *sinking of cold meteoric water* into the earth, and by its *contact with a volcanic focus*, is afforded by the volcano Jorullo in Mexico. In September, 1759, *Jorullo was suddenly elevated into a mountain* 1,183 feet high. *Two small rivers* the Rio de de Cuitimbo, and Rio de San Pedro *disappeared*, and some time afterwards *burst forth again as hot springs*, whose temperature he found in 1803 to be 186·4°F.—*Cosmos* vol i, p. 219, and vol. v. p. 313.

70. In the afternoon of the day preceding the great Lisbon earthquake of 1755 the *water of a fountain* at Colares, twenty miles from Lisbon, was *greatly decreased*. On the *morning of the earthquake* it ran *very muddy* and *after* the earthquake it *returned to its usual state both in quantity and clearness* . . . . This earthquake took its rise from under the sea (p. 458).—Rev. John Michell, *Phil. Trans. R. S.*, 1760, p. 463.

71. On Feb. 2, 1828, the whole island of Ischia was shaken by an *earthquake*. The *hot spring of Rita*, which was nearest the centre of the movement, was ascertained by M. Covelli to have *increased its temperature*.—*Principles*, p. 456.

## Volcanoes, Earthquakes, Hot Water and increasing Temperature of Hot Springs, sometimes all connected together.

72. M. Abich has proved the connection which exists between the thermal springs of Sarcin, and the earthquakes which frequently visit the elevated districts in every second year. In October, 1848, an *undulatory movement* of the earth which lasted for a whole hour, *caused the temperature* of the spring, which is between 111° and 115° F., *to rise immediately to a most painful scalding heat*.— *Cosmos*, vol. v, p. 175.

73. Charpentier observed that the *temperature* of the sulphurous spring of Lavey (above S. Maurice, on the bank of the

Rhone), *rose from* 87·8° *to* 97·3° F., *during the Swiss earthquake* of August 25th, 1851.—*Cosmos*, vol. v, p. 175, note.

74. A tremendous earthquake, which destroyed a great part of St. Domingo in 1770, caused innumerable fissures throughout the island, from which mephitic vapours emanated. *Hot springs burst out where there had been no water before*, but after a time they ceased to flow.—*Principles*, p. 494.

75. In the cases of Stromboli, Etna, the volcanoes of the isle of Bourbon, and Kirauea, in Owhyhee, melted matter of unknown depth, covered for the most part with a thin pellicle of scoriform lava, and *emitting copious volumes of steam or gas*, was perceived in the craters.—*Dr. Daubeny*, p. 662.

76. The violent earthquake which devastated Syria in January, 1837, was felt on a line 500 miles in length by 90 miles in breadth; more than 6000 persons perished; deep rents were caused in solid rocks, and *new hot springs burst out* at Tabereah.

77. "The town of Chittagong, in Bengal, was violently shaken by an earthquake on the 2nd of April 1762, the *earth opening* in many places, and *throwing up water and mud* of a sulphurous smell."—*Principles*, p. 494.

The following, especially the parts in italics, are very striking and significant. Has the water sunk so as to be now in process of conversion into steam?

### Expected Eruption of Vesuvius.

78. "In the townships under Vesuvius," says a letter from Naples, "I find an uneasy feeling prevailing, and a general expectation of an earthquake. The less educated classes say that as the cholera in 1856, was followed by an earthquake, so we may look out for another now. Among persons better educated, one said, 'I never go to bed without apprehension, and sleep with my door open.' The reasons for such apprehensions, when they are adduced are these:—Vesuvius has long been dormant. Of late it has been making some ineffectual efforts to relieve itself, but nothing beyond a line of smoke by day and an occasional tongue of fire by night is perceptible. Then, *all round Vesuvius*, extending even to Castellamare, there is a *perfect dearth of water*, so much so that the arsenal of that place, which has always derived its water from mountain springs that have never failed even in summer, is now compelled to send to a considerable distance for water. Perhaps the most *startling fact* is the *depression of the sea all round the bay*. I have examined it at various places, and find that this *depression* is *at least two palms beneath the ordinary level*. We have certainly had a month's calm weather, but, still, this is scarcely sufficient to account for the fact now stated."—*British Press* (Jersey), Jan. 12, 1866. Is the water sinking down to the melted lava?

## Remarks on the Seventy-eight Evidences.

Observe, in the preceding 78 evidences, how closely and inextricably *all* the species of natural disturbances of the earth's crust are commingled and combined together, as if they were all produced by one and the same cause. And how very probable that *steam*, produced by the contact of lava and water, is their cause!

It is an interesting question whether volcanic operations originate from the internal heat of the globe, or from certain chemical operations going on beneath and around us. Perhaps the truth is that both contribute more or less. Be that as it may, heat, whether derived from one source or the other, will certainly produce steam when brought into contact with water. And it is impossible to overlook or ignore the tremendous power of highly heated, saturated steam, let the origin of its heat be what it will. Is it possible to imagine that such steam does nothing?

Pumice, scoriæ and smoke, having come up, as we have seen, from volcanoes in very deep water, prove the presence of melted lava, and one of two things must necessarily have happened. Either the water with its immense pressure and quantity extinguished the lava (producing steam at the same time), and in that case there could have been no action afterwards; or otherwise the lava was sufficient in bulk to convert the water into steam again and again at several miles in depth of water, and even to remain as melted lava afterwards; which latter we must suppose to have been the case. Because we have seen in No. 40, that a submarine volcano (producing pumice) is known to have been active for 2,000 years, and we have seen also in Nos. 41, 42, 43, that volcanoes (producing scoriæ and smoke) occur *periodically*, in water of as much as 2,800 and 3,000 fathoms deep. The internal fire is therefore a vast mass, or masses, which the ocean with its variously estimated average depth of from two to five miles cannot quench. The ocean is but as a very thin film, its depth being only about a one thousandth part of the earth's radius. It is probable there are vast areas of fire, consisting (say) of melted lava, and of *hundreds of miles in depth*; else they would necessarily have been extinguished long ago by the statical depth of three or four miles of water. As a matter of fact, the ocean does *not* extinguish the fires, and steam must necessarily be produced: which in its turn will necessarily produce those shocks which we call earthquakes. Professor Bischoff calculated that one eruption of a volcano in Iceland ejected as much lava as the bulk of Mont Blanc.* And yet, more was left behind, for the geysers continue to act with undiminished vigour. I believe, with Mr. Hopkins, that the present condition of the shell of the earth is, that it is a solid mass of 800 or 1,000 miles thick, containing numerous cavities filled with fluid incandescent matter

* Lyell's "Principles of Geology," 1853, p. 427.

(and some of them, I say, also with steam, and perhaps others with steam and gases), and either entirely insulated, or perhaps communicating in some cases by obstructed channels.* Such cavities must be distant from the surface of the earth, in countries free from volcanoes, earthquakes, geysers, &c.; but so near the surface in the disturbed localities, that water gets access to the lava and steam is produced. The heat of the molten lava in these cavities was perhaps what led Humboldt to believe that in consequence of the progressive increase of 1° F. in every 40, 50, or 60ft. (as the case may be), as we descend into deep mines, that the nucleus itself was only about twenty-five miles below the surface. These respective increases of 1° in 40, 50, or 60ft. as you descend mines in *different* countries would seem to signify that the fluid lava exists at *various depths* in different localities and countries, as the hypothesis requires. The dividing walls of the cavities perhaps consist of granites, and elvans containing black non-lithia micas, which Sir H. de la Beche and Mr. Dillwyn found could not be melted by the greatest heat of a smith's forge,† which is probably from 3,000° to 3,300° F. If any reliance can be placed on the following hypothesis, we may not believe that the interior nucleus (of about 6,000 miles in diameter) has a very much higher temperature than these, else also would it not melt the solid crust? and on the other hand we may not believe the nucleus has much less temperature than those named, else it would have abstracted heat from the fluid lava in the cavities, and would have solidified it.

### Hypothesis, as to the present Temperature of the Earth's Nucleus.

If we make a large hemispherical coal fire on the ground, it will not, perhaps, very badly represent a hemisphere of the earth. The late Professer Daniell, F.R.S., determined for us that the heat of it will be 1,141° F., that is to say of its centre. *The heat, also, at half the distance from the centre to the sides will be sensibly the same.* That is to say, the eye cannot detect that the fire approaches nearer to a *white* heat (which is the measure of its temperature) at the centre, than at half the distance towards the sides. And it may be a question whether attempts at actual measurement would succeed in proving that the centre was the hottest. The comparatively cool outside of the fire would not badly represent the crust of the earth. Take, again, the case of a large mass of melted cast iron, run out into a mould, which the same authority has determined to be 2786° F. The exterior surface in contact with the sand would immediately part with a portion of its heat and become solid; but *the centre part and the parts at half the distance thence to the sides would remain at* 2,786°

* Brit. Assn. Report 1847, pp. 51 and 54.

† Sir H. de la Beche's *Cornwall*, &c., p. 191.

*for a certain period.* The case does not appear to be more difficult if we venture to speculate on the refrigeration of the earth. Let it be supposed, then, as it has often been supposed before, that the earth with its waters, its atmosphere, and its gases, was originally a vast spheroid of vapour with the enormous temperature due to such a state. Let it also be supposed that the universal law of gravitation then prevailed, and that the body of vapour revolved on its axis, and circulated in an orbit, no matter of what form or dimensions, nor what was the nearest approach to the central body. The space traversed by our vaporous body in its orbit must have been of a lower temperature than the body itself, else the vapour could never have cooled into a fluid much less into a solid. And we know indeed as a matter of fact, that the space traversed by the earth in its orbit, is not only not intensely heated, but not even heated at all—for it does not heat the earth's atmosphere.* After a short geological period, a comparatively thin stratum all over the surface of the spheroid would have so far cooled down as to become fluid instead of vaporous, *by which its specific gravity would be greatly increased*, and it would immediately fall like a shower of rain, the heaviest parts being foremost, along radii of the spheroid towards the centre of gravity. But it would fail to reach that centre, *because it would soon become vaporous again*, from a double cause, namely, from the heat it would absorb from the vapour by which it would have become surrounded, and by the conversion of its own rapid motion into heat. Very soon after, in due order, another, and another, and another shower of fluid would be precipitated toward the centre of gravity to be again, and again, and again, reconverted into vapour by the two combined causes. But this process could not be repeated for ever; the whole spheriod of vapour would part with more and more of its heat, and become fluid in process of time, and would consequently *diminish in volume;* and the showers of lava would descend nearer and nearer to the centre of gravity, which some of them would at length reach, and *there they would remain;* because they would be heavier than anything else, and would, in fact, be the commencement of the nucleus. This commencement of the nucleus we will call the end of the first stage of the process of conversion.

*Note.*—Some of Lord Rosse's beautiful drawings of nebulæ in *Phil. Trans. R.S.*, 1861, part 3, will well serve as diagrams, by their forms and textures and incipient nuclei, to illustrate this hypothesis. The following figures or drawings are especially referred to, viz., H 15, H 262, H 311, H 327, H 1,111, and 1,113, H 1,946, and H 2,075. Whether there is any real resemblance in the nature and present condition of any of those vast systems to the hypothetical primitive condition of our earth is more than I know, but Messrs. Miller and Huggins throw light on the subject.

It would appear to be very probable from the following extract from a very striking paper, "On the Spectra of some of the Heavenly Bodies," by Professor W. A. Miller, V.P.R.S., and W. Huggins, F.R.A.S., that the earth really was a planetary nebula when in its primitive condition :—"The third and most remarkable part of this communication was that which referred to the spectra of nebulæ; and the observations in this field were stated to have been conducted solely by Mr. Huggins. The nebulæ examined were chiefly those denominated planetary nebulæ. It was scarcely expected that the extremely faint light of these bodies would be sufficient to produce any spectrum at all; nor would it have done so had their construction been that which has been usually assigned to them. But to the surprise of the observer he beheld, not a continuous spectrum, such as that which proceeds from a solid, interspersed with dark lines due to atmospheric absorption, but a spectrum consisting of a few bright lines, *such as that which proceeds from an intensely heated gas*. It was, indeed, the smallness in number of these component lines that enabled any success to be obtained; and the result from three or four of these nebulæ revealed the fact that they were in each case *composed of glowing gas*, probably hydrogen and nitrogen, without any solid nucleus whatever. But what can be the origin of this high temperature, since, upon the principle of the conservation of energy, some other form of motion must be destroyed in order to produce the luminosity? The origin of the light of the heavenly bodies thus becomes more perplexing than ever, and seems to point to some law regarding which we are still in the dark.—"British Association Report, 1864, Transactions of the Sections," p. 12.

Must we not, perforce, answer this question by other questions? Supposing (as Mr. Huggins and the present writer agree) that a primary condition of the earth was, that it consisted of vapour, gases, nebulous matter, highly heated. Must we not be content with that condition as the most rudimentary to which human intellect can reach? How can hydrogen and nitrogen be analysed so as to resolve them into still more primitive elements? Man's researches must from the very necessity of the case stop short of the very beginning. Have we any choice except to suppose that it was in the vaporous, highly heated condition, stated in the hypothesis that our earth was first projected into space as a planetary nebula, direct from the hands of the Creator? This conclusion however is intended to be *provisional* only. And it will not in point of fact, and of course it is not intended to impede, much less to stop, the progress of scientific investigation on the part of those who may happen to think the ultimatum of possible human knowledge, in this direction, has not yet been reached.

To proceed with the hypothesis, which is by no means identical with Sir W. Herschel's nebular hypothesis:—A long geological period would elapse before the first stage of the process was reached, and a farther long period may perhaps have elapsed before the remaining parts which are *now* either solids or fluid lavas, *had all changed from the vaporous to the fluid condition,* and the earth had become reduced nearly to its present dimensions. By the time this second stage had been accomplished, *the rapid circulation which has been sketched would have brought all except an extremely thin shell of the surface to a uniform temperature of about* 3,000° Fahr.; or to something else not widely differing from that amount. And our spheroid of fluid lava would then begin, as a third process, to cool on the outside and form a *cavernous* crust. Emphatically a "cavernous" crust, because those parts which contained non-lithia micas would solidify at higher temperatures than those others which consisted of felspar, for example*:—Must not the immense nucleus of the earth therefore even now be fluid lava, and of not greatly higher temperatures than those named, and consisting of ingredients of a certain average specific gravity such that the average specific gravity of the whole *present* spheroid would of necessity be about 6·565, as the Astronomer Royal eliminated from his experiments at the Harton mine, which cannot be far from the truth? His figures indicate a specific gravity intermediate between the gravities of the commoner metals, viz., copper, brass, iron, tin, and zinc, which all range between 8·91 and 7·19—and those of stones, viz., marble, granite, Purbeck, Portland, Bristol, mill-stone-grit, and sandstone, which all range between 2·72 and 2·143. We may not, therefore, suppose that the amount of metals (especially not of the precious metals) contained in the nucleus, is relatively great, for that would make the specific gravity too high. And we may not even suppose that the nucleus is composed of material as heavy as melted stone at the surface of the earth, because the pressure due to the enormous depth down to the centre of gravity, would *compress*, and make even that too much. Apparently we are compelled to suppose that some such light material as *pumice* constitutes an important part of its bulk, and we actually know, in point of fact, that pumice *is* an abundant product of volcanoes.

This hypothesis of a uniform heat of the earth's vast nucleus, is most favorable to the fact of the absence of all appreciable secular refrigeration since the time of Hipparchus, a period of 2,000 years. If such refrigeration had occured, the earth's bulk would have diminished, and its revolution on its axis would have been performed in a shorter time, that is to say, the day would have shortened. Whereas astronomers know that the length of the day has not diminished by 1-100th of a second within that period.

* We shall see presently in No. 9 that when granite is passing from a plastic to a solid state, a contraction of more than 10 per cent. takes place, which would leave a cavity of that dimension. We shall see also plenty more reasons why there must be cavities.

## ELEVEN REASONS WHY THERE MUST BE CAVITIES IN THE CRUST OF THE EARTH.

I.

The well known aperature on the shore of Cephalonia into which the sea has been running for ages (see *Evidence* No. 24), seems to give incontestable proof that there is a cavity beneath, and that it must be a large one, if we suppose with Sir Charles Lyell, that the water is converted into steam and escapes upwards. In which case the nearest known vents, Etna, and the Lipari Isles being each 300 miles distant from Cephalonia, that distance must be the length of the cavity. If Vesuvius is the vent, the length will be 360 miles. Of course the *breadth* and *depth* of the passage may be either great or small, we do not know. Or otherwise it must also be a large one, for if the water does not escape as steam, the cavity must be so vast that even *ages* of constant flow of water have not sufficed to fill it, Such an idea as this latter cannot be entertained.

2.

Marine fossils have been found at an elevation of more than 8,000ft. in the Pyrenees, 10,000ft. in the Alps, 12,000ft. in the Andes. Captain R. J. Strachey found oolitic fossils 18,400ft. high in the Himalayas.* And the late Professor Forbes says that Illampu or Sorata (Andes) 24,812ft. high, is fossiliferous up to its summit. † When these were elevated must not large cavities have been left behind? And the like with other fossiliferous, and with all igneous ranges? Unless collapse took place about the bases of all mountains and ranges of hills, which we have no reason to believe, lava, which is at most semi-fluid, could only partly fill the cavity, and even then it must have formed more cavity at the places from whence it had flowed.

3.

We have seen in *Evidence* No. 3, that there must be a communication underground nearly 200 miles long between Skaptár Jokul and Nyöe. And in *Evidence* No 58, that there must be underground communication between the volcano of Pasto and the volcanoes of Quito, which are sixty-five leagues distant.

4.

We saw at p. 24 that a force of 243.2 tons per square inch would be required to propel a column of granite 9ft. thick, to a vertical height of four miles. This was on the

* Lyell's Manual of Geology, p. 4.

† Quarterly Review, January, 1863.

supposition, however, that it *was entirely unconnected with the adjoining ground*, and not impeded either, by the friction of contact with the adjoining ground. Now, to propel a column 9ft. thick through a height of four miles, is equal to propelling a column four miles thick through a height of 9ft. The terms are convertible, the one into the other. And if we make allowance for *cohesion of the column to the adjoining ground*, we may scarcely affirm that a supposed force of 800 or 900 tons per square inch will do more than propel the mass of 9ft. thick through, say twice that distance, or eight miles of vertical height, so as to produce undulation. Mr. Mallett, C.E., F.R.S., states that the focus of the great Neapolitan earthquake of 1857, is at 5·64 geographical miles, which however he conceives to be somewhat below the true depth, as a closer examination of the various wave paths led him to conclude that the probable vertical depth of the focal cavity itself does not exceed three geographical miles. * We may, at all events, be pretty sure that so far as evidence has yet been gathered, either from the distances to which masses of rock have been hurled, or from dislocations observed by geologists in the Alps and elsewhere; that the maximum force can hardly be supposed to exceed 800 or 900 tons per square inch, and that it would scarcely do more after allowing for the uncertain amounts of cohesion and friction, than project a mass eight miles thick through a space of 9ft. Now to apply ~~three~~ considerations. these

The average diameter of the earth, omitting fractions of a mile is 7912 miles, † and the outside circle of the figure at p. 22 represents that diameter on a scale of 1,000 miles to $\frac{1}{3}$ in., and the thickness of the line forming the outer circle is ten miles, or $\frac{1}{300}$in., as nearly as may be. The two interior circles are respectively at 800 and 1,000 miles below the surface of the earth, on the same scale; and one or other of them defines the thickness of the crust according to Mr. Hopkin's calculations based on precession and nutation. Now it is clear, on a mere inspection of the figure, that earthquake shocks taking place at foci within the thickness of the line forming the outside circle, which represents ten miles by the scale, could not cause the undulations which are so frequently the accompaniments of earthquakes, *if the crust were solid*, and 800 or 1,000 miles thick. The mass of the crust would have too great a rigidity to be capable of being made to undulate, by a force acting within the thickness of the exterior line. We *must* suppose, therefore, that there are cavities (some filled with melted lava, and others with vapour, perhaps), else the undulations could not take place. For the force could at the utmost, only take effect, say, ten miles upwards and ten miles

* "Great Neapolitan Earthquake of 1857," by Robert Mallett, C.E., F.R.S., 2 vols.

† "Herschel's Outlines of Astronomy," 1864, p. 139

downward, leaving hundreds of miles of solid crust below, quite unaffected; and consequently the whole solid mass of 800 or 1,000 miles thick would be unmoved and immoveable by a force so comparatively puny and insignificant as 800 or 900 tons per square inch. Undulations could not take place, even if the crust were a solid of only twenty-five geographical miles thick, as Humboldt supposed it to be. That is to say, it is immaterial to the present argument whether the thickness of the crust is twenty-five miles, or 800, or 1,000 miles, or something intermediate. Provided it abounds with cavities, and a sufficient number of them be filled with nothing more substantial than air, steam or gases, the ground might then undulate in either case, as in point of fact it actually does.

5.

If the crust of the earth were a homogeneous solid, and if the interior nucleus were homogeneous also, the plumb line when freely suspended, would always hang in a direction pointing to the centre of the earth. As a matter of fact. however, it never does so point in the several instances about to be quoted, which are all I have been able to collect. Now this circumstance may mean either of two things, viz.: First, the crust may be cavernous or porous on that side from which the plummet is drawn away. Or second, the deficiency in attraction may be due only to material of less specific gravity. May we not fairly and reasonably conclude that the phenomenon is sometimes due to the first cause and sometimes to the second? Obviously, whether cavernous or only porous, either would hold steam; though of course the latter would not allow sinkings of ground.

*Instances of deflections of the plumb line.* It will be observed that deflection is the rule and not the exception, the line is *always* deflected more or less. M. Schweitzer, director of the Observatory at Moscow, found that a difference of 8″ in latitude existed between the result determined by direct observation, and that observed by triangulation from distant well known points. And by observation at very numerous stations in the neighbourhood, it was found that a line existed to the South of Moscow where observations of all kinds agreed; but that to the north there was a difference in one direction, and to the south in another. And that in the direction of the *meridian* the tract of country affected seemed about *seventy-four miles* in extent, but that in the line of *east and west* the extent was greater, and had not yet been reached. The effect was that plumb lines at the two extremes converged $\frac{1}{50}$ part less than they ought, and the only explanation which could be given was, that a large trough of the earth was less in density than the surrounding country. There are no mountains, nor large surface of sea, to disturb the general effect of gravity, as those features were sometimes known to do.* Another account says that M. Schweitzer's more recent researches have confirmed the observations of the Russian geodesists, and established the existence of a local deviation to the extraordinary amount of 19 seconds within a very short distance of Moscow. At that city the plumb line deviates 8″ from the spheroidal perpendicular towards the north. At 25 versts (13 English miles) to the north of Moscow this deviation ceases. It ceases also at 12 versts (8 miles) to the south of Moscow; but on going further south, it recommences in a contrary direction, and at 25 versts (16 miles) to the south of the city, it is converted into a southern deviation of 11″. Proceeding from Moscow in either an easterly or westerly direction, similar phenomena are observed. As there is nothing deserving the name of a mountain in the neighbourhood of Moscow, it follows as a necessary consequence from these facts:—

1st. That there exist beneath Moscow, enormous cavities, occupied by air, or perhaps by water (or as the present writer suggests, perhaps sometimes by steam, and at other times by steam and gases), Or,

2nd. That strata of some substance of very small specific gravity exist beneath the city, Or,

3rd. That there extends over the whole of the country surrounding Moscow, a generally loose, unconsolidated mass of geological formations (which would contain steam as well as cavities would) at a depth hopelessly beyond what human labour can ever expect to penetrate. †

*Deviations of the plumb line in India.* Archdeacon Pratt ‡ found by calculation that the deflexions were as follows at the three places named:—

| | Kaliana. | Kalianpur. | Damargida. |
|---|---|---|---|
| | ″ | ″ | ″ |
| In the meridian …… | 27·853 | 11·968 | 6·909 |
| In prime vertical …… | 16·942 | 4·763 | 2·723 |
| Total deflections …… | 32·601 | 12·88 | 7·426 (p. 94). |

On these the Astronomer Royal of England, in another paper immediately following (p. 101), says "there is nothing surprising in Pratt's conclusion, it ought to have been anticipated, instead of expecting a positive effect of attraction of a large mountain mass upon a station at a considerable distance from it, we ought to be prepared to expect no effect whatever, or in some cases even a small negative effect . . . Most physicists suppose, either that the interior of the earth is now fluid, or that it was fluid when the mountains took their present forms."

* Intellectual Observer, May, 1863, p. 305.

† "Cornhill Magazine," October, 1862, p. 550.

‡ Phil. Trans., R. S., 1855.

~~100.~~ An arc of the meridian was triangulated a few years ago from Dunnose in the Isle of Wight to Burleigh Moor in Yorkshire. And the deflexions of the plumb line at each extremity, and at three intermediate stations were noted. And it is remarkable that at not one of these five stations did the plumb line point, as prima facie it might have been expected to do, towards the centre of the earth. The deviations are as follows:—Dunnose 1″·767 *south*; Greenwich, 1″·27 *north*; Arbury Hill, 1″·692 *north*; Clifton, 2″·864 *south*; and Burleigh Moor 3″·855 *south*.—*Paper* by Captain Clarke, R.E. Phil. Trans., R.S., 1858, p. 789.

The deflexion being towards the *south* instead of the north at Dunnose, is not a little remarkable. The low level of the sea and the less specific gravity of its water than so much earth, chalk, or rock, would naturally have suggested that the plumb line would have been deflected towards the *north*; in consequence of the large mass of the island and its considerably greater specific gravity than that of sea water. The sp. gr. of chalk is 2·781, Sea water only 1·028, distilled water being 1·000

The deflexion of the plumb line at Arthur's seat is 5″·25, and at the Royal Observatory at Edinburgh, it amounts to 5″·63, both to the south. Phil. Trans., R.S., 1856, p. 591, by Col. James.

Early during the present century the headland eastward of Portsoy, on Cowhythe in Banffshire was visited by an officer of the Royal Engineers with the zenith sector., constructed for the Ordnance survey of this country by the celebrated Ramsden; and from the observations made with that instrument to determine the latitude of the trigonometrical station there, it was found that the plumb line, instead of being vertical was deflected northward of the zenith, and southward of the earth's centre, fully nine seconds of angular measure. By way of verification, a party of the same corps, some sixteen years back (1848), furnished with a new zenith sector, designed by the present Astronomer Royal, and constructed by Troughton and Simms, visited the same spot, More observations and to a greater number of stars, resulted in confirming the first or earlier determination.—Artizan, Nov., 1864, p. 259.

Cavities of various sizes, and positions, and at various depths, would perfectly account for all these deflexions of the plumb line.

6.

*Densities as observed by the pendulum.*—In the Phil. Trans. R.S. for 1856, p. 42; the following table is given by Archdeacon Pratt, who takes it from Col. Sabine's volume on the pendulum. They are quoted as given. How can it be otherwise than that there are cavities ?

| Stations | Excess or defect of Vibrations. | Scale of density of Strata beneath. |
|---|---|---|
| St. Thomas .............. | + 5·58 | 100 |
| Ascension .............. | + 5·04 | 94 |
| Spitzbergen.............. | + 3·50 | 79 |
| Jamaica ................ | + 0·28 | 45 |
| New York .............. | 0·00 | 43 |
| Greenland .............. | — ·08 | 43 |
| Sierra Leone ........... | — ·12 | 42 |
| London ................ | — ·28 | 41 |
| Hammerfest ........... | — ·52 | 37 |
| Bahia .................... | — 1·80 | 26 |
| Drontheim .............. | — 3·10 | 12 |
| Trinidad ................ | — 4·12 | 2 |
| Maranham .............. | — 4·34 | 1 |

These great variations are consistent enough with the deviations of the plumb line in various and opposite directions, and with the existence of cavities.

7.

*The vast masses of materials ejected by volcanoes must have caused cavities beneath.* The volume of lava ejected by the Skaptàr Jokul in Iceland, in 1783, was very immense. " Of the two branches, which flowed in nearly opposite directions, the greatest was fifty and the lesser forty miles in length. The extreme breadth which the Skaptâr branch attained in the low countries, was from twelve to fifteen miles, that of the other about seven. The ordinary height of both currents was 100ft., but in narrow defiles it sometimes amounted to 600." And Sir Charles then mentions Professor Bischoff's calculations, which we have referred to before, that the mass of lava brought up from the subterranean regions by this single eruption, surpassed in magnitude the bulk of Mont Blanc.* This *must* have left a large cavity behind.

8.

In Bohn's translation of " Humboldt's Cosmos," vol. v., p. 170, 171, and notes, we read that cavities have been attributed to the elevation of enormous, sharp-edged, perfectly hardened rocks.

9.

*Cavities must be caused by the solidifying and consequent contraction of melted stone.* We learn from " Principles of Geology," p. 562-3, and a reference is there given to " Bulletin de la Soc. Géol.," 2nd series, vol. iv, p. 1312 ; that " according to the ex-

* " Lyell's Principles of Geology," p. 427, who quotes Jameson's " Phil. Journ," vol. xxvi, p. 291.

periments of Deville and calculations of Bischoff, the contraction of granite when passing from a melted or plastic, to a solid and crystalline state, must be *more than ten per cent.*" which would certainly leave cavities.

10.

The aggregate subsidences or sinkings of land, must have been all along at least as great as the aggregate elevations, else the mean diameter of the earth would have been increased, and the day would have lengthened—unless the equator had revolved more rapidly, which we have no right to suppose.

Hear Sir John Herschell:—"The time occupied by one complete rotation of the earth on its axis, or the mean sidereal day, may be shewn on dynamical principles, to be subject to no variation from any external cause, and although its duration would be *shortened* by contraction in the dimensions of the globe itself, (and *vice versa* would be *lengthened* by increase of those dimensions), such as might arise from the gradual escape of its internal heat, and consequent refrigeration and sinking of the whole mass, yet theory on the one hand, has rendered it almost certain that this cause cannot have effected any perceptible amount of change during the history of the human race;* and on the other, the comparison of ancient and modern observations affords every corroboration to this conclusion. From such comparisons, Laplace has concluded that the sidereal day has not changed by so much as 1-100th of a second since the time of Hipparchus.†

When we refer to Lyell's "Principles of ~~Astronomy~~," chap. xxvii., "On earthquakes and their effects," we find that the recorded sinkings are for the most part only from 2 to 10ft. in depth. Surely there must be a vast aggregate amount of sinkings yet undiscovered! And if so, must there not have been, and may there not be still, vast cavities?

11.

Some very extensive and deep sinkings have accordingly been discovered within a very short period (and doubtless more such discoveries are on the eve of being made). For example, "At a recent meeting of Geological Society, a paper was read by Mr. Robert Dawson, relating to the occurence of dead littoral shells in the bed of the German Ocean, *forty miles* from the coast of Aberdeen. From the fact of four species having been dredged in one day, Mr. Dawson considered that it was probable that they had lived and died where they were found, and did not owe their pre-

* The hypothesis at p. 42, according to which the nucleus is of uniform temperature, accounts for the non-refrigeration and consequent non-shrinking of the bulk of the earth since Hipparchus' time.

† "Outlines of Astronomy," 1864, p. 667. NOTE.—Hipparchus flourished 2,000 years ago.

sence at that depth and distance from land to any mere accident."—*Illustrated London News*, March, 3, 1866, p. 212. Also from a private letter from an F. G. S. who was present at the discussion on Mr. Dawson's paper.

Again, it appears from a "further report on Shetland Dredgings," by J. Gwyn Jeffreys Esq., F.R.S. *Report of British Association* for 1864, p. 329. He says:—"More quasi-fossil shells were dredged, and for the first time in this district *Lepeta cæca*, dead, but apparently as fresh as any Scandinavian specimen. A perfect specimen of *Rhynconella psittacea* was also obtained at a depth of 86 fathoms; but it had two tell tale associates. One was *Pecten Islandicus*, and the other *Spirorbis granulatus*, var. *heterostropha*, of much larger size than specimens of the same Annelid from the southern coasts of England; the *Spirorbis* was also dead, and covered both the *Rhynconella* and *Pecten*. *S. granulatus* has not been found in a living state north of the Hebrides, so far as I have been able to discover. This appears to have been one of the numerous relics of the glacial or post-glacial epoch, it is *an inhabitant of Shallow water*, and affords another confirmatory proof of my hypothesis that *the Shetland sea-bed has sunk considerably during a comparatively recent period.*"

But there is a still more surprising circumstance which remains to be stated. I quote from a private letter dated the 22nd ult., in which my correspondent says:—"We had a talk last evening (also at the Geological Society's) about depression of land which had evidently taken place (but not in the historical period) between Malta and Jamaica." What the nature of the proof is, of this extraordinary depression, I cannot even conjecture. The Mid-Atlantic is too deep for dredging. But I have full confidence in the scientific knowledge and caution of my friendly correspondent.

~~Fourthly,~~ It will be my business in future papers to endeavour to convince the reader that some two or three thousand square miles of land and sea-bottom, have sunk fully 100ft., and were within the last 1,900 years, parts of the northerly and westerly coasts of France.

For some or one of the eleven reasons just given also, there *may* have been, and for some or one of the same eleven reasons, there *must* have been cavities elsewhere.

The following conclusions may, perhaps, be accepted, provisionally and hypothetically at least, until further facts, corroborative or negative, can be obtained, namely: The nucleus of the earth, has a uniform temperature of about 3000° F. This is probably sufficient to produce saturated steam, having a force or pressure of about 900 tons per square inch. Such force is powerful enough to account for any convulsions either of the coal period, or since, And, finally, that steam (assisted by other forces whose help is not essential) is the cause of all the natural disturbances of the earth's crust.

**Steam is the active agent in Volcanic Explosions of the greatest intensity.**

The following extract from the *Illustrated London News*, May 12th, p. 470, refers to something which occured at the Geological Society, in reference to the present eruption at Neo Kaimeni.

"M. Fouque's observations tend to support M. St. Claire Deville's law, that there exists a certain relation between the degree of intensity of a volcano in action and the nature of the volatile elements ejected. In an eruption of maximum intensity common salt, and salts of soda and potash predominate ; in one of the second order, hydrochloric acid and chloride of iron ; in one of the third degree, sulphuric acid and salts of ammonia ; and in fourth or most feeble phase, steam only, with carbonic acid and combustible gases."

On the contrary, we have seen not only in No. 57, but also in Evidences 2, 3, 8, 38, 41, 42, 43, 44, 51, 59, 66, 68, 70, that Steam was the chief, if not the only, agent in all of them. And they were all of very great intensity.

---

# SUMMARY.

Since the Birmingham meeting, the author had further considered the subject, and had made a full statement in the pamphlet just published. The following abstract gives the principal results. The Steam law set forth is empirical, because of the impracticability of making experiments with very high temperatures. Some of the reasons for believing that the law stated, is the true one, will now be given. :—

A. The Tables prove, that 240° Fahr. is the temperature, due to Steam pressure of 25lbs. per square inch, and 450·689° is the temperature due to a pressure of [illegible]lbs. per square inch. And that the pressure increases in the enormously rapid ratio, *as the* $4\frac{1}{2}$ *power of the temperature.* The last is the highest limit to which experiments have been carried, which was done by M. Regnault. A rigid reduction of his weights and measures to English, only proves that a correction of the formula by the trifling addition of 0·543°, or about half a unit *per cent.* to the temperatures, is requisite to produce the given pressures.

B. Seventy-eight Evidences recited, prove that Steam is the active agent in every species of natural disturbance of the earth's crust. From No. 43, of these, corroborated by others, it appears that two ships sailing near the equator at 600 miles distance from the nearest land, both experienced the shock of an earthquake. And since, troubled water, floating scoriæ, and columns of smoke have been observed at intervals since the middle of last century; apparently steam produced by lava is the cause of the shocks. These shocks occurred where, according to Lieut. Maury's chart, the water is 3000 fathoms deep, and consequently a force of more than $3\frac{1}{2}$ tons per square inch is required to overcome its pressure. And the steam must have exerted that great power, over and above whatever force was required to give the shocks to the ships, and to cause the ship DALLAS to lose her false keel by the collision.

C. But we may go further in illustrating the great power of Steam. Brass melts at 1869° Fahr. And we have had proof that in casting two brass cannon, the heat of the metal of the first gun, drove *so much damp* into the mould of the second which was near it, that as soon as the metal was let in, it blew up with the greatest violence, tearing up the ground some feet deep, breaking down the furnace, untiling the house, killing many spectators on the spot with the streams of the melted metal, and scalding many others in a most miserable manner.—Now the pressure due to Steam produced by melted brass, according to the formula, would exceed a hundred tons per square inch. And whether that is true or not (and he saw no reason for disbelieving it), the Steam was at any rate exceedingly powerful: for the whole effects were due to the Steam of a few ounces of water only, it being described merely as "damp."

D. It now became an interesting question to make an estimate in tons per square inch, of the force of ordinary volcanoes, and of volcanoes of the greatest intensity; in all of which be it remembered, Steam is the active agent. And it appeared by calculation, depending on the well-known laws of Falling and Ascending bodies, that a force of about 243 tons per square inch, which would propel a mass of granite 9 feet thick to a vertical height of 4 miles overcoming at the same time the resistance of the atmosphere—might be taken to represent the force of an ordinary volcano; and twice that force a volcano of the highest intensity. And even supposing the calculations by the steam formula, to be 48 per cent. in excess of the truth, steam of 3000° Fahr. would still give a force equal to that of a volcano of the highest intensity. For it has been seen in Evidence No. 57, that at Galangoon in Java, lapilli of the size of nuts were projected, apparently by steam, with such prodigious violence that large quantities fell more than 40 miles distant. And great blocks of basalt were thrown, by a still more violent valcano in which steam was also the active agent, to the distance of seven miles from the volcano. If these things be so, steam has sufficient power, and other forces co-operate where no help is required.

E. A hypothesis stated, would account satisfactorily for the absence of refrigeration of the earth during the last 2,000 years.

And first there appear to be good grounds for the hypothesis, which consists of this ; that primarily the earth was a planetary nebula. Mr. Huggins had examined the spectra of several planetary nebulæ, and found that they consisted of a few bright lines such as those which proceed from an intensely heated gas. And it is certain that the space passed through by the earth in its orbit, is cold, not hot : which is proved by the atmosphere not becoming heated, and by the perpetual existence of snow on all the loftiest mountains. He therefore concluded that the earth's nebula had gradually cooled down by passing through cold space, so as to become a fluid instead of vapour ; and of the heat of melted lava, say about 3000°, which he supposed is its present condition. Such uniformity of temperature would be favourable to the absence of secular refrigeration. The vast nucleus, which must be about 6000 miles diameter, if the crust is 800 or 1000 miles thick, must in large part consist af pumice (which is known to be an abundant product of volcanoes) or other light substance ; else the average specific gravity would be too great. And this hypothesis prevents the steam theory from proving too much, for he had shown that the steam could never exceed a pressure of from 900 to 1000 tons per square inch, which was due to the supposed maximum or rather *uniform* temperature of about 3000°.

F. And this brought him to the conclusion of his subject, in which he stated eleven reasons—old, or new, or newly put,—why there must be Cavities in the Crust of the Earth. The outside circle of the diagram, represented the average diameter of the earth, and the thickness of the line was 10 miles by the scale, which was about the extreme depth at which it appeared that steam of the highest pressure stated, had the power to overcome the inertia and tenacity of the earth's crust. If this be so, the crust must abound with cavities, else such comparatively puny shocks of earthquakes and volcanoes could never cause undulations, even if the crust was only 25 miles thick as Baron Humboldt has supposed. The interior circles were respectively at 800 and 1000 miles below the earth's surface, and represented the thickness of the crust according to Mr. Hopkins ; in which case of course it was far beyond the puny power of steam to cause undulations : unless there were numerous cavities filled say, with steam, smoke, or gases ; and at any rate, not with anything more solid than melted lava. And there *must*, in fact, be cavities, else sinkings of land, which had often occurred, could never have taken place. And these cavities may some of them be receptacles of Steam.

---

The author is sensible of the imperfection of the pamphlet. He has done what he could with the facts gathered up, in the absence of any steam experiments with very high temperatures.

---

Le Lievre, Bros., Machine Printers and Booksellers, 13, Halkett-place, Jersey.

www.ingramcontent.com/pod-product-compliance
Lightning Source LLC
Chambersburg PA
CBHW031410270326
41929CB00010BA/1396

* 9 7 8 3 3 3 7 2 0 2 4 8 4 *